MASS CALENDAR FOR 2017-2018

Using this Book in Prayer

You can use this book to help your prayer, alone or with your family and friends:

- Read the Gospel or other readings for last Sunday, and pray about them.
- Read the Gospel or other readings for next Sunday, and begin to pray about them.
- Think about God's Word: what is the Holy Spirit telling you?
- Pray the Responsorial Psalm from any of the Masses in the book.
- Reflect on the Collect from last Sunday's Mass, and pray it slowly.
- Use some of the prayers in the treasury.
- Say the Lord's Prayer slowly (page 72).

Handy Edge-Marking

This Missal belongs to

....

New *Saint Joseph*

SUNDAY MISSAL

PRAYERBOOK AND HYMNAL

CANADIAN MISSAL

For 2017 - 2018

Year B

How easy it is to use this Missal

- Refer to the Calendar inside the front cover for the page of the Sunday Mass (the "Proper").
- This arrow (↓) means continue to read. This arrow (→) indicates a reference back to the Order of Mass ("Ordinary") or to another part of the "Proper."
- Boldface type always indicates the people's parts that are to be recited aloud.

"Take this, all of you, and eat of it, for this is my Body, which will be given up for you."

CANADIAN EDITION

New . . . St. Joseph

SUNDAY MISSAL

PRAYERBOOK AND HYMNAL

For 2017 - 2018

THE COMPLETE MASSES FOR
SUNDAYS and the
SACRED PASCHAL TRIDUUM

With the People's Parts Printed in Boldface Type and Arranged for Parish Participation

The liturgical texts are approved by the Canadian Conference of Catholic Bishops.

IN ACCORD WITH THE THIRD TYPICAL EDITION OF THE ROMAN MISSAL

With the "NEW REVISED STANDARD VERSION" Text

Dedicated to St. Joseph
Patron of the Universal Church

CATHOLIC BOOK PUBLISHING CORP.
New Jersey

The *St. Joseph Sunday Missal for 2017-2018* is approved for use in Canada by the National Liturgy Office, Canadian Conference of Catholic Bishops.

Acknowledgements:

The St. Joseph Missals have been diligently prepared with the invaluable assistance of a special Board of Editors, including specialists in Liturgy and Sacred Scripture, Catechetics, and Sacred Music and Art.

(T-2118)

ISBN 978-1-941243-78-7

www.catholicbookpublishing.com

Printed in U.S.A.

PREFACE

IN the words of the Second Vatican Council in the *Constitution on the Sacred Liturgy*, the Mass "is an action of Christ the priest and of his body which is the Church; it is a sacred action surpassing all others; no other action of the Church can equal its efficacy by the same title and to the same degree" (art. 7). Hence the Mass is a sacred sign, something visible which brings the invisible reality of Christ to us in the worship of the Father.

The Mass was first instituted as a meal at the Last Supper and became a living memorial of Christ's sacrifice on the Cross:

"At the Last Supper, on the night when he was betrayed, our Saviour instituted the Eucharistic sacrifice of his body and blood. He did this in order to perpetuate the sacrifice of the Cross throughout the centuries until he should come again, and so to entrust to his beloved spouse, the Church, a memorial of his death and resurrection: a sacrament of love, a sign of unity, a bond of charity, a paschal banquet in which Christ is eaten, the mind is filled with grace, and a pledge of future glory is given to us.

"The Church, therefore, earnestly desires that Christ's faithful, when present at this mystery of faith, should not be there as strangers or silent spectators; on the contrary, through a good understanding of the rites and prayers they should take part in the sacred action conscious of what they are doing, with devotion and full collaboration. They should be instructed by God's word and be nourished at the table of the Lord's body; they should give thanks to God; by offering the immaculate Victim, not only through the hands of the priest, but also with him, they should learn also to offer themselves; through Christ the Mediator, they should be drawn day by day into ever more perfect union with God and with each other, so that . . . God may be all in all" (art. 47-48).

A simple method of identifying the various parts of the Mass has been designed using different typefaces:

(1) **boldface type**—clearly identifies all people's parts

(2) lightface type—indicates the Priest's, Deacon's, or reader's parts.

In order to enable the faithful to prepare for each Mass at home and so participate more actively at Mass, the editors have added short, helpful explanations of the scripture readings, geared to the spiritual needs of daily life. A large selection of hymns for congregational singing has been included, as well as a treasury of personal prayers.

We trust that all these special features will help Catholics who use this new St. Joseph Missal to be led—in keeping with the desire of the Church—"to that full, conscious, and active participation in liturgical celebrations which is demanded by the very nature of the liturgy. Such participation by the Christian people as a chosen race, a royal priesthood, a holy nation, a redeemed people (1 Pt 2, 9; cf. 2, 4-5), is their right and duty by reason of their baptism" (art. 14).

PLAN OF THE MASS

THE INTRODUCTORY RITES	1. Entrance Chant 2. Greeting 3. Rite for the Blessing and Sprinkling of Water 4. Penitential Act 5. Kyrie 6. Gloria 7. Collect **(Proper)**
THE LITURGY OF THE WORD	8. First Reading **(Proper)** 9. Responsorial Psalm **(Proper)** 10. Second Reading **(Proper)** 11. Gospel Acclamation **(Proper)** 12. Gospel Dialogue 13. Gospel Reading **(Proper)** 14. Homily 15. Profession of Faith **(Creed)** 16. Universal Prayer
THE LITURGY OF THE EUCHARIST	17. Presentation and Preparation of the Gifts 18. Invitation to Prayer 19. Prayer over the Offerings **(Proper)** 20. Eucharistic Prayer 21. Preface Dialogue 22. Preface 23. Preface Acclamation Eucharistic Prayer 1, 2, 3, 4 Reconciliation 1, 2 Various Needs 1, 2, 3, 4
The Communion Rite	24. The Lord's Prayer 25. Sign of Peace 26. Lamb of God 27. Invitation to Communion 28. Communion 29. Prayer after Communion **(Proper)**
THE CONCLUDING RITES	30. Solemn Blessing 31. Final Blessing 32. Dismissal

THE ORDER OF MASS

Options are indicated by A, B, C, D in the margin.

THE INTRODUCTORY RITES

Acts of prayer and penitence prepare us to meet Christ as he comes in Word and Sacrament. We gather as a worshipping community to celebrate our unity with him and with one another in faith.

1 ENTRANCE CHANT — STAND

If it is not sung, it is recited by all or some of the people.

Joined together as Christ's people, we open the celebration by raising our voices in praise of God who is present among us. This song should deepen our unity as it introduces the Mass we celebrate today.

→ Turn to Today's Mass

2 GREETING (3 forms)

When the Priest comes to the altar, he makes the customary reverence with the ministers and kisses the altar. Then, with the ministers, he goes to his chair. After the Entrance Chant, all make the Sign of the Cross:

Priest: In the name of the Father, and of the Son, and of the Holy Spirit.

PEOPLE: **Amen.**

The Priest welcomes us in the name of the Lord. We show our union with God, our neighbour, and the Priest by a united response to his greeting.

A

Priest: The grace of our Lord Jesus Christ,
and the love of God,
and the communion of the Holy Spirit
be with you all.

PEOPLE: **And with your spirit.**

B OR

Priest: Grace to you and peace from God our Father
and the Lord Jesus Christ.

PEOPLE: **And with your spirit.**

C OR

Priest: The Lord be with you.

PEOPLE: **And with your spirit.**

[Bishop: Peace be with you.

PEOPLE: **And with your spirit.**]

3 RITE FOR the BLESSING and SPRINKLING of WATER

From time to time on Sundays, especially in Easter Time, instead of the customary Penitential Act, the Blessing and Sprinkling of Water may take place (see pp. 78-81) as a reminder of Baptism.

4 PENITENTIAL ACT (3 forms)

(Omitted when the Rite for the Blessing and Sprinkling of Water [see pp. 78-81] has taken place or some part of the liturgy of the hours has preceded.)

Before we hear God's word, we acknowledge our sins humbly, ask for mercy, and accept his pardon.

Invitation to repent:

After the introduction to the day's Mass, the Priest invites the people to recall their sins and to repent of them in silence:

Priest: Brethren (brothers and sisters), let us acknowledge our sins,
and so prepare ourselves to celebrate the sacred mysteries.

Then, after a brief silence, one of the following forms is used.

Priest and **PEOPLE:**

I confess to almighty God
and to you, my brothers and sisters,
that I have greatly sinned,
in my thoughts and in my words,
in what I have done and in what I have failed to do,

They strike their breast:

through my fault, through my fault,
through my most grievous fault;

Then they continue:

therefore I ask blessed Mary ever-Virgin,
all the Angels and Saints,
and you, my brothers and sisters,
to pray for me to the Lord our God.

B — **OR** —

Priest: Have mercy on us, O Lord.

PEOPLE: **For we have sinned against you.**

Priest: Show us, O Lord, your mercy.

PEOPLE: **And grant us your salvation.**

C — **OR** —

Priest, or a Deacon or another minister:

You were sent to heal the contrite of heart:
Lord, have mercy.

PEOPLE: **Lord, have mercy.**

Priest or other minister:

You came to call sinners:
Christ, have mercy.

PEOPLE: **Christ, have mercy.**

Priest or other minister:

You are seated at the right hand of the Father to intercede for us:

Lord, have mercy.

PEOPLE: **Lord, have mercy.**

Absolution:

At the end of any of the forms of the Penitential Act:

Priest: May almighty God have mercy on us,
forgive us our sins,
and bring us to everlasting life.

PEOPLE: **Amen.**

5 KYRIE

Unless included in the Penitential Act, the Kyrie is sung or said by all, with alternating parts for the choir or cantor and for the people:

℣. Lord, have mercy.

℟. **Lord, have mercy.**

℣. Christ, have mercy.

℟. **Christ, have mercy.**

℣. Lord, have mercy.

℟. **Lord, have mercy.**

6 GLORIA

As the Church assembled in the Spirit we praise and pray to the Father and the Lamb.

When the Gloria is sung or said, the Priest or the cantors or everyone together may begin it:

Glory to God in the highest,
and on earth peace to people of good will.

We praise you,
we bless you,
we adore you,
we glorify you,
we give you thanks for your great glory,
Lord God, heavenly King,
O God, almighty Father.

Lord Jesus Christ, Only Begotten Son,
Lord God, Lamb of God, Son of the Father,
you take away the sins of the world,
have mercy on us;

you take away the sins of the world,
receive our prayer;
you are seated at the right hand of the Father,
have mercy on us.

For you alone are the Holy One,
you alone are the Lord,
you alone are the Most High,
Jesus Christ,
with the Holy Spirit,
in the glory of God the Father.
Amen.

7 COLLECT

The Priest invites us to pray silently for a moment and then, in our name, expresses the theme of the day's celebration and petitions God the Father through the mediation of Christ in the Holy Spirit.

Priest: Let us pray.

→ **Turn to Today's Mass**

Priest and people pray silently for a while. Then the Priest says the Collect prayer, at the end of which the people acclaim:

PEOPLE: **Amen.**

Liturgy of the WORD

The proclamation of God's Word is always centred on Christ, present through his Word. Old Testament writings prepare for him; New Testament books speak of him directly. All of scripture calls us to believe once more and to follow. After the reading we reflect on God's words and respond to them.

As in Today's Mass **SIT**

8 FIRST READING

At the end of the reading: Reader: The word of the Lord.

PEOPLE: **Thanks be to God.**

9 RESPONSORIAL PSALM

The people repeat the response sung by the cantor the first time and then after each verse.

10 SECOND READING

At the end of the reading: Reader: The word of the Lord.

PEOPLE: **Thanks be to God.**

11 GOSPEL ACCLAMATION **STAND**

Jesus will speak to us in the Gospel. We rise now out of respect and prepare for his message with the Alleluia.

The people repeat the Alleluia after the cantor's Alleluia and then after the verse. During Lent one of the following invocations is used as a response instead of the Alleluia:

(a) **Glory and praise to you, Lord Jesus Christ!**
(b) **Glory to you, Lord Jesus Christ, Wisdom of God the Father!**
(c) **Glory to you, Word of God, Lord Jesus Christ!**
(d) **Glory to you, Lord Jesus Christ, Son of the living God!**

(e) **Praise and honour to you, Lord Jesus Christ!**
(f) **Praise to you, Lord Jesus Christ, King of endless glory!**
(g) **Marvellous and great are your works, O Lord!**
(h) **Salvation, glory, and power to the Lord Jesus Christ!**

12 GOSPEL DIALOGUE

Before proclaiming the Gospel, the Deacon asks the Priest: Your blessing, Father. *The Priest says:*

May the Lord be in your heart and on your lips, that you may proclaim his Gospel worthily and well, in the name of the Father, and of the Son, ✠ and of the Holy Spirit. *The Deacon answers:* Amen.

If there is no Deacon, the Priest says inaudibly:

Cleanse my heart and my lips, almighty God,
that I may worthily proclaim your holy Gospel.

13 GOSPEL READING

Deacon (or Priest):
The Lord be with you.

PEOPLE: **And with your spirit.**

Deacon (or Priest):

✠ A reading from the holy Gospel according to N.

PEOPLE: **Glory to you, O Lord.**

At the end:

Deacon (or Priest):
The Gospel of the Lord.

PEOPLE: **Praise to you, Lord Jesus Christ.**

Then the Deacon (or Priest) kisses the book, saying inaudibly: Through the words of the Gospel may our sins be wiped away.

14 HOMILY

SIT

God's word is spoken again in the Homily. The Holy Spirit speaking through the lips of the preacher explains and applies today's biblical readings to the needs of this particular congregation. He calls us to respond to Christ through the life we lead.

15 PROFESSION OF FAITH (CREED) STAND

As a people we express our acceptance of God's message in the Scriptures and Homily. We summarize our faith by proclaiming a creed handed down from the early Church.

All say the Profession of Faith on Sundays.

THE NICENE CREED

I believe in one God,
the Father almighty,
maker of heaven and earth,
of all things visible and invisible.

I believe in one Lord Jesus Christ,
the Only Begotten Son of God,
born of the Father before all ages.
God from God, Light from Light,
true God from true God,
begotten, not made, consubstantial with the Father;
through him all things were made.
For us men and for our salvation
he came down from heaven,
and by the Holy Spirit was incarnate of the Virgin Mary,
and became man. } *bow*

For our sake he was crucified under Pontius Pilate,
he suffered death and was buried,
and rose again on the third day
in accordance with the Scriptures.
He ascended into heaven
and is seated at the right hand of the Father.
He will come again in glory
to judge the living and the dead
and his kingdom will have no end.

I believe in the Holy Spirit, the Lord, the giver of life,
who proceeds from the Father and the Son,
who with the Father and the Son is adored and glorified,
who has spoken through the prophets.

**I believe in one, holy, catholic and apostolic Church.
I confess one Baptism for the forgiveness of sins
and I look forward to the resurrection of the dead
and the life of the world to come. Amen.**

OR — APOSTLES' CREED

Especially during Lent and Easter Time, the Apostles' Creed may be said after the Homily.

**I believe in God,
the Father almighty,
Creator of heaven and earth,
and in Jesus Christ, his only Son, our Lord,
who was conceived by the Holy Spirit,
*born of the Virgin Mary,*** } *bow*
**suffered under Pontius Pilate,
was crucified, died and was buried;
he descended into hell;
on the third day he rose again from the dead;
he ascended into heaven,
and is seated at the right hand of God the Father almighty;
from there he will come to judge the living and the dead.**

**I believe in the Holy Spirit,
the holy catholic Church,
the communion of saints,
the forgiveness of sins,
the resurrection of the body,
and life everlasting. Amen.**

16 UNIVERSAL PRAYER (Prayer of the Faithful)

As a priestly people we unite with one another to pray for today's needs in the Church and the world.

After the Priest gives the introduction the Deacon or other minister sings or says the invocations.

PEOPLE: **Lord, hear our prayer.**

(or other response, according to local custom)
At the end the Priest says the concluding prayer:

PEOPLE: **Amen.**

THE LITURGY OF THE EUCHARIST

17 PRESENTATION AND PREPARATION OF THE GIFTS **SIT**

While the people's gifts are brought forward to the Priest and are placed on the altar, the Offertory Chant is sung.

Before placing the bread on the altar, the Priest says inaudibly:

Blessed are you, Lord God of all creation,
for through your goodness we have received
the bread we offer you:
fruit of the earth and work of human hands,
it will become for us the bread of life.

If there is no singing, the Priest may say this prayer aloud, and the people may respond:

PEOPLE: **Blessed be God for ever.**

When he pours wine and a little water into the chalice, the Deacon (or the Priest) says inaudibly:

By the mystery of this water and wine
may we come to share in the divinity of Christ
who humbled himself to share in our humanity.

Before placing the chalice on the altar, he says:

Blessed are you, Lord God of all creation,
for through your goodness we have received
the wine we offer you:
fruit of the vine and work of human hands,
it will become our spiritual drink.

If there is no singing, the Priest may say this prayer aloud, and the people may respond:

PEOPLE: **Blessed be God for ever.**

The Priest says inaudibly:

With humble spirit and contrite heart
may we be accepted by you, O Lord,
and may our sacrifice in your sight this day
be pleasing to you, Lord God.

Then he washes his hands, saying:

Wash me, O Lord, from my iniquity
and cleanse me from my sin.

18 INVITATION TO PRAYER

Priest: Pray, brethren (brothers and sisters),
that my sacrifice and yours
may be acceptable to God,
the almighty Father. **STAND**

PEOPLE:

May the Lord accept the sacrifice at your hands
for the praise and glory of his name,
for our good
and the good of all his holy Church.

19 PRAYER OVER THE OFFERINGS

The Priest, speaking in our name, asks the Father to bless and accept these gifts.

→ Turn to Today's Mass

At the end, PEOPLE: **Amen.**

20 EUCHARISTIC PRAYER

We begin the eucharistic service of praise and thanksgiving, the centre of the entire celebration, the central prayer of worship. We lift our hearts to God, and offer praise and thanks as the Priest addresses this prayer to the Father through Jesus Christ. Together we join Christ in his sacrifice, celebrating his memorial in the holy meal and acknowledging with him the wonderful works of God in our lives.

21 PREFACE DIALOGUE

Priest: The Lord be with you.
PEOPLE: And with your spirit.
Priest: Lift up your hearts.
PEOPLE: We lift them up to the Lord.
Priest: Let us give thanks to the Lord our God.
PEOPLE: It is right and just.

22 PREFACE

As indicated in the individual Masses of this Missal, the Priest may say one of the following Prefaces (listed in numerical order).

23 PREFACE ACCLAMATION

Priest and **PEOPLE:**

Holy, Holy, Holy Lord, God of hosts.
Heaven and earth are full of your glory.
Hosanna in the highest.
Blessed is he who comes in the name of the Lord.
Hosanna in the highest. **KNEEL**

Then the Priest continues with one of the following Eucharistic Prayers.

EUCHARISTIC PRAYER .... Choice of ten

1 EUCHARISTIC PRAYER No. 1

The Roman Canon

(This Eucharistic Prayer is especially suitable for Sundays and Masses with proper Communicantes *and* Hanc igitur.*)*

[The words within parentheses may be omitted.]

To you, therefore, most merciful Father,
we make humble prayer and petition
through Jesus Christ, your Son, our Lord:
that you accept
and bless ✠ these gifts, these offerings,
these holy and unblemished sacrifices,
which we offer you firstly
for your holy catholic Church.
Be pleased to grant her peace,
to guard, unite and govern her
throughout the whole world,
together with your servant *N.* our Pope,
and *N.* our Bishop,
and all those who, holding to the truth,
hand on the catholic and apostolic faith.

Remember, Lord, your servants *N.* and *N.*
and all gathered here,
whose faith and devotion are known to you.
For them, we offer you this sacrifice of praise
or they offer it for themselves
and all who are dear to them:
for the redemption of their souls,
in hope of health and well-being,
and paying their homage to you,
the eternal God, living and true.

In communion with those whose memory we venerate,
especially the glorious ever-Virgin Mary,
Mother of our God and Lord, Jesus Christ,
† and blessed Joseph, her Spouse,
your blessed Apostles and Martyrs
Peter and Paul, Andrew,
(James, John,
Thomas, James, Philip,
Bartholomew, Matthew,
Simon and Jude;
Linus, Cletus, Clement, Sixtus,
Cornelius, Cyprian,
Lawrence, Chrysogonus,
John and Paul,
Cosmas and Damian)
and all your Saints;
we ask that through their merits and prayers,
in all things we may be defended
by your protecting help.
(Through Christ our Lord. Amen.)

Therefore, Lord, we pray:*
graciously accept this oblation of our service,
that of your whole family;
order our days in your peace,
and command that we be delivered from eternal damnation
and counted among the flock of those you have chosen.
(Through Christ our Lord. Amen.)

Be pleased, O God, we pray,
to bless, acknowledge,
and approve this offering in every respect;

† * *See p. 95 for proper* Communicantes *and* Hanc igitur.

1 make it spiritual and acceptable,
so that it may become for us
the Body and Blood of your most beloved Son,
our Lord Jesus Christ.

On the day before he was to suffer,
he took bread in his holy and venerable hands,
and with eyes raised to heaven
to you, O God, his almighty Father,
giving you thanks, he said the blessing,
broke the bread
and gave it to his disciples, saying:

Take this, all of you, and eat of it,
for this is my Body,
which will be given up for you.

In a similar way when supper was ended,
he took this precious chalice
in his holy and venerable hands,
and once more giving you thanks, he said the blessing
and gave the chalice to his disciples, saying:

Take this, all of you, and drink from it,
for this is the chalice of my Blood,
the Blood of the new and eternal covenant,
which will be poured out for you and for many
for the forgiveness of sins.

Do this in memory of me.

Priest: The mystery of faith. *(Memorial Acclamation)*

PEOPLE:

A We proclaim your Death, O Lord,
and profess your Resurrection
until you come again.

B **When we eat this Bread and drink this Cup,
we proclaim your Death, O Lord,
until you come again.**

C **Save us, Saviour of the world,
for by your Cross and Resurrection
you have set us free.**

Therefore, O Lord,
as we celebrate the memorial of the blessed Passion,
the Resurrection from the dead,
and the glorious Ascension into heaven
of Christ, your Son, our Lord,
we your servants and your holy people,
offer to your glorious majesty
from the gifts that you have given us,
this pure victim,
this holy victim,
this spotless victim,
the holy Bread of eternal life
and the Chalice of everlasting salvation.

Be pleased to look upon these offerings
with a serene and kindly countenance,
and to accept them,
as once you were pleased to accept
the gifts of your servant Abel the just,
the sacrifice of Abraham, our father in faith,
and the offering of your high priest Melchizedek,
a holy sacrifice, a spotless victim.

In humble prayer we ask you, almighty God:
command that these gifts be borne
by the hands of your holy Angel
to your altar on high
in the sight of your divine majesty,

1 so that all of us, who through this participation at the altar
receive the most holy Body and Blood of your Son,
may be filled with every grace and heavenly blessing.
(Through Christ our Lord. Amen.)

Remember also, Lord, your servants, *N.* and *N.*,
who have gone before us with the sign of faith
and rest in the sleep of peace.
Grant them, O Lord, we pray,
and all who sleep in Christ,
a place of refreshment, light and peace.
(Through Christ our Lord. Amen.)

To us, also your servants, who, though sinners,
hope in your abundant mercies,
graciously grant some share
and fellowship with your holy Apostles and Martyrs:
with John the Baptist, Stephen,
Matthias, Barnabas,
(Ignatius, Alexander,
Marcellinus, Peter,
Felicity, Perpetua,
Agatha, Lucy,
Agnes, Cecilia, Anastasia)
and all your Saints;
admit us, we beseech you,
into their company,
not weighing our merits,
but granting us your pardon,
through Christ our Lord.

Through whom
you continue to make all these good things,
O Lord;
you sanctify them, fill them with life,
bless them, and bestow them upon us.

(Concluding Doxology)

Through him, and with him, and in him,
O God, almighty Father,
in the unity of the Holy Spirit,
all glory and honour is yours,
for ever and ever.

All reply: **Amen.**

Continue with the Mass, as on p. 72.

2 EUCHARISTIC PRAYER No. 2

(This Eucharistic Prayer is particularly suitable on Weekdays or for special circumstances.)

STAND

℣. The Lord be with you.
℟. **And with your spirit.**

℣. Lift up your hearts.
℟. **We lift them up to the Lord.**

℣. Let us give thanks to the Lord our God.
℟. **It is right and just.**

It is truly right and just, our duty and our salvation,
always and everywhere to give you thanks, Father most holy,
through your beloved Son, Jesus Christ,
your Word through whom you made all things,
whom you sent as our Saviour and Redeemer,
incarnate by the Holy Spirit and born of the Virgin.

Fulfilling your will
and gaining for you a holy people,
he stretched out his hands
as he endured his Passion,
so as to break the bonds of death
and manifest the resurrection.

And so, with the Angels and all the Saints
we declare your glory,
as with one voice we acclaim:

Holy, Holy, Holy Lord God of hosts.
Heaven and earth are full of your glory.
Hosanna in the highest.
Blessed is he who comes in the name of the Lord.
Hosanna in the highest.

KNEEL

You are indeed Holy, O Lord,
the fount of all holiness.

Make holy, therefore, these gifts, we pray,
by sending down your Spirit upon them like the dewfall,
so that they may become for us
the Body and ✠ Blood of our Lord Jesus Christ.

At the time he was betrayed
and entered willingly into his Passion,
he took bread and, giving thanks, broke it,
and gave it to his disciples, saying:

Take this, all of you, and eat of it,
for this is my Body,
which will be given up for you.

In a similar way, when supper was ended,
he took the chalice
and, once more giving thanks,
he gave it to his disciples, saying:

Take this, all of you, and drink from it,
for this is the chalice of my Blood,
the Blood of the new and eternal covenant,
which will be poured out for you and for many
for the forgiveness of sins.
Do this in memory of me.

2 Priest: The mystery of faith. *(Memorial Acclamation)*

PEOPLE:

A **We proclaim your Death, O Lord,
and profess your Resurrection
until you come again.**

B **When we eat this Bread and drink this Cup,
we proclaim your Death, O Lord,
until you come again.**

C **Save us, Saviour of the world,
for by your Cross and Resurrection
you have set us free.**

Therefore, as we celebrate
the memorial of his Death and Resurrection,
we offer you, Lord,
the Bread of life and the Chalice of salvation,
giving thanks that you have held us worthy
to be in your presence and minister to you.

Humbly we pray
that, partaking of the Body and Blood of Christ,
we may be gathered into one by the Holy Spirit.

Remember, Lord, your Church,
spread throughout the world,
and bring her to the fullness of charity,
together with *N.* our Pope and *N.* our Bishop
and all the clergy.

In Masses for the Dead the following may be added:

Remember your servant *N.*,
whom you have called (today)
from this world to yourself.

Grant that he (she) who was united with your Son in a death like his,
may also be one with him in his Resurrection.

Remember also our brothers and sisters
who have fallen asleep in the hope of the resurrection,
and all who have died in your mercy:
welcome them into the light of your face.
Have mercy on us all, we pray,
that with the Blessed Virgin Mary, Mother of God,
with blessed Joseph, her Spouse,
with the blessed Apostles,
and all the Saints who have pleased you throughout the ages,
we may merit to be co-heirs to eternal life,
and may praise and glorify you
through your Son, Jesus Christ.

(Concluding Doxology)

Through him, and with him, and in him,
O God, almighty Father,
in the unity of the Holy Spirit,
all glory and honour is yours,
for ever and ever.

All reply: **Amen.**

Continue with the Mass, as on p. 72.

3 EUCHARISTIC PRAYER No. 3

(This Eucharistic Prayer may be used with any Preface and preferably on Sundays and feast days.)

KNEEL

You are indeed Holy, O Lord,
and all you have created
rightly gives you praise,
for through your Son our Lord Jesus Christ,
by the power and working of the Holy Spirit,
you give life to all things and make them holy,
and you never cease to gather a people to yourself,
so that from the rising of the sun to its setting
a pure sacrifice may be offered to your name.

Therefore, O Lord, we humbly implore you:
by the same Spirit graciously make holy
these gifts we have brought to you for consecration,
that they may become the Body and ✠ Blood
of your Son our Lord Jesus Christ,
at whose command we celebrate these mysteries.

For on the night he was betrayed
he himself took bread,
and, giving you thanks, he said the blessing,
broke the bread and gave it to his disciples, saying:

Take this, all of you, and eat of it,
for this is my Body,
which will be given up for you.

In a similar way, when supper was ended,
he took the chalice,

and, giving you thanks, he said the blessing,
and gave the chalice to his disciples, saying:

*Take this, all of you, and drink from it,
for this is the chalice of my Blood,
the Blood of the new and eternal covenant,
which will be poured out for you and for many
for the forgiveness of sins.*

Do this in memory of me.

Priest: The mystery of faith. *(Memorial Acclamation)*

PEOPLE:

A **We proclaim your Death, O Lord,
and profess your Resurrection
until you come again.**

B **When we eat this Bread and drink this Cup,
we proclaim your Death, O Lord,
until you come again.**

C **Save us, Saviour of the world,
for by your Cross and Resurrection
you have set us free.**

Therefore, O Lord, as we celebrate the memorial
of the saving Passion of your Son,
his wondrous Resurrection
and Ascension into heaven,
and as we look forward to his second coming,
we offer you in thanksgiving
this holy and living sacrifice.

Look, we pray, upon the oblation of your Church
and, recognizing the sacrificial Victim by whose death
you willed to reconcile us to yourself,

grant that we, who are nourished
by the Body and Blood of your Son
and filled with his Holy Spirit,
may become one body, one spirit in Christ.

May he make us
an eternal offering to you,
so that we may obtain an inheritance with your elect,
especially with the most Blessed Virgin Mary, Mother of God,
with blessed Joseph, her Spouse,
with your blessed Apostles and glorious Martyrs
(with Saint *N.*: the Saint of the day or Patron Saint)
and with all the Saints,
on whose constant intercession in your presence
we rely for unfailing help.

May this Sacrifice of our reconciliation,
we pray, O Lord,
advance the peace and salvation of all the world.
Be pleased to confirm in faith and charity
your pilgrim Church on earth,
with your servant *N.* our Pope and *N.* our Bishop,
the Order of Bishops, all the clergy,
and the entire people you have gained for your own.

Listen graciously to the prayers of this family,
whom you have summoned before you:
in your compassion, O merciful Father,
gather to yourself all your children
scattered throughout the world.

† To our departed brothers and sisters
and to all who were pleasing to you
at their passing from this life,
give kind admittance to your Kingdom.

There we hope to enjoy for ever the fullness of your glory
through Christ our Lord,
through whom you bestow on the world all that is good. †

(Concluding Doxology)

Through him, and with him, and in him,
O God, almighty Father,
in the unity of the Holy Spirit,
all glory and honour is yours,
for ever and ever.

All reply: **Amen.**

Continue with the Mass, as on p. 72.

---

* *In Masses for the Dead the following may be said:*

† Remember your servant *N.*
whom you have called (today)
from this world to yourself.
Grant that he (she) who was united with your Son in a death like his,
may also be one with him in his Resurrection,
when from the earth
he will raise up in the flesh those who have died,
and transform our lowly body
after the pattern of his own glorious body.
To our departed brothers and sisters, too,
and to all who were pleasing to you
at their passing from this life,
give kind admittance to your Kingdom.
There we hope to enjoy for ever the fullness of your glory,
when you will wipe away every tear from our eyes.
For seeing you, our God, as you are,
we shall be like you for all the ages
and praise you without end,
through Christ our Lord,
through whom you bestow on the world all that is good. †

4 EUCHARISTIC PRAYER No. 4

STAND

℣. The Lord be with you.
℟. **And with your spirit.**

℣. Lift up your hearts.
℟. **We lift them up to the Lord.**

℣. Let us give thanks to the Lord our God.
℟. **It is right and just.**

It is truly right to give you thanks,
truly just to give you glory, Father most holy,
for you are the one God living and true,
existing before all ages and abiding for all eternity,
dwelling in unapproachable light;
yet you, who alone are good, the source of life,
have made all that is,
so that you might fill your creatures with blessings
and bring joy to many of them by the glory of your light.

And so, in your presence are countless hosts of Angels,
who serve you day and night
and, gazing upon the glory of your face,
glorify you without ceasing.

With them we, too, confess your name in exultation,
giving voice to every creature under heaven,
as we acclaim:

Holy, Holy, Holy Lord God of hosts.
Heaven and earth are full of your glory.
Hosanna in the highest.

Blessed is he who comes in the name of the Lord.
Hosanna in the highest. 4

KNEEL

We give you praise, Father most holy,
for you are great
and you have fashioned all your works
in wisdom and in love.
You formed man in your own image
and entrusted the whole world to his care,
so that in serving you alone, the Creator,
he might have dominion over all creatures.
And when through disobedience he had lost your friendship,
you did not abandon him to the domain of death.
For you came in mercy to the aid of all,
so that those who seek might find you.
Time and again you offered them covenants
and through the prophets
taught them to look forward to salvation.

And you so loved the world, Father most holy,
that in the fullness of time
you sent your Only Begotten Son to be our Saviour.
Made incarnate by the Holy Spirit
and born of the Virgin Mary,
he shared our human nature
in all things but sin.
To the poor he proclaimed the good news of salvation,
to prisoners, freedom,
and to the sorrowful of heart, joy.
To accomplish your plan,
he gave himself up to death,
and, rising from the dead,
he destroyed death and restored life.

4 And that we might live no longer for ourselves
but for him who died and rose again for us,
he sent the Holy Spirit from you, Father,
as the first fruits for those who believe,
so that, bringing to perfection his work in the world,
he might sanctify creation to the full.

Therefore, O Lord, we pray:
may this same Holy Spirit
graciously sanctify these offerings,
that they may become
the Body and ✠ Blood of our Lord Jesus Christ
for the celebration of this great mystery,
which he himself left us
as an eternal covenant.

For when the hour had come
for him to be glorified by you, Father most holy,
having loved his own who were in the world,
he loved them to the end:
and while they were at supper,
he took bread, blessed and broke it,
and gave it to his disciples, saying:

Take this, all of you, and eat of it,
for this is my Body,
which will be given up for you.

In a similar way,
taking the chalice filled with the fruit of the vine,
he gave thanks,
and gave the chalice to his disciples, saying:

Take this, all of you, and drink from it,
for this is the chalice of my Blood,
the Blood of the new and eternal covenant,

which will be poured out for you and for many
for the forgiveness of sins.

Do this in memory of me.

Priest: The mystery of faith. *(Memorial Acclamation)*

PEOPLE:

A **We proclaim your Death, O Lord,**
and profess your Resurrection
until you come again.

B **When we eat this Bread and drink this Cup,**
we proclaim your Death, O Lord,
until you come again.

C **Save us, Saviour of the world,**
for by your Cross and Resurrection
you have set us free.

Therefore, O Lord,
as we now celebrate the memorial of our redemption,
we remember Christ's Death
and his descent to the realm of the dead,
we proclaim his Resurrection
and his Ascension to your right hand,
and, as we await his coming in glory,
we offer you his Body and Blood,
the sacrifice acceptable to you
which brings salvation to the whole world.

Look, O Lord, upon the Sacrifice
which you yourself have provided for your Church,
and grant in your loving kindness
to all who partake of this one Bread and one Chalice
that, gathered into one body by the Holy Spirit,

4 they may truly become a living sacrifice in Christ
to the praise of your glory.

Therefore, Lord, remember now
all for whom we offer this sacrifice:
especially your servant *N.* our Pope,
N. our Bishop, and the whole Order of Bishops,
all the clergy,
those who take part in this offering,
those gathered here before you,
your entire people,
and all who seek you with a sincere heart.

Remember also
those who have died in the peace of your Christ
and all the dead,
whose faith you alone have known.

To all of us, your children,
grant, O merciful Father,
that we may enter into a heavenly inheritance
with the Blessed Virgin Mary, Mother of God,
with blessed Joseph, her Spouse,
and with your Apostles and Saints in your Kingdom.
There, with the whole of creation,
freed from the corruption of sin and death,
may we glorify you through Christ our Lord,
through whom you bestow on the world all that is good.

(Concluding Doxology)

Through him, and with him, and in him,
O God, almighty Father,
in the unity of the Holy Spirit,
all glory and honour is yours,
for ever and ever.

All reply: **Amen.**

Continue with the Mass, as on p. 72.

EUCHARISTIC PRAYER FOR RECONCILIATION I

R 1

STAND

℣. The Lord be with you.
℟. **And with your spirit.**

℣. Lift up your hearts.
℟. **We lift them up to the Lord.**

℣. Let us give thanks to the Lord our God.
℟. **It is right and just.**

It is truly right and just
that we should always give you thanks,
Lord, holy Father, almighty and eternal God.

For you do not cease to spur us on
to possess a more abundant life
and, being rich in mercy,
you constantly offer pardon
and call on sinners
to trust in your forgiveness alone.

Never did you turn away from us,
and, though time and again we have broken your covenant,
you have bound the human family to yourself
through Jesus your Son, our Redeemer,
with a new bond of love so tight
that it can never be undone.

Even now you set before your people
a time of grace and reconciliation,
and, as they turn back to you in spirit,
you grant them hope in Christ Jesus
and a desire to be of service to all,

R1

while they entrust themselves
more fully to the Holy Spirit.

And so, filled with wonder,
we extol the power of your love,
and, proclaiming our joy
at the salvation that comes from you,
we join in the heavenly hymn of countless hosts,
as without end we acclaim:

Holy, Holy, Holy Lord God of hosts.
Heaven and earth are full of your glory.
Hosanna in the highest.
Blessed is he who comes in the name of the Lord.
Hosanna in the highest.

KNEEL

You are indeed Holy, O Lord,
and from the world's beginning
are ceaselessly at work,
so that the human race may become holy,
just as you yourself are holy.

Look, we pray, upon your people's offerings
and pour out on them the power of your Spirit,
that they may become the Body and ✠ Blood
of your beloved Son, Jesus Christ,
in whom we, too, are your sons and daughters.

Indeed, though we once were lost
and could not approach you,
you loved us with the greatest love:
for your Son, who alone is just,
handed himself over to death,

and did not disdain to be nailed for our sake
to the wood of the Cross.

But before his arms were outstretched between heaven and earth,
to become the lasting sign of your covenant,
he desired to celebrate the Passover with his disciples.

As he ate with them,
he took bread
and, giving you thanks, he said the blessing,
broke the bread and gave it to them, saying:

Take this, all of you, and eat of it,
for this is my Body,
which will be given up for you.

In a similar way, when supper was ended,
knowing that he was about to reconcile all things in himself
through his Blood to be shed on the Cross,
he took the chalice, filled with the fruit of the vine,
and once more giving you thanks,
handed the chalice to his disciples, saying:

Take this, all of you, and drink from it,
for this is the chalice of my Blood,
the Blood of the new and eternal covenant,
which will be poured out for you and for many
for the forgiveness of sins.

Do this in memory of me.

R1

Priest: The mystery of faith. *(Memorial Acclamation)*

PEOPLE:

A **We proclaim your Death, O Lord,**
and profess your Resurrection
until you come again.

B **When we eat this Bread and drink this Cup,**
we proclaim your Death, O Lord,
until you come again.

C **Save us, Saviour of the world,**
for by your Cross and Resurrection
you have set us free.

Therefore, as we celebrate
the memorial of your Son Jesus Christ,
who is our Passover and our surest peace,
we celebrate his Death and Resurrection from the dead,
and looking forward to his blessed Coming,
we offer you, who are our faithful and merciful God,
this sacrificial Victim
who reconciles to you the human race.

Look kindly, most compassionate Father,
on those you unite to yourself
by the Sacrifice of your Son,
and grant that, by the power of the Holy Spirit,
as they partake of this one Bread and one Chalice,
they may be gathered into one Body in Christ,
who heals every division.

Be pleased to keep us always
in communion of mind and heart,
together with *N.* our Pope and *N.* our Bishop.
Help us to work together
for the coming of your Kingdom,
until the hour when we stand before you,
Saints among the Saints in the halls of heaven,
with the Blessed Virgin Mary, Mother of God,
the blessed Apostles and all the Saints,
and with our deceased brothers and sisters,
whom we humbly commend to your mercy.

Then, freed at last from the wound of corruption
and made fully into a new creation,
we shall sing to you with gladness
the thanksgiving of Christ,
who lives for all eternity.

(Concluding Doxology)

Through him, and with him, and in him,
O God, almighty Father,
in the unity of the Holy Spirit,
all glory and honour is yours,
for ever and ever.

The people respond: **Amen.**

Continue with the Mass, as on p. 72.

R 2

EUCHARISTIC PRAYER FOR RECONCILIATION II

STAND

℣. The Lord be with you.
℟. **And with your spirit.**

℣. Lift up your hearts.
℟. **We lift them up to the Lord.**

℣. Let us give thanks to the Lord our God.
℟. **It is right and just.**

It is truly right and just
that we should give you thanks and praise,
O God, almighty Father,
for all you do in this world,
through our Lord Jesus Christ.

For though the human race
is divided by dissension and discord,
yet we know that by testing us
you change our hearts
to prepare them for reconciliation.

Even more, by your Spirit you move human hearts
that enemies may speak to each other again,
adversaries join hands,
and peoples seek to meet together.

By the working of your power
it comes about, O Lord,
that hatred is overcome by love,
revenge gives way to forgiveness,
and discord is changed to mutual respect.

Therefore, as we give you ceaseless thanks
with the choirs of heaven,

we cry out to your majesty on earth,
and without end we acclaim:

**Holy, Holy, Holy Lord God of hosts.
Heaven and earth are full of your glory.
Hosanna in the highest.
Blessed is he who comes in the name of the Lord.
Hosanna in the highest.**

KNEEL

You, therefore, almighty Father,
we bless through Jesus Christ your Son,
who comes in your name.
He himself is the Word that brings salvation,
the hand you extend to sinners,
the way by which your peace is offered to us.
When we ourselves had turned away from you
on account of our sins,
you brought us back to be reconciled, O Lord,
so that, converted at last to you,
we might love one another
through your Son,
whom for our sake you handed over to death.

And now, celebrating the reconciliation
Christ has brought us,
we entreat you:
sanctify these gifts by the outpouring of your Spirit,
that they may become the Body and ✠ Blood of your Son,
whose command we fulfill
when we celebrate these mysteries.

For when about to give his life to set us free,
as he reclined at supper,

R2 he himself took bread into his hands,
and, giving you thanks, he said the blessing,
broke the bread and gave it to his disciples, saying:

Take this, all of you, and eat of it,
for this is my Body,
which will be given up for you.

In a similar way, on that same evening,
he took the chalice of blessing in his hands,
confessing your mercy,
and gave the chalice to his disciples, saying:

Take this, all of you, and drink from it,
for this is the chalice of my Blood,
the Blood of the new and eternal covenant,
which will be poured out for you and for many
for the forgiveness of sins.

Do this in memory of me.

Priest: The mystery of faith. *(Memorial Acclamation)*

PEOPLE:

A **We proclaim your Death, O Lord,**
and profess your Resurrection
until you come again.

B **When we eat this Bread and drink this Cup,**
we proclaim your Death, O Lord,
until you come again.

C **Save us, Saviour of the world,**
for by your Cross and Resurrection
you have set us free.

Celebrating, therefore, the memorial
of the Death and Resurrection of your Son,
who left us this pledge of his love,
we offer you what you have bestowed on us,
the Sacrifice of perfect reconciliation.

Holy Father, we humbly beseech you
to accept us also, together with your Son,
and in this saving banquet
graciously to endow us with his very Spirit,
who takes away everything
that estranges us from one another.

May he make your Church a sign of unity
and an instrument of your peace among all people
and may he keep us in communion
with *N.* our Pope and *N.* our Bishop
and all the Bishops
and your entire people.

Just as you have gathered us now at the table of your Son,
so also bring us together,
with the glorious Virgin Mary, Mother of God,
with your blessed Apostles and all the Saints,
with our brothers and sisters
and those of every race and tongue
who have died in your friendship.
Bring us to share with them the unending banquet of unity
in a new heaven and a new earth,
where the fullness of your peace will shine forth
in Christ Jesus our Lord.

(Concluding Doxology)

Through him, and with him, and in him,
O God, almighty Father,
in the unity of the Holy Spirit,
all glory and honour is yours,
for ever and ever.

The people respond: **Amen.**

Continue with the Mass, as on p. 72.

VI EUCHARISTIC PRAYER FOR USE IN MASSES FOR VARIOUS NEEDS I

STAND

℣. The Lord be with you.
℟. **And with your spirit.**

℣. Lift up your hearts.
℟. **We lift them up to the Lord.**

℣. Let us give thanks to the Lord our God.
℟. **It is right and just.**

It is truly right to give you thanks
and raise to you a hymn of glory and praise,
O Lord, Father of infinite goodness.

For by the word of your Son's Gospel
you have brought together one Church
from every people, tongue, and nation,
and, having filled her with life by the power of your Spirit,
you never cease through her
to gather the whole human race into one.

Manifesting the covenant of your love,
she dispenses without ceasing
the blessed hope of your Kingdom
and shines bright as the sign of your faithfulness,
which in Christ Jesus our Lord
you promised would last for eternity.

And so, with all the Powers of heaven,
we worship you constantly on earth,
while, with all the Church,
as one voice we acclaim:

Holy, Holy, Holy Lord God of hosts.
Heaven and earth are full of your glory.
Hosanna in the highest.
Blessed is he who comes in the name of the Lord.
Hosanna in the highest.

KNEEL

You are indeed Holy and to be glorified, O God,
who love the human race
and who always walk with us on the journey of life.
Blessed indeed is your Son,
present in our midst
when we are gathered by his love,
and when, as once for the disciples, so now for us,
he opens the Scriptures and breaks the bread.

Therefore, Father most merciful,
we ask that you send forth your Holy Spirit
to sanctify these gifts of bread and wine,
that they may become for us
the Body and ✠ Blood
of our Lord Jesus Christ.

On the day before he was to suffer,
on the night of the Last Supper,
he took bread and said the blessing,
broke the bread and gave it to his disciples, saying:

Take this, all of you, and eat of it,
for this is my Body,
which will be given up for you.

In a similar way, when supper was ended,
he took the chalice, gave you thanks
and gave the chalice to his disciples, saying:

V1

Take this, all of you, and drink from it,
for this is the chalice of my Blood,
the Blood of the new and eternal covenant,
which will be poured out for you and for many
for the forgiveness of sins.

Do this in memory of me.

Priest: The mystery of faith. *(Memorial Acclamation)*

PEOPLE:

A **We proclaim your Death, O Lord,**
and profess your Resurrection
until you come again.

B **When we eat this Bread and drink this Cup,**
we proclaim your Death, O Lord,
until you come again.

C **Save us, Saviour of the world,**
for by your Cross and Resurrection
you have set us free.

Therefore, holy Father,
as we celebrate the memorial of Christ your Son,
our Saviour,
whom you led through his Passion and Death on the Cross
to the glory of the Resurrection,
and whom you have seated at your right hand,
we proclaim the work of your love until he comes again
and we offer you the Bread of life
and the Chalice of blessing.

Look with favour on the oblation of your Church,
in which we show forth

the paschal Sacrifice of Christ that has been handed on to us,
and grant that, by the power of the Spirit of your love,
we may be counted now and until the day of eternity
among the members of your Son,
in whose Body and Blood we have communion.

Lord, renew your Church (which is in *N.*)
by the light of the Gospel.
Strengthen the bond of unity
between the faithful and the pastors of your people,
together with *N.* our Pope, *N.* our Bishop,
and the whole Order of Bishops,
that in a world torn by strife
your people may shine forth
as a prophetic sign of unity and concord.

Remember our brothers and sisters (*N.* and *N.*),
who have fallen asleep in the peace of your Christ,
and all the dead, whose faith you alone have known.
Admit them to rejoice in the light of your face,
and in the resurrection give them the fullness of life.

Grant also to us,
when our earthly pilgrimage is done,
that we may come to an eternal dwelling place
and live with you for ever;
there, in communion with the Blessed Virgin Mary, Mother of God,
with the Apostles and Martyrs,

V1

(with Saint *N.*: the Saint of the day or Patron)
and with all the Saints,
we shall praise and exalt you
through Jesus Christ, your Son.

(Concluding Doxology)

Through him, and with him, and in him,
O God, almighty Father,
in the unity of the Holy Spirit,
all glory and honour is yours,
for ever and ever.

The people respond: **Amen.**

Continue with the Mass, as on p. 72.

EUCHARISTIC PRAYER FOR USE IN MASSES FOR VARIOUS NEEDS II

STAND

℣. The Lord be with you.
℟. **And with your spirit.**

℣. Lift up your hearts.
℟. **We lift them up to the Lord.**

℣. Let us give thanks to the Lord our God.
℟. **It is right and just.**

It is truly right and just, our duty and our salvation,
always and everywhere to give you thanks,
Lord, holy Father,
creator of the world and source of all life.

For you never forsake the works of your wisdom,
but by your providence are even now at work in our midst.
With mighty hand and outstretched arm
you led your people Israel through the desert.
Now, as your Church makes her pilgrim journey in the world,
you always accompany her
by the power of the Holy Spirit
and lead her along the paths of time
to the eternal joy of your Kingdom,
through Christ our Lord.

And so, with the Angels and Saints,
we, too, sing the hymn of your glory,
as without end we acclaim:

V2

Holy, Holy, Holy Lord God of hosts.
Heaven and earth are full of your glory.
Hosanna in the highest.
Blessed is he who comes in the name of the Lord.
Hosanna in the highest.

KNEEL

You are indeed Holy and to be glorified, O God,
who love the human race
and who always walk with us on the journey of life.
Blessed indeed is your Son,
present in our midst
when we are gathered by his love,
and when, as once for the disciples, so now for us,
he opens the Scriptures and breaks the bread.

Therefore, Father most merciful,
we ask that you send forth your Holy Spirit
to sanctify these gifts of bread and wine,
that they may become for us
the Body and ✠ Blood
of our Lord Jesus Christ.

On the day before he was to suffer,
on the night of the Last Supper,
he took bread and said the blessing,
broke the bread and gave it to his disciples, saying:

Take this, all of you, and eat of it,
for this is my Body,
which will be given up for you.

In a similar way, when supper was ended,
he took the chalice, gave you thanks
and gave the chalice to his disciples, saying:

Take this, all of you, and drink from it,
for this is the chalice of my Blood,
the Blood of the new and eternal covenant,
which will be poured out for you and for many
for the forgiveness of sins.

Do this in memory of me.

Priest: The mystery of faith. *(Memorial Acclamation)*

PEOPLE:

A **We proclaim your Death, O Lord,**
and profess your Resurrection
until you come again.

B **When we eat this Bread and drink this Cup,**
we proclaim your Death, O Lord,
until you come again.

C **Save us, Saviour of the world,**
for by your Cross and Resurrection
you have set us free.

Therefore, holy Father,
as we celebrate the memorial of Christ your Son, our Saviour,
whom you led through his Passion and Death on the Cross
to the glory of the Resurrection,
and whom you have seated at your right hand,
we proclaim the work of your love until he comes again
and we offer you the Bread of life
and the Chalice of blessing.

Look with favour on the oblation of your Church,
in which we show forth

V2

the paschal Sacrifice of Christ that has been handed on to us,
and grant that, by the power of the Spirit of your love,
we may be counted now and until the day of eternity
among the members of your Son,
in whose Body and Blood we have communion.

And so, having called us to your table, Lord,
confirm us in unity,
so that, together with *N.* our Pope and *N.* our Bishop,
with all Bishops, Priests and Deacons,
and your entire people,
as we walk your ways with faith and hope,
we may strive to bring joy and trust into the world.

Remember our brothers and sisters (*N.* and *N.*),
who have fallen asleep in the peace of your Christ,
and all the dead, whose faith you alone have known.
Admit them to rejoice in the light of your face,
and in the resurrection give them the fullness of life.

Grant also to us,
when our earthly pilgrimage is done,
that we may come to an eternal dwelling place
and live with you for ever;
there, in communion with the Blessed Virgin Mary, Mother of God,
with the Apostles and Martyrs,
(with Saint *N.*: the Saint of the day or Patron)

and with all the Saints,
we shall praise and exalt you
through Jesus Christ, your Son.

(Concluding Doxology)

Through him, and with him, and in him,
O God, almighty Father,
in the unity of the Holy Spirit,
all glory and honour is yours,
for ever and ever.

The people respond: **Amen.**

Continue with the Mass, as on p. 72.

V 3

EUCHARISTIC PRAYER FOR USE IN MASSES FOR VARIOUS NEEDS III

STAND

℣. The Lord be with you.
℟. **And with your spirit.**

℣. Lift up your hearts.
℟. **We lift them up to the Lord.**

℣. Let us give thanks to the Lord our God.
℟. **It is right and just.**

It is truly right and just, our duty and our salvation,
always and everywhere to give you thanks,
holy Father, Lord of heaven and earth,
through Christ our Lord.

For by your Word you created the world
and you govern all things in harmony.
You gave us the same Word made flesh as Mediator,
and he has spoken your words to us
and called us to follow him.
He is the way that leads us to you,
the truth that sets us free,
the life that fills us with gladness.

Through your Son
you gather men and women,
whom you made for the glory of your name,
into one family,
redeemed by the Blood of his Cross
and signed with the seal of the Spirit.

Therefore, now and for ages unending,
with all the Angels,

we proclaim your glory,
as in joyful celebration we acclaim:

Holy, Holy, Holy Lord God of hosts.
Heaven and earth are full of your glory.
Hosanna in the highest.
Blessed is he who comes in the name of the Lord.
Hosanna in the highest.

KNEEL

You are indeed Holy and to be glorified, O God,
who love the human race
and who always walk with us on the journey of life.
Blessed indeed is your Son,
present in our midst
when we are gathered by his love,
and when, as once for the disciples, so now for us,
he opens the Scriptures and breaks the bread.

Therefore, Father most merciful,
we ask that you send forth your Holy Spirit
to sanctify these gifts of bread and wine,
that they may become for us
the Body and ✠ Blood
of our Lord Jesus Christ.

On the day before he was to suffer,
on the night of the Last Supper,
he took bread and said the blessing,
broke the bread and gave it to his disciples, saying:

Take this, all of you, and eat of it,
for this is my Body,
which will be given up for you.

V3

In a similar way, when supper was ended,
he took the chalice, gave you thanks
and gave the chalice to his disciples, saying:

Take this, all of you, and drink from it,
for this is the chalice of my Blood,
the Blood of the new and eternal covenant,
which will be poured out for you and for many
for the forgiveness of sins.

Do this in memory of me.

Priest: The mystery of faith. *(Memorial Acclamation)*

PEOPLE:

A **We proclaim your Death, O Lord,**
and profess your Resurrection
until you come again.

B **When we eat this Bread and drink this Cup,**
we proclaim your Death, O Lord,
until you come again.

C **Save us, Saviour of the world,**
for by your Cross and Resurrection
you have set us free.

Therefore, holy Father,
as we celebrate the memorial of Christ your Son, our Saviour,
whom you led through his Passion and Death on the Cross
to the glory of the Resurrection,
and whom you have seated at your right hand,
we proclaim the work of your love until he comes again
and we offer you the Bread of life
and the Chalice of blessing.

Look with favour on the oblation of your Church,
in which we show forth
the paschal Sacrifice of Christ that has been handed on to us,
and grant that, by the power of the Spirit of your love,
we may be counted now and until the day of eternity
among the members of your Son,
in whose Body and Blood we have communion.

By our partaking of this mystery, almighty Father,
give us life through your Spirit,
grant that we may be conformed to the image of your Son,
and confirm us in the bond of communion,
together with *N.* our Pope and *N.* our Bishop,
with all other Bishops,
with Priests and Deacons,
and with your entire people.

Grant that all the faithful of the Church,
looking into the signs of the times by the light of faith,
may constantly devote themselves
to the service of the Gospel.

Keep us attentive to the needs of all
that, sharing their grief and pain,
their joy and hope,
we may faithfully bring them the good news of salvation
and go forward with them
along the way of your Kingdom.

V3

Remember our brothers and sisters (*N.* and *N.*),
who have fallen asleep in the peace of your Christ,
and all the dead, whose faith you alone have known.
Admit them to rejoice in the light of your face,
and in the resurrection give them the fullness of life.

Grant also to us,
when our earthly pilgrimage is done,
that we may come to an eternal dwelling place
and live with you for ever;
there, in communion with the Blessed Virgin Mary, Mother of God,
with the Apostles and Martyrs,
(with Saint *N.*: the Saint of the day or Patron)
and with all the Saints,
we shall praise and exalt you
through Jesus Christ, your Son.

(Concluding Doxology)

Through him, and with him, and in him,
O God, almighty Father,
in the unity of the Holy Spirit,
all glory and honour is yours,
for ever and ever.

The people respond: **Amen.**

Continue with the Mass, as on p. 72.

EUCHARISTIC PRAYER FOR USE IN MASSES FOR VARIOUS NEEDS IV

V 4

STAND

℣. The Lord be with you.
℟. **And with your spirit.**

℣. Lift up your hearts.
℟. **We lift them up to the Lord.**

℣. Let us give thanks to the Lord our God.
℟. **It is right and just.**

It is truly right and just, our duty and our salvation,
always and everywhere to give you thanks,
Father of mercies and faithful God.

For you have given us Jesus Christ, your Son,
as our Lord and Redeemer.

He always showed compassion
for children and for the poor,
for the sick and for sinners,
and he became a neighbour
to the oppressed and the afflicted.

By word and deed he announced to the world
that you are our Father
and that you care for all your sons and daughters.

And so, with all the Angels and Saints,
we exalt and bless your name
and sing the hymn of your glory,
as without end we acclaim:

V4

**Holy, Holy, Holy Lord God of hosts.
Heaven and earth are full of your glory.
Hosanna in the highest.
Blessed is he who comes in the name of the Lord.
Hosanna in the highest.**

KNEEL

You are indeed Holy and to be glorified, O God,
who love the human race
and who always walk with us on the journey of life.
Blessed indeed is your Son,
present in our midst
when we are gathered by his love
and when, as once for the disciples, so now for us,
he opens the Scriptures and breaks the bread.

Therefore, Father most merciful,
we ask that you send forth your Holy Spirit
to sanctify these gifts of bread and wine,
that they may become for us
the Body and ✠ Blood
of our Lord Jesus Christ.

On the day before he was to suffer,
on the night of the Last Supper,
he took bread and said the blessing,
broke the bread and gave it to his disciples, saying:

*Take this, all of you, and eat of it,
for this is my Body,
which will be given up for you.*

In a similar way, when supper was ended,
he took the chalice, gave you thanks
and gave the chalice to his disciples, saying:

V4

Take this, all of you, and drink from it,
for this is the chalice of my Blood,
the Blood of the new and eternal covenant,
which will be poured out for you and for many
for the forgiveness of sins.
Do this in memory of me.

Priest: The mystery of faith. *(Memorial Acclamation)*

PEOPLE:

A **We proclaim your Death, O Lord,**
and profess your Resurrection
until you come again.

B **When we eat this Bread and drink this Cup,**
we proclaim your Death, O Lord,
until you come again.

C **Save us, Saviour of the world,**
for by your Cross and Resurrection
you have set us free.

Therefore, holy Father,
as we celebrate the memorial of Christ your Son, our Saviour,
whom you led through his Passion and Death on the Cross
to the glory of the Resurrection,
and whom you have seated at your right hand,
we proclaim the work of your love until he comes again
and we offer you the Bread of life
and the Chalice of blessing.

Look with favour on the oblation of your Church,
in which we show forth

V4

the paschal Sacrifice of Christ that has been handed on to us,
and grant that, by the power of the Spirit of your love,
we may be counted now and until the day of eternity
among the members of your Son,
in whose Body and Blood we have communion.

Bring your Church, O Lord,
to perfect faith and charity,
together with *N.* our Pope and *N.* our Bishop,
with all Bishops, Priests and Deacons,
and the entire people you have made your own.

Open our eyes
to the needs of our brothers and sisters;
inspire in us words and actions
to comfort those who labour and are burdened.
Make us serve them truly,
after the example of Christ and at his command.
And may your Church stand as a living witness
to truth and freedom,
to peace and justice,
that all people may be raised up to a new hope.

Remember our brothers and sisters (*N.* and *N.*),
who have fallen asleep in the peace of your Christ,
and all the dead, whose faith you alone have known.
Admit them to rejoice in the light of your face,
and in the resurrection give them the fullness of life.

Grant also to us,
when our earthly pilgrimage is done,
that we may come to an eternal dwelling place
and live with you for ever;
there, in communion with the Blessed Virgin Mary,
Mother of God,
with the Apostles and Martyrs,
(with Saint *N.*: the Saint of the day or Patron)
and with all the Saints,
we shall praise and exalt you
through Jesus Christ, your Son.

(Concluding Doxology)

Through him, and with him, and in him,
O God, almighty Father,
in the unity of the Holy Spirit,
all glory and honour is yours,
for ever and ever.

The people respond: **Amen.**

Continue with the Mass, as on p. 72.

THE COMMUNION RITE

To prepare for the paschal meal, to welcome the Lord, we pray for forgiveness and exchange a sign of peace. Before eating Christ's Body and drinking his Blood, we must be one with him and with all our brothers and sisters in the Church.

24 THE LORD'S PRAYER

STAND

Priest: At the Saviour's command
and formed by divine teaching,
we dare to say:

Priest and **PEOPLE**:

**Our Father, who art in heaven,
hallowed be thy name;
thy kingdom come;
thy will be done
on earth as it is in heaven.
Give us this day our daily bread,
and forgive us our trespasses,
as we forgive those who trespass against us;
and lead us not into temptation,
but deliver us from evil.**

Priest: Deliver us, Lord, we pray, from every evil,
graciously grant us peace in our days,
that, by the help of your mercy,
we may be always free from sin
and safe from all distress,
as we await the blessed hope
and the coming of our Saviour, Jesus Christ.

PEOPLE: **For the kingdom,
the power and the glory are yours
now and for ever.**

25 SIGN OF PEACE

The Church is a community of Christians joined by the Spirit in love. It needs to express, deepen, and restore its peaceful unity before eating the one Body of the Lord and drinking from the one cup of salvation. We do this by a sign of peace.

The Priest says the prayer for peace:

Lord Jesus Christ,
who said to your Apostles:
Peace I leave you, my peace I give you,
look not on our sins,
but on the faith of your Church,
and graciously grant her peace and unity
in accordance with your will.
Who live and reign for ever and ever.

PEOPLE: **Amen.**

Priest: The peace of the Lord be with you always.

PEOPLE: **And with your spirit.**

Deacon (or Priest):
Let us offer each other the sign of peace.

The people exchange a sign of peace, communion and charity, according to local customs.

26 LAMB OF GOD

Christians are gathered for the "breaking of the bread," another name for the Mass. In Communion, though many we are made one body in the one bread, which is Christ.

The Priest breaks the host over the paten and places a small piece in the chalice, saying quietly:

May this mingling of the Body and Blood
of our Lord Jesus Christ
bring eternal life to us who receive it.

Meanwhile the following is sung or said:

PEOPLE:

Lamb of God, you take away the sins of the world,
have mercy on us.
Lamb of God, you take away the sins of the world,
have mercy on us.
Lamb of God, you take away the sins of the world,
grant us peace.

The invocation may even be repeated several times if the breaking of the bread is prolonged. Only the final time, however, is grant us peace *said.*

We pray in silence and then voice words of humility and hope as our final preparation before meeting Christ in the Eucharist.

Before Communion, the Priest says quietly one of the following prayers:

Lord Jesus Christ, Son of the living God,
who, by the will of the Father
and the work of the Holy Spirit,
through your Death gave life to the world,
free me by this, your most holy Body and Blood,
from all my sins and from every evil;
keep me always faithful to your commandments,
and never let me be parted from you.

OR

May the receiving of your Body and Blood,
Lord Jesus Christ,
not bring me to judgment and condemnation,
but through your loving mercy
be for me protection in mind and body
and a healing remedy.

27 INVITATION TO COMMUNION

The Priest genuflects, takes the host and, holding it slightly raised above the paten or above the chalice, while facing the people, says aloud:

Priest: Behold the Lamb of God,
behold him who takes away the sins of the world.
Blessed are those called to the supper of the Lamb.

Priest and **PEOPLE** (once only):

Lord, I am not worthy
that you should enter under my roof,
but only say the word
and my soul shall be healed.

Before reverently consuming the Body of Christ, the Priest says quietly:

May the Body of Christ
keep me safe for eternal life.

Then, before reverently consuming the Blood of Christ, he takes the chalice and says quietly:

May the Blood of Christ
keep me safe for eternal life.

28 COMMUNION

He then gives Communion to the people.

Priest: The Body of Christ. Communicant: **Amen.**
Priest: The Blood of Christ. Communicant: **Amen.**

The Communion Psalm or other appropriate chant is sung while Communion is given to the faithful. If there is no singing, the Communion Antiphon is said.

→ Turn to Today's Mass

The vessels are purified by the Priest or Deacon or acolyte. Meanwhile he says quietly:

What has passed our lips as food, O Lord,
may we possess in purity of heart,
that what has been given to us in time
may be our healing for eternity.

After Communion there may be a period of sacred silence, or a canticle of praise or a hymn may be sung.

29 PRAYER AFTER COMMUNION **STAND**

The Priest prays in our name that we may live the life of faith since we have been strengthened by Christ himself. Our *Amen* makes his prayer our own.

Priest: Let us pray.

Priest and people may pray silently for a while unless silence has just been observed. Then the Priest says the Prayer after Communion.

→ Turn to Today's Mass

At the end, **PEOPLE: Amen.**

THE CONCLUDING RITES

We have heard God's Word and eaten the Body of Christ. Now it is time for us to leave, to do good works, to praise and bless the Lord in our daily lives.

30 SOLEMN BLESSING STAND

After any brief announcements, the Blessing and Dismissal follow:

Priest: The Lord be with you.

PEOPLE: **And with your spirit.**

31 FINAL BLESSING

Priest: May almighty God bless you,
the Father, and the Son, ✠ and the Holy Spirit.

PEOPLE: **Amen.**

On certain days or occasions, this formula of blessing is preceded, in accordance with the rubrics, by another more solemn formula of blessing (pp. 97-105) or by a prayer over the people (pp. 105-110).

32 DISMISSAL

Deacon (or Priest):

A Go forth, the Mass is ended.

B Go and announce the Gospel of the Lord.

C Go in peace, glorifying the Lord by your life.

D Go in peace.

PEOPLE: **Thanks be to God.**

If any liturgical service follows immediately, the rites of dismissal are omitted.

RITE FOR THE BLESSING AND SPRINKLING OF WATER

If this rite is celebrated during Mass, it takes the place of the usual Penitential Act at the beginning of Mass.

After the greeting, the Priest stands at his chair and faces the people. With a vessel containing the water to be blessed before him, he calls upon the people to pray in these or similar words:

Dear brethren (brothers and sisters),
let us humbly beseech the Lord our God
to bless this water he has created,
which will be sprinkled on us
as a memorial of our Baptism.
May he help us by his grace
to remain faithful to the Spirit we have received.

And after a brief pause for silence, he continues with hands joined:

Almighty ever-living God,
who willed that through water,
the fountain of life and the source of purification,
even souls should be cleansed
and receive the gift of eternal life;
be pleased, we pray, to ✠ bless this water,
by which we seek protection on this your day, O Lord.
Renew the living spring of your grace within us
and grant that by this water we may be defended
from all ills of spirit and body,
and so approach you with hearts made clean
and worthily receive your salvation.
Through Christ our Lord. ℟. **Amen.**

Or:

Almighty Lord and God,
who are the source and origin of all life,

whether of body or soul,
we ask you to ✠ bless this water,
which we use in confidence
to implore forgiveness for our sins
and to obtain the protection of your grace
against all illness and every snare of the enemy.
Grant, O Lord, in your mercy,
that living waters may always spring up for our salvation,
and so may we approach you with a pure heart
and avoid all danger to body and soul.
Through Christ our Lord. ℟. **Amen.**

Or (during Easter Time):

Lord our God,
in your mercy be present to your people's prayers,
and, for us who recall the wondrous work of our creation
and the still greater work of our redemption,
graciously ✠ bless this water.
For you created water to make the fields fruitful
and to refresh and cleanse our bodies.
You also made water the instrument of your mercy:
for through water you freed your people from slavery
and quenched their thirst in the desert;
through water the Prophets proclaimed the new covenant
you were to enter upon with the human race;
and last of all,
through water, which Christ made holy in the Jordan,
you have renewed our corrupted nature
in the bath of regeneration.
Therefore, may this water be for us
a memorial of the Baptism we have received,
and grant that we may share
in the gladness of our brothers and sisters
who at Easter have received their Baptism.
Through Christ our Lord. ℟. **Amen.**

Where the circumstances of the place or the custom of the people suggest that the mixing of salt be preserved in the blessing of water, the Priest may bless salt, saying:

We humbly ask you, almighty God:
be pleased in your faithful love to bless ✠ this salt
you have created,
for it was you who commanded the prophet Elisha
to cast salt into water,
that impure water might be purified.
Grant, O Lord, we pray,
that, wherever this mixture of salt and water is sprinkled,
every attack of the enemy may be repulsed
and your Holy Spirit may be present
to keep us safe at all times.
Through Christ our Lord. ℟. **Amen.**

Then he pours the salt into the water, without saying anything.

Afterward, taking the aspergillum, the Priest sprinkles himself and the ministers, then the clergy and people, moving through the church, if appropriate.

Meanwhile, one of the following chants, or another appropriate chant is sung.

Outside Easter Time

ANTIPHON 1 Ps. 51(50).9

Sprinkle me with hyssop, O Lord, and I shall be cleansed; wash me and I shall be whiter than snow.

ANTIPHON 2 Ez. 36.25-26

I will pour clean water upon you, and you will be made clean of all your impurities, and I shall give you a new spirit, says the Lord.

HYMN Cf. 1 Pt. 1.3-5

Blessed be the God and Father of our Lord Jesus Christ, who in his great mercy has given us new birth into a living hope through the Resurrection of Jesus Christ from

the dead, into an inheritance that will not perish, preserved for us in heaven for the salvation to be revealed in the last time!

During Easter Time

ANTIPHON 1 Cf. Ez. 47.1-2, 9

I saw water flowing from the Temple, from its right-hand side, alleluia: and all to whom this water came were saved and shall say: Alleluia, alleluia.

ANTIPHON 2 Cf. Zeph. 3.8; Ez. 36.25

On the day of my resurrection, says the Lord, alleluia, I will gather the nations and assemble the kingdoms and I will pour clean water upon you, alleluia.

ANTIPHON 3 Cf. Dn. 3.77, 79

You springs and all that moves in the waters, sing a hymn to God, alleluia.

ANTIPHON 4 1 Pt. 2.9

O chosen race, royal priesthood, holy nation, proclaim the mighty works of him who called you out of darkness into his wonderful light, alleluia.

ANTIPHON 5

From your side, O Christ, bursts forth a spring of water, by which the squalor of the world is washed away and life is made new again, alleluia.

When he returns to his chair and the singing is over, the Priest stands facing the people and, with hands joined, says:

May almighty God cleanse us of our sins,
and through the celebration of this Eucharist
make us worthy to share at the table of his Kingdom.
℟. **Amen.**

Then, when it is prescribed, the hymn Gloria in excelsis (Glory to God in the highest) *is sung or said.*

PREFACES

PREFACE I OF ADVENT (1)

The two comings of Christ

(From the First Sunday of Advent to December 16)

It is truly right and just, our duty and our salvation,
always and everywhere to give you thanks,
Lord, holy Father, almighty and eternal God,
through Christ our Lord.

For he assumed at his first coming
the lowliness of human flesh,
and so fulfilled the design you formed long ago,
and opened for us the way to eternal salvation,
that, when he comes again in glory and majesty
and all is at last made manifest,
we who watch for that day
may inherit the great promise
in which now we dare to hope.

And so, with Angels and Archangels,
with Thrones and Dominions,
and with all the hosts and Powers of heaven,
we sing the hymn of your glory,
as without end we acclaim: → No. 23, p. 23

PREFACE II OF ADVENT (2)

The twofold expectation of Christ

(From December 17 to December 24)

It is truly right and just, our duty and our salvation,
always and everywhere to give you thanks,
Lord, holy Father, almighty and eternal God,
through Christ our Lord.

For all the oracles of the prophets foretold him,
the Virgin Mother longed for him
with love beyond all telling,

John the Baptist sang of his coming
and proclaimed his presence when he came.

It is by his gift that already we rejoice
at the mystery of his Nativity,
so that he may find us watchful in prayer
and exultant in his praise.

And so, with Angels and Archangels,
with Thrones and Dominions,
and with all the hosts and Powers of heaven,
we sing the hymn of your glory,
as without end we acclaim: → No. 23, p. 23

PREFACE I OF THE NATIVITY OF THE LORD (3)

Christ the Light

(For the Nativity of the Lord, its Octave Day and within the Octave)

It is truly right and just, our duty and our salvation,
always and everywhere to give you thanks,
Lord, holy Father, almighty and eternal God.

For in the mystery of the Word made flesh
a new light of your glory has shone upon the eyes of our mind,
so that, as we recognize in him God made visible,
we may be caught up through him in love of things invisible.

And so, with Angels and Archangels,
with Thrones and Dominions,
and with all the hosts and Powers of heaven,
we sing the hymn of your glory,
as without end we acclaim: → No. 23, p. 23

PREFACE II OF THE NATIVITY OF THE LORD (4)

The restoration of all things in the Incarnation

(For the Nativity of the Lord, its Octave Day and within the Octave)

It is truly right and just, our duty and our salvation,
always and everywhere to give you thanks,
Lord, holy Father, almighty and eternal God,
through Christ our Lord.

For on the feast of this awe-filled mystery,
though invisible in his own divine nature,

he has appeared visibly in ours;
and begotten before all ages,
he has begun to exist in time;
so that, raising up in himself all that was cast down,
he might restore unity to all creation
and call straying humanity back to the heavenly Kingdom.

And so, with all the Angels, we praise you,
as in joyful celebration we acclaim: → No. 23, p. 23

PREFACE III OF THE NATIVITY OF THE LORD (5)

The exchange in the Incarnation of the Word

(For the Nativity of the Lord, its Octave Day and within the Octave)

It is truly right and just, our duty and our salvation,
always and everywhere to give you thanks,
Lord, holy Father, almighty and eternal God,
through Christ our Lord.

For through him the holy exchange that restores our life
has shone forth today in splendour:
when our frailty is assumed by your Word
not only does human mortality receive unending honour
but by this wondrous union we, too, are made eternal.

And so, in company with the choirs of Angels,
we praise you, and with joy we proclaim: → No. 23, p. 23

PREFACE I OF LENT (8)

The spiritual meaning of Lent

It is truly right and just, our duty and our salvation,
always and everywhere to give you thanks,
Lord, holy Father, almighty and eternal God,
through Christ our Lord.

For by your gracious gift each year
your faithful await the sacred paschal feasts
with the joy of minds made pure,
so that, more eagerly intent on prayer
and on the works of charity,
and participating in the mysteries
by which they have been reborn,

they may be led to the fullness of grace
that you bestow on your sons and daughters.

And so, with Angels and Archangels,
with Thrones and Dominions,
and with all the hosts and Powers of heaven,
we sing the hymn of your glory,
as without end we acclaim: → No. 23, p. 23

PREFACE II OF LENT (9)

Spiritual penance

It is truly right and just, our duty and our salvation,
always and everywhere to give you thanks,
Lord, holy Father, almighty and eternal God.

For you have given your children a sacred time
for the renewing and purifying of their hearts,
that, freed from disordered affections,
they may so deal with the things of this passing world
as to hold rather to the things that eternally endure.

And so, with all the Angels and Saints,
we praise you, as without end we acclaim: → No. 23, p. 23

PREFACE I OF EASTER I (21)

The Paschal Mystery

(Easter Vigil, Easter Sunday and during the Octave and Easter Time)

(At the Easter Vigil, is said "on this night"; on Easter Sunday and throughout the Octave of Easter, is said "on this day"; on other days of Easter Time, is said "in this time.")

It is truly right and just, our duty and our salvation,
at all times to acclaim you, O Lord,
but (on this night / on this day / in this time) above all
to laud you yet more gloriously,
when Christ our Passover has been sacrificed.

For he is the true Lamb
who has taken away the sins of the world;
by dying he has destroyed our death,
and by rising, restored our life.

Therefore, overcome with paschal joy,
every land, every people exults in your praise
and even the heavenly Powers, with the angelic hosts,
sing together the unending hymn of your glory,
as they acclaim: → No. 23, p. 23

PREFACE II OF EASTER (22)

New life in Christ

It is truly right and just, our duty and our salvation,
at all times to acclaim you, O Lord,
but in this time above all to laud you yet more gloriously,
when Christ our Passover has been sacrificed.

Through him the children of light rise to eternal life
and the halls of the heavenly Kingdom
are thrown open to the faithful;
for his Death is our ransom from death,
and in his rising the life of all has risen.

Therefore, overcome with paschal joy,
every land, every people exults in your praise
and even the heavenly Powers, with the angelic hosts,
sing together the unending hymn of your glory,
as they acclaim: → No. 23, p. 23

PREFACE III OF EASTER (23)

Christ living and always interceding for us

It is truly right and just, our duty and our salvation,
at all times to acclaim you, O Lord,
but in this time above all to laud you yet more gloriously,
when Christ our Passover has been sacrificed.

He never ceases to offer himself for us
but defends us and ever pleads our cause before you:
he is the sacrificial Victim who dies no more,
the Lamb, once slain, who lives for ever.

Therefore, overcome with paschal joy,
every land, every people exults in your praise
and even the heavenly Powers, with the angelic hosts,
sing together the unending hymn of your glory,
as they acclaim: → No. 23, p. 23

PREFACE IV OF EASTER (24)

The restoration of the universe through the Paschal Mystery

It is truly right and just, our duty and our salvation,
at all times to acclaim you, O Lord,

but in this time above all to laud you yet more gloriously,
when Christ our Passover has been sacrificed.

For, with the old order destroyed,
a universe cast down is renewed,
and integrity of life is restored to us in Christ.

Therefore, overcome with paschal joy,
every land, every people exults in your praise
and even the heavenly Powers, with the angelic hosts,
sing together the unending hymn of your glory,
as they acclaim: → No. 23, p. 23

PREFACE V OF EASTER (25)

Christ, Priest and Victim

It is truly right and just, our duty and our salvation,
at all times to acclaim you, O Lord,
but in this time above all to laud you yet more gloriously,
when Christ our Passover has been sacrificed.

By the oblation of his Body,
he brought the sacrifices of old to fulfillment
in the reality of the Cross
and, by commending himself to you for our salvation,
showed himself the Priest, the Altar, and the Lamb of sacrifice.

Therefore, overcome with paschal joy,
every land, every people exults in your praise
and even the heavenly Powers, with the angelic hosts,
sing together the unending hymn of your glory,
as they acclaim: → No. 23, p. 23

PREFACE I OF THE ASCENSION OF THE LORD (26)

The mystery of the Ascension

(Ascension to the Saturday before Pentecost inclusive)

It is truly right and just, our duty and our salvation,
always and everywhere to give you thanks,
Lord, holy Father, almighty and eternal God.

For the Lord Jesus, the King of glory,
conqueror of sin and death,

ascended (today) to the highest heavens,
as the Angels gazed in wonder.

Mediator between God and man,
judge of the world and Lord of hosts,
he ascended, not to distance himself from our lowly state
but that we, his members, might be confident of following
where he, our Head and Founder, has gone before.

Therefore, overcome with paschal joy,
every land, every people exults in your praise
and even the heavenly Powers, with the angelic hosts,
sing together the unending hymn of your glory,
as they acclaim: → No. 23, p. 23

PREFACE II OF THE ASCENSION OF THE LORD (27)

The mystery of the Ascension

(Ascension to the Saturday before Pentecost inclusive)

It is truly right and just, our duty and our salvation,
always and everywhere to give you thanks,
Lord, holy Father, almighty and eternal God,
through Christ our Lord.

For after his Resurrection
he plainly appeared to all his disciples
and was taken up to heaven in their sight,
that he might make us sharers in his divinity.

Therefore, overcome with paschal joy,
every land, every people exults in your praise
and even the heavenly Powers, with the angelic hosts,
sing together the unending hymn of your glory,
as they acclaim: → No. 23, p. 23

PREFACE I OF THE SUNDAYS IN ORDINARY TIME (29)

The Paschal Mystery and the People of God

It is truly right and just, our duty and our salvation,
always and everywhere to give you thanks,
Lord, holy Father, almighty and eternal God,
through Christ our Lord.

For through his Paschal Mystery,
he accomplished the marvellous deed,

by which he has freed us from the yoke of sin and death,
summoning us to the glory of being now called
a chosen race, a royal priesthood,
a holy nation, a people for your own possession,
to proclaim everywhere your mighty works,
for you have called us out of darkness
into your own wonderful light.

And so, with Angels and Archangels,
with Thrones and Dominions,
and with all the hosts and Powers of heaven,
we sing the hymn of your glory,
as without end we acclaim: → No. 23, p. 23

PREFACE II OF THE SUNDAYS IN ORDINARY TIME (30)

The mystery of salvation

It is truly right and just, our duty and our salvation,
always and everywhere to give you thanks,
Lord, holy Father, almighty and eternal God,
through Christ our Lord.

For out of compassion for the waywardness that is ours,
he humbled himself and was born of the Virgin;
by the passion of the Cross he freed us from unending death,
and by rising from the dead he gave us life eternal.

And so, with Angels and Archangels,
with Thrones and Dominions,
and with all the hosts and Powers of heaven,
we sing the hymn of your glory,
as without end we acclaim: → No. 23, p. 23

PREFACE III OF THE SUNDAYS IN ORDINARY TIME (31)

The salvation of man by a man

It is truly right and just, our duty and our salvation,
always and everywhere to give you thanks,
Lord, holy Father, almighty and eternal God.

For we know it belongs to your boundless glory,
that you came to the aid of mortal beings with your divinity
and even fashioned for us a remedy out of mortality itself,
that the cause of our downfall

might become the means of our salvation,
through Christ our Lord.

Through him the host of Angels adores your majesty
and rejoices in your presence for ever.
May our voices, we pray, join with theirs
in one chorus of exultant praise, as we acclaim:

→ No. 23, p. 23

PREFACE IV OF THE SUNDAYS IN ORDINARY TIME (32)

The history of salvation

It is truly right and just, our duty and our salvation,
always and everywhere to give you thanks,
Lord, holy Father, almighty and eternal God,
through Christ our Lord.

For by his birth he brought renewal
to humanity's fallen state,
and by his suffering, cancelled out our sins;
by his rising from the dead
he has opened the way to eternal life,
and by ascending to you, O Father,
he has unlocked the gates of heaven.

And so, with the company of Angels and Saints,
we sing the hymn of your praise,
as without end we acclaim:

→ No. 23, p. 23

PREFACE V OF THE SUNDAYS IN ORDINARY TIME (33)

Creation

It is truly right and just, our duty and our salvation,
always and everywhere to give you thanks,
Lord, holy Father, almighty and eternal God.

For you laid the foundations of the world
and have arranged the changing of times and seasons;
you formed man in your own image
and set humanity over the whole world in all its wonder,
to rule in your name over all you have made
and for ever praise you in your mighty works,
through Christ our Lord.

And so, with all the Angels, we praise you,
as in joyful celebration we acclaim: → No. 23, p. 23

PREFACE VI OF THE SUNDAYS IN ORDINARY TIME (34)

The pledge of the eternal Passover

It is truly right and just, our duty and our salvation,
always and everywhere to give you thanks,
Lord, holy Father, almighty and eternal God.

For in you we live and move and have our being,
and while in this body
we not only experience the daily effects of your care,
but even now possess the pledge of life eternal.

For, having received the first fruits of the Spirit,
through whom you raised up Jesus from the dead,
we hope for an everlasting share in the Paschal Mystery.

And so, with all the Angels, we praise you,
as in joyful celebration we acclaim: → No. 23, p. 23

PREFACE VII OF THE SUNDAYS IN ORDINARY TIME (35)

Salvation through the obedience of Christ

It is truly right and just, our duty and our salvation,
always and everywhere to give you thanks,
Lord, holy Father, almighty and eternal God.

For you so loved the world
that in your mercy you sent us the Redeemer,
to live like us in all things but sin,
so that you might love in us what you loved in your Son,
by whose obedience we have been restored to those gifts of yours
that, by sinning, we had lost in disobedience.

And so, Lord, with all the Angels and Saints,
we, too, give you thanks, as in exultation we acclaim:
→ No. 23, p. 23

PREFACE VIII OF THE SUNDAYS IN ORDINARY TIME (36)

The Church united by the unity of the Trinity

It is truly right and just, our duty and our salvation,
always and everywhere to give you thanks,
Lord, holy Father, almighty and eternal God.

For, when your children were scattered afar by sin,
through the Blood of your Son and the power of the Spirit,
you gathered them again to yourself,
that a people, formed as one by the unity of the Trinity,
made the body of Christ and the temple of the Holy Spirit,
might, to the praise of your manifold wisdom,
be manifest as the Church.

And so, in company with the choirs of Angels,
we praise you, and with joy we proclaim: → No. 23, p. 23

PREFACE I OF THE MOST HOLY EUCHARIST (47)

The Sacrifice and the Sacrament of Christ

It is truly right and just, our duty and our salvation,
always and everywhere to give you thanks,
Lord, holy Father, almighty and eternal God,
through Christ our Lord.

For he is the true and eternal Priest,
who instituted the pattern of an everlasting sacrifice
and was the first to offer himself as the saving Victim,
commanding us to make this offering as his memorial.
As we eat his flesh that was sacrificed for us,
we are made strong,
and, as we drink his Blood that was poured out for us,
we are washed clean.

And so, with Angels and Archangels,
with Thrones and Dominions,
and with all the hosts and Powers of heaven,
we sing the hymn of your glory,
as without end we acclaim: → No. 23, p. 23

PREFACE II OF THE MOST HOLY EUCHARIST (48)

The fruits of the Most Holy Eucharist

It is truly right and just, our duty and our salvation,
always and everywhere to give you thanks,
Lord, holy Father, almighty and eternal God,
through Christ our Lord.

For at the Last Supper with his Apostles,
establishing for the ages to come the saving memorial of the Cross,
he offered himself to you as the unblemished Lamb,
the acceptable gift of perfect praise.

Nourishing your faithful by this sacred mystery,
you make them holy, so that the human race,
bounded by one world,
may be enlightened by one faith
and united by one bond of charity.

And so, we approach the table of this wondrous Sacrament,
so that, bathed in the sweetness of your grace,
we may pass over to the heavenly realities here foreshadowed.

Therefore, all creatures of heaven and earth
sing a new song in adoration,
and we, with all the host of Angels,
cry out, and without end we acclaim: → No. 23, p. 23

PREFACE I FOR THE DEAD (77)

The hope of resurrection in Christ

It is truly right and just, our duty and our salvation,
always and everywhere to give you thanks,
Lord, holy Father, almighty and eternal God,
through Christ our Lord.

In him the hope of blessed resurrection has dawned,
that those saddened by the certainty of dying
might be consoled by the promise of immortality to come.
Indeed for your faithful, Lord,
life is changed not ended,
and, when this earthly dwelling turns to dust,
an eternal dwelling is made ready for them in heaven.

And so, with Angels and Archangels,
with Thrones and Dominions,
and with all the hosts and Powers of heaven,
we sing the hymn of your glory,
as without end we acclaim: → No. 23, p. 23

PREFACE II FOR THE DEAD (78)

Christ died so that we might live

It is truly right and just, our duty and our salvation,
always and everywhere to give you thanks,
Lord, holy Father, almighty and eternal God,
through Christ our Lord.

For as one alone he accepted death,
so that we might all escape from dying;
as one man he chose to die,
so that in your sight we all might live for ever.

And so, in company with the choirs of Angels,
we praise you, and with joy we proclaim: → No. 23, p. 23

PREFACE III FOR THE DEAD (79)

Christ, the salvation and the life

It is truly right and just, our duty and our salvation,
always and everywhere to give you thanks,
Lord, holy Father, almighty and eternal God,
through Christ our Lord.

For he is the salvation of the world,
the life of the human race,
the resurrection of the dead.

Through him the host of Angels adores your majesty
and rejoices in your presence for ever.
May our voices, we pray, join with theirs
in one chorus of exultant praise, as we acclaim:

→ No. 23, p. 23

PREFACE IV FOR THE DEAD (80)

From earthly life to heavenly glory

It is truly right and just, our duty and our salvation,
always and everywhere to give you thanks,
Lord, holy Father, almighty and eternal God.

For it is at your summons that we come to birth,
by your will that we are governed,
and at your command that we return,
on account of sin,
to that earth from which we came.

And when you give the sign,
we who have been redeemed by the Death of your Son
shall be raised up to the glory of his Resurrection.

And so, with the company of Angels and Saints,
we sing the hymn of your praise,
as without end we acclaim: → No. 23, p. 23

PREFACE V FOR THE DEAD (81)

Our resurrection through the victory of Christ

It is truly right and just, our duty and our salvation,
always and everywhere to give you thanks,
Lord, holy Father, almighty and eternal God.

For even though by our own fault we perish,
yet by your compassion and your grace,
when seized by death according to our sins,
we are redeemed through Christ's great victory,
and with him called back into life.

And so, with the Powers of heaven,
we worship you constantly on earth,
and before your majesty
without end we acclaim: → No. 23, p. 23

PROPER COMMUNICANTES AND HANC IGITUR

FOR EUCHARISTIC PRAYER I (THE ROMAN CANON)

Communicantes for the Nativity of the Lord and throughout the Octave

Celebrating the most sacred night (day)
on which blessed Mary the immaculate Virgin
brought forth the Saviour for this world,
and in communion with those whose memory we venerate,
especially the glorious ever-Virgin Mary,
Mother of our God and Lord, Jesus Christ,† etc., p. 25.

Communicantes for the Epiphany of the Lord

Celebrating the most sacred day
on which your Only Begotten Son,
eternal with you in your glory,
appeared in a human body, truly sharing our flesh,

and in communion with those whose memory we venerate,
especially the glorious ever-Virgin Mary,
Mother of our God and Lord, Jesus Christ,† etc., p. 25.

Communicantes for Easter

Celebrating the most sacred night (day)
of the Resurrection of our Lord Jesus Christ in the flesh,
and in communion with those whose memory we venerate,
especially the glorious ever-Virgin Mary,
Mother of our God and Lord, Jesus Christ,† etc., p. 25.

Hanc Igitur for the Easter Vigil until the Second Sunday of Easter

Therefore, Lord, we pray:
graciously accept this oblation of our service,
that of your whole family,
which we make to you
also for those to whom you have been pleased to give
the new birth of water and the Holy Spirit,
granting them forgiveness of all their sins;
order our days in your peace,
and command that we be delivered from eternal damnation
and counted among the flock of those you have chosen.
(Through Christ our Lord. Amen.) → *Canon*, p. 25.

Communicantes for the Ascension of the Lord

Celebrating the most sacred day
on which your Only Begotten Son, our Lord,
placed at the right hand of your glory
our weak human nature,
which he had united to himself,
and in communion with those whose memory we venerate,
especially the glorious ever-Virgin Mary,
Mother of our God and Lord, Jesus Christ,† etc., p. 25.

Communicantes for Pentecost Sunday

Celebrating the most sacred day of Pentecost,
on which the Holy Spirit
appeared to the Apostles in tongues of fire,
and in communion with those whose memory we venerate,
especially the glorious ever-Virgin Mary,
Mother of our God and Lord, Jesus Christ,† etc., p. 25.

BLESSINGS AT THE END OF MASS AND PRAYERS OVER THE PEOPLE

SOLEMN BLESSINGS

The following blessings may be used, at the discretion of the Priest, at the end of the celebration of Mass, or of a Liturgy of the Word, or of the Office, or of the Sacraments.

The Deacon or, in his absence, the Priest himself, says the invitation: Bow down for the blessing. *Then the Priest, with hands extended over the people, says the blessing, with all responding:* **Amen**.

I. For Celebrations in the Different Liturgical Times

1. ADVENT

May the almighty and merciful God,
by whose grace you have placed your faith
in the First Coming of his Only Begotten Son
and yearn for his coming again,
sanctify you by the radiance of Christ's Advent
and enrich you with his blessing. ℟. **Amen.**

As you run the race of this present life,
may he make you firm in faith,
joyful in hope and active in charity. ℟. **Amen.**

So that, rejoicing now with devotion.
at the Redeemer's coming in the flesh,
you may be endowed with the rich reward of eternal life
when he comes again in majesty. ℟. **Amen.**

And may the blessing of almighty God,
the Father, and the Son, ✠ and the Holy Spirit,
come down on you and remain with you for ever. ℟. **Amen.**

2. THE NATIVITY OF THE LORD

May the God of infinite goodness,
who by the Incarnation of his Son has driven darkness from the world

and by that glorious Birth has illumined this most holy night (day),
drive far from you the darkness of vice
and illumine your hearts with the light of virtue. ℟. **Amen.**

May God, who willed that the great joy
of his Son's saving Birth
be announced to shepherds by the Angel,
fill your minds with the gladness he gives
and make you heralds of his Gospel. ℟. **Amen.**

And may God, who by the Incarnation
brought together the earthly and heavenly realm,
fill you with the gift of his peace and favour
and make you sharers with the Church in heaven. ℟. **Amen.**

And may the blessing of almighty God,
the Father, and the Son, ✠ and the Holy Spirit,
come down on you and remain with you for ever. ℟. **Amen.**

3. THE BEGINNING OF THE YEAR

May God, the source and origin of all blessing,
grant you grace,
pour out his blessing in abundance,
and keep you safe from harm throughout the year. ℟. **Amen.**

May he give you integrity in the faith,
endurance in hope,
and perseverance in charity
with holy patience to the end. ℟. **Amen.**

May he order your days and your deeds in his peace,
grant your prayers in this and in every place,
and lead you happily to eternal life. ℟. **Amen.**

And may the blessing of almighty God,
the Father, and the Son, ✠ and the Holy Spirit,
come down on you and remain with you for ever. ℟. **Amen.**

4. THE EPIPHANY OF THE LORD

May God, who has called you
out of darkness into his wonderful light,
pour out in kindness his blessing upon you
and make your hearts firm
in faith, hope and charity. ℟. **Amen.**

And since in all confidence you follow Christ,
who today appeared in the world
as a light shining in darkness,
may God make you, too,
a light for your brothers and sisters. ℟. **Amen.**

And so when your pilgrimage is ended,
may you come to him
whom the Magi sought as they followed the star
and whom they found with great joy, the Light from Light,
who is Christ the Lord. ℟. **Amen.**

And may the blessing of almighty God,
the Father, and the Son, ✠ and the Holy Spirit,
come down on you and remain with you for ever. ℟. **Amen.**

5. THE PASSION OF THE LORD

May God, the Father of mercies,
who has given you an example of love
in the Passion of his Only Begotten Son,
grant that, by serving God and your neighbour,
you may lay hold of the wondrous gift of his blessing. ℟. **Amen.**

So that you may receive the reward of everlasting life from him,
through whose earthly Death
you believe that you escape eternal death. ℟. **Amen.**

And by following the example of his self-abasement,
may you possess a share in his Resurrection. ℟. **Amen.**

And may the blessing of almighty God,
the Father, and the Son, ✠ and the Holy Spirit,
come down on you and remain with you for ever. ℟. **Amen.**

6. EASTER TIME

May God, who by the Resurrection of his Only Begotten Son
was pleased to confer on you
the gift of redemption and of adoption,
give you gladness by his blessing. ℟. **Amen.**

May he, by whose redeeming work
you have received the gift of everlasting freedom,
make you heirs to an eternal inheritance. ℟. **Amen.**

And may you, who have already risen with Christ
in Baptism through faith,
by living in a right manner on this earth,
be united with him in the homeland of heaven. ℟. **Amen.**

And may the blessing of almighty God,
the Father, and the Son, ✠ and the Holy Spirit,
come down on you and remain with you for ever. ℟. **Amen.**

7. THE ASCENSION OF THE LORD

May almighty God bless you,
for on this very day his Only Begotten Son
pierced the heights of heaven
and unlocked for you the way
to ascend to where he is. ℟. **Amen.**

May he grant that,
as Christ after his Resurrection
was seen plainly by his disciples,
so when he comes as Judge
he may show himself merciful to you for all eternity. ℟. **Amen.**

And may you, who believe he is seated
with the Father in his majesty,
know with joy the fulfillment of his promise
to stay with you until the end of time. ℟. **Amen.**

And may the blessing of almighty God,
the Father, and the Son, ✠ and the Holy Spirit,
come down on you and remain with you for ever. ℟. **Amen.**

8. THE HOLY SPIRIT

May God, the Father of lights,
who was pleased to enlighten the disciples' minds
by the outpouring of the Spirit, the Paraclete,
grant you gladness by his blessing
and make you always abound with the gifts of the same Spirit. ℟. **Amen.**

May the wondrous flame that appeared above the disciples,
powerfully cleanse your hearts from every evil
and pervade them with its purifying light. ℟. **Amen.**

And may God, who has been pleased to unite many tongues
in the profession of one faith,
give you perseverance in that same faith
and, by believing, may you journey from hope to clear vision. ℟. **Amen.**

And may the blessing of almighty God,
the Father, and the Son, ✠ and the Holy Spirit,
come down on you and remain with you for ever. ℟. **Amen.**

9. ORDINARY TIME I

May the Lord bless you and keep you. ℟. **Amen.**

May he let his face shine upon you
and show you his mercy. ℟. **Amen.**

May he turn his countenance towards you
and give you his peace. ℟. **Amen.**

And may the blessing of almighty God,
the Father, and the Son, ✠ and the Holy Spirit,
come down on you and remain with you for ever. ℟. **Amen.**

10. ORDINARY TIME II

May the peace of God,
which surpasses all understanding,
keep your hearts and minds
in the knowledge and love of God,
and of his Son, our Lord Jesus Christ. ℟. **Amen.**

And may the blessing of almighty God,
the Father, and the Son, ✠ and the Holy Spirit,
come down on you and remain with you for ever. ℟. **Amen.**

11. ORDINARY TIME III

May almighty God bless you in his kindness
and pour out saving wisdom upon you. ℟. **Amen.**

May he nourish you always with the teachings of the faith
and make you persevere in holy deeds. ℟. **Amen.**

May he turn your steps towards himself
and show you the path of charity and peace. ℟. **Amen.**

And may the blessing of almighty God,
the Father, and the Son, ✠ and the Holy Spirit,
come down on you and remain with you for ever. ℟. **Amen.**

12. ORDINARY TIME IV

May the God of all consolation order your days in his peace
and grant you the gifts of his blessing. ℟. **Amen.**

May he free you always from every distress
and confirm your hearts in his love. ℟. **Amen.**

So that on this life's journey
you may be effective in good works,
rich in the gifts of hope, faith and charity,
and may come happily to eternal life. ℟. **Amen.**

And may the blessing of almighty God,
the Father, and the Son, ✠ and the Holy Spirit,
come down on you and remain with you for ever. ℟. **Amen.**

13. ORDINARY TIME V

May almighty God always keep every adversity far from you
and in his kindness pour out upon you the gifts of his blessing. ℟. **Amen.**

May God keep your hearts attentive to his words,
that they may be filled with everlasting gladness. ℟. **Amen.**

And so, may you always understand what is good and right,
and be found ever hastening along
in the path of God's commands,
made co-heirs with the citizens of heaven. ℟. **Amen.**

And may the blessing of almighty God,
the Father, and the Son, ✠ and the Holy Spirit,
come down on you and remain with you for ever. ℟. **Amen.**

14. ORDINARY TIME VI

May God bless you with every heavenly blessing,
make you always holy and pure in his sight,
pour out in abundance upon you the riches of his glory,
and teach you with the words of truth;
may he instruct you in the Gospel of salvation,
and ever endow you with fraternal charity.
Through Christ our Lord. ℟. **Amen.**

And may the blessing of almighty God,
the Father, and the Son, ✠ and the Holy Spirit,
come down on you and remain with you for ever. ℟. **Amen.**

II. For Celebrations of the Saints

15. THE BLESSED VIRGIN MARY

May God, who through the childbearing of the Blessed Virgin Mary
willed in his great kindness to redeem the human race,
be pleased to enrich you with his blessing. ℟. **Amen.**

May you know always and everywhere the protection of her,
through whom you have been found worthy to receive the author of life. ℟. **Amen.**

May you, who have devoutly gathered on this day,
carry away with you the gifts of spiritual joys and heavenly rewards. ℟. **Amen.**

And may the blessing of almighty God,
the Father, and the Son, ✠ and the Holy Spirit,
come down on you and remain with you for ever. ℟. **Amen.**

16. SAINTS PETER AND PAUL, APOSTLES

May almighty God bless you,
for he has made you steadfast in Saint Peter's saving confession
and through it has set you on the solid rock of the Church's faith. ℟. **Amen.**

And having instructed you
by the tireless preaching of Saint Paul,
may God teach you constantly by his example
to win brothers and sisters for Christ. ℟. **Amen.**

So that by the keys of Saint Peter and the words of Saint Paul,
and by the support of their intercession,
God may bring us happily to that homeland
that Peter attained on a cross
and Paul by the blade of a sword. ℟. **Amen.**

And may the blessing of almighty God,
the Father, and the Son, ✠ and the Holy Spirit,
come down on you and remain with you for ever. ℟. **Amen.**

17. THE APOSTLES

May God, who has granted you
to stand firm on apostolic foundations,
graciously bless you through the glorious merits
of the holy Apostles *N.* and *N.* (the holy Apostle *N.*).
℟. **Amen.**

And may he, who endowed you
with the teaching and example of the Apostles,
make you, under their protection,
witnesses to the truth before all. ℟. **Amen.**

So that through the intercession of the Apostles,
you may inherit the eternal homeland,
for by their teaching you possess firmness of faith. ℟. **Amen.**

And may the blessing of almighty God,
the Father, and the Son, ✠ and the Holy Spirit,
come down on you and remain with you for ever. ℟. **Amen.**

18. ALL SAINTS

May God, the glory and joy of the Saints,
who has caused you to be strengthened
by means of their outstanding prayers,
bless you with unending blessings. ℟. **Amen.**

Freed through their intercession from present ills
and formed by the example of their holy way of life,
may you be ever devoted
to serving God and your neighbour. ℟. **Amen.**

So that, together with all,
you may possess the joys of the homeland,
where Holy Church rejoices
that her children are admitted in perpetual peace
to the company of the citizens of heaven. ℟. **Amen.**

And may the blessing of almighty God,
the Father, and the Son, ✠ and the Holy Spirit,
come down on you and remain with you for ever. ℟. **Amen.**

III. Other Blessings

19. FOR THE DEDICATION OF A CHURCH

May God, the Lord of heaven and earth,
who has gathered you today for the dedication of this church,
make you abound in heavenly blessings. ℟. **Amen.**

And may he, who has willed that all his scattered children
should be gathered together in his Son,
grant that you may become his temple
and the dwelling place of the Holy Spirit. ℟. **Amen.**

And so, when you are thoroughly cleansed,
may God dwell within you
and grant you to possess with all the Saints
the inheritance of eternal happiness. ℟. **Amen.**

And may the blessing of almighty God,
the Father, ✠ and the Son, ✠ and the Holy ✠ Spirit,
come down on you and remain with you for ever. ℟. **Amen.**

20. IN CELEBRATIONS FOR THE DEAD

May the God of all consolation bless you,
for in his unfathomable goodness he created the human race,
and in the Resurrection of his Only Begotten Son
he has given believers the hope of rising again. ℟. **Amen.**

To us who are alive, may God grant pardon for our sins,
and to all the dead, a place of light and peace. ℟. **Amen.**

So may we all live happily for ever with Christ,
whom we believe truly rose from the dead. ℟. **Amen.**

And may the blessing of almighty God,
the Father, and the Son, ✠ and the Holy Spirit,
come down on you and remain with you for ever. ℟. **Amen.**

PRAYERS OVER THE PEOPLE

The following prayers may be used, at the discretion of the Priest, at the end of the celebration of Mass, or of a Liturgy of the Word, or of the Office, or of the Sacraments.

The Deacon or, in his absence, the Priest himself, says the invitation: Bow down for the blessing. *Then the Priest, with hands outstretched over the people, says the prayer, with all responding:* **Amen**.

After the prayer, the Priest always adds: And may the blessing of almighty God, the Father, and the Son, ✠ and the Holy Spirit, come down on you and remain with you for ever. ℟. **Amen.**

1. Be gracious to your people, O Lord,
and do not withhold consolation on earth
from those you call to strive for heaven.
Through Christ our Lord.

2. Grant, O Lord, we pray,
that the Christian people
may understand the truths they profess
and love the heavenly liturgy
in which they participate.
Through Christ our Lord.

3. May your people receive your holy blessing,
O Lord, we pray,
and, by that gift,
spurn all that would harm them
and obtain what they desire.
Through Christ our Lord.

4. Turn your people to you with all their heart,
O Lord, we pray,
for you protect even those who go astray,
but when they serve you with undivided heart,
you sustain them with still greater care.
Through Christ our Lord.

5. Graciously enlighten your family, O Lord, we pray,
that by holding fast to what is pleasing to you,
they may be worthy to accomplish all that is good.
Through Christ our Lord.

6. Bestow pardon and peace, O Lord, we pray,
upon your faithful,
that they may be cleansed from every offence

and serve you with untroubled hearts.
Through Christ our Lord.

7. May your heavenly favour, O Lord, we pray,
increase in number the people subject to you
and make them always obedient to your commands.
Through Christ our Lord.

8. Be propitious to your people, O God,
that, freed from every evil,
they may serve you with all their heart
and ever stand firm under your protection.
Through Christ our Lord.

9. May your family always rejoice together, O God,
over the mysteries of redemption they have celebrated,
and grant its members the perseverance
to attain the effects that flow from them.
Through Christ our Lord.

10. Lord God, from the abundance of your mercies
provide for your servants and ensure their safety,
so that, strengthened by your blessings,
they may at all times abound in thanksgiving
and bless you with unending exultation.
Through Christ our Lord.

11. Keep your family, we pray, O Lord,
in your constant care,
so that, under your protection,
they may be free from all troubles
and by good works show dedication to your name.
Through Christ our Lord.

12. Purify your faithful, both in body and in mind,
O Lord, we pray,
so that, feeling the compunction you inspire,
they may be able to avoid harmful pleasures
and ever feed upon your delights.
Through Christ our Lord.

13. May the effects of your sacred blessing, O Lord,
make themselves felt among your faithful,

to prepare with spiritual sustenance the minds of all,
that they may be strengthened by the power of your love
to carry out works of charity.
Through Christ our Lord.

14. The hearts of your faithful submitted to your name,
entreat your help, O Lord,
and since without you they can do nothing that is just,
grant by your abundant mercy
that they may both know what is right
and receive all that they need for their good.
Through Christ our Lord.

15. Hasten to the aid of your faithful people
who call upon you, O Lord, we pray,
and graciously give strength in their human weakness,
so that, being dedicated to you in complete sincerity,
they may find gladness in your remedies
both now and in the life to come.
Through Christ our Lord.

16. Look with favour on your family, O Lord,
and bestow your endless mercy on those who seek it:
and just as without your mercy
they can do nothing truly worthy of you,
so through it,
may they merit to obey your saving commands.
Through Christ our Lord.

17. Bestow increase of heavenly grace
on your faithful, O Lord;
may they praise you with their lips,
with their souls, with their lives;
and since it is by your gift that we exist,
may our whole lives be yours.
Through Christ our Lord.

18. Direct your people, O Lord, we pray,
with heavenly instruction,
that by avoiding every evil
and pursuing all that is good,
they may earn not your anger

but your unending mercy.
Through Christ our Lord.

19. Be near to those who call on you, O Lord,
and graciously grant your protection
to all who place their hope in your mercy,
that they may remain faithful in holiness of life
and, having enough for their needs in this world,
they may be made full heirs of your promise for eternity.
Through Christ our Lord.

20. Bestow the grace of your kindness
upon your supplicant people, O Lord,
that, formed by you, their Creator,
and restored by you, their sustainer,
through your constant action they may be saved.
Through Christ our Lord.

21. May your faithful people, O Lord, we pray,
always respond to the promptings of your love
and, moved by wholesome compunction,
may they do gladly what you command,
so as to receive the things you promise.
Through Christ our Lord.

22. May the weakness of your devoted people
stir your compassion, O Lord, we pray,
and let their faithful pleading win your mercy,
that what they do not presume upon by their merits
they may receive by your generous pardon.
Through Christ our Lord.

23. In defence of your children, O Lord, we pray,
stretch forth the right hand of your majesty,
so that, obeying your fatherly will,
they may have the unfailing protection
of your fatherly care.
Through Christ our Lord.

24. Look, O Lord, on the prayers of your family,
and grant them the assistance they humbly implore,
so that, strengthened by the help they need,
they may persevere in confessing your name.
Through Christ our Lord.

25. Keep your family safe, O Lord, we pray,
and grant them the abundance of your mercies,
that they may find growth
through the teachings and the gifts of heaven.
Through Christ our Lord.

26. May your faithful people rejoice, we pray, O Lord,
to be upheld by your right hand,
and, progressing in the Christian life,
may they delight in good things
both now and in the time to come.
Through Christ our Lord.

ON FEASTS OF SAINTS

27. May the Christian people exult, O Lord,
at the glorification of the illustrious members of your Son's Body,
and may they gain a share in the eternal lot
of the Saints on whose feast day
they reaffirm their devotion to you,
rejoicing with them for ever in your glory.
Through Christ our Lord.

28. Turn the hearts of your people
always to you, O Lord, we pray,
and, as you give them the help of such great patrons as these,
grant also the unfailing help of your protection.
Through Christ our Lord.

"What I say to you I say to all: Keep awake."

YEAR B

DECEMBER 3, 2017

1st SUNDAY OF ADVENT

ENTRANCE ANTIPHON Cf. Ps. 24:1-3

To you, I lift up my soul, O my God. In you, I have trusted; let me not be put to shame. Nor let my enemies exult over me; and let none who hope in you be put to shame. → No. 2, p. 10 (Omit Gloria)

COLLECT

Grant your faithful, we pray, almighty God,
the resolve to run forth to meet your Christ
with righteous deeds at his coming,
so that, gathered at his right hand,
they may be worthy to possess the heavenly Kingdom.
Through our Lord Jesus Christ, your Son,

who lives and reigns with you in the unity of the
Holy Spirit,
one God, for ever and ever. ℟. **Amen.** ↓

FIRST READING Isa. 63.16b-17; 64.1, 3-8

God is our Father. We are sinful, and you, O God, are hidden from our eyes. We are the work of your hands.

A reading from the book of the Prophet Isaiah.

YOU, O Lord, are our father;
"Our Redeemer from of old" is your name.
Why, O Lord, do you make us stray from your ways
and harden our heart, so that we do not fear you?
Turn back for the sake of your servants,
for the sake of the tribes that are your heritage.

O that you would tear open the heavens and come down,
so that the mountains would quake at your presence.
When you did awesome deeds that we did not expect,
you came down, the mountains quaked at your presence.
From ages past no one has heard,
no ear has perceived,
no eye has seen any God besides you,
who works for those who wait for him.

You meet those who gladly do right,
those who remember you in your ways.

But you were angry, and we sinned;
because you hid yourself we transgressed.
We have all become like one who is unclean,
and all our righteous deeds are like a filthy cloth.

We all fade like a leaf,
and our iniquities, like the wind, take us away.
There is no one who calls on your name,
or attempts to take hold of you;
for you have hidden your face from us,
and have delivered us into the hand of our iniquity.

Yet, O Lord, you are our Father;
we are the clay, and you are our potter;
we are all the work of your hand.

The word of the Lord. ℟. **Thanks be to God.** ↓

RESPONSORIAL PSALM Ps. 80

Gloria Gassi

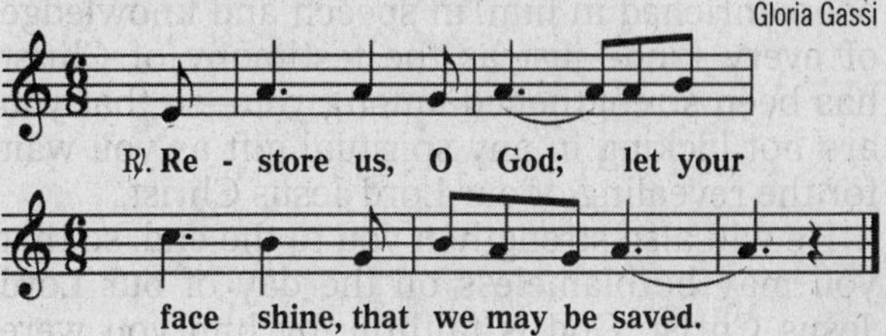
℟. Re - store us, O God; let your
face shine, that we may be saved.

Give ear, O Shepherd of Israel,
you who are enthroned upon the cherubim, shine forth.
Stir up your might,
and come to save us.—℟.

Turn again, O God of hosts;
look down from heaven, and see;
have regard for this vine,
the stock that your right hand has planted.—℟.

But let your hand be upon the man at your right,
the son of man you have made strong for yourself.
Then we will never turn back from you;
give us life, and we will call on your name.—℟. ↓

SECOND READING 1 Cor. 1.3-9

Jesus gives us faith and the strength to persevere. God calls us into the fellowship of Christ.

A reading from the first Letter of Saint Paul to the Corinthians.

BROTHERS and sisters: Grace to you and peace from God our Father and the Lord Jesus Christ.

I give thanks to my God always for you because of the grace of God that has been given you in Christ Jesus, for in every way you have been enriched in him, in speech and knowledge of every kind—just as the testimony of Christ has been strengthened among you—so that you are not lacking in any spiritual gift as you wait for the revealing of our Lord Jesus Christ.

He will also strengthen you to the end, so that you may be blameless on the day of our Lord Jesus Christ. God is faithful; by him you were called into fellowship with his Son, Jesus Christ our Lord.—The word of the Lord. ℟. **Thanks be to God.** ↓

GOSPEL ACCLAMATION Ps. 85.7

℣. Alleluia. ℟. **Alleluia.**
℣. Show us your steadfast love, O Lord,
and grant us your salvation.
℟. **Alleluia.** ↓

GOSPEL Mk. 13.33-37

Be on guard always. We do not know at what time or hour God will come.

℣. The Lord be with you. ℟. **And with your spirit.**
✠ A reading from the holy Gospel according to Mark. ℟. **Glory to you, O Lord.**

JESUS said to his disciples: "Beware, keep alert; for you do not know when the time will come.

It is like a man going on a journey, when he leaves home and puts his slaves in charge, each with a particular task, and commands the doorkeeper to be on the watch. Therefore, keep awake—for you do not know when the master of the house will come, in the evening, or at midnight, or at cockcrow, or at dawn, or else he may find you asleep when he comes suddenly.

And what I say to you I say to all: Keep awake."—The Gospel of the Lord. ℟. **Praise to you, Lord Jesus Christ.** → No. 15, p. 18

PRAYER OVER THE OFFERINGS

Accept, we pray, O Lord, these offerings we make,
gathered from among your gifts to us,
and may what you grant us to celebrate devoutly
here below
gain for us the prize of eternal redemption.
Through Christ our Lord.
℟. **Amen.** → No. 21, p. 22 (Pref. 1)

COMMUNION ANTIPHON Ps. 84.13

The Lord will bestow his bounty, and our earth shall yield its increase. ↓

PRAYER AFTER COMMUNION

May these mysteries, O Lord,
in which we have participated,
profit us, we pray,
for even now, as we walk amid passing things,
you teach us by them
to love the things of heaven
and hold fast to what endures.
Through Christ our Lord.
℟. **Amen.** → No. 30, p. 77

Optional Solemn Blessings, p. 97, and Prayers over the People, p. 105

"Prepare the way of the Lord. . . ."

DECEMBER 10

2nd SUNDAY OF ADVENT

ENTRANCE ANTIPHON Cf. Isa. 30.19, 30

O people of Sion, behold, the Lord will come to save the nations, and the Lord will make the glory of his voice heard in the joy of your heart.

→ No. 2, p. 10 (Omit Gloria)

COLLECT

Almighty and merciful God,
may no earthly undertaking hinder those
who set out in haste to meet your Son,
but may our learning of heavenly wisdom
gain us admittance to his company.
Who lives and reigns with you in the unity of the
Holy Spirit,
one God, for ever and ever. ℟. **Amen.** ↓

FIRST READING Isa. 40.1-5, 9-11

Make ready the way for the Messiah. Make known the good news, for God is near.

A reading from the book of the Prophet Isaiah.

COMFORT, O comfort my people,
says your God.
Speak tenderly to Jerusalem,
and cry to her
that she has served her term,
that her penalty is paid,
that she has received from the Lord's hand
double for all her sins.

A voice cries out:
"In the wilderness prepare the way of the Lord,
make straight in the desert a highway for our God.
Every valley shall be lifted up,
and every mountain and hill be made low;
the uneven ground shall become level,
and the rough places a plain.
Then the glory of the Lord shall be revealed,
and all people shall see it together,
for the mouth of the Lord has spoken."

Get you up to a high mountain,
O Zion, herald of good tidings;
lift up your voice with strength,
O Jerusalem, herald of good tidings,
lift it up, do not fear;
say to the cities of Judah,
"Here is your God!"

See, the Lord God comes with might,
and his arm rules for him;
his reward is with him,
and his recompense before him.

He will feed his flock like a shepherd;
he will gather the lambs in his arms,
and carry them in his bosom,
and gently lead the mother sheep.

The word of the Lord. ℟. **Thanks be to God. ↓**

RESPONSORIAL PSALM Ps. 85 Gloria Gassi

℟. Show us your stead-fast love, O
Lord, and grant us your sal - va - tion.

Let me hear what God the Lord will speak,
for he will speak peace to his people.
Surely his salvation is at hand for those who fear
him,
that his glory may dwell in our land. —℟.

Steadfast love and faithfulness will meet;
righteousness and peace will kiss each other.
Faithfulness will spring up from the ground,
and righteousness will look down from the sky.—℟.

The Lord will give what is good,
and our land will yield its increase.
Righteousness will go before him,
and will make a path for his steps.—℟. ↓

SECOND READING 2 Pet. 3.8-14

There is no counting of time with God, who does not want anyone to perish. We await a new heaven and earth, relying on the justice of God.

A reading from the second Letter of Saint Peter.

DO not ignore this one fact, beloved, that with the Lord one day is like a thousand years, and a thousand years are like one day. The Lord is not slow about his promise, as some think of slowness, but is patient with you, not wanting any to perish, but all to come to repentance.

But the day of the Lord will come like a thief, and then the heavens will pass away with a loud noise, and the elements will be dissolved with fire, and the earth and everything that is done on it will be disclosed.

Since all these things are to be dissolved in this way, what sort of persons ought you to be in leading lives of holiness and godliness, waiting for and hastening the coming of the day of God, because of which the heavens will be set ablaze and dissolved, and the elements will melt with fire? But, in accordance with his promise, we wait for new heavens and a new earth, where righteousness is at home.

Therefore, beloved, while you are waiting for these things, strive to be found by him at peace.—The word of the Lord. ℟. **Thanks be to God.** ↓

GOSPEL ACCLAMATION Lk. 3.4, 6

℣. Alleluia. ℟. **Alleluia.**

℣. Prepare the way of the Lord, make straight
his paths:
all people shall see the salvation of God.
℟. **Alleluia.** ↓

GOSPEL Mk. 1.1-8

John the Baptist announced the coming of Jesus. John called for repentance and promised that the Messiah would baptize in the Holy Spirit.

℣. The Lord be with you. ℟. **And with your spirit.**
✠ A reading from the holy Gospel according to Mark. ℟. **Glory to you, O Lord.**

THE beginning of the good news of Jesus Christ, the Son of God.

As it is written in the Prophet Isaiah,
"See, I am sending my messenger ahead of
you,
who will prepare your way;
the voice of one crying out in the wilderness:
'Prepare the way of the Lord,
make his paths straight.'"

John the Baptist appeared in the wilderness, proclaiming a baptism of repentance for the forgiveness of sins. And people from the whole Judean countryside and all the people of Jerusalem were going out to him, and were baptized by him in the river Jordan, confessing their sins.

Now John was clothed with camel's hair, with a leather belt around his waist, and he ate locusts and wild honey.

He proclaimed, "The one who is more powerful than I is coming after me; I am not worthy to stoop down and untie the thong of his sandals. I have baptized you with water; but he will baptize you with the Holy Spirit."—The Gospel of the Lord. ℟. **Praise to you, Lord Jesus Christ.**

→ No. 15, p. 18

PRAYER OVER THE OFFERINGS

Be pleased, O Lord, with our humble prayers and offerings,
and, since we have no merits to plead our cause,
come, we pray, to our rescue
with the protection of your mercy.
Through Christ our Lord.
℟. **Amen.** → No. 21, p. 22 (Pref. 1)

COMMUNION ANTIPHON Bar. 5.5; 4.36

Jerusalem, arise and stand upon the heights, and behold the joy which comes to you from God. ↓

PRAYER AFTER COMMUNION

Replenished by the food of spiritual nourishment,
we humbly beseech you, O Lord,
that, through our partaking in this mystery,
you may teach us to judge wisely the things of earth
and hold firm to the things of heaven.
Through Christ our Lord.
℟. **Amen.** → No. 30, p. 77

Optional Solemn Blessings, p. 97, and Prayers over the People, p. 105

"I baptize with water. Among you stands . . . the one who is coming after me."

DECEMBER 17

3rd SUNDAY OF ADVENT

ENTRANCE ANTIPHON Phil. 4.4, 5

Rejoice in the Lord always; again I say, rejoice. Indeed, the Lord is near.

→ No. 2, p. 10 (Omit Gloria)

COLLECT

O God, who see how your people
faithfully await the feast of the Lord's Nativity,
enable us, we pray,
to attain the joys of so great a salvation
and to celebrate them always
with solemn worship and glad rejoicing.
Through our Lord Jesus Christ, your Son,
who lives and reigns with you in the unity of the Holy Spirit,
one God, for ever and ever. ℟. **Amen.** ↓

FIRST READING Isa. 61.1-2a, 10-11

Isaiah has been sent to proclaim good news to those in need. He rejoices in the Lord who will be shown to be the God of justice and peace.

A reading from the book of the Prophet Isaiah.

THE spirit of the Lord God is upon me,
because the Lord has anointed me;
he has sent me to bring good news to the oppressed,
to bind up the brokenhearted,
to proclaim liberty to the captives,
and release to the prisoners;
to proclaim the year of the Lord's favour.

I will greatly rejoice in the Lord,
my soul shall exult in my God;
for he has clothed me with the garments of salvation,
he has covered me with the robe of righteousness,
as a bridegroom decks himself with a garland,
and as a bride adorns herself with her jewels.

For as the earth brings forth its shoots,
and as a garden causes what is sown in it to spring up,
so the Lord God will cause righteousness and praise
to spring up before all the nations.

The word of the Lord. ℟. **Thanks be to God.** ↓

RESPONSORIAL PSALM Lk. 1

Normand L. Blanchard

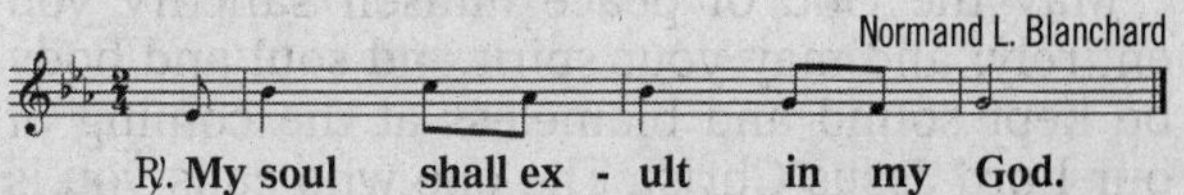
℟. My soul shall ex - ult in my God.

My soul magnifies the Lord
and my spirit rejoices in God my Saviour,
for he has looked with favour on the lowliness of his servant.
Surely, from now on all generations will call me blessed.
℟. **My soul shall exult in my God.**

For the Mighty One has done great things for me,
and holy is his name.
His mercy is for those who fear him
from generation to generation.—℟.

The Lord has filled the hungry with good things
and sent the rich away empty.
He has helped his servant Israel,
in remembrance of his mercy.—℟. ↓

SECOND READING 1 Thess. 5.16-24

Paul admonishes that Christians should rejoice. He prays that the Christ-bearer will be free from any semblance of evil, but rather will grow in holiness.

A reading from the first Letter of Saint Paul to the Thessalonians.

BROTHERS and sisters, rejoice always, pray without ceasing, give thanks in all circumstances; for this is the will of God in Christ Jesus for you.

Do not quench the Spirit. Do not despise the words of Prophets, but test everything; hold fast to what is good; abstain from every form of evil.

May the God of peace himself sanctify you entirely; and may your spirit and soul and body be kept sound and blameless at the coming of our Lord Jesus Christ. The one who calls you is faithful, and he will do this.—The word of the Lord. ℟. **Thanks be to God.** ↓

GOSPEL ACCLAMATION Lk. 4.18 (Isa. 61.1)

℣. Alleluia. ℟. **Alleluia.**
℣. The Spirit of the Lord is upon me;
he has sent me to bring good news to the poor.
℟. **Alleluia.** ↓

GOSPEL Jn. 1.6-8, 19-28

John the Baptist is the forerunner of Jesus. John gives witness to Jesus by his preaching.

℣. The Lord be with you. ℟. **And with your spirit.**
✠ A reading from the holy Gospel according to John. ℟. **Glory to you, O Lord.**

THERE was a man sent from God, whose name was John. He came as a witness to testify to the light, so that all might believe through him. He himself was not the light, but he came to testify to the light.

This is the testimony given by John when the Jews sent priests and Levites from Jerusalem to ask him, "Who are you?"

He confessed and did not deny it, but confessed, "I am not the Messiah." And they asked him, "What then? Are you Elijah?" He said, "I am not." "Are you the Prophet?" He answered, "No."

Then they said to him, "Who are you? Let us have an answer for those who sent us. What do you say about yourself?" He said,

"I am the voice of one crying out in the
wilderness,

'Make straight the way of the Lord,'"
as the Prophet Isaiah said.

Now they had been sent from the Pharisees. They asked him, "Why then are you baptizing if you are neither the Messiah, nor Elijah, nor the Prophet?" John answered them, "I baptize with water. Among you stands one whom you do not know, the one who is coming after me; I am not worthy to untie the thong of his sandal." This took place in Bethany across the Jordan where John was baptizing.—The Gospel of the Lord.
℟. **Praise to you, Lord Jesus Christ.** → No. 15, p. 18

PRAYER OVER THE OFFERINGS

May the sacrifice of our worship, Lord, we pray,
be offered to you unceasingly,
to complete what was begun in sacred mystery
and powerfully accomplish for us your saving work.
Through Christ our Lord.
℟. **Amen.** → No. 21, p. 22 (Pref. 1 or 2)

COMMUNION ANTIPHON Cf. Isa. 35.4

Say to the faint of heart: Be strong and do not fear. Behold, our God will come, and he will save us. ↓

PRAYER AFTER COMMUNION

We implore your mercy, Lord,
that this divine sustenance may cleanse us of our faults
and prepare us for the coming feasts.
Through Christ our Lord.
℟. **Amen.** → No. 30, p. 77

Optional Solemn Blessings, p. 97, and Prayers over the People, p. 105

"Do not be afraid, Mary, for you have found favour with God."

DECEMBER 24

4th SUNDAY OF ADVENT

ENTRANCE ANTIPHON Cf. Isa. 45.8

Drop down dew from above, you heavens, and let the clouds rain down the Just One; let the earth be opened and bring forth a Saviour.

→ No. 2, p. 10 (Omit Gloria)

COLLECT

Pour forth, we beseech you, O Lord,
your grace into our hearts,
that we, to whom the Incarnation of Christ your Son
was made known by the message of an Angel,
may by his Passion and Cross
be brought to the glory of his Resurrection.

Who lives and reigns with you in the unity of the Holy Spirit,
one God, for ever and ever. ℟. **Amen.** ↓

FIRST READING 2 Sam. 7.1-5, 8b-12, 14a, 16

David wishes to build a temple to house the "ark of God," but God speaks to him promising to exalt and secure the house of David forever. The Lord will bring peace.

A reading from the second book of Samuel.

NOW when David, the king, was settled in his house, and the Lord had given him rest from all his enemies around him, the king said to the Prophet Nathan, "See now, I am living in a house of cedar, but the ark of God stays in a tent." Nathan said to the king, "Go, do all that you have in mind, for the Lord is with you."

But that same night the word of the Lord came to Nathan: "Go and tell my servant David: 'Thus says the Lord: Are you the one to build me a house to live in? I took you from the pasture, from following the sheep to be prince over my people Israel: and I have been with you wherever you went, and have cut off all your enemies from before you; and I will make for you a great name, like the name of the great ones of the earth.

And I will appoint a place for my people Israel and will plant them, so that they may live in their own place, and be disturbed no more; and evildoers shall afflict them no more, as formerly, from the time that I appointed judges over my people Israel; and I will give you rest from all your enemies.

Moreover the Lord declares to you, David, that the Lord will make you a house. When your days are fulfilled and you lie down with your ancestors, I will raise up your offspring after you, who shall come forth from your body, and I will establish his kingdom.

I will be a father to him, and he shall be a son to me. Your house and your kingdom shall be made sure forever before me; your throne, David, shall be established forever.'"—The word of the Lord. ℟. **Thanks be to God.** ↓

RESPONSORIAL PSALM Ps. 89 Gloria Gassi

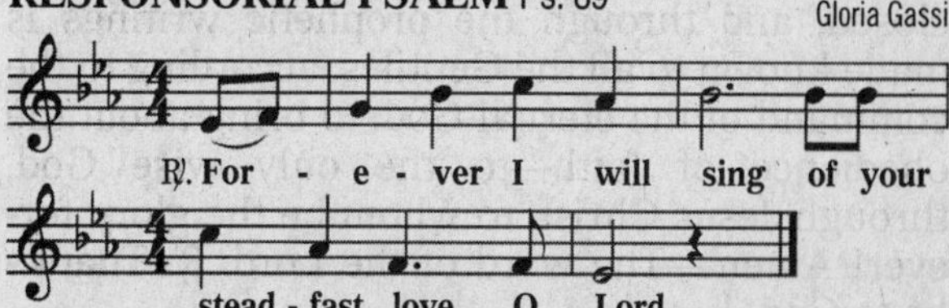
℟. For - e - ver I will sing of your
stead - fast love, O Lord.

I will sing of your steadfast love, O Lord, forever;
with my mouth I will proclaim your faithfulness to all generations.
I declare that your steadfast love is established forever;
your faithfulness is as firm as the heavens.—℟.

You said, "I have made a covenant with my chosen one,
I have sworn to my servant David:
I will establish your descendants forever,
and build your throne for all generations."—℟.

He shall cry to me, "You are my Father,
my God, and the Rock of my salvation!"
Forever I will keep my steadfast love for him,
and my covenant with him will stand firm.—℟. ↓

SECOND READING Rom. 16.25-27

God has revealed the divine plan of salvation through the coming of God's Son, Jesus Christ. It is made known to all human beings that they may believe and obey.

A reading from the Letter of Saint Paul to the Romans.

BROTHERS and sisters: To the One who is able to strengthen you according to my Gospel and the proclamation of Jesus Christ, according to the revelation of the mystery that was kept secret for long ages but is now disclosed, and through the prophetic writings is made known to all the Gentiles, according to the command of the eternal God, to bring about the obedience of faith—to the only wise God, through Jesus Christ, to whom be the glory forever! Amen.—The word of the Lord. ℟. **Thanks be to God.** ↓

GOSPEL ACCLAMATION Lk. 1.38

℣. Alleluia. ℟. **Alleluia.**
℣. Here am I, the servant of the Lord:
let it be done to me according to your word.
℟. **Alleluia.** ↓

GOSPEL Lk. 1.26-38

Gabriel speaks to Mary, announcing that she who is a virgin shall conceive through the Holy Spirit and give birth to a Son. Mary agrees to God's request.

℣. The Lord be with you. ℟. **And with your spirit.**
✠ A reading from the holy Gospel according to Luke. ℟. **Glory to you, O Lord.**

THE Angel Gabriel was sent by God to a town in Galilee called Nazareth, to a virgin engaged to a man whose name was Joseph, of the house of David. The virgin's name was Mary.

And he came to her and said, "Hail, full of grace! The Lord is with you." But she was much perplexed by his words and pondered what sort of greeting this might be.

The Angel said to her, "Do not be afraid, Mary, for you have found favour with God. And now, you will conceive in your womb and bear a son, and you will name him Jesus.

He will be great, and will be called the Son of the Most High, and the Lord God will give to him the throne of his father David. He will reign over the house of Jacob forever, and of his kingdom there will be no end."

Mary said to the Angel, "How can this be, since I am a virgin?" The Angel said to her, "The Holy Spirit will come upon you, and the power of the Most High will overshadow you; therefore the child to be born will be holy; he will be called Son of God.

And now, your relative Elizabeth in her old age has also conceived a son; and this is the sixth month for her who was said to be barren. For nothing will be impossible with God." Then Mary said, "Here am I, the servant of the Lord; let it be done to me according to your word." Then the Angel departed from her.—The Gospel of the Lord. ℟. **Praise to you, Lord Jesus Christ.**

→ No. 15, p. 18

PRAYER OVER THE OFFERINGS

May the Holy Spirit, O Lord,
sanctify these gifts laid upon your altar,
just as he filled with his power the womb of the Blessed Virgin Mary.
Through Christ our Lord.
℟. **Amen.** → No. 21, p. 22 (Pref. 2)

COMMUNION ANTIPHON Isa. 7.14

Behold, a Virgin shall conceive and bear a son; and his name will be called Emmanuel. ↓

PRAYER AFTER COMMUNION

Having received this pledge of eternal redemption,
we pray, almighty God,
that, as the feast day of our salvation draws ever nearer,
so we may press forward all the more eagerly
to the worthy celebration of the mystery of your Son's Nativity.
Who lives and reigns for ever and ever.
℟. **Amen.** → No. 30, p. 77

Optional Solemn Blessings, p. 97, and Prayers over the People, p. 105

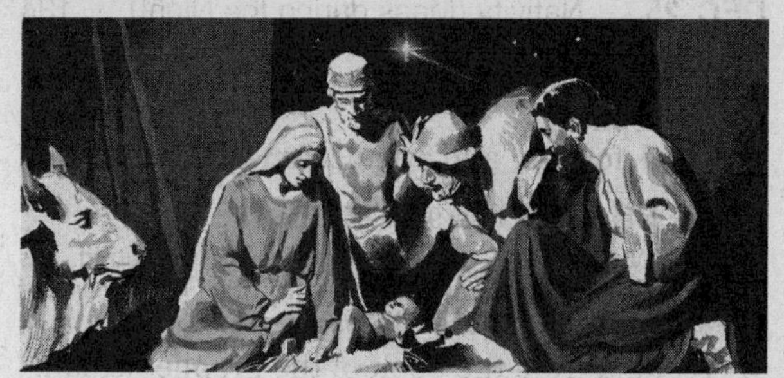

The Word is made flesh.

DECEMBER 25

CHRISTMAS: THE NATIVITY OF THE LORD

Solemnity

AT THE MASS DURING THE NIGHT

ENTRANCE ANTIPHON Ps. 2.7

The Lord said to me: You are my Son. It is I who have begotten you this day. → No. 2, p. 10

OR

Let us all rejoice in the Lord, for our Saviour has been born in the world. Today true peace has come down to us from heaven. → No. 2, p. 10

COLLECT

O God, who have made this most sacred night
radiant with the splendour of the true light,
grant, we pray, that we, who have known the mysteries of his light on earth,
may also delight in his gladness in heaven.

Who lives and reigns with you in the unity of the Holy Spirit,
one God, for ever and ever. ℟. **Amen.** ↓

FIRST READING Isa. 9.2-4, 6-7

The Messiah is a promise of peace for the world. His reign shall be vast and filled with justice. The power of God is revealed through the weakness of humans.

A reading from the book of the Prophet Isaiah.

THE people who walked in darkness have seen a great light;
those who lived in a land of deep darkness—
on them light has shone.
You have multiplied the nation,
you have increased its joy;
they rejoice before you
as with joy at the harvest,
as people exult when dividing plunder.

For the yoke of their burden,
and the bar across their shoulders,
the rod of their oppressor,
you have broken as on the day of Midian.

For a child has been born for us,
a son given to us;
authority rests upon his shoulders;
and he is named
Wonderful Counsellor, Mighty God,
Everlasting Father, Prince of Peace.
His authority shall grow continually,
and there shall be endless peace
for the throne of David and his kingdom.
He will establish and uphold it
with justice and with righteousness

from this time onward and forevermore.
The zeal of the Lord of hosts will do this.

The word of the Lord. ℟. **Thanks be to God.** ↓

RESPONSORIAL PSALM Ps. 96

Leo Marchildon

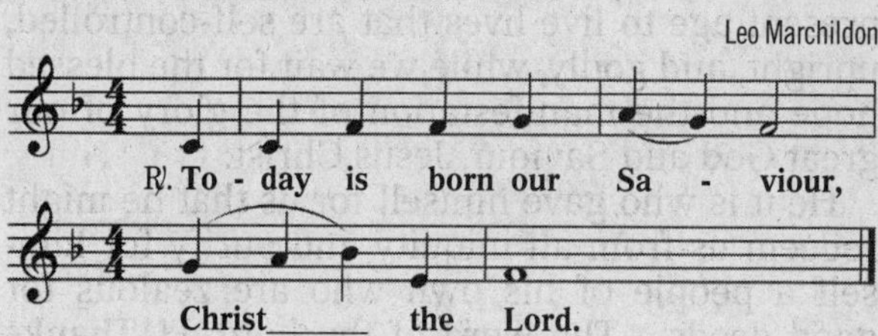
℟. To - day is born our Sa - viour,
Christ the Lord.

O sing to the Lord a new song;
sing to the Lord, all the earth.
Sing to the Lord, bless his name;
tell of his salvation from day to day.—℟.

Declare his glory among the nations,
his marvellous works among all the peoples.
For great is the Lord, and greatly to be praised;
he is to be revered above all gods.—℟.

Let the heavens be glad, and let the earth rejoice;
let the sea roar, and all that fills it;
let the field exult, and everything in it.
Then shall all the trees of the forest sing for joy.—℟.

Rejoice before the Lord; for he is coming,
for he is coming to judge the earth.
He will judge the world with righteousness,
and the peoples with his truth.—℟. ↓

SECOND READING Tit. 2.11-14

God offers salvation to all people. His way asks us to reject worldly desires—to live temperately and justly. He even asked the only Son to sacrifice himself to redeem us.

A reading from the Letter of Saint Paul to Titus.

BELOVED: The grace of God has appeared, bringing salvation to all, training us to renounce impiety and worldly passions, and in the present age to live lives that are self-controlled, upright, and godly, while we wait for the blessed hope and the manifestation of the glory of our great God and Saviour, Jesus Christ.

He it is who gave himself for us that he might redeem us from all iniquity and purify for himself a people of his own who are zealous for good deeds.—The word of the Lord. ℟. **Thanks be to God.** ↓

GOSPEL ACCLAMATION Lk. 2.10-11

℣. Alleluia. ℟. **Alleluia.**
℣. Good news and great joy to all the world:
today is born our Saviour, Christ the Lord.
℟. **Alleluia.** ↓

GOSPEL Lk. 2.1-16

Caesar Augustus desired a world census. Joseph and Mary go to Bethlehem where Jesus, the Lord of the universe, is born in a stable. Glory to God and peace on earth!

℣. The Lord be with you. ℟. **And with your spirit.**
✠ A reading from the holy Gospel according to Luke. ℟. **Glory to you, O Lord.**

IN those days a decree went out from Caesar Augustus that all the world should be registered. This was the first registration and was taken while Quirinius was governor of Syria. All went to their own towns to be registered. Joseph also went from the town of Nazareth in Galilee to Judea, to the city of David called Bethlehem, because he was descended from the house and family of David. He went to be registered with Mary, to whom he was engaged and who was expecting a child.

While they were there, the time came for her to deliver her child. And she gave birth to her firstborn son and wrapped him in swaddling clothes, and laid him in a manger, because there was no place for them in the inn.

In that region there were shepherds living in the fields, keeping watch over their flock by night. Then an Angel of the Lord stood before them, and the glory of the Lord shone around them, and they were terrified. But the Angel said to them, "Do not be afraid; for see—I am bringing you good news of great joy for all the people: to you is born this day in the city of David a Saviour, who is the Christ, the Lord. This will be a sign for you: you will find a child wrapped in swaddling clothes and lying in a manger."

And suddenly there was with the Angel a multitude of the heavenly host, praising God and saying,

"Glory to God in the highest heaven,
and on earth peace among those whom he favours!"

When the Angels had left them and gone into heaven, the shepherds said to one another, "Let us go now to Bethlehem and see this thing that has taken place, which the Lord has made known to us." So they went with haste and found Mary and Joseph, and the child lying in the manger.—The Gospel of the Lord. ℟. **Praise to you, Lord Jesus Christ.** → No. 15, p. 18

The Creed is said. All kneel at the words and by the Holy Spirit was incarnate.

PRAYER OVER THE OFFERINGS

May the oblation of this day's feast
be pleasing to you, O Lord, we pray,
that through this most holy exchange
we may be found in the likeness of Christ,
in whom our nature is united to you.
Who lives and reigns for ever and ever.
℟. **Amen.** → No. 21, p. 22 (Pref. 3-5)

When the Roman Canon is used, the proper form of the Communicantes (In communion with those) *is said.*

COMMUNION ANTIPHON Jn. 1.14

The Word became flesh, and we have seen his glory. ↓

PRAYER AFTER COMMUNION

Grant us, we pray, O Lord our God,
that we, who are gladdened by participation
in the feast of our Redeemer's Nativity,
may through an honourable way of life become worthy of union with him.
Who lives and reigns for ever and ever.
℟. **Amen.** → No. 30, p. 77

Optional Solemn Blessings, p. 97, and Prayers over the People, p. 105

AT THE MASS AT DAWN

ENTRANCE ANTIPHON Cf. Isa. 9.1, 5; Lk. 1.33

Today a light will shine upon us, for the Lord is born for us; and he will be called Wondrous God, Prince of peace, Father of future ages: and his reign will be without end. → No. 2, p. 10

COLLECT

Grant, we pray, almighty God,
that, as we are bathed in the new radiance of your incarnate Word,
the light of faith, which illumines our minds,
may also shine through in our deeds.
Through our Lord Jesus Christ, your Son,
who lives and reigns with you in the unity of the Holy Spirit,
one God, for ever and ever. ℟. **Amen.** ↓

FIRST READING Isa. 62.11-12

Isaiah foretells the birth of the Saviour who will come to Zion. These people will be called holy, and they shall be redeemed.

A reading from the book of the Prophet Isaiah.

THE Lord has proclaimed to the end of the earth:
"Say to daughter Zion,
See, your salvation comes;
his reward is with him,
and his recompense before him.
They shall be called 'The Holy People,'
'The Redeemed of the Lord';
and you shall be called 'Sought Out,'
'A City Not Forsaken.'"

The word of the Lord. ℟. **Thanks be to God.** ↓

RESPONSORIAL PSALM Ps. 97 James Howells

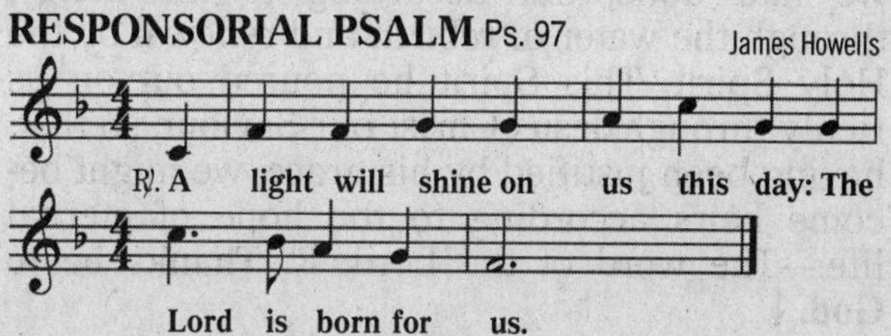
℟. A light will shine on us this day: The
Lord is born for us.

The Lord is king! Let the earth rejoice;
let the many coastlands be glad!
Clouds and thick darkness are all around him;
righteousness and justice are the foundation of his throne.
℟. **A light will shine on us this day: The Lord is born for us.**

The mountains melt like wax before the Lord,
before the Lord of all the earth.
The heavens proclaim his righteousness;
and all the peoples behold his glory.—℟.

Light dawns for the righteous,
and joy for the upright in heart.
Rejoice in the Lord, O you righteous,
and give thanks to his holy name!—℟. ↓

SECOND READING Tit. 3.4-7

Christians are saved not because of their own merits but because of the mercy of God. We are saved through baptism and renewal in the Holy Spirit.

A reading from the Letter of
Saint Paul to Titus.

WHEN the goodness and loving kindness of God our Saviour appeared, he saved us, not because of any works of righteousness that we had done, but according to his mercy, through the water of rebirth and renewal by the Holy Spirit. This Spirit he poured out on us richly through Jesus Christ our Saviour, so that, having been justified by his grace, we might become heirs according to the hope of eternal life.—The word of the Lord. ℟. **Thanks be to God.** ↓

GOSPEL ACCLAMATION Lk. 2.14

℣. Alleluia. ℟. **Alleluia.**
℣. Glory to God in the highest heaven;
peace on earth to people of good will.
℟. **Alleluia.** ↓

GOSPEL Lk. 2.15-20

The shepherds, the poor of the people of God, come to pay homage to Jesus. Mary ponders and prays over the great event of God becoming one of us.

℣. The Lord be with you. ℟. **And with your spirit.**
✠ A reading from the holy Gospel according to Luke. ℟. **Glory to you, O Lord.**

WHEN the Angels had left them and gone into heaven, the shepherds said to one another, "Let us go now to Bethlehem and see this thing that has taken place, which the Lord has made known to us."

So they went with haste and found Mary and Joseph, and the child lying in the manger. When they saw this, they made known what had been told them about this child; and all who heard it were amazed at what the shepherds told them.

But Mary treasured all these words and pondered them in her heart. The shepherds returned, glorifying and praising God for all they had heard and seen, as it had been told them.—The Gospel of the Lord. ℟. **Praise to you, Lord Jesus Christ.** → No. 15, p. 18

The Creed is said. All kneel at the words and by the Holy Spirit was incarnate.

PRAYER OVER THE OFFERINGS

May our offerings be worthy, we pray, O Lord,
of the mysteries of the Nativity this day,
that, just as Christ was born a man and also shone forth as God,
so these earthly gifts may confer on us what is divine.
Through Christ our Lord.
℟. **Amen.** → No. 21, p. 22 (Pref. 3-5)

When the Roman Canon is used, the proper form of the Communicantes (In communion with those) *is said.*

COMMUNION ANTIPHON Cf. Zech. 9.9

Rejoice, O Daughter Sion; lift up praise, Daughter Jerusalem: Behold, your King will come, the Holy One and Saviour of the world. ↓

PRAYER AFTER COMMUNION

Grant us, Lord, as we honour with joyful devotion
the Nativity of your Son,
that we may come to know with fullness of faith
the hidden depths of this mystery
and to love them ever more and more.
Through Christ our Lord.
℟. **Amen.** → No. 30, p. 77

Optional Solemn Blessings, p. 97, and Prayers over the People, p. 105

AT THE MASS DURING THE DAY

ENTRANCE ANTIPHON Cf. Isa. 9.5

A child is born for us, and a son is given to us; his sceptre of power rests upon his shoulder, and his name will be called Messenger of great counsel.

→ No. 2, p. 10

COLLECT

O God, who wonderfully created the dignity of human nature
and still more wonderfully restored it,
grant, we pray,
that we may share in the divinity of Christ,
who humbled himself to share in our humanity.
Who lives and reigns with you in the unity of the Holy Spirit,
one God, for ever and ever. ℟. **Amen.** ↓

FIRST READING Isa. 52.7-10

God shows salvation to all people. God brings peace and good news. God comforts and redeems the faithful.

A reading from the book of the Prophet Isaiah.

HOW beautiful upon the mountains
are the feet of the messenger who announces peace,
who brings good news,
who announces salvation,
who says to Zion, "Your God reigns."

Listen! Your watchmen lift up their voices,
together they sing for joy;
for in plain sight they see
the return of the Lord to Zion.

Break forth together into singing,
you ruins of Jerusalem;
for the Lord has comforted his people,
he has redeemed Jerusalem.
The Lord has bared his holy arm
before the eyes of all the nations;

and all the ends of the earth shall see the salvation of our God.

The word of the Lord. ℟. **Thanks be to God.** ↓

RESPONSORIAL PSALM Ps. 98 Normand L. Blanchard

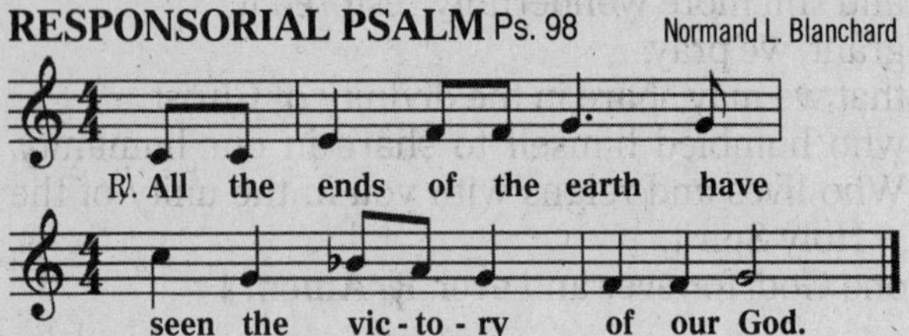
℟. All the ends of the earth have
seen the vic-to-ry of our God.

O sing to the Lord a new song,
for he has done marvellous things.
His right hand and his holy arm
have brought him victory.—℟.

The Lord has made known his victory;
he has revealed his vindication in the sight of the nations.
He has remembered his steadfast love
and faithfulness to the house of Israel.—℟.

All the ends of the earth have seen
the victory of our God.
Make a joyful noise to the Lord, all the earth;
break forth into joyous song and sing praises.—℟.

Sing praises to the Lord with the lyre,
with the lyre and the sound of melody.
With trumpets and the sound of the horn
make a joyful noise before the King, the Lord.—℟. ↓

SECOND READING Heb. 1.1-6

God now speaks through Jesus, the Son, who reflects God's glory. The Son cleanses us from sin. Heaven and earth should worship him.

A reading from the Letter to the Hebrews.

LONG ago God spoke to our ancestors in many and various ways by the Prophets, but in these last days he has spoken to us by the Son, whom he appointed heir of all things, through whom he also created the ages.

He is the reflection of God's glory and the exact imprint of God's very being, and he sustains all things by his powerful word. When he had made purification for sins, he sat down at the right hand of the Majesty on high, having become as much superior to Angels as the name he has inherited is more excellent than theirs.

For to which of the Angels did God ever say,
"You are my Son;
today I have begotten you"?
Or again,
"I will be his Father,
and he will be my Son"?
And again, when he brings the firstborn into the world, he says,
"Let all God's Angels worship him."

The word of the Lord. ℟. **Thanks be to God.** ↓

GOSPEL ACCLAMATION

℣. Alleluia. ℟. **Alleluia.**
℣. A holy day has dawned upon us.
Come you nations and adore the Lord.
Today a great light has come down upon the earth.
℟. **Alleluia.** ↓

GOSPEL Jn. 1.1-18 or 1.1-5, 9-14

John's opening words parallel the Book of Genesis. Jesus is the Word made flesh, the light of the world, who always was and will ever be.

[If the "Shorter Form" is used, the indented text in brackets is omitted.]

℣. The Lord be with you. ℟. **And with your spirit.**
✠ A reading from the holy Gospel according to John. ℟. **Glory to you, O Lord.**

IN the beginning was the Word, and the Word was with God, and the Word was God. He was in the beginning with God. All things came into being through him, and without him not one thing came into being. What has come into being in him was life, and the life was the light of the human race.

The light shines in the darkness, and the darkness did not overcome it.

> [There was a man sent from God, whose name was John. He came as a witness to testify to the light, so that all might believe through him. He himself was not the light, but he came to testify to the light.]

The true light, which enlightens everyone, was coming into the world. He was in the world, and the world came into being through him; yet the world did not know him. He came to what was his own, and his own people did not accept him. But to all who received him, who believed in his name, he gave power to become children of God, who were born, not of blood or of the will of the flesh or of the will of man, but of God. And the Word became flesh and lived among us, and we have seen his glory, the glory as of a father's only-begotten son, full of grace and truth.

> [John testified to him and cried out, "This was he of whom I said, 'He who comes after me ranks ahead of me because he was before me.'"

From his fullness we have all received, grace upon grace. The law indeed was given through Moses; grace and truth came through Jesus Christ.

No one has ever seen God. It is God the only-begotten Son, who is close to the Father's heart, who has made him known.]

The Gospel of the Lord. ℟. **Praise to you, Lord Jesus Christ.** → No. 15, p. 18

The Creed is said. All kneel at the words and by the Holy Spirit was incarnate.

PRAYER OVER THE OFFERINGS

Make acceptable, O Lord, our oblation on this solemn day,
when you manifested the reconciliation
that makes us wholly pleasing in your sight
and inaugurated for us the fullness of divine worship.
Through Christ our Lord.
℟. **Amen.** → No. 21, p. 22 (Pref. 3-5)

When the Roman Canon is used, the proper form of the Communicantes (In communion with those) *is said.*

COMMUNION ANTIPHON Cf. Ps. 97.3

All the ends of the earth have seen the salvation of our God. ↓

PRAYER AFTER COMMUNION

Grant, O merciful God,
that, just as the Saviour of the world, born this day,
is the author of divine generation for us,
so he may be the giver even of immortality.
Who lives and reigns for ever and ever.
℟. **Amen.** → No. 30, p. 77

Optional Solemn Blessings, p. 97, and Prayers over the People, p. 105

Simeon said, "This child is destined for the falling and the rising of many in Israel."

DECEMBER 31

THE HOLY FAMILY OF JESUS, MARY AND JOSEPH

Feast

ENTRANCE ANTIPHON Lk. 2.16

The shepherds went in haste, and found Mary and Joseph and the Infant lying in a manger.

→ No. 2, p. 10

COLLECT

O God, who were pleased to give us
the shining example of the Holy Family,
graciously grant that we may imitate them
in practising the virtues of family life and in the
  bonds of charity,
and so, in the joy of your house,
delight one day in eternal rewards.
Through our Lord Jesus Christ, your Son,

who lives and reigns with you in the unity of the Holy Spirit,
one God, for ever and ever. ℟. **Amen.** ↓

FIRST READING Gen. 15.1-6; 17.3b-5, 15-16; 21.1-7

Abraham believed God, and his faith was rewarded. Through a son born to him and Sarah in their old age, he became the father of many peoples.

A reading from the book of Genesis.

THE word of the Lord came to Abram in a vision, "Do not be afraid, Abram, I am your shield; your reward shall be very great." But Abram said, "O Lord God, what will you give me, for I continue childless, and the heir of my house is Eliezer of Damascus?" And Abram said, "You have given me no offspring, and so a slave born in my house is to be my heir." But the word of the Lord came to him, "This man shall not be your heir; no one but your very own issue shall be your heir."

The Lord brought him outside and said, "Look toward heaven and count the stars, if you are able to count them." Then he said to him, "So shall your descendants be." And he believed the Lord; and the Lord reckoned it to him as righteousness.

God said to him, "As for me, this is my covenant with you: You shall be the father of a multitude of nations. No longer shall your name be Abram, but your name shall be Abraham; for I have made you the father of a multitude of nations."

God said to Abraham, "As for Sarah your wife, you shall not call her Sarai, but Sarah shall be her name. I will bless her, and moreover I will give you a son by her. I will bless her, and she shall give rise to nations; kings of peoples shall come from her."

The Lord dealt with Sarah as he had said, and the Lord did for Sarah as he had promised. Sarah conceived and bore Abraham a son in his old age, at the time of which God had spoken to him. Abraham gave the name Isaac to his son whom Sarah bore him. And Abraham circumcised his son Isaac when he was eight days old, as God had commanded him. Abraham was a hundred years old when his son Isaac was born to him. Now Sarah said, "God has brought laughter for me; everyone who hears will laugh with me." And she said, "Who would ever have said to Abraham that Sarah would nurse children? Yet I have borne him a son in his old age."—The word of the Lord. ℟. **Thanks be to God.** ↓

RESPONSORIAL PSALM Ps. 105

Normand L. Blanchard

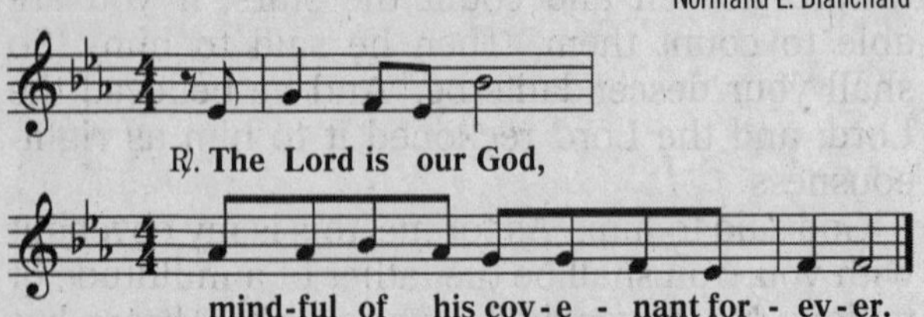
℟. The Lord is our God,
mind-ful of his cov-e - nant for - ev-er.

O give thanks to the Lord, call on his name,
make known his deeds among the peoples.
Sing to him, sing praises to him;
tell of all his wonderful works.—℟.

Glory in his holy name;
let the hearts of those who seek the Lord rejoice.
Seek the Lord and his strength;
seek his presence continually.—℟.

Remember the wonderful works he has done,
his miracles, and the judgments he uttered,
O offspring of his servant Abraham,
children of Jacob, his chosen ones.—℟.

He is mindful of his covenant forever,
of the word that he commanded, for a thousand generations,
the covenant that he made with Abraham,
his sworn promise to Isaac.—℟. ↓

SECOND READING Heb. 11.8, 11-12, 17-19

We are called to emulate the faith of Abraham. For God is "able even to raise someone from the dead."

A reading from the Letter to the Hebrews.

BY faith Abraham obeyed when he was called to set out for a place that he was to receive as an inheritance; and he set out, not knowing where he was going.

By faith Sarah herself, though barren, received power to conceive, even when she was too old, because she considered him faithful who had promised.

Therefore from one person, and this one as good as dead, descendants were born, "as many as the stars of heaven and as the innumerable grains of sand by the seashore."

By faith Abraham, when put to the test, offered up Isaac. He who had received the promises was ready to offer up his only-begotten son, of whom he had been told, "It is through Isaac that descendants shall be named for you." Abraham considered the fact that God is able even to raise someone from the dead—and figuratively speaking, he did receive him back.—The word of the Lord. ℟. **Thanks be to God.** ↓

GOSPEL ACCLAMATION Heb. 1.1-2

℣. Alleluia. ℟. **Alleluia.**

℣. Long ago God spoke to our ancestors by the Prophets;
in these last days he has spoken to us by the Son.
℟. **Alleluia.** ↓

GOSPEL Lk. 2.22-40 or 2.22, 25-27, 34-35, 39-40

Joseph and Mary take Jesus to the temple in Jerusalem to be presented to the Lord. Simeon recognizes him as the Anointed of the Lord and blesses him. The child returns to Nazareth and grows to maturity.

[If the "Shorter Form" is used, the indented text in brackets is omitted.]

℣. The Lord be with you. ℟. **And with your spirit.**
✠ A reading from the holy Gospel according to Luke. ℟. **Glory to you, O Lord.**

WHEN the time came for their purification according to the law of Moses, Mary and Joseph brought the child Jesus up to Jerusalem to present him to the Lord, [(as it is written in the law of the Lord, "Every firstborn male shall be designated as holy to the Lord"), and they offered a sacrifice according to what is stated in the law of the Lord, "a pair of turtledoves or two young pigeons."]

Now there was a man in Jerusalem whose name was Simeon; this man was righteous and devout, looking forward to the consolation of Israel, and the Holy Spirit rested on him. It had been revealed to him by the Holy Spirit that he would not see death before he had seen the Christ of the Lord. Guided by the Spirit, Simeon came into the temple; and when the parents brought in the child Jesus, to do for him what was customary under the law,

[Simeon took him in his arms and praised God, saying, "Master, now you are dismissing your servant in peace, according to your word; for my eyes have seen your salvation, which you have prepared in the presence of all peoples, a light for revelation to the Gentiles and for glory to your people Israel."

And the child's father and mother were amazed at what was being said about him.]

[Then] Simeon blessed them and said to his mother Mary, "This child is destined for the falling and the rising of many in Israel, and to be a sign that will be opposed so that the inner thoughts of many will be revealed—and a sword will pierce your own soul too."

[There was also a Prophet, Anna the daughter of Phanuel, of the tribe of Asher. She was of a great age, having lived with her husband seven years after her marriage, then as a widow to the age of eighty-four. She never left the temple but worshipped there with fasting and prayer night and day. At that moment she came, and began to praise God and to speak about the child to all who were looking for the redemption of Jerusalem.]

When Mary and Joseph had finished everything required by the law of the Lord, they returned to Galilee, to their own town of Nazareth. The child grew and became strong, filled with wisdom; and the favour of God was upon him.—The Gospel of the Lord. ℟. **Praise to you, Lord Jesus Christ.** → No. 15, p. 18

PRAYER OVER THE OFFERINGS

We offer you, Lord, the sacrifice of conciliation,
humbly asking that,
through the intercession of the Virgin Mother of God and Saint Joseph,
you may establish our families firmly in your grace and your peace.
Through Christ our Lord.
℟. **Amen.** → No. 21, p. 22 (Pref. 3-5)

When the Roman Canon is used, the proper form of the Communicantes (In communion with those) *is said.*

COMMUNION ANTIPHON Bar. 3.38

Our God has appeared on the earth, and lived among us. ↓

PRAYER AFTER COMMUNION

Bring those you refresh with this heavenly Sacrament,
most merciful Father,
to imitate constantly the example of the Holy Family,
so that, after the trials of this world,
we may share their company for ever.
Through Christ our Lord.
℟. **Amen.** → No. 30, p. 77

Optional Solemn Blessings, p. 97, and Prayers over the People, p. 105

"He was called Jesus. . . ."

JANUARY 1, 2018

The Octave Day of the Nativity of the Lord SOLEMNITY OF MARY, THE HOLY MOTHER OF GOD

ENTRANCE ANTIPHON

Hail, Holy Mother, who gave birth to the King who rules heaven and earth for ever. → No. 2, p. 10

OR Cf. Isa. 9.1, 5; Lk. 1.33

Today a light will shine upon us, for the Lord is born for us; and he will be called Wondrous God, Prince of peace, Father of future ages: and his reign will be without end. → No. 2, p. 10

COLLECT

O God, who through the fruitful virginity of Blessed Mary
bestowed on the human race
the grace of eternal salvation,
grant, we pray,

that we may experience the intercession of her,
through whom we were found worthy
to receive the author of life,
our Lord Jesus Christ, your Son.
Who lives and reigns with you in the unity of the Holy Spirit,
one God, for ever and ever. ℟. **Amen.** ↓

FIRST READING Num. 6.22-27

Aaron and the Israelites are to pray that God will answer their prayers with blessings.

A reading from the book of Numbers.

THE Lord spoke to Moses:
Speak to Aaron and his sons, saying,
Thus you shall bless the children of Israel:
You shall say to them,

The Lord bless you and keep you;
the Lord make his face to shine upon you,
and be gracious to you;
the Lord lift up his countenance upon you,
and give you peace.

So they shall put my name on the children of Israel,
and I will bless them.

The word of the Lord. ℟. **Thanks be to God.** ↓

RESPONSORIAL PSALM Ps. 67

Paul K. McKay

℟. May God be gra - cious to
us and bless us.

May God be gracious to us and bless us
and make his face to shine upon us,

that your way may be known upon earth,
your saving power among all nations.
℟. **May God be gracious to us and bless us.**

Let the nations be glad and sing for joy,
for you judge the peoples with equity
and guide the nations upon earth.
Let the peoples praise you, O God;
let all the peoples praise you.—℟.

The earth has yielded its increase;
God, our God, has blessed us.
May God continue to bless us;
let all the ends of the earth revere him.—℟. ↓

SECOND READING Gal. 4.4-7

God sent Jesus, his Son, born of Mary, to deliver all people from the bondage of sin and slavery of the law. By God's choice we are heirs of heaven.

A reading from the Letter of Saint Paul to the Galatians.

BROTHERS and sisters: When the fullness of time had come, God sent his Son, born of a woman, born under the law, in order to redeem those who were under the law, so that we might receive adoption to sonship.

And because you are sons and daughters, God has sent the Spirit of his Son into our hearts, crying, "Abba! Father!" So you are no longer slave but son, and if son then also heir, through God.—The word of the Lord. ℟. **Thanks be to God.** ↓

GOSPEL ACCLAMATION Heb. 1.1-2

℣. Alleluia. ℟. **Alleluia.**
℣. Long ago God spoke to our ancestors by the Prophets;

in these last days he has spoken to us by the Son.
℟. **Alleluia.** ↓

GOSPEL Lk. 2.16-21

When the shepherds came to Bethlehem, they began to understand the message of the angels. Mary prayed about this great event. Jesus received his name according to the Jewish ritual of circumcision.

℣. The Lord be with you. ℟. **And with your spirit.**
✠ A reading from the holy Gospel according to Luke. ℟. **Glory to you, O Lord.**

THE shepherds went with haste to Bethlehem and found Mary and Joseph, and the child lying in the manger. When they saw this, they made known what had been told them about this child; and all who heard it were amazed at what the shepherds told them. But Mary treasured all these words and pondered them in her heart.

The shepherds returned, glorifying and praising God for all they had heard and seen, as it had been told them.

After eight days had passed, it was time to circumcise the child; and he was called Jesus, the name given by the Angel before he was conceived in the womb.—The Gospel of the Lord.
℟. **Praise to you, Lord Jesus Christ.** → No. 15, p. 18

PRAYER OVER THE OFFERINGS

O God, who in your kindness begin all good things
and bring them to fulfilment,
grant to us, who find joy in the Solemnity of the holy Mother of God,

that, just as we glory in the beginnings of your grace,
so one day we may rejoice in its completion.
Through Christ our Lord.
℟. **Amen.** ↓

PREFACE (56)

℣. The Lord be with you. ℟. **And with your spirit.**
℣. Lift up your hearts. ℟. **We lift them up to the Lord.** ℣. Let us give thanks to the Lord our God.
℟. **It is right and just.**

It is truly right and just, our duty and our salvation,
always and everywhere to give you thanks,
Lord, holy Father, almighty and eternal God,
and to praise, bless, and glorify your name
on the Solemnity of the Motherhood
of the Blessed ever-Virgin Mary.

For by the overshadowing of the Holy Spirit
she conceived your Only Begotten Son,
and without losing the glory of virginity,
brought forth into the world the eternal Light,
Jesus Christ our Lord.

Through him the Angels praise your majesty,
Dominions adore and Powers tremble before you.
Heaven and the Virtues of heaven and the blessed Seraphim
worship together with exultation.
May our voices, we pray, join with theirs
in humble praise, as we acclaim: → No. 23, p. 23

When the Roman Canon is used, the proper form of the Communicantes (In communion with those) *is said.*

COMMUNION ANTIPHON Heb. 13.8

Jesus Christ is the same yesterday, today, and for ever. ↓

PRAYER AFTER COMMUNION

We have received this heavenly Sacrament with joy, O Lord:
grant, we pray,
that it may lead us to eternal life,
for we rejoice to proclaim the blessed ever-Virgin Mary
Mother of your Son and Mother of the Church.
Through Christ our Lord.
℟. **Amen.** → No. 30, p. 77

Optional Solemn Blessings, p. 97, and Prayers over the People, p. 105

"They knelt down and paid him homage."

JANUARY 7

THE EPIPHANY OF THE LORD

Solemnity

AT THE VIGIL MASS (January 6)

ENTRANCE ANTIPHON Cf. Bar. 5.5

Arise, Jerusalem, and look to the East and see your children gathered from the rising to the setting of the sun. → No. 2, p. 10

COLLECT

May the splendour of your majesty, O Lord, we pray,
shed its light upon our hearts,
that we may pass through the shadows of this world
and reach the brightness of our eternal home.
Through our Lord Jesus Christ, your Son,
who lives and reigns with you in the unity of the Holy Spirit,
one God, for ever and ever. ℟. **Amen.** ↓

The readings for this Mass can be found beginning on p. 165.

PRAYER OVER THE OFFERINGS

Accept we pray, O Lord, our offerings,
in honour of the appearing of your Only Begotten Son
and the first fruits of the nations,
that to you praise may be rendered
and eternal salvation be ours.
Through Christ our Lord. ℟. **Amen.** ↓

PREFACE (6)

℣. The Lord be with you. ℟. **And with your spirit.** ℣. Lift up your hearts. ℟. **We lift them up to the Lord.** ℣. Let us give thanks to the Lord our God. ℟. **It is right and just.**

It is truly right and just, our duty and our salvation,
always and everywhere to give you thanks,
Lord, holy Father, almighty and eternal God.

For today you have revealed the mystery
of our salvation in Christ
as a light for the nations,
and, when he appeared in our mortal nature,
you made us new by the glory of his immortal nature.

And so, with Angels and Archangels,
with Thrones and Dominions,
and with all the hosts and Powers of heaven,
we sing the hymn of your glory,
as without end we acclaim: → No. 23, p. 23

COMMUNION ANTIPHON Cf. Rev. 21.23

The brightness of God illumined the holy city Jerusalem, and the nations will walk by its light. ↓

PRAYER AFTER COMMUNION

Renewed by sacred nourishment,
we implore your mercy, O Lord,
that the star of your justice
may shine always bright in our minds
and that our true treasure may ever consist in our confession of you.
Through Christ our Lord.
℟. **Amen.** → No. 30, p. 77

Optional Solemn Blessings, p. 97, and Prayers over the People, p. 105

AT THE MASS DURING THE DAY

ENTRANCE ANTIPHON Cf. Mal. 3.1; 1 Chr. 29.12

Behold, the Lord, the Mighty One, has come; and kingship is in his grasp, and power and dominion. → No. 2, p. 10

COLLECT

O God, who on this day
revealed your Only Begotten Son to the nations
by the guidance of a star,
grant in your mercy
that we, who know you already by faith,
may be brought to behold the beauty of your sublime glory.
Through our Lord Jesus Christ, your Son,
who lives and reigns with you in the unity of the Holy Spirit,
one God, for ever and ever. ℟. **Amen.** ↓

FIRST READING Isa. 60.1-6

Jerusalem is favoured by the Lord. Kings and peoples will come there, and the riches of the earth will be placed at its gates.

A reading from the book of the
Prophet Isaiah.

ARISE, shine, for your light has come,
and the glory of the Lord has risen upon you!
For darkness shall cover the earth,
and thick darkness the peoples;

but the Lord will arise upon you,
and his glory will appear over you.

Nations shall come to your light,
and kings to the brightness of your dawn.
Lift up your eyes and look around;
they all gather together, they come to you;
your sons shall come from far away,
and your daughters shall be carried on their nurses' arms.

Then you shall see and be radiant;
your heart shall thrill and rejoice,
because the abundance of the sea shall be brought to you,
the wealth of the nations shall come to you.
A multitude of camels shall cover you,
the young camels of Midian and Ephah;
all those from Sheba shall come.
They shall bring gold and frankincense,
and shall proclaim the praise of the Lord.

The word of the Lord. ℟. **Thanks be to God.** ↓

RESPONSORIAL PSALM Ps. 72

David Szanto

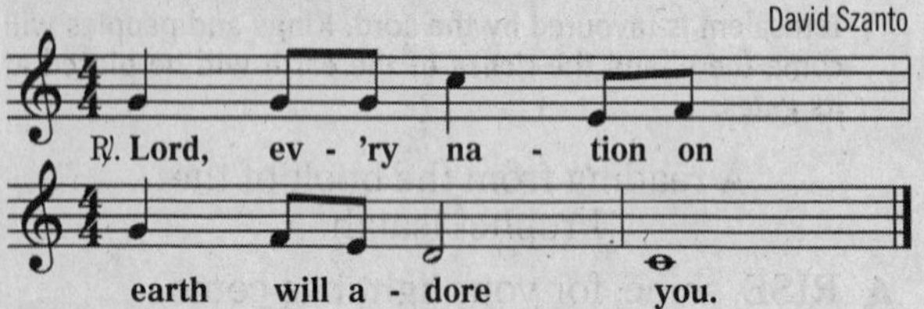
℟. Lord, ev - 'ry na - tion on
earth will a - dore you.

Give the king your justice, O God,
and your righteousness to a king's son.
May he judge your people with righteousness,
and your poor with justice.—℟.

In his days may righteousness flourish
and peace abound, until the moon is no more.
May he have dominion from sea to sea,
and from the River to the ends of the earth.—℟.

May the kings of Tarshish and of the isles render
 him tribute,
may the kings of Sheba and Seba bring gifts.
May all kings fall down before him,
all nations give him service.—℟.

For he delivers the needy one who calls,
the poor and the one who has no helper.
He has pity on the weak and the needy,
and saves the lives of the needy.—℟. ↓

SECOND READING Eph. 3.2-3a, 5-6

God has revealed the divine plan of salvation. The whole world will share in the good news.

A reading from the Letter of Saint Paul
to the Ephesians.

BROTHERS and sisters: Surely you have already heard of the commission of God's grace that was given me for you, and how the mystery was made known to me by revelation.

In former generations this mystery was not made known to humankind as it has now been revealed to his holy Apostles and Prophets by the Spirit: that is, the Gentiles have become fellow heirs, members of the same body, and sharers in the promise in Christ Jesus through the Gospel.—The word of the Lord. ℟. **Thanks be to God.** ↓

GOSPEL ACCLAMATION See Mt. 2.2

℣. Alleluia. ℟. **Alleluia.**
℣. We observed his star at its rising,
and have come to pay homage to the Lord.
℟. **Alleluia.** ↓

GOSPEL Mt. 2.1-12

The wise men from the East followed the star to Bethlehem, from which a ruler was to come.

℣. The Lord be with you. ℟. **And with your spirit.**
✠ A reading from the holy Gospel according to Matthew. ℟. **Glory to you, O Lord.**

IN the time of King Herod, after Jesus was born in Bethlehem of Judea, wise men from the East came to Jerusalem, asking, "Where is the child who has been born king of the Jews? For we observed his star at its rising, and have come to pay him homage."

When King Herod heard this, he was frightened, and all Jerusalem with him; and calling together all the chief priests and scribes of the people, he inquired of them where the Messiah was to be born. They told him, "In Bethlehem of Judea; for so it has been written by the Prophet:

'And you, Bethlehem, in the land of Judah,
are by no means least among the rulers of Judah;
for from you shall come a ruler
who is to shepherd my people Israel.'"

Then Herod secretly called for the wise men and learned from them the exact time when the star had appeared. Then he sent them to Bethlehem, saying, "Go and search diligently for the child; and when you have found him, bring me word so that I may also go and pay him homage."

When they had heard the king, they set out; and there, ahead of them, went the star that they had seen at its rising, until it stopped over the place where the child was. When they saw that the star had stopped, they were overwhelmed with joy.

On entering the house, they saw the child with Mary his mother; and they knelt down and paid him homage. Then, opening their treasure chests, they offered him gifts of gold, frankincense, and myrrh. And having been warned in a dream not to return to Herod, they left for their own country by another road.—The Gospel of the Lord. ℟. **Praise to you, Lord Jesus Christ.** → No. 15, p. 18

PRAYER OVER THE OFFERINGS

Look with favour, Lord, we pray,
on these gifts of your Church,
in which are offered now not gold or
frankincense or myrrh,
but he who by them is proclaimed,
sacrificed and received, Jesus Christ.
Who lives and reigns for ever and ever. ℟. **Amen.**

→ Pref. 6, p. 163

When the Roman Canon is used, the proper form of the Communicantes (In communion with those) *is said.*

COMMUNION ANTIPHON Cf. Mt. 2.2

We have seen his star in the East, and have come with gifts to adore the Lord. ↓

PRAYER AFTER COMMUNION

Go before us with heavenly light, O Lord,
always and everywhere,
that we may perceive with clear sight
and revere with true affection
the mystery in which you have willed us to participate.
Through Christ our Lord.
℟. **Amen.** → No. 30, p. 77

Optional Solemn Blessings, p. 97, and Prayers over the People, p. 105

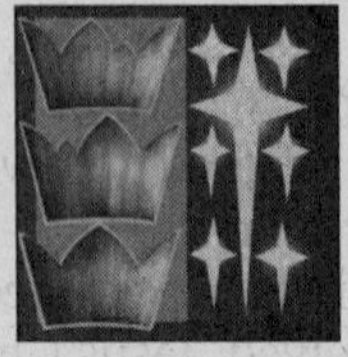

"Look, here is the Lamb of God!"

JANUARY 14

2nd SUNDAY IN ORDINARY TIME

ENTRANCE ANTIPHON Ps. 65.4

All the earth shall bow down before you, O God, and shall sing to you, shall sing to your name, O Most High! → No. 2, p. 10

COLLECT

Almighty ever-living God,
who govern all things,
both in heaven and on earth,
mercifully hear the pleading of your people
and bestow your peace on our times.
Through our Lord Jesus Christ, your Son,
who lives and reigns with you in the unity of the
  Holy Spirit,
one God, for ever and ever. ℟. **Amen.** ↓

FIRST READING 1 Sam. 3.3b-10, 19

The Lord called Samuel, but he did not recognize God's voice. Samuel receives advice from Eli, who is already a

prophet for the Lord. Following instructions from Eli, Samuel listens to the Lord.

A reading from the first book of Samuel.

SAMUEL was lying down in the temple of the Lord, where the ark of God was. Then the Lord called, "Samuel! Samuel!" and he said, "Here I am!" Samuel ran to Eli, and said, "Here I am, for you called me." But Eli said, "I did not call; lie down again." So he went and lay down.

The Lord called again, "Samuel!" Samuel got up and went to Eli, and said, "Here I am, for you called me." But he said, "I did not call, my son; lie down again." Now Samuel did not yet know the Lord, and the word of the Lord had not yet been revealed to him.

The Lord called Samuel again, a third time. And he got up and went to Eli, and said, "Here I am, for you called me." Then Eli perceived that the Lord was calling the boy. Therefore Eli said to Samuel, "Go, lie down; and if he calls you, you shall say, 'Speak, Lord, for your servant is listening.'" So Samuel went and lay down in his place.

Now the Lord came and stood there, calling as before, "Samuel! Samuel!" And Samuel said, "Speak, for your servant is listening."

As Samuel grew up, the Lord was with him and let none of his words fall to the ground.—The word of the Lord. ℟. **Thanks be to God.** ↓

RESPONSORIAL PSALM Ps. 40

Frank Lynch

℟. Here I am, Lord; I come to do your will.

I waited patiently for the Lord;
he inclined to me and heard my cry.
He put a new song in my mouth,
a song of praise to our God.—℟.

Sacrifice and offering you do not desire,
but you have given me an open ear.
Burnt offering and sin offering
you have not required.—℟.

Then I said, "Here I am;
in the scroll of the book it is written of me.
I delight to do your will, O my God;
your law is within my heart."—℟.

I have told the glad news of deliverance
in the great congregation;
see, I have not restrained my lips,
as you know, O Lord.—℟. ↓

SECOND READING 1 Cor. 6.13c-15a, 17-20

The body is made for the Lord. With the price of the cross Jesus redeemed all humanity. The Holy Spirit dwells within each person.

A reading from the first Letter of Saint Paul to the Corinthians.

BROTHERS and sisters: The body is meant not for fornication but for the Lord, and the Lord for the body. And God raised the Lord and will also raise us by his power.

Do you not know that your bodies are members of Christ? But anyone united to the Lord becomes one spirit with him. Shun fornication! Every sin that a person commits is outside the body; but the fornicator sins against the body itself.

Or do you not know that your body is a temple of the Holy Spirit within you, which you have from God, and that you are not your own? For you were bought with a price; therefore glorify God in your body.—The word of the Lord. ℟. **Thanks be to God.** ↓

GOSPEL ACCLAMATION Cf. Jn. 1.41, 17

℣. Alleluia. ℟. **Alleluia.**
℣. We have found the Messiah:
Jesus Christ, who brings us grace and truth.
℟. **Alleluia.** ↓

In place of the Gospel Acclamation given for each Sunday in Ordinary Time, another may be selected.

GOSPEL Jn. 1.35-42

It was John the Baptist's purpose to point out Jesus, the Messiah. Andrew and his companion go with Jesus. Andrew summons Peter. Jesus identifies Peter and gives him a new name.

℣. The Lord be with you. ℟. **And with your spirit.**
✠ A reading from the holy Gospel according to John. ℟. **Glory to you, O Lord.**

JOHN was standing with two of his disciples, and as he watched Jesus walk by, he exclaimed, "Look, here is the Lamb of God!" The two disciples heard him say this, and they followed Jesus.

When Jesus turned and saw them following, he said to them, "What are you looking for?" They said to him, "Rabbi" (which translated means Teacher), "where are you staying?" He said to them, "Come and see." They came and saw where he was staying, and they remained with him that day. It was about four o'clock in the afternoon.

One of the two who heard John speak and followed him was Andrew, Simon Peter's brother. He first found his brother Simon and said to him, "We have found the Messiah" (which is translated the Christ). He brought Simon to Jesus, who looked at him and said, "You are Simon son of John. You are to be called Cephas" (which is translated Peter).—The Gospel of the Lord. ℟. **Praise to you, Lord Jesus Christ.** → No. 15, p. 18

PRAYER OVER THE OFFERINGS

Grant us, O Lord, we pray,
that we may participate worthily in these mysteries,
for whenever the memorial of this sacrifice is celebrated
the work of our redemption is accomplished.
Through Christ our Lord.
℟. **Amen.** → No. 21, p. 22 (Pref. 29-36)

COMMUNION ANTIPHON Cf. Ps. 22.5

You have prepared a table before me, and how precious is the chalice that quenches my thirst. ↓

OR 1 Jn. 4.16

We have come to know and to believe in the love that God has for us. ↓

PRAYER AFTER COMMUNION

Pour on us, O Lord, the Spirit of your love,
and in your kindness
make those you have nourished

by this one heavenly Bread
one in mind and heart.
Through Christ our Lord.
℟. **Amen.** → No. 30, p. 77

Optional Solemn Blessings, p. 97, and Prayers over the People, p. 105

"Follow me and I will make you fishers of people."

JANUARY 21

3rd SUNDAY IN ORDINARY TIME

ENTRANCE ANTIPHON Cf. Ps. 95.1, 6

O sing a new song to the Lord; sing to the Lord, all the earth. In his presence are majesty and splendour, strength and honour in his holy place.

→ No. 2, p. 10

COLLECT

Almighty ever-living God,
direct our actions according to your good pleasure,

that in the name of your beloved Son
we may abound in good works.
Through our Lord Jesus Christ, your Son,
who lives and reigns with you in the unity of the Holy Spirit,
one God, for ever and ever. ℟. **Amen.** ↓

FIRST READING Jon. 3.1-5, 10

The mercy of God is shown to the people of Nineveh. The Lord sends Jonah to them to preach penance for sin. The king proclaims a universal fast to appease the Lord.

A reading from the book of the
Prophet Jonah.

THE word of the Lord came to Jonah, saying, "Get up, go to Nineveh, that great city, and proclaim to it the message that I tell you." So Jonah set out and went to Nineveh, according to the word of the Lord.

Now Nineveh was an exceedingly large city, a three days' walk across. Jonah began to go into the city, going a day's walk. And he cried out, "Forty days more, and Nineveh shall be overthrown!" And the people of Nineveh believed God; they proclaimed a fast, and everyone, great and small, put on sackcloth.

When God saw what they did, how they turned from their evil ways, God changed his mind about the calamity that he had said he would bring upon them; and he did not do it.—The word of the Lord.

℟. **Thanks be to God.** ↓

RESPONSORIAL PSALM Ps. 25

Normand L. Blanchard
℟. Lord, make me know your ways.

Make me to know your ways, O Lord;
teach me your paths.
Lead me in your truth, and teach me,
for you are the God of my salvation.—℟.

Be mindful of your mercy, O Lord, and of your
steadfast love,
for they have been from of old.
According to your steadfast love remember me,
for the sake of your goodness, O Lord!—℟.

Good and upright is the Lord;
therefore he instructs sinners in the way.
He leads the humble in what is right,
and teaches the humble his way.—℟. ↓

SECOND READING 1 Cor. 7.29-31

Paul warns the Corinthians of the shortness of time in this world. All must conduct themselves worthily in the eyes of God and be detached from this world's pleasures.

A reading from the first Letter of Saint Paul to the Corinthians.

BROTHERS and sisters, the appointed time has grown short; from now on, let even those who have wives be as though they had none, and those who mourn as though they were not mourning, and those who rejoice as though they were not rejoicing, and those who buy as though they had no possessions, and those who deal with the world as though they had no dealings with it. For the present form of this world is passing away.—The word of the Lord. ℟. **Thanks be to God.** ↓

GOSPEL ACCLAMATION Mk. 1.15

℣. Alleluia. ℟. **Alleluia.**
℣. The kingdom of God has come near:
repent and believe the good news!
℟. **Alleluia.** ↓

GOSPEL Mk. 1.14-20

Jesus began to preach the good news of salvation. He called Simon and Andrew, James and John, to follow him. Immediately, they accepted the call to become "fishers of people."

℣. The Lord be with you. ℟. **And with your spirit.**
✠ A reading from the holy Gospel according to Mark. ℟. **Glory to you, O Lord.**

AFTER John was arrested, Jesus came to Galilee, proclaiming the good news of God, and saying, "The time is fulfilled, and the kingdom of God has come near; repent, and believe in the good news."

As Jesus passed along the Sea of Galilee, he saw Simon and his brother Andrew casting a net into the sea—for they were fishermen. And Jesus said to them, "Come follow me and I will make you fishers of people." And immediately they left their nets and followed him.

As Jesus went a little farther, he saw James son of Zebedee and his brother John, who were in their boat mending the nets. Immediately he called them; and they left their father Zebedee in the boat with the hired men, and followed him.—The Gospel of the Lord. ℟. **Praise to you, Lord Jesus Christ.** → No. 15, p. 18

PRAYER OVER THE OFFERINGS

Accept our offerings, O Lord, we pray,
and in sanctifying them
grant that they may profit us for salvation.
Through Christ our Lord.
℟. **Amen.** → No. 21, p. 22 (Pref. 29-36)

COMMUNION ANTIPHON Cf. Ps. 33.6

Look toward the Lord and be radiant; let your faces not be abashed. ↓

OR Jn. 8.12

I am the light of the world, says the Lord; whoever follows me will not walk in darkness, but will have the light of life. ↓

PRAYER AFTER COMMUNION

Grant, we pray, almighty God,
that, receiving the grace
by which you bring us to new life,
we may always glory in your gift.
Through Christ our Lord.
℟. **Amen.** → No. 30, p. 77

Optional Solemn Blessings, p. 97, and Prayers over the People, p. 105

"He commands even the unclean spirits. . . ."

JANUARY 28

4th SUNDAY IN ORDINARY TIME

ENTRANCE ANTIPHON Ps. 105.47

Save us, O Lord our God! And gather us from the nations, to give thanks to your holy name, and make it our glory to praise you. → No. 2, p. 10

COLLECT

Grant us, Lord our God,
that we may honour you with all our mind,
and love everyone in truth of heart.
Through our Lord Jesus Christ, your Son,
who lives and reigns with you in the unity of the
Holy Spirit,
one God, for ever and ever. ℟. **Amen.** ↓

FIRST READING Deut. 18.15-20

The Lord promises to select a prophet from among the people who will speak for him.

A reading from the book of Deuteronomy.

MOSES spoke to the people; he said: "The Lord your God will raise up for you a Prophet like me from among your own kin; you shall heed such a Prophet. This is what you requested of the Lord your God at Horeb on the day of the assembly when you said: 'Let me not hear the voice of the Lord my God any more, or ever again see this great fire, lest I die.'

Then the Lord replied to me: 'They are right in what they have said. I will raise up for them a Prophet like you from among their own kin; I will put my words in his mouth, and he shall speak to them everything that I command him.

'Anyone who does not heed the words that he shall speak in my name, I myself will hold him accountable. But any Prophet who speaks in the name of other gods, or who presumes to speak in my name a word that I have not commanded him to speak—that Prophet shall die.'"—The word of the Lord. ℟. **Thanks be to God.** ↓

RESPONSORIAL PSALM Ps. 95

Normand L. Blanchard

℟. O that to - day you would lis - ten to the
voice of the Lord.
Do not hard - en your hearts!

O come, let us sing to the Lord;
let us make a joyful noise to the rock of our salvation!
Let us come into his presence with thanksgiving;
let us make a joyful noise to him with songs of praise!—℟.

O come, let us worship and bow down,
let us kneel before the Lord, our Maker!
For he is our God, and we are the people of his pasture,
and the sheep of his hand.—℟.

O that today you would listen to his voice!
Do not harden your hearts, as at Meribah,
as on the day at Massah in the wilderness,
when your ancestors tested me,
and put me to the proof,
though they had seen my work.—℟. ↓

SECOND READING 1 Cor. 7.32-35

Paul speaks about the value of a celibate life. He is anxious to promote what helps us live entirely for the Lord.

A reading from the first Letter of Saint Paul to the Corinthians.

BROTHERS and sisters, I want you to be free from anxieties. The unmarried man is anxious about the affairs of the Lord, how to please the Lord; but the married man is anxious about the affairs of the world, how to please his wife, and his interests are divided.

The unmarried woman and the virgin are concerned about the affairs of the Lord, so that they may be holy in body and spirit; but the married woman is concerned about the affairs of the world, how to please her husband.

I say this for your own benefit, not to put any restraint upon you, but to promote good order and unhindered devotion to the Lord.—The word of the Lord. ℟. **Thanks be to God.** ↓

GOSPEL ACCLAMATION Mt. 4.16

℣. Alleluia. ℟. **Alleluia.**
℣. The people who sat in darkness have seen a great light,
and for those who sat in the region and shadow of death, light has dawned.
℟. **Alleluia.** ↓

GOSPEL Mk. 1.21-28

Jesus teaches in the synagogue with outstanding authority. The people are amazed.

℣. The Lord be with you. ℟. **And with your spirit.**
✠ A reading from the holy Gospel according to Mark. ℟. **Glory to you, O Lord.**

THE disciples went to Capernaum; and when the Sabbath came, Jesus entered the synagogue and taught. They were astounded at his teaching, for he taught them as one having authority, and not as the scribes. Just then there was in their synagogue a man with an unclean spirit, and he cried out, "What have you to do with us, Jesus of Nazareth? Have you come to destroy us? I know who you are, the Holy One of God."

But Jesus rebuked him, saying, "Be silent, and come out of him!" And the unclean spirit, convulsing the man and crying with a loud voice, came out of him. They were all amazed, and they kept on asking one another, "What is this?

A new teaching—with authority! He commands even the unclean spirits, and they obey him."

At once Jesus' fame began to spread throughout the surrounding region of Galilee.—The Gospel of the Lord. ℟. **Praise to you, Lord Jesus Christ.** → No. 15, p. 18

PRAYER OVER THE OFFERINGS

O Lord, we bring to your altar
these offerings of our service:
be pleased to receive them, we pray,
and transform them
into the Sacrament of our redemption.
Through Christ our Lord.
℟. **Amen.** → No. 21, p. 22 (Pref. 29-36)

COMMUNION ANTIPHON Cf. Ps. 30.17-18

Let your face shine on your servant. Save me in your merciful love. O Lord, let me never be put to shame, for I call on you. ↓

OR Mt 5.3-4

Blessed are the poor in spirit, for theirs is the Kingdom of Heaven. Blessed are the meek, for they shall possess the land.↓

PRAYER AFTER COMMUNION

Nourished by these redeeming gifts,
we pray, O Lord,
that through this help to eternal salvation
true faith may ever increase.
Through Christ our Lord.
℟. **Amen.** → No. 30, p. 77

Optional Solemn Blessings, p. 97, and Prayers over the People, p. 105

"He came. . . . Then the fever left her."

FEBRUARY 4

5th SUNDAY IN ORDINARY TIME

ENTRANCE ANTIPHON Ps. 94.6-7

O come, let us worship God and bow low before the God who made us, for he is the Lord our God.

→ No. 2, p. 10

COLLECT

Keep your family safe, O Lord, with unfailing care,
that, relying solely on the hope of heavenly grace,
they may be defended always by your protection.
Through our Lord Jesus Christ, your Son,
who lives and reigns with you in the unity of the Holy Spirit,
one God, for ever and ever. ℟. **Amen.** ↓

FIRST READING Job 7.1-4, 6-7

Job describes our life on earth. The days of our life come to a swift end.

A reading from the book of Job.

JOB spoke to his friends:
"Does not the human being have a hard service on earth,
and are not their days like the days of a labourer?
Like a slave who longs for the shadow,
and like a labourer who looks for their wages,
so I am allotted months of emptiness,
and nights of misery are apportioned to me.

When I lie down I say, 'When shall I rise?'
But the night is long,
and I am full of tossing until dawn.

My days are swifter than a weaver's shuttle,
and come to their end without hope.
Remember that my life is a breath;
my eye will never again see good."

The word of the Lord. ℟. **Thanks be to God.** ↓

RESPONSORIAL PSALM Ps. 147

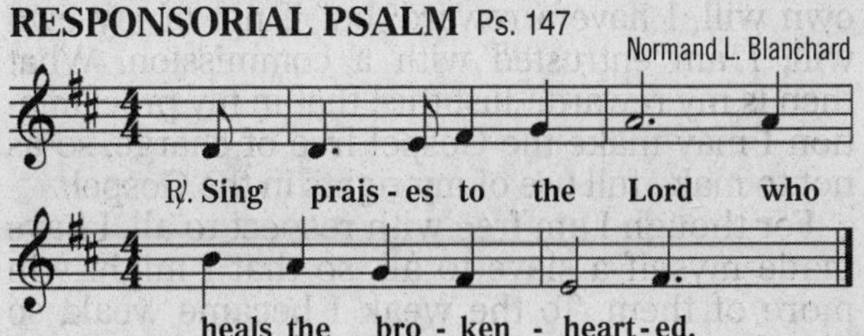
Normand L. Blanchard
℟. Sing prais - es to the Lord who
heals the bro - ken - heart - ed.

Or: ℟. **Alleluia!**

How good it is to sing praises to our God;
for he is gracious, and a song of praise is fitting.
The Lord builds up Jerusalem;
he gathers the outcasts of Israel.—℟.

The Lord heals the brokenhearted,
and binds up their wounds.

He determines the number of the stars;
he gives to all of them their names.
℟. **Sing praises to the Lord who heals the brokenhearted.**

Great is our Lord, and abundant in power;
his understanding is beyond measure.
The Lord lifts up the downtrodden;
he casts the wicked to the ground.—℟. ↓

SECOND READING 1 Cor. 9.16-19, 22-23

Paul writes that he must preach the gospel. He has tried to become one with his hearers to convince them of the saving message of the gospel.

A reading from the first Letter of Saint Paul to the Corinthians.

BROTHERS and sisters: If I proclaim the Gospel, this gives me no ground for boasting, for an obligation is laid on me, and woe to me if I do not proclaim the Gospel! For if I do this of my own will, I have a reward; but if not of my own will, I am entrusted with a commission. What then is my reward? Just this: that in my proclamation I may make the Gospel free of charge, so as not to make full use of my rights in the Gospel.

For though I am free with respect to all, I have made myself a slave to all, so that I might win more of them. To the weak I became weak, so that I might win the weak. I have become all things to all people, that I might by all means save some. I do it all for the sake of the Gospel, so that I may share in its blessings.—The word of the Lord. ℟. **Thanks be to God.** ↓

GOSPEL ACCLAMATION Mt. 8.17

℣. Alleluia. ℟. **Alleluia.**

℣. Christ took our infirmities,
and bore our diseases.
℟. **Alleluia.** ↓

GOSPEL Mk. 1.29-39

Jesus cures Simon's mother-in-law and the sick. Then he goes off to pray alone.

℣. The Lord be with you. ℟. **And with your spirit.**
✠ A reading from the holy Gospel according to Mark. ℟. **Glory to you, O Lord.**

AS soon as Jesus and his disciples left the synagogue, they entered the house of Simon and Andrew, with James and John. Now Simon's mother-in-law was in bed with a fever, and they told Jesus about her at once. He came and took her by the hand and lifted her up. Then the fever left her, and she began to serve them.

That evening, at sunset, they brought to Jesus all who were sick or possessed with demons. And the whole city was gathered around the door. And he cured many who were sick with various diseases, and cast out many demons; and he would not permit the demons to speak, because they knew him.

In the morning, while it was still very dark, Jesus got up and went out to a deserted place, and there he prayed. And Simon and his companions hunted for him. When they found him, they said to him, "Everyone is searching for you."

He answered, "Let us go on to the neighbouring towns, so that I may proclaim the message there also; for that is what I came out to do." And Jesus went throughout Galilee, proclaiming the message in their synagogues and casting out demons.—

The Gospel of the Lord. ℟. **Praise to you, Lord Jesus Christ.** → No. 15, p. 18

PRAYER OVER THE OFFERINGS

O Lord our God,
who once established these created things
to sustain us in our frailty,
grant, we pray,
that they may become for us now
the Sacrament of eternal life.
Through Christ our Lord.
℟. **Amen.** → No. 21, p. 22 (Pref. 29-36)

COMMUNION ANTIPHON Cf. Ps. 106.8-9

Let them thank the Lord for his mercy, his wonders for the children of men, for he satisfies the thirsty soul, and the hungry he fills with good things. ↓

OR Mt. 5.5-6

Blessed are those who mourn, for they shall be consoled. Blessed are those who hunger and thirst for righteousness, for they shall have their fill. ↓

PRAYER AFTER COMMUNION

O God, who have willed that we be partakers
in the one Bread and the one Chalice,
grant us, we pray, so to live
that, made one in Christ,
we may joyfully bear fruit
for the salvation of the world.
Through Christ our Lord.
℟. **Amen.** → No. 30, p. 77

Optional Solemn Blessings, p. 97, and Prayers over the People, p. 105

"Jesus stretched out his hand and touched him, and said, . . . 'Be made clean!' "

FEBRUARY 11

6th SUNDAY IN ORDINARY TIME

ENTRANCE ANTIPHON Cf. Ps. 30.3-4

Be my protector, O God, a mighty stronghold to save me. For you are my rock, my stronghold! Lead me, guide me, for the sake of your name.

→ No. 2, p. 10

COLLECT

O God, who teach us that you abide
in hearts that are just and true,
grant that we may be so fashioned by your grace
as to become a dwelling pleasing to you.
Through our Lord Jesus Christ, your Son,
who lives and reigns with you in the unity of the
  Holy Spirit,
one God, for ever and ever. ℟. **Amen.** ↓

FIRST READING Lev. 13.1-2, 45-46

The Lord instructs Moses and Aaron on the legal prescriptions that are to be followed by those who have leprosy.

A reading from the book of Leviticus.

THE Lord spoke to Moses and Aaron, saying: "When someone has on the skin of their body a swelling or an eruption or a spot, and it turns into a leprous disease on the skin of their body, that person shall be brought to Aaron the priest or to one of his sons the priests.

Anyone who has the leprous disease shall wear torn clothes and let the hair of their head be dishevelled and shall cover their upper lip and cry out, 'Unclean, unclean.' That person shall remain unclean as long as the disease persists; and being unclean, such a one shall live alone with their dwelling outside the camp."—The word of the Lord. ℟. **Thanks be to God.** ↓

RESPONSORIAL PSALM Ps. 32

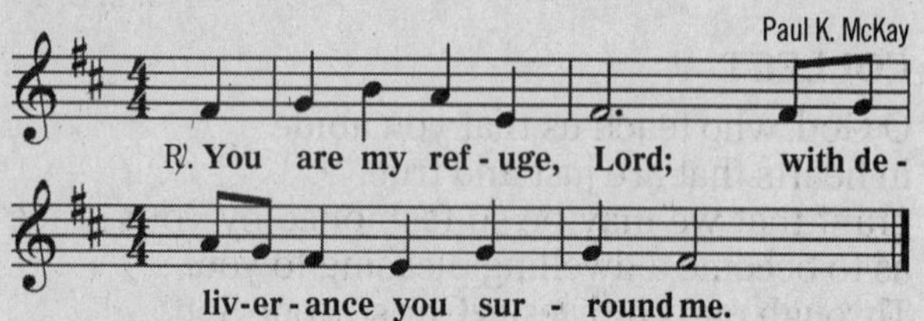
Paul K. McKay
℟. You are my ref - uge, Lord; with de -
liv-er - ance you sur - round me.

Blessed is the one whose transgression is forgiven,
whose sin is covered.
Blessed is the one to whom the Lord imputes no iniquity,
and in whose spirit there is no deceit.—℟.

I acknowledged my sin to you,
and I did not hide my iniquity;
I said, "I will confess my transgressions to the Lord,"
and you forgave the guilt of my sin.—℟.

Be glad in the Lord and rejoice, O righteous,
and shout for joy, all you upright in heart.—℟. ↓

SECOND READING 1 Cor. 10.31–11.1

Paul directs that whatever is done should be for the glory of God.

A reading from the first Letter of Saint Paul to the Corinthians.

BROTHERS and sisters: Whether you eat or drink, or whatever you do, do everything for the glory of God. Give no offense to Jews or to Greeks or to the Church of God, just as I try to please everyone in everything I do, not seeking my own advantage, but that of many, so that they may be saved.

Be imitators of me, as I am of Christ.—The word of the Lord. ℟. **Thanks be to God.** ↓

GOSPEL ACCLAMATION Lk. 7.16

℣. Alleluia. ℟. **Alleluia.**
℣. A great Prophet has risen among us;
God has looked favourably on his people.
℟. **Alleluia.** ↓

GOSPEL Mk. 1.40-45

Upon request, Jesus cured a leper reminding him to follow the directions of the Mosaic law and to tell no one.

℣. The Lord be with you. ℟. **And with your spirit.**
✠ A reading from the holy Gospel according to Mark. ℟. **Glory to you, O Lord.**

A MAN with leprosy came to Jesus begging him, and kneeling said to Jesus, "If you choose, you can make me clean." Moved with pity, Jesus stretched out his hand and touched him, and said to him, "I do choose. Be made clean!" Immediately the leprosy left him, and he was made clean.

After sternly warning him Jesus sent him away at once, saying to him, "See that you say nothing to anyone; but go, show yourself to the priest, and offer for your cleansing what Moses commanded, as a testimony to them."

But the man went out and began to proclaim it freely, and to spread the word, so that Jesus could no longer go into a town openly, but stayed out in the country; and people came to Jesus from every quarter.—The Gospel of the Lord. ℟. **Praise to you, Lord Jesus Christ.** → No. 15, p. 18

PRAYER OVER THE OFFERINGS

May this oblation, O Lord, we pray,
cleanse and renew us
and may it become for those who do your will
the source of eternal reward.
Through Christ our Lord.
℟. **Amen.** → No. 21, p. 22 (Pref. 29-36)

COMMUNION ANTIPHON Cf. Ps. 77.29-30

They ate and had their fill, and what they craved

the Lord gave them; they were not disappointed in what they craved. ↓

OR Jn. 3.16

God so loved the world that he gave his Only Begotten Son, so that all who believe in him may not perish, but may have eternal life. ↓

PRAYER AFTER COMMUNION

Having fed upon these heavenly delights,
we pray, O Lord,
that we may always long
for that food by which we truly live.
Through Christ our Lord.
℟. **Amen.** → No. 30, p. 77

Optional Solemn Blessings, p. 97, and Prayers over the People, p. 105

"Whenever you fast, do not look dismal, like the hypocrites."

FEBRUARY 14

ASH WEDNESDAY

ENTRANCE ANTIPHON Wis. 11.24, 25, 27

You are merciful to all, O Lord, and despise nothing that you have made. You overlook people's sins, to bring them to repentance, and you spare them, for you are the Lord our God. → No. 2, p. 10 (Omit Penitential Act)

COLLECT

Grant, O Lord, that we may begin with holy fasting
this campaign of Christian service,
so that, as we take up battle against spiritual evils,
we may be armed with weapons of self-restraint.
Through our Lord Jesus Christ, your Son,
who lives and reigns with you in the unity of the Holy Spirit,
one God, for ever and ever.
℟. **Amen.** ↓

FIRST READING Jl. 2.12-18

The prophet points to the fact that "works" of penance, if not related to that inner conversion to God in love, are worthless.

A reading from the book of the Prophet Joel.

EVEN now, says the Lord,
return to me with all your heart,
with fasting, with weeping, and with mourning;
rend your hearts and not your clothing.
Return to the Lord, your God,
for he is gracious and merciful,
slow to anger, and abounding in steadfast love,
and relents from punishing.
Who knows whether the Lord will not turn and relent,
and leave a blessing behind him:
a grain offering and a drink offering
to be presented to the Lord, your God?

Blow the trumpet in Zion;
sanctify a fast;
call a solemn assembly;
gather the people.
Sanctify the congregation;
assemble the aged;
gather the children, even infants at the breast.
Let the bridegroom leave his room,
and the bride her canopy.

Between the vestibule and the altar
let the priests, the ministers of the Lord, weep.
Let them say, "Spare your people, O Lord,
and do not make your heritage a mockery,
a byword among the nations.
Why should it be said among the peoples,
'Where is their God?'"

Then the Lord became jealous for his land,
and had pity on his people.

The word of the Lord. ℟. **Thanks be to God.** ↓

RESPONSORIAL PSALM Ps. 51

Michel Guimont

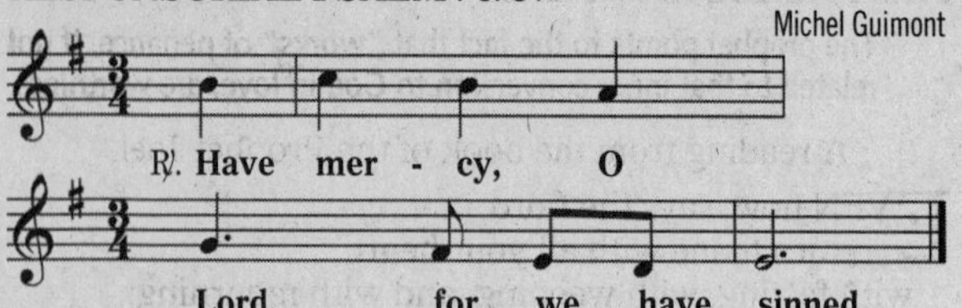
℟. Have mer - cy, O
Lord, for we have sinned.

Have mercy on me, O God,
according to your steadfast love;
according to your abundant mercy
blot out my transgressions
Wash me thoroughly from my iniquity,
and cleanse me from my sin.—℟.

For I know my transgressions,
and my sin is ever before me.
Against you, you alone, have I sinned,
and done what is evil in your sight.—℟.

Create in me a clean heart, O God,
and put a new and right spirit within me.
Do not cast me away from your presence,
and do not take your holy spirit from me.—℟.

Restore to me the joy of your salvation,
and sustain in me a willing spirit.
O Lord, open my lips,
and my mouth will declare your praise.—℟. ↓

SECOND READING 2 Cor. 5.20—6.2

Paul insists on conversion now! Forgiveness is available. Ask for it now! "Now is the acceptable time!"

A reading from the second Letter of Saint Paul to the Corinthians.

BROTHERS and sisters: We are ambassadors for Christ, since God is making his appeal through us; we entreat you on behalf of Christ, be reconciled to God. For our sake God made Christ to be sin who knew no sin, so that in Christ we might become the righteousness of God.

As we work together with him, we urge you also not to accept the grace of God in vain. For the Lord says, "At an acceptable time I have listened to you, and on a day of salvation I have helped you." See, now is the acceptable time; see, now is the day of salvation!—The word of the Lord. ℟. **Thanks be to God.** ↓

GOSPEL ACCLAMATION Ps. 95.7-8

℣. Praise to you, Lord Jesus Christ, King of endless glory! *

℟. **Praise to you, Lord Jesus Christ, King of endless glory!**

℣. Today, do not harden your hearts,
but listen to the voice of the Lord.

℟. **Praise to you, Lord Jesus Christ, King of endless glory!** ↓

GOSPEL Mt. 6.1-6, 16-18

External works of penance have no value in themselves. You must relate them to the real penance, your conversion to God.

℣. The Lord be with you. ℟. **And with your spirit.**

✠ A reading from the holy Gospel according to Matthew.

℟. **Glory to you, O Lord.**

JESUS said to his disciples: "Beware of practising your piety before people in order to be seen by them; for then you have no reward from your Father in heaven.

So whenever you give alms, do not sound a trumpet before you, as the hypocrites do in the synagogues and in the streets, so that they may be praised by others. Truly I tell you, they have received their reward. But when you give alms, do not let your left hand know what your right hand is doing, so that your alms may be done in secret; and your Father who sees in secret will reward you.

---

* *See p. 16 for other Gospel Acclamations.*

And whenever you pray, do not be like the hypocrites; for they love to stand and pray in the synagogues and on the street corners, so that they may be seen by others. Truly I tell you, they have received their reward. But whenever you pray, go into your room and shut the door and pray to your Father who is in secret; and your Father who sees in secret will reward you.

And whenever you fast, do not look dismal, like the hypocrites, for they disfigure their faces so as to show others that they are fasting. Truly I tell you, they have received their reward. But when you fast, put oil on your head and wash your face, so that your fasting may be seen not by others but by your Father who is in secret; and your Father who sees in secret will reward you."—The Gospel of the Lord. ℟. **Praise to you, Lord Jesus Christ.** ↓

BLESSING AND DISTRIBUTION OF ASHES

After the Homily, the Priest, standing with his hands joined, says:

Dear brethren (brothers and sisters), let us humbly ask God our Father
that he be pleased to bless with the abundance of his grace
these ashes, which we will put on our heads in penitence. ↓

After a brief prayer in silence, and, with hands extended, he continues:

O God, who are moved by acts of humility
and respond with forgiveness to works of penance,
lend your merciful ear to our prayers
and in your kindness pour out the grace of your ✠ blessing
on your servants who are marked with these ashes,
that, as they follow the Lenten observances,
they may be worthy to come with minds made pure
to celebrate the Paschal Mystery of your Son.
Through Christ our Lord. ℟. **Amen.** ↓

OR:

O God, who desire not the death of sinners,
but their conversion,
mercifully hear our prayers
and in your kindness be pleased to bless ✠ these ashes,
which we intend to receive upon our heads,
that we, who acknowledge we are but ashes
and shall return to dust,
may, through a steadfast observance of Lent,
gain pardon for sins and newness of life
after the likeness of your Risen Son.
Who lives and reigns for ever and ever. ℟. **Amen.** ↓

He sprinkles the ashes with holy water, without saying anything.

Then the Priest places ashes on the head of all those present who come to him, and says to each one:

Repent, and believe in the Gospel.

OR:

Remember that you are dust, and to dust you shall return.

Meanwhile, the following are sung.

ANTIPHON 1

Let us change our garments to sackcloth and ashes, let us fast and weep before the Lord, that our God, rich in mercy, might forgive us our sins.

ANTIPHON 2 Cf. Jl. 2.17; Est. 4.17

Let the priests, the ministers of the Lord, stand between the porch and the altar and weep and cry out: Spare, O Lord, spare your people; do not close the mouths of those who sing your praise, O Lord.

ANTIPHON 3 Ps. 51.3

Blot out my transgressions, O Lord.

*This may be repeated after each verse of Psalm 51 (*Have mercy on me, O God).

RESPONSORY Cf. Bar. 3.2; Ps. 79.9

℟. **Let us correct our faults which we have committed in ignorance, let us not be taken unawares by the day of our death, looking in vain for leisure to repent. Hear us, O Lord, and show us your mercy, for we have sinned against you.**

℣. **Help us, O God our Savior; for the sake of your name, O Lord, set us free. Hear us, O Lord . . .**

Another appropriate chant may also be sung.

After the distribution of ashes, the Priest washes his hands and proceeds to the Universal Prayer, and continues the Mass in the usual way.

The Creed is not said.

PRAYER OVER THE OFFERINGS

As we solemnly offer
the annual sacrifice for the beginning of Lent,
we entreat you, O Lord,
that, through works of penance and charity,
we may turn away from harmful pleasures
and, cleansed from our sins, may become worthy
to celebrate devoutly the Passion of your Son.
Who lives and reigns for ever and ever. ℟. **Amen.** ↓

PREFACE (10)

℣. The Lord be with you. ℟. **And with your spirit.** ℣. Lift up your hearts. ℟. **We lift them up to the Lord.** ℣. Let us give thanks to the Lord our God. ℟. **It is right and just.**

It is truly right and just, our duty and our salvation,
always and everywhere to give you thanks,
Lord, holy Father, almighty and eternal God.

For you will that our self-denial should give you thanks,
humble our sinful pride,
contribute to the feeding of the poor,
and so help us imitate you in your kindness.

And so we glorify you with countless Angels,
as with one voice of praise we acclaim: → No. 23, p. 23

OR:

PREFACE (11)

℣. The Lord be with you. ℟. **And with your spirit.** ℣. Lift up your hearts. ℟. **We lift them up to the Lord.** ℣. Let us give thanks to the Lord our God. ℟. **It is right and just.**

It is truly right and just, our duty and our salvation,
always and everywhere to give you thanks,
Lord, holy Father, almighty and eternal God.

For through bodily fasting you restrain our faults,
raise up our minds,
and bestow both virtue and its rewards,
through Christ our Lord.

Through him the Angels praise your majesty,
Dominions adore and Powers tremble before you.
Heaven and the Virtues of heaven and the blessed Seraphim
worship together with exultation.
May our voices, we pray, join with theirs
in humble praise, as we acclaim: → No. 23, p. 23

COMMUNION ANTIPHON Cf. Ps. 1.2-3

He who ponders the law of the Lord day and night will yield fruit in due season. ↓

PRAYER AFTER COMMUNION

May the Sacrament we have received sustain us, O Lord,
that our Lenten fast may be pleasing to you
and be for us a healing remedy.
Through Christ our Lord. ℟. **Amen. ↓**

PRAYER OVER THE PEOPLE

For the dismissal, the Priest stands facing the people and, extending his hands over them, says this prayer:

Pour out a spirit of compunction, O God,
on those who bow before your majesty,
and by your mercy may they merit the rewards you promise
to those who do penance.
Through Christ our Lord. ℟. **Amen.** → No. 32, p. 77

Jesus was "tempted by Satan."

FEBRUARY 18

1st SUNDAY OF LENT

ENTRANCE ANTIPHON Cf. Ps. 90.15-16

When he calls on me, I will answer him; I will deliver him and give him glory, I will grant him length of days. → No. 2, p. 10 (Omit Gloria)

COLLECT

Grant, almighty God,
through the yearly observances of holy Lent,
that we may grow in understanding
of the riches hidden in Christ
and by worthy conduct pursue their effects.
Through our Lord Jesus Christ, your Son,
who lives and reigns with you in the unity of the Holy Spirit,
one God, for ever and ever.
℟. **Amen.** ↓

FIRST READING Gen. 9.8-15

God promises Noah that the world will never again be destroyed by a flood. God gives a sign of this covenant—the rainbow among the clouds.

A reading from the book of Genesis.

GOD said to Noah and to his sons with him, "As for me, I am establishing my covenant with you and your descendants after you, and with every living creature that is with you, the birds, the domestic animals, and every animal of the earth with you, as many as came out of the ark. I establish my covenant with you, that never again shall all flesh be cut off by the waters of a flood, and never again shall there be a flood to destroy the earth."

God said, "This is the sign of the covenant that I make between me and you and every living creature that is with you, for all future generations: I have set my bow in the clouds, and it shall be a sign of the covenant between me and the earth. When I bring clouds over the earth and the bow is seen in the clouds, I will remember my covenant that is between me and you and every living creature of all flesh; and the waters shall never again become a flood to destroy all flesh."—The word of the Lord. ℟. **Thanks be to God.** ↓

RESPONSORIAL PSALM Ps. 25

Lawrence J. Folk

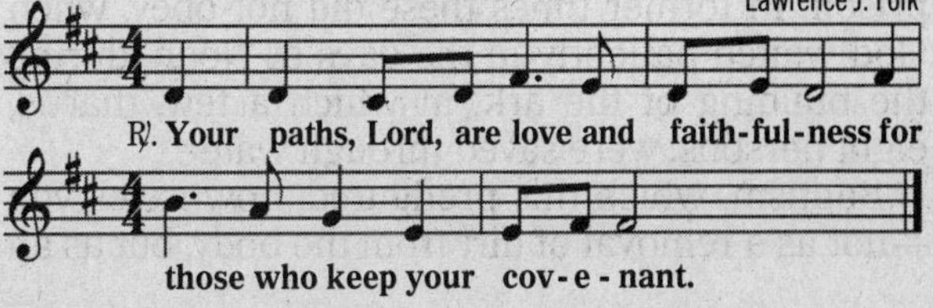

℟. Your paths, Lord, are love and faith-ful-ness for those who keep your cov-e-nant.

Make me to know your ways, O Lord;
teach me your paths.
Lead me in your truth, and teach me,
for you are the God of my salvation.
℟. **Your paths, Lord, are love and faithfulness for those who keep your covenant.**

Be mindful of your mercy, O Lord, and of your steadfast love,
for they have been from of old.
According to your steadfast love remember me,
for the sake of your goodness, O Lord!—℟.

Good and upright is the Lord;
therefore he instructs sinners in the way.
He leads the humble in what is right,
and teaches the humble his way.—℟. ↓

SECOND READING 1 Pet. 3.18-22

Christ died once for sin. Because of sin, God destroyed the earth by water. Now Christians are saved by the water of baptism. It becomes the pledge of resurrection.

A reading from the first Letter of Saint Peter.

BELOVED: Christ suffered for sins once for all, the righteous for the unrighteous, in order to bring you to God. He was put to death in the flesh, but made alive in the spirit, in which also he went and made a proclamation to the spirits in prison. In former times these did not obey, when God waited patiently in the days of Noah, during the building of the ark, in which a few, that is, eight persons, were saved through water.

Baptism, which this prefigured, now saves you —not as a removal of dirt from the body, but as an appeal to God for a good conscience through the resurrection of Jesus Christ, who has gone into heaven and is at the right hand of God, with Angels, Authorities, and Powers made subject to him.—The word of the Lord. ℟. **Thanks be to God.** ↓

GOSPEL ACCLAMATION Mt. 4.4

℣. Praise and honour to you, Lord Jesus Christ!*
℟. **Praise and honour to you, Lord Jesus Christ!**
℣. Man does not live by bread alone,
but by every word that comes from the mouth of God.
℟. **Praise and honour to you, Lord Jesus Christ!** ↓

GOSPEL Mk. 1.12-15

Jesus prayed in the desert for forty days. After John's arrest, Jesus came forth, announcing the time of fulfillment.

℣. The Lord be with you. ℟. **And with your spirit.**
✠ A reading from the holy Gospel according to Mark. ℟. **Glory to you, O Lord.**

AFTER Jesus was baptized, the Spirit drove him out into the wilderness. He was in the wilderness forty days, tempted by Satan; and he was with the wild beasts; and the Angels waited on him.

Now after John was arrested, Jesus came to Galilee, proclaiming the good news of God, and saying,

"The time is fulfilled, and the kingdom of God has come near; repent, and believe in the good

* *See p. 16 for other Gospel Acclamations.*

news."—The Gospel of the Lord. ℟. **Praise to you, Lord Jesus Christ.** → No. 15, p. 18

PRAYER OVER THE OFFERINGS

Give us the right dispositions, O Lord, we pray,
to make these offerings,
for with them we celebrate the beginning
of this venerable and sacred time.
Through Christ our Lord. ℟. **Amen.** ↓

PREFACE (12)

℣. The Lord be with you. ℟. **And with your spirit.** ℣. Lift up your hearts. ℟. **We lift them up to the Lord.** ℣. Let us give thanks to the Lord our God. ℟. **It is right and just.**

It is truly right and just, our duty and our salvation,
always and everywhere to give you thanks,
Lord, holy Father, almighty and eternal God,
through Christ our Lord.

By abstaining forty long days from earthly food,
he consecrated through his fast
the pattern of our Lenten observance
and, by overturning all the snares of the ancient serpent,
taught us to cast out the leaven of malice,
so that, celebrating worthily the Paschal Mystery,
we might pass over at last to the eternal paschal feast.

And so, with the company of Angels and Saints,
we sing the hymn of your praise,
as without end we acclaim: → No. 23, p. 23

COMMUNION ANTIPHON Mt. 4.4

One does not live by bread alone, but by every word that comes forth from the mouth of God. ↓

OR Cf. Ps. 90.4

The Lord will conceal you with his pinions, and under his wings you will trust. ↓

PRAYER AFTER COMMUNION

Renewed now with heavenly bread,
by which faith is nourished, hope increased,
and charity strengthened,
we pray, O Lord,
that we may learn to hunger for Christ,
the true and living Bread,
and strive to live by every word
which proceeds from your mouth.
Through Christ our Lord.
℟. **Amen. ↓**

The Deacon or, in his absence, the Priest himself, says the invitation: Bow down for the blessing.

PRAYER OVER THE PEOPLE

May bountiful blessing, O Lord, we pray,
come down upon your people,
that hope may grow in tribulation,
virtue be strengthened in temptation,
and eternal redemption be assured.
Through Christ our Lord.
℟. **Amen.** → No. 32, p. 77

"There appeared to them Elijah and Moses, who were talking with Jesus."

FEBRUARY 25

2nd SUNDAY OF LENT

ENTRANCE ANTIPHON Cf. Ps. 26.8-9

Of you my heart has spoken: Seek his face. It is your face, O Lord, that I seek; hide not your face from me. → No. 2, p. 10 (Omit Gloria)

OR Cf. Ps. 24.6, 2, 22

Remember your compassion, O Lord, and your merciful love, for they are from of old. Let not our enemies exult over us. Redeem us, O God of Israel, from all our distress.

→ No. 2, p. 10 (Omit Gloria)

COLLECT

O God, who have commanded us
to listen to your beloved Son,
be pleased, we pray,
to nourish us inwardly by your word,
that, with spiritual sight made pure,

we may rejoice to behold your glory.
Through our Lord Jesus Christ, your Son,
who lives and reigns with you in the unity of the Holy Spirit,
one God, for ever and ever. ℟. **Amen.** ↓

FIRST READING Gen. 22.1-2, 9-13, 15-18

Abraham and his son, Isaac, prefigure God, the Father, and Jesus, his divine Son. God tests Abraham's faith, and because of it, God promises abundant blessings on the family of Abraham and all his descendants.

A reading from the book of Genesis.

GOD tested Abraham. He said to him, "Abraham!" And Abraham said, "Here I am."

God said, "Take your son, your only son Isaac, whom you love, and go to the land of Moriah, and offer him there as a burnt offering on one of the mountains that I shall show you."

When Abraham and Isaac came to the place that God had shown him, Abraham built an altar there and laid the wood in order. He bound his son Isaac, and laid him on the altar, on top of the wood. Then Abraham reached out his hand and took the knife to kill his son.

But the Angel of the Lord called to him from heaven, and said, "Abraham, Abraham!" And he said, "Here I am." The Angel said, "Do not lay your hand on the boy or do anything to him; for now I know that you fear God, since you have not withheld your son, your only son, from me."

Abraham looked up and saw a ram, caught in a thicket by its horns. Abraham went and took the ram and offered it up as a burnt offering instead of his son.

The Angel of the Lord called to Abraham a second time from heaven, and said, "By myself I have sworn, says the Lord: Because you have done this, and have not withheld your son, your only son, I will indeed bless you, and I will make your offspring as numerous as the stars of heaven and as the sand that is on the seashore. And your offspring shall possess the gate of their enemies, and by your offspring shall all the nations of the earth gain blessing for themselves, because you have obeyed my voice."—The word of the Lord. ℟. **Thanks be to God.** ↓

RESPONSORIAL PSALM Ps. 116

Frank Lynch

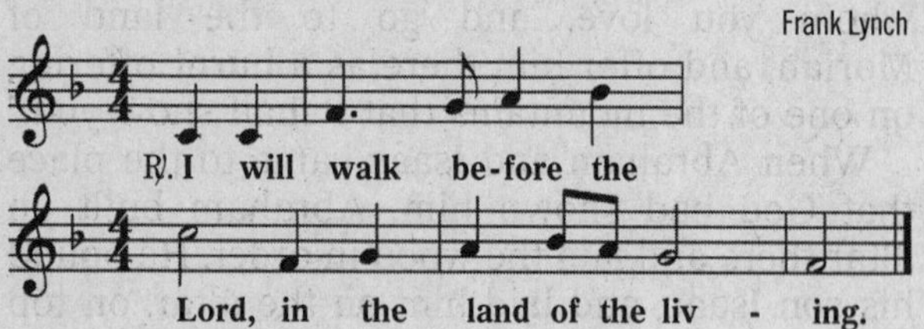
℟. I will walk be-fore the
Lord, in the land of the liv - ing.

I kept my faith, even when I said,
"I am greatly afflicted."
Precious in the sight of the Lord
is the death of his faithful ones.—℟.

O Lord, I am your servant.
You have loosed my bonds.
I will offer to you a thanksgiving sacrifice
and call on the name of the Lord.—℟.

I will pay my vows to the Lord
in the presence of all his people,

in the courts of the house of the Lord,
in your midst, O Jerusalem.—℟. ↓

SECOND READING Rom. 8.31b-35, 37

Who is going to judge God's chosen ones? Is this not the right of Jesus, who loves those to whom he gave his life?

A reading from the Letter of Saint Paul
to the Romans.

BROTHERS and sisters: If God is for us, who is against us? He who did not withhold his own Son, but gave him up for all of us, will he not with him also give us everything else?

Who will bring any charge against God's elect? It is God who justifies. Who is to condemn? It is Christ Jesus, who died, yes, who was raised, who is at the right hand of God, who indeed intercedes for us.

Who will separate us from the love of Christ? Will hardship, or distress, or persecution, or famine, or nakedness, or peril, or sword?

No, in all these things we are more than conquerors through him who loved us.—The word of the Lord. ℟. **Thanks be to God.** ↓

GOSPEL ACCLAMATION See Lk. 9.35

℣. Praise and honour to you, Lord Jesus Christ!*
℟. **Praise and honour to you, Lord Jesus Christ!**
℣. From the bright cloud the Father's voice is heard:
This is my Son, the Beloved, listen to him.
℟. **Praise and honour to you, Lord Jesus Christ!** ↓

* *See p. 16 for other Gospel Acclamations.*

GOSPEL Mk. 9.2-10

Jesus becomes transfigured and God speaks to us: "This is my Son, the Beloved; listen to him."

℣. The Lord be with you. ℟. **And with your spirit.**
✠ A reading from the holy Gospel according to Mark. ℟. **Glory to you, O Lord.**

JESUS took with him Peter and James and John, and led them up a high mountain apart, by themselves. And he was transfigured before them, and his clothes became dazzling white, such as no one on earth could bleach them.

And there appeared to them Elijah and Moses, who were talking with Jesus. Then Peter said to Jesus, "Rabbi, it is good for us to be here; let us make three dwellings, one for you, one for Moses, and one for Elijah." Peter did not know what to say, for they were terrified.

Then a cloud overshadowed them, and from the cloud there came a voice, "This is my Son, the Beloved; listen to him!" Suddenly when they looked around, they saw no one with them any more, but only Jesus.

As they were coming down the mountain, he ordered them to tell no one about what they had seen, until after the Son of Man had risen from the dead.

So they kept the matter to themselves, questioning what this rising from the dead could mean.—The Gospel of the Lord. ℟. **Praise to you, Lord Jesus Christ.** → No. 15, p. 18

PRAYER OVER THE OFFERINGS

May this sacrifice, O Lord, we pray,
cleanse us of our faults

and sanctify your faithful in body and mind
for the celebration of the paschal festivities.
Through Christ our Lord. ℟. **Amen.** ↓

PREFACE (13)

℣. The Lord be with you. ℟. **And with your spirit.** ℣. Lift up your hearts. ℟. **We lift them up to the Lord.** ℣. Let us give thanks to the Lord our God. ℟. **It is right and just.**

It is truly right and just, our duty and our salvation,
always and everywhere to give you thanks,
Lord, holy Father, almighty and eternal God,
through Christ our Lord.

For after he had told the disciples of his coming Death,
on the holy mountain he manifested to them his glory,
to show, even by the testimony of the law and the prophets,
that the Passion leads to the glory of the Resurrection.

And so, with the Powers of heaven,
we worship you constantly on earth,
and before your majesty
without end we acclaim: → No. 23, p. 23

COMMUNION ANTIPHON Mt. 17.5

This is my beloved Son, with whom I am well pleased; listen to him. ↓

PRAYER AFTER COMMUNION

As we receive these glorious mysteries,
we make thanksgiving to you, O Lord,

for allowing us while still on earth
to be partakers even now of the things of heaven.
Through Christ our Lord.
℟. **Amen.** ↓

The Deacon or, in his absence, the Priest himself, says the invitation: Bow down for the blessing.

PRAYER OVER THE PEOPLE

Bless your faithful, we pray, O Lord,
with a blessing that endures for ever,
and keep them faithful
to the Gospel of your Only Begotten Son,
so that they may always desire and at last attain
that glory whose beauty he showed in his own Body,
to the amazement of his Apostles.
Through Christ our Lord.
℟. **Amen.** → No. 32, p. 77

"Stop making my Father's house a marketplace!"

MARCH 4

3rd SUNDAY OF LENT

On this Sunday is celebrated the First Scrutiny in preparation for the Baptism of the catechumens who are to be admitted to the Sacraments of Christian Initiation at the Easter Vigil. The Ritual Mass for the First Scrutiny is found on p. 223.

ENTRANCE ANTIPHON Cf. Ps. 24.15-16

My eyes are always on the Lord, for he rescues my feet from the snare. Turn to me and have mercy on me, for I am alone and poor.

→ No. 2, p. 10 (Omit Gloria)

OR Ez. 36.23-26

When I prove my holiness among you, I will gather you from all the foreign lands; and I will pour clean water upon you and cleanse you from all your impurities, and I will give you a new spirit, says the Lord. → No. 2, p. 10 (Omit Gloria)

COLLECT

O God, author of every mercy and of all goodness,
who in fasting, prayer and almsgiving
have shown us a remedy for sin,
look graciously on this confession of our lowliness,
that we, who are bowed down by our conscience,
may always be lifted up by your mercy.
Through our Lord Jesus Christ, your Son,
who lives and reigns with you in the unity of the
Holy Spirit,
one God, for ever and ever. ℟. **Amen.** ↓

FIRST READING Ex. 20.1-17 or 20.1-3, 7-8, 12-17

God speaks to the people and gives them a code of life to follow—the commandments. The first three describe how God is to be worshipped and the others outline how the people are to respect and live with one another.

[If the "Shorter Form" is used, the indented text in brackets is omitted.]

A reading from the book of Exodus.

GOD spoke all these words: I am the Lord your God, who brought you out of the land of Egypt, out of the house of slavery; you shall have no other gods before me.

[You shall not make for yourself an idol, whether in the form of anything that is in heaven above, or that is on the earth beneath, or that is in the water under the earth. You shall not bow down to them or worship them; for I the Lord your God am a jealous God, punishing children for the iniquity of parents, to the third and the fourth generation of those who reject me, but showing steadfast love to the thousandth generation of those who love me and keep my commandments.]

You shall not make wrongful use of the name of the Lord your God, for the Lord will not acquit anyone who misuses his name.

Remember the Sabbath day, and keep it holy. [Six days you shall labour and do all your work. But the seventh day is a Sabbath to the Lord your God; you shall not do any work—you, your son or your daughter, your male or female slave, your livestock, or the alien resident in your towns. For in six days the Lord made heaven and earth, the sea, and all that is in them, but rested the seventh day; therefore the Lord blessed the Sabbath day and consecrated it.]

Honour your father and your mother, so that your days may be long in the land that the Lord your God is giving you. You shall not murder.

You shall not commit adultery. You shall not steal.

You shall not bear false witness against your neighbour. You shall not covet your neighbour's house; you shall not covet your neighbour's wife, or male or female slave, or ox, or donkey, or anything that belongs to your neighbour.— The word of the Lord. ℟. **Thanks be to God.** ↓

RESPONSORIAL PSALM Ps. 19

Gloria Gassi

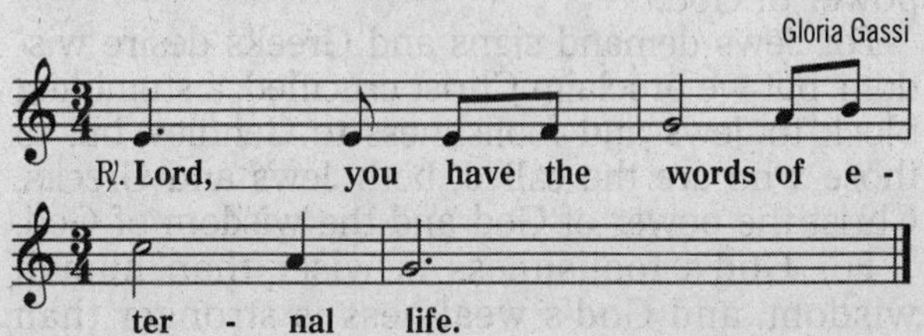
℟. Lord, you have the words of e - ter - nal life.

The law of the Lord is perfect,
reviving the soul;
the decrees of the Lord are sure,
making wise the simple.
℟. **Lord, you have the words of eternal life.**

The precepts of the Lord are right,
rejoicing the heart;
the commandment of the Lord is clear,
enlightening the eyes.—℟.

The fear of the Lord is pure,
enduring forever;
the ordinances of the Lord are true
and righteous altogether.—℟.

More to be desired are they than gold,
even much fine gold;
sweeter also than honey,
and drippings of the honeycomb.—℟. ↓

SECOND READING 1 Cor. 1.18, 22-25

Paul admits that the preaching of Christ crucified is regarded as absurd by some. Still, for those who have faith, Christ is the power and wisdom of God.

A reading from the first Letter of Saint Paul to the Corinthians.

BROTHERS and sisters: The message about the Cross is foolishness to those who are perishing, but to us who are being saved it is the power of God.

For Jews demand signs and Greeks desire wisdom, but we proclaim Christ crucified, a stumbling block to Jews and foolishness to Gentiles, but to those who are the called, both Jews and Greeks, Christ the power of God and the wisdom of God.

For God's foolishness is wiser than human wisdom, and God's weakness is stronger than human strength.—The word of the Lord. ℟. **Thanks be to God.** ↓

GOSPEL ACCLAMATION Jn. 3.16

℣. Praise and honour to you, Lord Jesus Christ!*
℟. **Praise and honour to you, Lord Jesus Christ!**
℣. God so loved the world that he gave his only Son,
that everyone who believes in him may have eternal life.
℟. **Praise and honour to you, Lord Jesus Christ!** ↓

GOSPEL Jn. 2.13-25

Jesus becomes angry when the temple, which is to be a house of prayer, is turned into a place of business.

℣. The Lord be with you. ℟. **And with your spirit.**
✠ A reading from the holy Gospel according to John. ℟. **Glory to you, O Lord.**

THE Passover of the Jews was near, and Jesus went up to Jerusalem. In the temple he found people selling cattle, sheep, and doves, and the money changers seated at their tables. Making a whip of cords, he drove all of them out of the temple, both the sheep and the cattle. He also poured out the coins of the money changers and overturned their tables. He told those who were selling the doves, "Take these things out of here! Stop making my Father's house a marketplace!"

His disciples remembered that it was written, "Zeal for your house will consume me."

The Jews then said to him, "What sign can you show us for doing this?" Jesus answered them,

* *See p. 16 for other Gospel Acclamations.*

"Destroy this temple, and in three days I will raise it up." They then said, "This temple has been under construction for forty-six years, and will you raise it up in three days?" But Jesus was speaking of the temple of his body.

After he was raised from the dead, his disciples remembered that he had said this; and they believed the Scripture and the word that Jesus had spoken.

When he was in Jerusalem during the Passover festival, many believed in his name because they saw the signs that he was doing. But Jesus on his part would not entrust himself to them, because he knew all people and needed no one to testify about human nature, for he himself knew what was within the human person.—The Gospel of the Lord. ℟. **Praise to you, Lord Jesus Christ.**

→ No. 15, p. 18

PRAYER OVER THE OFFERINGS

Be pleased, O Lord, with these sacrificial offerings,
and grant that we who beseech pardon for our own sins,
may take care to forgive our neighbour.
Through Christ our Lord.
℟. **Amen.** → No. 21, p. 22 (Pref. 8-9)

COMMUNION ANTIPHON Ps. 83.4-5

The sparrow finds a home, and the swallow a nest for her young: by your altars, O Lord of hosts, my King and my God. Blessed are they who dwell in your house, for ever singing your praise. ↓

PRAYER AFTER COMMUNION

As we receive the pledge
of things yet hidden in heaven
and are nourished while still on earth
with the Bread that comes from on high,
we humbly entreat you, O Lord,
that what is being brought about in us in mystery
may come to true completion.
Through Christ our Lord.
℟. **Amen.** ↓

The Deacon or, in his absence, the Priest himself, says the invitation: Bow down for the blessing.

PRAYER OVER THE PEOPLE

Direct, O Lord, we pray, the hearts of your faithful,
and in your kindness grant your servants this grace:
that, abiding in the love of you and their neighbour,
they may fulfill the whole of your commands.
Through Christ our Lord.
℟. **Amen.** → No. 32, p. 77

MARCH 4

MASS FOR THE FIRST SCRUTINY

This Mass is celebrated when the First Scrutiny takes place during the Rite of Christian Initiation of Adults, usually on the 3rd Sunday of Lent.

ENTRANCE ANTIPHON Ez. 36.23-26

When I prove my holiness among you, I will gather you from all the foreign lands and I will pour clean water

upon you and cleanse you from all your impurities, and I will give you a new spirit, says the Lord.

→ No. 2 p. 10 (Omit Gloria)

OR Cf. Isa. 55.1

Come to the waters, you who are thirsty, says the Lord; you who have no money, come and drink joyfully.

→ No. 2 p. 10 (Omit Gloria)

COLLECT

Grant, we pray, O Lord,
that these chosen ones may come worthily and wisely
to the confession of your praise,
so that in accordance with that first dignity
which they lost by original sin
they may be fashioned anew through your glory.
Through our Lord Jesus Christ, your Son,
who lives and reigns with you in the unity of the Holy
Spirit,
one God, for ever and ever. ℟. **Amen.** ↓

FIRST READING Ex. 17.3-7

The Israelites murmured against God in their thirst. God directs Moses to strike a rock with his staff, and water issues forth.

A reading from the book of Exodus.

IN the wilderness the people thirsted for water; and the people complained against Moses and said, "Why did you bring us out of Egypt, to kill us and our children and livestock with thirst?" So Moses cried out to the Lord, "What shall I do with this people? They are almost ready to stone me."

The Lord said to Moses, "Go on ahead of the people, and take some of the elders of Israel with you; take in your hand the staff with which you struck the Nile, and go. I will be standing there in front of you on the rock at Horeb. Strike the rock, and water will come out of it, so that the people may drink." Moses did so, in the sight of the elders of Israel.

He called the place Massah and Meribah, because the children of Israel quarrelled and tested the Lord, saying, "Is the Lord among us or not?"—The word of the Lord.
℟. **Thanks be to God.** ↓

RESPONSORIAL PSALM Ps. 95

Michael Gauthier

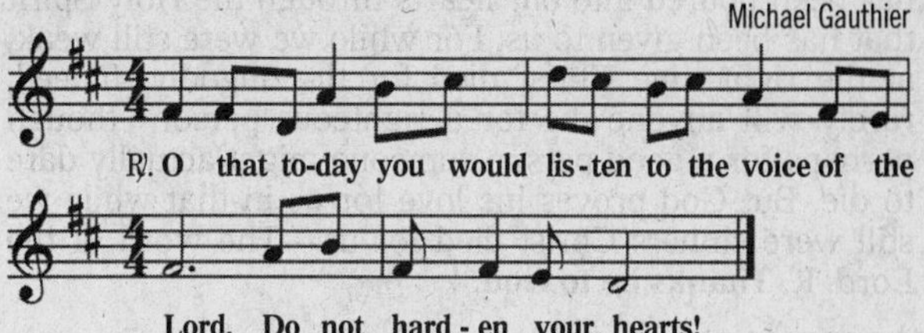
℟. O that to-day you would lis-ten to the voice of the
Lord. Do not hard-en your hearts!

O come, let us sing to the Lord;
let us make a joyful noise to the rock of our salvation!
Let us come into his presence with thanksgiving;
let us make a joyful noise to him with songs of praise!—℟.

O come, let us worship and bow down,
let us kneel before the Lord, our Maker!
For he is our God, and we are the people of his pasture,
and the sheep of his hand.—℟.

O that today you would listen to his voice!
Do not harden your hearts, as at Meribah,
as on the day at Massah in the wilderness,
when your ancestors tested me,
and put me to the proof,
though they had seen my work.—℟. ↓

SECOND READING Rom. 5.1-2, 5-8

Through Jesus we have received the grace of faith. The love of God has been poured upon us. Jesus laid down his life for us while we were still sinners.

A reading from the Letter of Saint Paul to the Romans.

BROTHERS and sisters: Since we are justified by faith, we have peace with God through our Lord Jesus Christ, through whom we have obtained access to this grace in which we stand; and we boast in our hope of sharing the glory of God.

And hope does not disappoint us, because God's love has been poured into our hearts through the Holy Spirit that has been given to us. For while we were still weak, at the right time Christ died for the ungodly. Indeed, rarely will anyone die for a righteous person—though perhaps for a good person someone might actually dare to die. But God proves his love for us in that while we still were sinners Christ died for us.—The word of the Lord. ℟. **Thanks be to God.** ↓

GOSPEL ACCLAMATION Jn. 4.42, 15

℣. Glory to you, Word of God, Lord Jesus Christ!*
℟. **Glory to you, Word of God, Lord Jesus Christ!**
℣. Lord, you are truly the Saviour of the world;
give me living water, that I may never be thirsty.
℟. **Glory to you, Word of God, Lord Jesus Christ!** ↓

GOSPEL Jn. 4.5-42 or 4.5-15, 19-26, 39a, 40-42

> **Jesus speaks to the Samaritan woman at the well. He searches her soul, and she recognizes him as a prophet. Jesus speaks of the water of eternal life.**

[If the "Shorter Form" is used, the indented text in brackets is omitted.]

℣. The Lord be with you. ℟. **And with your spirit.**
✠ A reading from the holy Gospel according to John.
℟. **Glory to you, O Lord.**

JESUS came to a Samaritan city called Sychar, near the plot of ground that Jacob had given to his son Joseph. Jacob's well was there, and Jesus, tired out by his journey, was sitting by the well. It was about noon.

---

* *See p. 16 for other Gospel Acclamations.*

A Samaritan woman came to draw water, and Jesus said to her, "Give me a drink." (His disciples had gone to the city to buy food.)

The Samaritan woman said to him, "How is it that you, a Jew, ask a drink of me, a woman of Samaria?" (Jews do not share things in common with Samaritans.) Jesus answered her, "If you knew the gift of God, and who it is that is saying to you, 'Give me a drink,' you would have asked him, and he would have given you living water."

The woman said to him, "Sir, you have no bucket, and the well is deep. Where do you get that living water? Are you greater than our father Jacob, who gave us the well, and with his children and his flocks drank from it?" Jesus said to her, "Everyone who drinks of this water will be thirsty again, but the one who drinks of the water that I will give will never be thirsty. The water that I will give him will become in him a spring of water gushing up to eternal life." The woman said to him, "Sir, give me this water, so that I may never be thirsty or have to keep coming here to draw water."

> [Jesus said to her, "Go, call your husband, and come back." The woman answered him, "I have no husband." Jesus said to her, "You are right in saying, 'I have no husband'; for you have had five husbands, and the one you have now is not your husband. What you have said is true!"]

The woman said to him, "Sir, I see that you are a Prophet. Our ancestors worshipped on this mountain, but you say that the place where people must worship is in Jerusalem."

Jesus said to her, "Woman, believe me, the hour is coming when you will worship the Father neither on this mountain nor in Jerusalem. You worship what you do not know; we worship what we know, for salvation is from the Jews. But the hour is coming, and is now here, when the true worshippers will worship the Father in spirit and truth, for the Father seeks such as these to worship him. God is spirit, and those who worship him must worship in spirit and truth."

The woman said to him, "I know that the Messiah is coming" (who is called the Christ). "When he comes, he will proclaim all things to us." Jesus said to her, "I am he, the one who is speaking to you."

[Just then his disciples came. They were astonished that he was speaking with a woman, but no one said, "What do you want?" or, "Why are you speaking with her?" Then the woman left her water jar and went back to the city. She said to the people, "Come and see a man who told me everything I have ever done! He cannot be the Messiah, can he?" They left the city and were on their way to him. Meanwhile the disciples were urging him, "Rabbi, eat something." But he said to them, "I have food to eat that you do not know about." So the disciples said to one another, "Surely no one has brought him something to eat?"

Jesus said to them, "My food is to do the will of him who sent me and to complete his work. Do you not say, 'Four months more, then comes the harvest'? But I tell you, look around you, and see how the fields are ripe for harvesting. The reaper is already receiving wages and is gathering fruit for eternal life, so that sower and reaper may rejoice together. For here the saying holds true, 'One sows and another reaps.' I sent you to reap that for which you did not labour. Others have laboured, and you have entered into their labour."]

Many Samaritans from that city believed in Jesus [because of the woman's testimony, "He told me everything I have ever done."]

So when the Samaritans came to him, they asked him to stay with them; and he stayed there two days. And many more believed because of his word. They said to the woman, "It is no longer because of what you said that we believe, for we have heard for ourselves, and we know that this is truly the Saviour of the world."—The Gospel of the Lord. ℟. **Praise to you, Lord Jesus Christ.**

→ No. 15, p. 18

PRAYER OVER THE OFFERINGS

May your merciful grace prepare your servants, O Lord,
for the worthy celebration of these mysteries
and lead them to it by a devout way of life.
Through Christ our Lord. ℟. **Amen.** ↓

PREFACE (14)

℣. The Lord be with you. ℟. **And with your spirit.**
℣. Lift up your hearts. ℟. **We lift them up to the Lord.**
℣. Let us give thanks to the Lord our God. ℟. **It is right and just.**

It is truly right and just, our duty and our salvation,
always and everywhere to give you thanks,
Lord, holy Father, almighty and eternal God,
through Christ our Lord.

For when he asked the Samaritan woman for water to drink,
he had already created the gift of faith within her
and so ardently did he thirst for her faith,
that he kindled in her the fire of divine love.

And so we, too, give you thanks
and with the Angels
praise your mighty deeds, as we acclaim:

→ No. 23, p. 23

When the Roman Canon is used, in the section Memento, Domine *(*Remember, Lord, your servants*) there is a commemoration of the godparents, and the proper form of the* Hanc igitur *(*Therefore, Lord, we pray*) is said.*

Remember, Lord, your servants
who are to present your chosen ones
for the holy grace of your Baptism,

Here the names of the godparents are read out.

and all gathered here,
whose faith and devotion are known to you . . . (p. 24).

Therefore, Lord, we pray:
graciously accept this oblation

which we make to you for your servants,
whom you have been pleased
to enrol, choose and call for eternal life
and for the blessed gift of your grace.
(Through Christ our Lord. Amen.)

The rest follows the Roman Canon, pp. 25-29.

When Eucharistic Prayer II is used, after the words and all the clergy, *the following is added:*

Remember also, Lord, your servants
who are to present these chosen ones
at the font of rebirth.

When Eucharistic Prayer III is used, after the words the entire people you have gained for your own, *the following is added:*

Assist your servants with your grace,
O Lord, we pray,
that they may lead these chosen ones by word and example
to new life in Christ, our Lord.

COMMUNION ANTIPHON Jn. 4.14

For anyone who drinks it, says the Lord, the water I shall give will become in him a spring welling up to eternal life. ↓

PRAYER AFTER COMMUNION

Give help, O Lord, we pray,
by the grace of your redemption
and be pleased to protect and prepare
those you are to initiate
through the Sacraments of eternal life.
Through Christ our Lord.
℟. **Amen.** → No. 30, p. 77

Optional Solemn Blessings, p. 97, and Prayers over the People, p. 105

"The light has come into the world, and people loved darkness rather than light."

MARCH 11

4th SUNDAY OF LENT

On this Sunday is celebrated the Second Scrutiny in preparation for the Baptism of the catechumens who are to be admitted to the Sacraments of Christian Initiation at the Easter Vigil. The Ritual Mass for the Second Scrutiny is found on p. 237.

ENTRANCE ANTIPHON Cf. Isa. 66.10-11

Rejoice, Jerusalem, and all who love her. Be joyful, all who were in mourning; exult and be satisfied at her consoling breast.

→ No. 2, p. 10 (Omit Gloria)

COLLECT

O God, who through your Word
reconcile the human race to yourself in a wonderful way,
grant, we pray,
that with prompt devotion and eager faith
the Christian people may hasten

toward the solemn celebrations to come.
Through our Lord Jesus Christ, your Son,
who lives and reigns with you in the unity of the
Holy Spirit,
one God, for ever and ever. ℟. **Amen.** ↓

FIRST READING 2 Chr. 36.14-17a, 19-23

The Israelites were repeatedly unfaithful to God. They ignored the prophets sent to them. God allowed them to fall to the Chaldeans, which Jeremiah had foretold.

A reading from the second book of Chronicles.

ALL the leading priests and the people were exceedingly unfaithful, following all the abominations of the nations; and they polluted the house of the Lord that he had consecrated in Jerusalem.

The Lord, the God of their ancestors, persistently sent his messengers to them, because he had compassion on his people and on his dwelling place; but they kept mocking the messengers of God, despising his words, and scoffing at his Prophets, until the wrath of the Lord against his people became so great that there was no remedy.

Therefore the Lord brought up against them the king of the Chaldeans, who burned the house of God, broke down the wall of Jerusalem, burned all its palaces with fire, and destroyed all its precious vessels. The king took into exile in Babylon those who had escaped from the sword, and they became servants to him and to his sons until the establishment of the kingdom of Persia, to fulfill the word of the Lord by the mouth of Jeremiah, until the land had made up for its Sabbaths. All the days that it lay desolate it kept Sabbath, to fulfill seventy years.

In the first year of King Cyrus of Persia, in fulfilment of the word of the Lord spoken by Jeremiah, the Lord stirred up the spirit of King Cyrus of Persia so that he sent a herald throughout all his kingdom and also declared in a written edict:

"Thus says King Cyrus of Persia: The Lord, the God of heaven, has given me all the kingdoms of the earth, and he has charged me to build him a house at Jerusalem, which is in Judah. Whoever is among you of all his people, may the Lord his God be with him! Let him go up."—The word of the Lord. ℟. **Thanks be to God.** ↓

RESPONSORIAL PSALM Ps. 137

Lawrence J. Folk

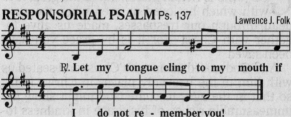

℟. Let my tongue cling to my mouth if I do not re - mem-ber you!

By the rivers of Babylon—
there we sat down and there we wept
when we remembered Zion.
On the willows there we hung up our harps.—℟.

For there our captors
asked us for songs,
and our tormentors asked for mirth, saying,
"Sing us one of the songs of Zion!"—℟.

How could we sing the Lord's song
in a foreign land?
If I forget you, O Jerusalem,
let my right hand wither!—℟.

Let my tongue cling to the roof of my mouth,
if I do not remember you,

if I do not set Jerusalem
above my highest joy.
℟. **Let my tongue cling to my mouth if I do not remember you!** ↓

SECOND READING Eph. 2.4-10

God's mercy and love brought Jesus into the world. Salvation is God's gift, not our human work. Jesus leads all people to perform good works.

A reading from the Letter of Saint Paul to the Ephesians.

GOD, who is rich in mercy, out of the great love with which he loved us even when we were dead through our trespasses, made us alive together with Christ—for it is by grace you have been saved.

And God raised us up with Christ and seated us with him in the heavenly places in Christ Jesus, so that in the ages to come God might show the immeasurable riches of his grace in kindness toward us in Christ Jesus.

For by grace you have been saved through faith, and this is not your own doing; it is the gift of God. This is not the result of works, so that no one may boast. For we are what he has made us, created in Christ Jesus for good works, which God prepared beforehand to be our way of life.—The word of the Lord. ℟. **Thanks be to God.** ↓

GOSPEL ACCLAMATION Jn. 3.16

℣. Praise and honour to you, Lord Jesus Christ!*
℟. **Praise and honour to you, Lord Jesus Christ!**
℣. God so loved the world that he gave his only Son,

* *See p. 16 for other Gospel Acclamations.*

that everyone who believes in him may have eternal life.

℟. **Praise and honour to you, Lord Jesus Christ!** ↓

GOSPEL Jn. 3.14-21

Jesus is to die on the cross—the proof of God's unlimited love for us. God sent Jesus that all people might believe. Through belief in him we will be saved.

℣. The Lord be with you. ℟. **And with your spirit.**
✠ A reading from the holy Gospel according to John. ℟. **Glory to you, O Lord.**

JESUS said to Nicodemus: "Just as Moses lifted up the serpent in the wilderness, so must the Son of Man be lifted up, that whoever believes in him may have eternal life. For God so loved the world that he gave his only-begotten Son, so that everyone who believes in him may not perish but may have eternal life.

Indeed, God did not send the Son into the world to condemn the world, but in order that the world might be saved through him. The one who believes in him is not condemned; but the one who does not believe is condemned already, for not having believed in the name of the only-begotten Son of God.

And this is the judgment, that the light has come into the world, and people loved darkness rather than light because their deeds were evil. For all who do evil hate the light and do not come to the light, so that their deeds may not be exposed. But those who do what is true come to the light, so that it may be clearly seen that their deeds have been done in God."—The Gospel of the Lord. ℟. **Praise to you, Lord Jesus Christ.**

→ No. 15, p. 18

PRAYER OVER THE OFFERINGS

We place before you with joy these offerings,
which bring eternal remedy, O Lord,
praying that we may both faithfully revere them
and present them to you, as is fitting,
for the salvation of all the world.
Through Christ our Lord.
℟. **Amen.**

→ No. 21, p. 22 (Pref. 8-9)

COMMUNION ANTIPHON Cf. Ps. 121.3-4

Jerusalem is built as a city bonded as one together. It is there that the tribes go up, the tribes of the Lord, to praise the name of the Lord. ↓

PRAYER AFTER COMMUNION

O God, who enlighten everyone who comes into this world,
illuminate our hearts, we pray,
with the splendour of your grace,
that we may always ponder
what is worthy and pleasing to your majesty
and love you in all sincerity.
Through Christ our Lord. ℟. **Amen.** ↓

The Deacon or, in his absence, the Priest himself, says the invitation: Bow down for the blessing.

PRAYER OVER THE PEOPLE

Look upon those who call to you, O Lord,
and sustain the weak;
give life by your unfailing light

to those who walk in the shadow of death,
and bring those rescued by your mercy from every evil
to reach the highest good.
Through Christ our Lord.
℟. **Amen.** → No. 32, p. 77

MARCH 11

MASS FOR THE SECOND SCRUTINY

This Mass is celebrated when the Second Scrutiny takes place in the Rite of Christian Initiation of Adults, usually on the 4th Sunday of Lent.

ENTRANCE ANTIPHON Cf. Ps. 24.15-16

My eyes are always on the Lord, for he rescues my feet from the snare. Turn to me and have mercy on me, for I am alone and poor. → No. 2, p. 10 (Omit Gloria)

COLLECT

Almighty ever-living God,
give to your Church an increase in spiritual joy,
so that those once born of earth
may be reborn as citizens of heaven.
Through our Lord Jesus Christ, your Son,
who lives and reigns with you in the unity of the Holy Spirit,
one God, for ever and ever. ℟. **Amen.** ↓

FIRST READING 1 Sam. 16.1b, 6-7, 10-13

God directs Samuel to anoint David king. God looks into the heart of each person.

A reading from the first book of Samuel.

THE Lord said to Samuel, "Fill your horn with oil and set out; I will send you to Jesse of Bethlehem, for I have provided for myself a king among his sons."

When the sons of Jesse came, Samuel looked on Eliab and thought, "Surely the Lord's anointed is now before the Lord." But the Lord said to Samuel, "Do not look on his appearance or on the height of his stature, because I have rejected him; for the Lord does not see as the human sees; the human looks on the outward appearance, but the Lord looks on the heart."

Jesse made seven of his sons pass before Samuel, and Samuel said to Jesse, "The Lord has not chosen any of these." Samuel said to Jesse, "Are all your sons here?" And he said, "There remains yet the youngest, but he is keeping the sheep." And Samuel said to Jesse, "Send and bring him; for we will not sit down until he comes here." Jesse sent and brought David in. Now he was ruddy, and had beautiful eyes, and was handsome. The Lord said, "Rise and anoint him; for this is the one."

Then Samuel took the horn of oil, and anointed him in the presence of his brothers; and the spirit of the Lord came mightily upon David from that day forward.—The word of the Lord. ℟. **Thanks be to God.** ↓

RESPONSORIAL PSALM Ps. 23

Michel Guimont

℟. The Lord is my
shep - herd; I shall not want.

The Lord is my shepherd, I shall not want.
He makes me lie down in green pastures;
he leads me beside still waters;
he restores my soul.—℟.

He leads me in right paths for his name's sake.
Even though I walk through the darkest valley, I fear
no evil;

for you are with me;
your rod and your staff—they comfort me.—℟.

You prepare a table before me
in the presence of my enemies;
you anoint my head with oil;
my cup overflows.—℟.

Surely goodness and mercy shall follow me
all the days of my life,
and I shall dwell in the house of the Lord
my whole life long.—℟. ↓

SECOND READING Eph. 5.8-14

We are to walk in the light which shows goodness, justice, and truth. Evil deeds are condemned. Christ gives this light whereby we live.

A reading from the Letter of Saint Paul
to the Ephesians.

BROTHERS and sisters: Once you were darkness, but now in the Lord you are light. Live as children of light—for the fruit of the light is found in all that is good and right and true.

Try to find out what is pleasing to the Lord. Take no part in the unfruitful works of darkness, but instead expose them. For it is shameful even to mention what such people do secretly; but everything exposed by the light becomes visible, for everything that becomes visible is light. Therefore it is said, "Sleeper, awake! Rise from the dead, and Christ will shine on you."—The word of the Lord. ℟. **Thanks be to God.** ↓

GOSPEL ACCLAMATION Jn. 8.12

℣. Praise and honour to you, Lord Jesus Christ!*
℟. **Praise and honour to you, Lord Jesus Christ!**

* *See p. 16 for other Gospel Acclamations.*

℣. I am the light of the world, says the Lord;
whoever follows me will have the light of life.
℟. **Praise and honour to you, Lord Jesus Christ!** ↓

GOSPEL Jn. 9.1-41 or 9.1, 6-9, 13-17, 34-38

Jesus is the light. He cures a man born blind by bringing him to see. Jesus identifies himself as the Son of Man.

[If the "Shorter Form" is used, the indented text in brackets is omitted.]

℣. The Lord be with you. ℟. **And with your spirit.**
✠ A reading from the holy Gospel according to John.
℟. **Glory to you, O Lord.**

AS Jesus walked along, he saw a man blind from birth.

[His disciples asked him, "Rabbi, who sinned, this man or his parents, that he was born blind?"

Jesus answered, "Neither this man nor his parents sinned; he was born blind so that God's works might be revealed in him. We must work the works of him who sent me while it is day; night is coming when no one can work. As long as I am in the world, I am the light of the world." When he had said this,]

he spat on the ground and made mud with the saliva and spread the mud on the man's eyes, saying to him, "Go, wash in the pool of Siloam" (which means Sent).

Then the man who was blind went and washed, and came back able to see. The neighbours and those who had seen him before as a beggar began to ask, "Is this not the man who used to sit and beg?" Some were saying, "It is he." Others were saying, "No, but it is someone like him." He kept saying, "I am the man."

[But they kept asking him, "Then how were your eyes opened?" He answered, "The man called Jesus made mud, spread it on my eyes, and said to me, 'Go to Siloam and wash.' Then I went and washed and received my sight." They said to him, "Where is he?" He said, "I do not know."]

They brought to the Pharisees the man who had formerly been blind. Now it was a Sabbath day when Jesus made the mud and opened his eyes. Then the Pharisees also began to ask him how he had received his sight. He said to them, "He put mud on my eyes. Then I washed, and now I see." Some of the Pharisees said, "This man is not from God, for he does not observe the Sabbath." But others said, "How can a man who is a sinner perform such signs?" And they were divided. So they said again to the blind man, "What do you say about him? It was your eyes he opened." He said, "He is a Prophet."

[They did not believe that he had been blind and had received his sight until they called the parents of the man who had received his sight and asked them, "Is this your son, who you say was born blind? How then does he now see?" His parents answered, "We know that this is our son, and that he was born blind; but we do not know how it is that now he sees, nor do we know who opened his eyes. Ask him; he is of age. He will speak for himself." His parents said this because they were afraid of the Jewish authorities, who had already agreed that anyone who confessed Jesus to be the Messiah would be put out of the synagogue. Therefore his parents said, "He is of age; ask him."

So for the second time they called the man who had been blind, and they said to him, "Give glory to God! We know that this man is a sinner." He answered, "I do not know whether he is a sinner. One thing I do know, that though I was blind, now I see." They said to him, "What did he do to you? How did he open your eyes?" He answered them, "I have told you already, and you would not listen. Why do you want to hear it again? Do you also want to become his disciples?" Then they reviled him, saying, "You are his disciple, but we are disciples of Moses. We know that God has spoken to Moses, but as for this man, we do not know where he comes from."

The man answered, "Here is an astonishing thing! You do not know where he comes from, and yet he opened my eyes. We know that God does not listen to sinners, but he does listen to one who worships him and obeys his will. Never since the world began has it been heard that anyone opened the eyes of a person born blind. If this man were not from God, he could do nothing."]

They answered him, "You were born entirely in sins, and are you trying to teach us?" And they drove him out.

Jesus heard that they had driven him out, and when he found him, he said, "Do you believe in the Son of Man?" He answered, "And who is he, sir? Tell me, so that I may believe in him." Jesus said to him, "You have seen him, and the one speaking with you is he." He said, "Lord, I believe." And he worshipped him.

[Jesus said, "I came into this world for judgment so that those who do not see may see, and those who do see may become blind." Some of the Pharisees near him heard this and said to him, "Surely we are not blind, are we?" Jesus said to them, "If you were blind, you would have no sin. But now that you say, 'We see,' your sin remains."]

The Gospel of the Lord. ℟. **Praise to you, Lord Jesus Christ.** → No. 15, p. 18

PRAYER OVER THE OFFERINGS

We place before you with joy these offerings,
which bring eternal remedy, O Lord,
praying that we may both faithfully revere them
and present them to you, as is fitting,
for those who seek salvation.
Through Christ our Lord. ℟. **Amen.** ↓

PREFACE (15)

℣. The Lord be with you. ℟. **And with your spirit.**
℣. Lift up your hearts. ℟. **We lift them up to the Lord.**
℣. Let us give thanks to the Lord our God. ℟. **It is right and just.**

It is truly right and just, our duty and our salvation,
always and everywhere to give you thanks,
Lord, holy Father, almighty and eternal God,
through Christ our Lord.

By the mystery of the Incarnation,
he has led the human race that walked in darkness
into the radiance of the faith
and has brought those born in slavery to ancient sin
through the waters of regeneration
to make them your adopted children.

Therefore, all creatures of heaven and earth
sing a new song in adoration,
and we, with all the host of Angels,
cry out, and without end acclaim: → No. 23, p. 23

The commemoration of the godparents in the Eucharistic Prayers takes place as above (pp. 229, 230) and, if the Roman Canon is used, the proper form of the Hanc igitur (Therefore, Lord, we pray) *is said, as in the First Scrutiny (p. 229).*

The rest follows the Roman Canon, pp. 25-29.

COMMUNION ANTIPHON Cf. Jn. 9.11, 38

The Lord anointed my eyes; I went, I washed, I saw and I believed in God. ↓

PRAYER AFTER COMMUNION

Sustain your family always in your kindness,
O Lord, we pray,
correct them, set them in order,
graciously protect them under your rule,
and in your unfailing goodness
direct them along the way of salvation.
Through Christ our Lord.
℟. **Amen.** → No. 30, p. 77

Optional Solemn Blessings, p. 97, and Prayers over the People, p. 105

Some bystanders heard a voice from heaven.

MARCH 18

5th SUNDAY OF LENT

On this Sunday is celebrated the Third Scrutiny in preparation for the Baptism of the catechumens who are to be admitted to the Sacraments of Christian Initiation at the Easter Vigil. The Ritual Mass for the Third Scrutiny is found on p. 249.

ENTRANCE ANTIPHON Cf. Ps. 42.1-2

Give me justice, O God, and plead my cause against a nation that is faithless. From the deceitful and cunning rescue me, for you, O God, are my strength. → No. 2, p. 10 (Omit Gloria)

COLLECT

By your help, we beseech you, Lord our God,
may we walk eagerly in that same charity
with which, out of love for the world,
your Son handed himself over to death.
Through our Lord Jesus Christ, your Son,
who lives and reigns with you in the unity of the
  Holy Spirit,
one God, for ever and ever. ℟. **Amen.** ↓

FIRST READING Jer. 31.31-34

The Lord promises a new covenant in which God's law will be written in people's hearts.

A reading from the book of the Prophet Jeremiah.

THE days are surely coming, says the Lord, when I will make a new covenant with the house of Israel and the house of Judah. It will not be like the covenant that I made with their fathers when I took them by the hand to bring them out of the land of Egypt—a covenant that they broke, though I was their husband, says the Lord.

But this is the covenant that I will make with the house of Israel after those days, says the Lord: I will put my law within them, and I will write it on their hearts; and I will be their God, and they shall be my people. No longer shall they teach one another, or say to each other, "Know the Lord," for they shall all know me, from the least of them to the greatest, says the Lord; for I will forgive their iniquity, and remember their sin no more.—The word of the Lord. ℟. **Thanks be to God.** ↓

RESPONSORIAL PSALM Ps. 51

Michel Guimont

℟. Cre - ate in me, cre - ate in me a
clean heart, O God.

Have mercy on me, O God,
according to your steadfast love;
according to your abundant mercy
blot out my transgressions.

Wash me thoroughly from my iniquity,
and cleanse me from my sin.
℟. **Create in me, create in me a clean heart, O God.**

Create in me a clean heart, O God,
and put a new and right spirit within me.
Do not cast me away from your presence,
and do not take your holy spirit from me.—℟.

Restore to me the joy of your salvation,
and sustain in me a willing spirit.
Then I will teach transgressors your ways,
and sinners will return to you.—℟. ↓

SECOND READING Heb. 5.7-9

We recall how Jesus prayed to his Father. Through obedience to suffering, Jesus became perfect and is the source of salvation for all who obey him.

A reading from the Letter to the Hebrews.

IN the days of his flesh, Jesus offered up prayers and supplications, with loud cries and tears, to the one who was able to save him from death, and he was heard because of his reverent submission. Although he was a Son, he learned obedience through what he suffered; and having been made perfect, he became the source of eternal salvation for all who obey him.—The word of the Lord. ℟. **Thanks be to God.** ↓

GOSPEL ACCLAMATION Jn. 12.26

℣. Praise and honour to you, Lord Jesus Christ!*
℟. **Praise and honour to you, Lord Jesus Christ!**

* *See p. 16 for other Gospel Acclamations.*

℣. Whoever serves me must follow me, says the Lord;
where I am, there will my servant be also.
℟. **Praise and honour to you, Lord Jesus Christ!** ↓

GOSPEL Jn. 12.20-33

Jesus predicts his glorification. It comes by dying like the grain of wheat. Those who love their life lose it. The Father from heaven answers Jesus.

℣. The Lord be with you. ℟. **And with your spirit.**
✠ A reading from the holy Gospel according to John. ℟. **Glory to you, O Lord.**

AMONG those who went up to worship at the festival were some Greeks. They came to Philip, who was from Bethsaida in Galilee, and said to him, "Sir, we wish to see Jesus."

Philip went and told Andrew; then Andrew and Philip went and told Jesus.

Jesus answered them, "The hour has come for the Son of Man to be glorified. Very truly, I tell you, unless a grain of wheat falls into the earth and dies, it remains just a single grain; but if it dies, it bears much fruit. The person who loves their life loses it, and the person who hates their life in this world will keep it for eternal life.

"Whoever serves me must follow me, and where I am, there will my servant be also. Whoever serves me, the Father will honour.

"Now my soul is troubled. And what should I say—'Father, save me from this hour'? No, it is for this reason that I have come to this hour. Father, glorify your name."

Then a voice came from heaven, "I have glorified it, and I will glorify it again."

The crowd standing there heard it and said that it was thunder. Others said, "An Angel has spoken to him." Jesus answered, "This voice has come for your sake, not for mine. Now is the judgment of this world; now the ruler of this world will be driven out. And I, when I am lifted up from the earth, will draw all people to myself." Jesus said this to indicate the kind of death he was to die.—The Gospel of the Lord. ℟. **Praise to you, Lord Jesus Christ.** → No. 15, p. 18

PRAYER OVER THE OFFERINGS

Hear us, almighty God,
and, having instilled in your servants
the teachings of the Christian faith,
graciously purify them
by the working of this sacrifice.
Through Christ our Lord.
℟. **Amen.** → No. 21, p. 22 (Pref. 8-9)

COMMUNION ANTIPHON Jn. 12.24

Amen, Amen I say to you: Unless a grain of wheat falls to the ground and dies, it remains a single grain. But if it dies, it bears much fruit. ↓

PRAYER AFTER COMMUNION

We pray, almighty God,
that we may always be counted among the members of Christ,
in whose Body and Blood we have communion.
Who lives and reigns for ever and ever.
℟. **Amen. ↓**

The Deacon or, in his absence, the Priest himself, says the invitation: Bow down for the blessing.

PRAYER OVER THE PEOPLE

Bless, O Lord, your people,
who long for the gift of your mercy,
and grant that what, at your prompting, they desire
they may receive by your generous gift.
Through Christ our Lord.
℟. **Amen.** → No. 32, p. 77

MARCH 18

MASS FOR THE THIRD SCRUTINY

This Mass is celebrated when the Third Scrutiny takes place in the Rite of Christian Initiation of Adults, usually on the 5th Sunday of Lent.

ENTRANCE ANTIPHON Cf. Ps. 17.5-7

The waves of death rose about me; the pains of the netherworld surrounded me. In my anguish I called to the Lord; and from his holy temple he heard my voice.

→ No. 2, p. 10 (Omit Gloria)

COLLECT

Grant, O Lord, to these chosen ones
that, instructed in the holy mysteries,
they may receive new life at the font of Baptism
and be numbered among the members of your Church.
Through our Lord Jesus Christ, your Son,
who lives and reigns with you in the unity of the Holy Spirit,
one God, for ever and ever. ℟. **Amen.** ↓

FIRST READING Ez. 37.12-14

The Lord promises to bring God's people back to their homeland. He will be with them and they will know him.

A reading from the book of the Prophet Ezekiel.

THUS says the Lord God: "I am going to open your graves, and bring you up from your graves, O my people; and I will bring you back to the land of Israel. And you shall know that I am the Lord, when I open your graves, and bring you up from your graves, O my people.

I will put my spirit within you, and you shall live, and I will place you on your own soil; then you shall know that I, the Lord, have spoken and will act," says the Lord.—The word of the Lord. ℟. **Thanks be to God.** ↓

RESPONSORIAL PSALM Ps. 130

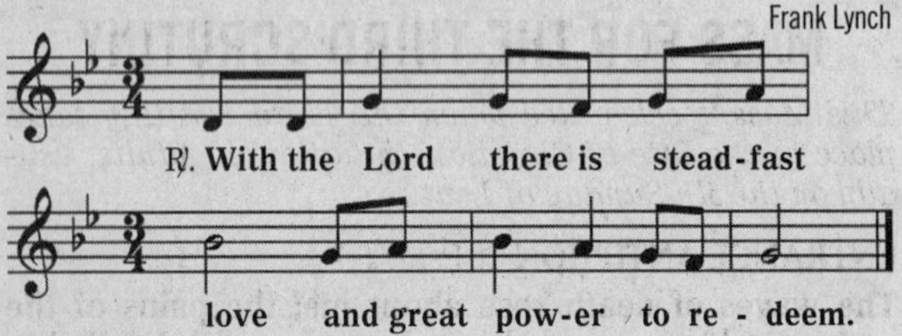
Frank Lynch
℟. With the Lord there is stead-fast
love and great pow-er to re - deem.

Out of the depths I cry to you, O Lord.
Lord, hear my voice!
Let your ears be attentive
to the voice of my supplications!—℟.

If you, O Lord, should mark iniquities,
Lord, who could stand?
But there is forgiveness with you,
so that you may be revered.—℟.

I wait for the Lord,
my soul waits, and in his word I hope;
my soul waits for the Lord
more than watchmen for the morning.—℟.

For with the Lord there is steadfast love,
and with him is great power to redeem.
It is he who will redeem Israel
from all its iniquities.—℟. ↓

SECOND READING Rom. 8.8-11

The followers of Jesus live in the Spirit of God. The same Spirit who brought Jesus back to life will bring mortal bodies to life since God's Spirit dwells in them.

A reading from the Letter of Saint Paul to the Romans.

BROTHERS and sisters: Those who are in the flesh cannot please God. But you are not in the flesh; you are in the Spirit, since the Spirit of God dwells in you. Anyone who does not have the Spirit of Christ does not belong to him.

But if Christ is in you, though the body is dead because of sin, the Spirit is life because of righteousness.

If the Spirit of God who raised Jesus from the dead dwells in you, he who raised Christ from the dead will give life to your mortal bodies also through his Spirit that dwells in you.—The word of the Lord. ℟. **Thanks be to God.** ↓

GOSPEL ACCLAMATION Jn. 11.25, 26

℣. Glory and praise to you, Lord Jesus Christ!*
℟. **Glory and praise to you, Lord Jesus Christ!**
℣. I am the resurrection and the life, says the Lord: whoever believes in me will never die.
℟. **Glory and praise to you, Lord Jesus Christ!** ↓

GOSPEL Jn. 11.1-45 or 11.3-7, 17, 20-27, 33b-45

Lazarus, the brother of Martha and Mary, died and was buried. When Jesus came, he assured them that he was the resurrection and the life. Jesus gave life back to Lazarus.

[If the "Shorter Form" is used, the indented text in brackets is omitted.]

℣. The Lord be with you. ℟. **And with your spirit.**
✠ A reading from the holy Gospel according to John.
℟. **Glory to you, O Lord.**

* *See p. 16 for other Gospel Acclamations.*

[NOW a certain man, Lazarus, was ill. He was from Bethany, the village of Mary and her sister Martha. Mary was the one who anointed the Lord with perfume and wiped his feet with her hair; her brother Lazarus was ill.]

[So] the sisters [of Lazarus] sent a message to Jesus, "Lord, he whom you love is ill." But when Jesus heard this, he said, "This illness does not lead to death; rather it is for God's glory, so that the Son of God may be glorified through it." Accordingly, though Jesus loved Martha and her sister and Lazarus, after having heard that Lazarus was ill, he stayed two days longer in the place where he was.

Then after this he said to the disciples, "Let us go to Judea again."

[The disciples said to him, "Rabbi, the people there were just now trying to stone you, and are you going there again?" Jesus answered, "Are there not twelve hours of daylight? Those who walk during the day do not stumble, because they see the light of this world. But those who walk at night stumble, because the light is not in them."

After saying this, he told them, "Our friend Lazarus has fallen asleep, but I am going there to awaken him." The disciples said to him, "Lord, if he has fallen asleep, he will be all right." Jesus, however, had been speaking about his death, but they thought that he was referring merely to sleep. Then Jesus told them plainly, "Lazarus is dead. For your sake I am glad I was not there, so that you may believe. But let us go to him." Thomas, who was called the Twin, said to his fellow disciples, "Let us also go, that we may die with him."]

When Jesus arrived, he found that Lazarus had already been in the tomb four days.

[Now Bethany was near Jerusalem, some two miles away, and many Jews had come to Martha and Mary to console them about their brother.]

When Martha heard that Jesus was coming, she went and met him, while Mary stayed at home. Martha said to Jesus, "Lord, if you had been here, my brother would not have died. But even now I know that God will give you whatever you ask of him." Jesus said to her, "Your brother will rise again." Martha said to him, "I know that he will rise again in the resurrection on the last day." Jesus said to her, "I am the resurrection and the life. Whoever believes in me, even though they die, will live, and everyone who lives and believes in me will never die. Do you believe this?" She said to him, "Yes, Lord, I believe that you are the Christ, the Son of God, the one coming into the world."

> [When she had said this, she went back and called her sister Mary, and told her privately, "The Teacher is here and is calling for you." And when Mary heard it, she got up quickly and went to him. Now Jesus had not yet come to the village, but was still at the place where Martha had met him. The Jews who were with her in the house, consoling her, saw Mary get up quickly and go out. They followed her because they thought that she was going to the tomb to weep there.
>
> When Mary came where Jesus was and saw him, she knelt at his feet and said to him, "Lord, if you had been here, my brother would not have died." When Jesus saw her weeping, and the Jews who came with her also weeping, he]

[Jesus] was greatly disturbed in spirit and deeply moved. He said, "Where have you laid him?" They said to him, "Lord, come and see." Jesus began to weep. So the Jews said, "See how he loved him!" But some of them said, "Could not he who opened the eyes of the blind man have kept this man from dying?"

Then Jesus, again greatly disturbed, came to the tomb. It was a cave, and a stone was lying against it. Jesus said, "Take away the stone." Martha, the sister of the dead man, said to him, "Lord, already there is a stench because he has been dead four days." Jesus said to her,

"Did I not tell you that if you believed, you would see the glory of God?" So they took away the stone. And Jesus looked upward and said, "Father, I thank you for having heard me. I knew that you always hear me, but I have said this for the sake of the crowd standing here, so that they may believe that you sent me."

When he had said this, he cried with a loud voice, "Lazarus, come out!" The dead man came out, his hands and feet bound with strips of cloth, and his face wrapped in a cloth. Jesus said to them, "Unbind him, and let him go."

Many of the Jews therefore, who had come with Mary and had seen what Jesus did, believed in him.—The Gospel of the Lord. ℟. **Praise to you, Lord Jesus Christ.**

→ No. 15, p. 18

PRAYER OVER THE OFFERINGS

Hear us, almighty God,
and, having instilled in your servants
the first fruits of the Christian faith,
graciously purify them by the working of this sacrifice.
Through Christ our Lord. ℟. **Amen.** ↓

PREFACE (16)

℣. The Lord be with you. ℟. **And with your spirit.**
℣. Lift up your hearts. ℟. **We lift them up to the Lord.**
℣. Let us give thanks to the Lord our God. ℟. **It is right and just.**

It is truly right and just, our duty and our salvation,
always and everywhere to give you thanks,
Lord, holy Father, almighty and eternal God,
through Christ our Lord.

For as true man he wept for Lazarus his friend
and as eternal God raised him from the tomb,
just as, taking pity on the human race,
he leads us by sacred mysteries to new life.

Through him the host of Angels adores your majesty
and rejoices in your presence for ever.

May our voices, we pray, join with theirs
in one chorus of exultant praise, as we acclaim:

→ No. 23, p. 23

The commemoration of the godparents in the Eucharistic Prayers takes place as above (pp. 229, 230) and, if the Roman Canon is used, the proper form of the Hanc igitur (Therefore, Lord, we pray) *is said, as in the First Scrutiny (p. 229).*

The rest follows the Roman Canon, pp. 25-29.

COMMUNION ANTIPHON Cf. Jn. 11.26

Everyone who lives and believes in me will not die for ever, says the Lord. ↓

PRAYER AFTER COMMUNION

May your people be at one, O Lord, we pray,
and in wholehearted submission to you
may they obtain this grace:
that, safe from all distress,
they may readily live out their joy at being saved
and remember in loving prayer those to be reborn.
Through Christ our Lord.
℟. **Amen.**

→ No. 30, p. 77

Optional Solemn Blessings, p. 97, and Prayers over the People, p. 105

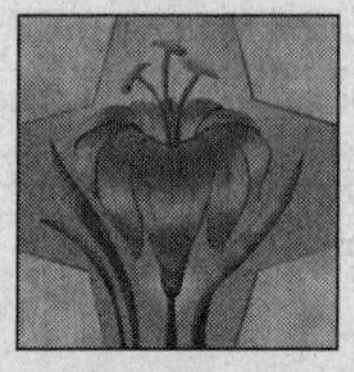

"Blessed are you, who have come in your abundant mercy!"

MARCH 25

PALM SUNDAY OF THE LORD'S PASSION

The Commemoration of the Lord's Entrance into Jerusalem

FIRST FORM: THE PROCESSION

At an appropriate hour, a gathering takes place at a smaller church or other suitable place other than inside the church to which the procession will go. The faithful hold branches in their hands.

Wearing the red sacred vestments as for Mass, the Priest and the Deacon, accompanied by other ministers, approach the place where the people are gathered. Instead of the chasuble, the Priest may wear a cope, which he leaves aside when the procession is over, and puts on a chasuble.

Meanwhile, the following antiphon or another appropriate chant is sung.

ANTIPHON Mt. 21.9

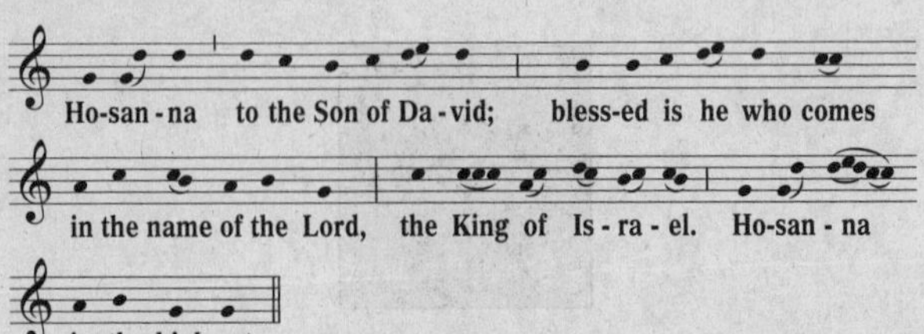
Ho-san-na to the Son of Da-vid; bless-ed is he who comes
in the name of the Lord, the King of Is-ra-el. Ho-san-na
in the high-est.

OR:

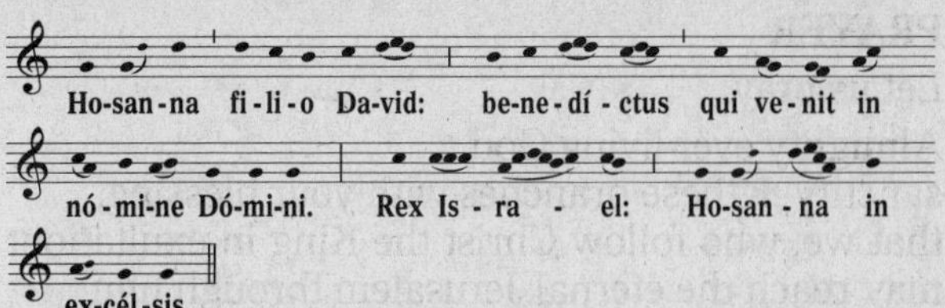
Ho-san-na fi-li-o Da-vid: be-ne-dí-ctus qui ve-nit in
nó-mi-ne Dó-mi-ni. Rex Is-ra-el: Ho-san-na in
ex-cél-sis.

After this, the Priest and people sign themselves, while the Priest says: In the name of the Father, and of the Son, and of the Holy Spirit. *Then he greets the people in the usual way. A brief address is given, in which the faithful are invited to participate actively and consciously in the celebration of this day, in these or similar words:*

Dear brethren (brothers and sisters),
since the beginning of Lent until now
we have prepared our hearts by penance and charitable works.
Today we gather together to herald with the whole Church
the beginning of the celebration
of our Lord's Paschal Mystery,
that is to say, of his Passion and Resurrection.
For it was to accomplish this mystery
that he entered his own city of Jerusalem.
Therefore, with all faith and devotion,
let us commemorate
the Lord's entry into the city for our salvation,
following in his footsteps,
so that, being made by his grace partakers of the Cross,
we may have a share also in his Resurrection and in his life.

After the address, the Priest says one of the following prayers with hands extended.

PRAYER

Let us pray.

Almighty ever-living God,
sanctify ✠ these branches with your blessing,
that we, who follow Christ the King in exultation,
may reach the eternal Jerusalem through him.
Who lives and reigns for ever and ever.
℟. **Amen.** ↓

OR

Increase the faith of those who place their hope in you, O God,
and graciously hear the prayers of those who call on you,
that we, who today hold high these branches
to hail Christ in his triumph,
may bear fruit for you by good works accomplished in him.
Who lives and reigns for ever and ever.
℟. **Amen.** ↓

The Priest sprinkles the branches with holy water without saying anything.

Then a Deacon or, if there is no Deacon, a Priest proclaims in the usual way the Gospel concerning the Lord's entrance according to one of the four Gospels.

GOSPEL Mk. 11.1-10

In triumphant glory Jesus comes into Jerusalem. The people spread their cloaks on the ground for him, wave palm branches and sing in his honour.

℣. The Lord be with you. ℟. **And with your spirit.**
✠ A reading from the holy Gospel according to Mark (*or* John). ℟. **Glory to you, O Lord.**

WHEN they were approaching Jerusalem, at Bethphage and Bethany, near the Mount of Olives, Jesus sent two of his disciples and said to them, "Go into the village ahead of you, and immediately as you enter it, you will find tied there a colt that has never been ridden; untie it and bring it. If anyone says to you, 'Why are you doing this?' just say this, 'The Lord needs it and will send it back here immediately.'"

They went away and found a colt tied near a door, outside in the street. As they were untying it, some of the bystanders said to them, "What are you doing, untying the colt?" The disciples told them what Jesus had said; and they allowed them to take it.

Then they brought the colt to Jesus and threw their cloaks on it; and he sat on it. Many people spread their cloaks on the road, and others spread leafy branches that they had cut in the fields.

Then those who went ahead and those who followed were shouting, "Hosanna! Blessed is the one who comes in the name of the Lord! Blessed is the coming kingdom of our father David! Hosanna in the highest heaven!"—The Gospel of the Lord. ℟. **Praise to you, Lord Jesus Christ.**

OR Jn. 12.12-16

THE great crowd that had come to the festival heard that Jesus was coming to Jerusalem. So they took branches of palm trees and went out to meet him, shouting,

"Hosanna!
Blessed is the one who comes in the name of the Lord—
the King of Israel!"

Jesus found a young donkey and sat on it; as it is written:

"Do not be afraid, daughter of Zion.
Look, your king is coming,
sitting on a donkey's colt!"

His disciples did not understand these things at first; but when Jesus was glorified, then they remembered that these things had been written of him and had been done to him.—The Gospel of the Lord. ℟. **Praise to you, Lord Jesus Christ.** ↓

After the Gospel, a brief homily may be given. Then, to begin the Procession, an invitation may be given by a Priest or a Deacon or a lay minister, in these or similar words:

Dear brethren (brothers and sisters),
like the crowds who acclaimed Jesus in Jerusalem,
let us go forth in peace.

OR

Let us go forth in peace.
℟. **In the name of Christ. Amen.**

The Procession to the church where Mass will be celebrated then sets off in the usual way. If incense is used, the thurifer goes first, carrying a thurible with burning incense, then an acolyte or another minister, carrying a cross decorated with palm branches according to local custom, between two ministers with lighted candles. Then follow the Deacon carrying the Book of Gospels, the Priest with the ministers, and, after them, all the faithful carrying branches.

As the Procession moves forward, the following or other suitable chants in honour of Christ the King are sung by the choir and people.

ANTIPHON 1

The children of the Hebrews, carrying olive branches,
went to meet the Lord, crying out and saying:
Hosanna in the highest.

If appropriate, this antiphon is repeated between the strophes (verses) of the following Psalm.

PSALM 23(24)

The LORD's is the earth and its fullness,
the world, and those who dwell in it.
It is he who set it on the seas;
on the rivers he made it firm.

(The antiphon is repeated.)

Who shall climb the mountain of the LORD?
The clean of hands and pure of heart,
whose soul is not set on vain things,
who has not sworn deceitful words.

(The antiphon is repeated.)

Blessings from the LORD shall he receive,
and right reward from the God who saves him.
Such are the people who seek him,
who seek the face of the God of Jacob.

(The antiphon is repeated.)

O gates, lift high your heads;
grow higher, ancient doors.
Let him enter, the king of glory!
Who is this king of glory?

The Lord, the mighty, the valiant;
the Lord, the valiant in war.

(The antiphon is repeated.)

O gates, lift high your heads;
grow higher, ancient doors.
Let him enter, the king of glory!
Who is this king of glory?
He, the Lord of hosts,
he is the king of glory. *(The antiphon is repeated.)*

ANTIPHON 2

The children of the Hebrews spread their garments on the road,
crying out and saying: Hosanna to the Son of David;
blessed is he who comes in the name of the Lord.

If appropriate, this antiphon is repeated between the strophes (verses) of the following Psalm.

PSALM 46(47)

All peoples, clap your hands.
Cry to God with shouts of joy!
For the Lord, the Most high, is awesome,
the great king over all the earth.

(The antiphon is repeated.)

He humbles peoples under us
and nations under our feet.
Our heritage he chose for us,
the pride of Jacob whom he loves.
God goes up with shouts of joy.
The Lord goes up with trumpet blast.

(The antiphon is repeated.)

Sing praise for God; sing praise!
Sing praise to our king; sing praise!
God is king of all earth.
Sing praise with all your skill.
(The antiphon is repeated.)

God reigns over the nations.
God sits upon his holy throne.
The princes of the peoples are assembled
with the people of the God of Abraham.
The rulers of the earth belong to God,
who is greatly exalted. *(The antiphon is repeated.)*

Hymn to Christ the King

Chorus:
Glory and honour and praise be to you, Christ, King and Redeemer,
to whom young children cried out loving Hosannas with joy.

All repeat: **Glory and honour . . .**

Chorus:
Israel's King are you, King David's magnificent offspring;
you are the ruler who come blest in the name of the Lord.

All repeat: **Glory and honour . . .**

Chorus:
Heavenly hosts on high unite in singing your praises;
men and women on earth and all creation join in.

All repeat: **Glory and honour . . .**

Chorus:
Bearing branches of palm, Hebrews came crowding to greet you;

see how with prayers and hymns we come to pay you our vows.

All repeat: **Glory and honour . . .**

Chorus:

They offered gifts of praise to you, so near to your Passion;
see how we sing this song now to you reigning on high.

All repeat: **Glory and honour . . .**

Chorus:

Those you were pleased to accept, now accept our gifts of devotion,
good and merciful King, lover of all that is good.

All repeat: **Glory and honour . . .**

As the procession enters the church, there is sung the following responsory or another chant, which should speak of the Lord's entrance.

RESPONSORY

℟. As the Lord entered the holy city, the children of the Hebrews proclaimed the resurrection of life. Waving their branches of palm, they cried: Hosanna in the Highest.

℣. When the people heard that Jesus was coming to Jerusalem, they went out to meet him. Waving their branches of palm, they cried: Hosanna in the Highest.

When the Priest arrives at the altar, he venerates it and, if appropriate, incenses it. Then he goes to the chair, where he puts aside the cope, if he has worn one, and puts on the chasuble. Omitting the other Introductory Rites of the Mass and, if appropriate, the Kyrie (Lord, have mercy)*, he says the Collect of the Mass, and then continues the Mass in the usual way.*

SECOND FORM: THE SOLEMN ENTRANCE

When a procession outside the church cannot take place, the entrance of the Lord is celebrated inside the church by means of a Solemn Entrance before the principal Mass.

Holding branches in their hands, the faithful gather either outside, in front of the church door, or inside the church itself. The Priest and ministers and a representative group of the faithful go to a suitable place in the church outside the sanctuary, where at least the greater part of the faithful can see the rite.

While the Priest approaches the appointed place, the antiphon Hosanna *or another appropriate chant is sung. Then the blessing of branches and the proclamation of the Gospel of the Lord's entrance into Jerusalem take place as above (pp. 258-260). After the Gospel, the Priest processes solemnly with the ministers and the representative group of the faithful through the church to the sanctuary, while the responsory* As the Lord entered *(p. 264) or another appropriate chant is sung.*

Arriving at the altar, the Priest venerates it. He then goes to the chair and, omitting the Introductory Rites of the Mass and, if appropriate, the Kyrie *(*Lord, have mercy*), he says the Collect of the Mass, and then continues the Mass in the usual way.*

THIRD FORM: THE SIMPLE ENTRANCE

At all other Masses of this Sunday at which the Solemn Entrance is not held, the memorial of the Lord's entrance into Jerusalem takes place by means of a Simple Entrance.

While the Priest proceeds to the altar, the Entrance Antiphon with its Psalm (p. 266) or another chant on the same theme is sung. Arriving at the altar, the Priest venerates it and goes to the chair. After the Sign of the Cross, he greets the people and continues the Mass in the usual way.

At other Masses, in which singing at the entrance cannot take place, the Priest, as soon as he has arrived at the altar and venerated it, greets the people, reads the Entrance Antiphon, and continues the Mass in the usual way.

ENTRANCE ANTIPHON Cf. Jn. 12.1, 12-13; Ps. 23.9-10

Six days before the Passover, when the Lord came into the city of Jerusalem, the children ran to meet him; in their hands they carried palm branches and with a loud voice cried out: Hosanna in the highest! Blessed are you, who have come in your abundant mercy!

O gates, lift high your heads; grow higher, ancient doors. Let him enter, the king of glory! Who is this king of glory? He, the Lord of hosts, he is the king of glory. Hosanna in the highest! Blessed are you, who have come in your abundant mercy!

AT THE MASS

After the Procession or Solemn Entrance the Priest begins the Mass with the Collect.

COLLECT

Almighty ever-living God,
who as an example of humility for the human race to follow
caused our Saviour to take flesh and submit to the Cross,
graciously grant that we may heed his lesson of patient suffering
and so merit a share in his Resurrection.
Who lives and reigns with you in the unity of the Holy Spirit,
one God, for ever and ever. ℟. **Amen.** ↓

FIRST READING Isa. 50.4-7

The suffering servant was persecuted and struck by his own people; he was spit upon and beaten. He proclaims the true faith and suffers to atone for the sins of his people. Here we see a foreshadowing of the true servant of God.

A reading from the book of the Prophet Isaiah.

THE servant of the Lord said:
"The Lord God has given me the tongue of a teacher,
that I may know how to sustain the weary with a word.
Morning by morning he wakens—
wakens my ear to listen as those who are taught.
The Lord God has opened my ear,
and I was not rebellious,
I did not turn backward.

I gave my back to those who struck me,
and my cheeks to those who pulled out the beard;
I did not hide my face
from insult and spitting.

The Lord God helps me;
therefore I have not been disgraced;
therefore I have set my face like flint,
and I know that I shall not be put to shame."

The word of the Lord. ℟. **Thanks be to God.** ↓

RESPONSORIAL PSALM Ps. 22

John Bouz

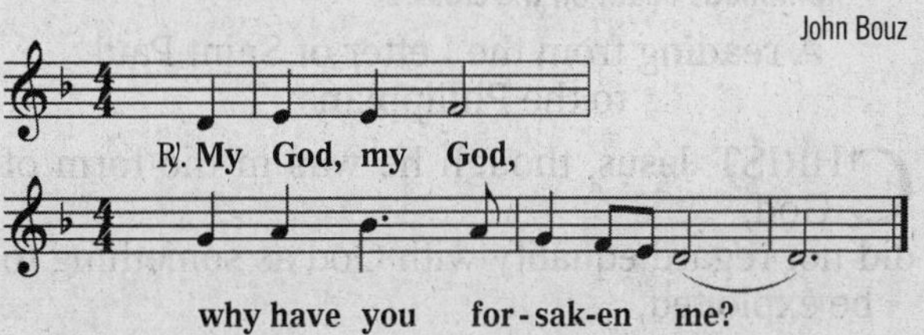
℟. My God, my God,
why have you for-sak-en me?

All who see me mock at me;
they make mouths at me, they shake their heads;
"Commit your cause to the Lord; let him deliver;
let him rescue the one in whom he delights!"
℟. **My God, my God, why have you forsaken me?**

For dogs are all around me;
a company of evildoers encircles me.
My hands and feet have shrivelled;
I can count all my bones.—℟.

They divide my clothes among themselves,
and for my clothing they cast lots.
But you, O Lord, do not be far away!
O my help, come quickly to my aid!—℟.

I will tell of your name to my brothers and sisters;
in the midst of the congregation I will praise you:
You who fear the Lord, praise him!
All you offspring of Jacob, glorify him;
stand in awe of him, all you offspring of Israel!
—℟. ↓

SECOND READING Phil. 2.6-11

Paul urges us to humility, by which we are made like Christ our Lord. He put off the majesty of his divinity and became man and humbled himself in obedience to an ignominious death on the cross.

A reading from the Letter of Saint Paul
to the Philippians.

CHRIST Jesus, though he was in the form of God,
did not regard equality with God as something to be exploited,

but emptied himself, taking the form of a slave,
being born in human likeness.
And being found in human form,
he humbled himself
and became obedient to the point of death—
even death on a cross.

Therefore God highly exalted him
and gave him the name that is above every name,
so that at the name of Jesus every knee should bend,
in heaven and on earth and under the earth,
and every tongue should confess that Jesus Christ is Lord,
to the glory of God the Father.

The word of the Lord. ℟. **Thanks be to God.** ↓

GOSPEL ACCLAMATION Phil. 2.8-9

℣. Praise and honour to you, Lord Jesus Christ!*
℟. **Praise and honour to you, Lord Jesus Christ!**
℣. Christ became obedient for us to death, even death on a Cross.
Therefore God exalted him and gave him the name above every name.
℟. **Praise and honour to you, Lord Jesus Christ!** ↓

GOSPEL Mk. 14.1—15.47 or 15.1-39

Mark recounts the events that led up to the betrayal of Jesus and his final condemnation—his death on the cross. At the Last Supper, Jesus gives us the Holy Eucharist.

---

* *See p. 16 for other Gospel Acclamations.*

The Passion of the Lord may also be divided into three parts in the traditional manner, the parts being read or sung by three persons. Preferably it is to be proclaimed by a priest or deacons, but in their absence, it may be proclaimed by lectors, the part of Jesus being reserved to a priest.

The Passion begins directly, without introduction.

We participate in the passion narrative in several ways: by reading it and reflecting on it during the week ahead; by listening with faith as it is proclaimed; by singing acclamations at appropriate places in the text; by respectful posture during the narrative; by reverent silence after the passage about Christ's death. We do not hold the palms during the reading on Palm Sunday.

Who caused the death of Jesus? In listening to God's word today, we must remember that our Lord died to save every human person. By our sins we have contributed to his suffering and Death. The authorities of his time bear responsibility for carrying out his execution; this charge must not be laid against all the Jewish people of Jesus' day or of our own. We are all responsible for sin and for our Lord's suffering.

This week we are challenged by the passion narrative to reflect on the way we are living up to our baptismal promises of dying with Christ to sin and living with him for God.

Note: A shorter version (15.1-39) is indicated by asterisks at the beginning and the end (pp. 276-279).

N. THE Passion of our Lord Jesus Christ according to Mark.

JESUS IS ANOINTED BEFORE HIS DEATH

N. IT was two days before the Passover and the festival of Unleavened Bread. The chief priests and the scribes were looking for a way to arrest Jesus by stealth and kill him; for they said, **S. "Not during the festival, or there may be a riot among the people."**

N. While Jesus was at Bethany in the house of Simon the leper, as he sat at the table, a woman came with an alabaster jar of very costly ointment of nard, and she broke open the jar and poured the ointment on his head. But some were there who said to one another in anger, **S. "Why was the ointment wasted in this way? For this ointment could have been sold for more than three hundred denarii, and the money given to the poor." N.** And they scolded her.

But Jesus said, **J.** *"Let her alone; why do you trouble her? She has performed a good service for me. For you always have the poor with you, and you can show kindness to them whenever you wish; but you will not always have me. She has done what she could; she has anointed my body beforehand for its burial. Truly I tell you, wherever the good news is proclaimed in the whole world, what she has done will be told in remembrance of her."*

BETRAYED BY A DISCIPLE

N. THEN Judas Iscariot, who was one of the twelve, went to the chief priests in order to betray him to them. When they heard it, they were greatly pleased, and promised to give him money. So he began to look for an opportunity to betray him.

AT THE LAST SUPPER

N. ON the first day of Unleavened Bread, when the Passover lamb is sacrificed, the disciples said to Jesus, **S. "Where do you want us to go and make the preparations for you to**

eat the Passover?" N. So he sent two of his disciples, saying to them, **J.** *"Go into the city, and a man carrying a jar of water will meet you; follow him, and wherever he enters, say to the owner of the house, 'The Teacher asks, "Where is my guest room where I may eat the Passover with my disciples?"' He will show you a large room upstairs, furnished and ready. Make preparations for us there."* **N.** So the disciples set out and went to the city, and found everything as he had told them; and they prepared the Passover meal.

When it was evening, Jesus came with the twelve. And when they had taken their places and were eating, Jesus said, **J.** *"Truly I tell you, one of you will betray me, one who is eating with me."* **N.** They began to be distressed and to say to him one after another, **S. "Surely, not I?"**

N. He said to them, **J.** *"It is one of the twelve, one who is dipping bread into the bowl with me. For the Son of Man goes as it is written of him, but woe to that one by whom the Son of Man is betrayed! It would have been better for that one not to have been born."*

N. While they were eating, he took a loaf of bread, and after blessing it he broke it, gave it to them, and said, **J.** *"Take; this is my Body."* **N.** Then he took a cup, and after giving thanks he gave it to them, and all of them drank from it. He said to them, **J.** *"This is my Blood of the covenant, which is poured out for many. Truly I tell you, I will never again drink of the fruit of the vine until that day when I drink it new in the kingdom of God."*

N. When they had sung the hymn, they went out to the Mount of Olives. And Jesus said to them, **J.** *"You will all become deserters; for it is written,*

'I will strike the shepherd,
and the sheep will be scattered.'

But after I am raised up, I will go before you to Galilee."

N. Peter said to him, **S. "Even though all become deserters, I will not."** [**N.** Jesus said to him,] **J.** *"Truly I tell you, this day, this very night, before the cock crows twice, you will deny me three times."* **N.** But he said vehemently, **S. "Even though I must die with you, I will not deny you." N.** And all of them said the same.

At this point all may join in singing an appropriate acclamation.

JESUS IN THE GARDEN

N. THEY went to a place called Gethsemane; and Jesus said to his disciples, **J.** *"Sit here while I pray."* **N.** He took with him Peter and James and John, and began to be distressed and agitated. And he said to them, **J.** *"I am deeply grieved, even to death; remain here, and keep awake."* **N.** And going a little farther, he threw himself on the ground and prayed that, if it were possible, the hour might pass from him. [He said,] **J.** *"Abba, Father, for you all things are possible; remove this cup from me; yet, not what I want, but what you want."* **N.** Jesus came and found them sleeping; and he said to Peter, **J.** *"Simon, are you asleep? Could you not keep awake one hour? Keep awake and pray that you may not come* *into temptation; the spirit indeed is willing, but the flesh is weak."*

N. And again he went away and prayed, saying the same words. And once more he came and found them sleeping, for their eyes were very heavy; and they did not know what to say to him. He came a third time and said to them, **J.** *"Are you still sleeping and taking your rest? Enough! The hour has come; the Son of Man is betrayed into the hands of sinners. Get up, let us be going. See, my betrayer is at hand."*

JESUS IS ARRESTED

N. IMMEDIATELY, while he was still speaking, Judas, one of the twelve, arrived; and with him there was a crowd with swords and clubs, from the chief priests, the scribes, and the elders. Now the betrayer had given them a sign, saying, **S. "The one I will kiss is the man; arrest him and lead him away under guard." N.** So when he came, he went up to Jesus at once and said, **S. "Rabbi!" N.** and kissed him. Then they laid hands on him and arrested him. But one of those who stood near drew his sword and struck the slave of the high priest, cutting off his ear.

Then Jesus said to them, **J.** *"Have you come out with swords and clubs to arrest me as though I were a bandit? Day after day I was with you in the temple teaching, and you did not arrest me. But let the Scriptures be fulfilled."* **N.** All of them deserted him and fled. A certain young man was following Jesus, wearing nothing but a linen cloth. They caught hold of him, but he left the linen cloth and ran off naked.

TRIAL IN THE HIGH PRIEST'S HOUSE

N. THEY took Jesus to the high priest; and all the chief priests, the elders, and the scribes were assembled.

Peter had followed him at a distance, right into the courtyard of the high priest; and he was sitting with the guards, warming himself at the fire.

Now the chief priests and the whole council were looking for testimony against Jesus to put him to death; but they found none. For many gave false testimony against him, and their testimony did not agree. Some stood up and gave false testimony against him, saying, **S. "We heard him say, 'I will destroy this temple that is made with hands, and in three days I will build another, not made with hands.' "** **N.** But even on this point their testimony did not agree. Then the high priest stood up before them and asked Jesus, **S. "Have you no answer? What is it that they testify against you?"** **N.** But he was silent and did not answer. Again the high priest asked him, **S. "Are you the Christ, the Son of the Blessed One?"** [Jesus said,] **J.** *"I am; and 'you will see the Son of Man seated at the right hand of the Power,' and 'coming with the clouds of heaven.' "* **N.** Then the high priest tore his clothes and said, **S. "Why do we still need witnesses? You have heard his blasphemy! What is your decision?"** **N.** All of them condemned him as deserving death. Some began to spit on him, to blindfold him, and to strike him, saying to him, **S. "Prophesy!" N.** The guards also took him over and beat him.

PETER DENIES THE LORD JESUS

N. WHILE Peter was below in the courtyard, one of the servant girls of the high priest came by. When she saw Peter warming himself, she stared at him and said, **S. "You also were with Jesus, the man from Nazareth." N.** But he denied it, saying, **S. "I do not know or understand what you are talking about." N.** And he went out into the forecourt. Then the cock crowed. And the servant girl, on seeing him, began again to say to the bystanders, **S. "This man is one of them." N.** But again he denied it.

Then after a little while the bystanders again said to Peter, **S. "Certainly you are one of them; for you are a Galilean." N.** But he began to curse, and he swore an oath, **S. "I do not know this man you are talking about." N.** At that moment the cock crowed for the second time. Then Peter remembered that Jesus had said to him, "Before the cock crows twice, you will deny me three times." And he broke down and wept.

At this point all may join in singing an appropriate acclamation.

TRIAL BEFORE PILATE

***N.** AS soon as it was morning, the chief priests held a consultation with the elders and scribes and the whole council. They bound Jesus, led him away, and handed him over to Pilate. Pilate asked him, **S. "Are you the King of the Jews?"** [He answered him,] **J.** *"You say so."* **N.** Then the chief priests accused him of many things. Pilate asked him again, **S. "Have you no answer? See how many charges they bring against you." N.** But Jesus made no further reply, so that Pilate was amazed.

Now at the festival he used to release a prisoner for them, anyone for whom they asked. Now a man called Barabbas was in prison with the rebels who had committed murder during the insurrection. So the crowd came and began to ask Pilate to do for them according to his custom. Then he answered them, **S. "Do you want me to release for you the King of the Jews?" N.** For he realized that it was out of jealousy that the chief priests had handed him over.

But the chief priests stirred up the crowd to have him release Barabbas for them instead. Pilate spoke to them again, **S. "Then what do you wish me to do with the man you call the King of the Jews?" N.** They shouted back, **S. "Crucify him!" N.** Pilate asked them, **S. "Why, what evil has he done?" N.** But they shouted all the more, **S. "Crucify him!" N.** So Pilate, wishing to satisfy the crowd, released Barabbas for them; and after flogging Jesus, he handed him over to be crucified.

Then the soldiers led him into the courtyard of the palace (that is, the governor's headquarters); and they called together the whole cohort. And they clothed him in a purple cloak; and after twisting some thorns into a crown, they put it on him. And they began saluting him, **S. "Hail, King of the Jews!" N.** They struck his head with a reed, spat upon him, and knelt down in homage to him. After mocking him, they stripped him of the purple cloak and put his own clothes on him. Then they led him out to crucify him.

ON THE WAY TO CALVARY

N. THEY compelled a passer-by, who was coming in from the country, to carry his Cross; it was Simon of Cyrene, the father of Alexander and Rufus. Then they brought Jesus to the place called Golgotha (which means the Place of a Skull).

JESUS IS CRUCIFIED AND DIES FOR US

N. AND they offered him wine mixed with myrrh; but he did not take it. And they crucified him, and divided his clothes among them, casting lots to decide what each should take.

It was nine o'clock in the morning when they crucified him. The inscription of the charge against him read, "The King of the Jews." And with him they crucified two bandits, one on his right and one on his left. Those who passed by derided him, shaking their heads and saying, **S. "Aha! You would destroy the temple and build it in three days; save yourself, and come down from the Cross!" N.** In the same way the chief priests, along with the scribes, were also mocking him among themselves and saying, **S. "He saved others; he cannot save himself. Let the Christ, the King of Israel, come down from the Cross now, so that we may see and believe." N.** Those who were crucified with him also taunted him.

When it was noon, darkness came over the whole land until three in the afternoon. At three o'clock Jesus cried out with a loud voice, **J.** *"Eloi, Eloi, lema sabachthani?"* **N.** which means, "My God, my God, why have you forsaken me?" When some of the bystanders heard it, they said, **S. "Listen, he is calling for Elijah." N.** And someone ran, filled a sponge with sour wine, put it on a stick, and gave it to him to drink, saying, **S. "Wait, let us see whether Elijah will come to take him down." N.** Then Jesus gave a loud cry and breathed his last.

Here all kneel and pause for a short time.

EVENTS AFTER JESUS' DEATH

N. AND the curtain of the temple was torn in two, from top to bottom. Now when the centurion, who stood facing him, saw that in this way he breathed his last, he said, **S. "Truly this man was God's Son!"** *

N. There were also women looking on from a distance; among them were Mary Magdalene, and Mary the mother of James the younger and of Joses, and Salome. These used to follow him and provided for him when he was in Galilee; and there were many other women who had come up with him to Jerusalem.

JESUS' BODY IS PLACED IN THE TOMB

N. WHEN evening had come, and since it was the day of Preparation, that is, the day before the Sabbath, Joseph of Arimathea, a respected member of the council, who was also himself waiting expectantly for the kingdom of God, went boldly to Pilate and asked for the body of Jesus. Then Pilate wondered if he were already dead; and summoning the centurion, he asked him whether he had been dead for some time. When he learned from the centurion that Jesus was dead, he granted the body to Joseph.

Then Joseph bought a linen cloth, and taking down the body, wrapped it in the linen cloth, and laid it in a tomb that had been hewn out of the rock. He then rolled a stone against the door of the tomb. Mary Magdalene and Mary the mother of Joses saw where the body was laid.

→ No. 15, p. 18

PRAYER OVER THE OFFERINGS

Through the Passion of your Only Begotten Son, O Lord,
may our reconciliation with you be near at hand,
so that, though we do not merit it by our own deeds,
yet by this sacrifice made once for all,
we may feel already the effects of your mercy.
Through Christ our Lord.
℟. **Amen.** ↓

PREFACE (19)

℣. The Lord be with you. ℟. **And with your spirit.** ℣. Lift up your hearts. ℟. **We lift them up to the Lord.** ℣. Let us give thanks to the Lord our God. ℟. **It is right and just.**

It is truly right and just, our duty and our salvation,
always and everywhere to give you thanks,
Lord, holy Father, almighty and eternal God,
through Christ our Lord.

For, though innocent, he suffered willingly for sinners
and accepted unjust condemnation to save the guilty.
His Death has washed away our sins,
and his Resurrection has purchased our justification.

And so, with all the Angels,
we praise you, as in joyful celebration we acclaim:

→ No. 23, p. 23

COMMUNION ANTIPHON Mt. 26.42

Father, if this chalice cannot pass without my drinking it, your will be done. ↓

PRAYER AFTER COMMUNION

Nourished with these sacred gifts,
we humbly beseech you, O Lord,
that, just as through the death of your Son
you have brought us to hope for what we believe,
so by his Resurrection

you may lead us to where you call.
Through Christ our Lord.
℟. **Amen.** ↓

The Deacon or, in his absence, the Priest himself, says the invitation: Bow down for the blessing.

PRAYER OVER THE PEOPLE

Look, we pray, O Lord, on this your family,
for whom our Lord Jesus Christ
did not hesitate to be delivered into the hands of the wicked
and submit to the agony of the Cross.
Who lives and reigns for ever and ever.
℟. **Amen.** → No. 32, p. 77

"This is my body that is for you.
Do this in remembrance of me."

THE SACRED PASCHAL TRIDUUM

MARCH 29

THURSDAY OF THE LORD'S SUPPER [HOLY THURSDAY]

AT THE EVENING MASS

The Mass of the Lord's Supper is celebrated in the evening, at a convenient time, with the full participation of the whole local community and with all the Priests and ministers exercising their office.

ENTRANCE ANTIPHON Cf. Gal. 6.14

We should glory in the Cross of our Lord Jesus Christ, in whom is our salvation, life and resurrection, through whom we are saved and delivered. → No. 2, p. 10

The Gloria in excelsis *(*Glory to God in the highest*) is said. While the hymn is being sung, bells are rung, and when it is finished, they remain silent until the* Gloria in excelsis *of the Easter Vigil, unless, if appropriate, the*

Diocesan Bishop has decided otherwise. Likewise, during this same period, the organ and other musical instruments may be used only so as to support the singing.

COLLECT

O God, who have called us to participate
in this most sacred Supper,
in which your Only Begotten Son,
when about to hand himself over to death,
entrusted to the Church a sacrifice new for all eternity,
the banquet of his love,
grant, we pray,
that we may draw from so great a mystery,
the fullness of charity and of life.
Through our Lord Jesus Christ, your Son,
who lives and reigns with you in the unity of the Holy Spirit,
one God, for ever and ever. ℟. **Amen.** ↓

FIRST READING Ex. 12.1-8, 11-14

The people are instructed to prepare for the Passover meal. By the blood of the lamb they are saved from death.

A reading from the book of Exodus.

THE Lord said to Moses and Aaron in the land of Egypt: This month shall mark for you the beginning of months; it shall be the first month of the year for you. Tell the whole congregation of Israel that on the tenth of this month they are to take a lamb for each family, a lamb for each household. If a household is too small for a whole lamb, it shall join its closest neighbour in obtaining one; the lamb shall be divided in proportion to the number of people who eat of it.

Your lamb shall be without blemish, a year-old male; you may take it from the sheep or from the goats. You shall keep it until the fourteenth day of this month; then the whole assembled congregation of Israel shall slaughter it at twilight. They shall take some of the blood and put it on the two doorposts and the lintel of the houses in which they eat it. They shall eat the lamb that same night; they shall eat it roasted over the fire with unleavened bread and bitter herbs.

This is how you shall eat it: your loins girded, your sandals on your feet, and your staff in your hand; and you shall eat it hurriedly. It is the Passover of the Lord. For I will pass through the land of Egypt that night, and I will strike down every firstborn in the land of Egypt, both human beings and animals; on all the gods of Egypt I will execute judgments: I am the Lord. The blood shall be a sign for you on the houses where you live: when I see the blood, I will pass over you, and no plague shall destroy you when I strike the land of Egypt.

This day shall be a day of remembrance for you. You shall celebrate it as a festival to the Lord; throughout your generations you shall observe it as a perpetual ordinance.—The word of the Lord.

℟. **Thanks be to God.** ↓

RESPONSORIAL PSALM Ps. 116 Normand L. Blanchard

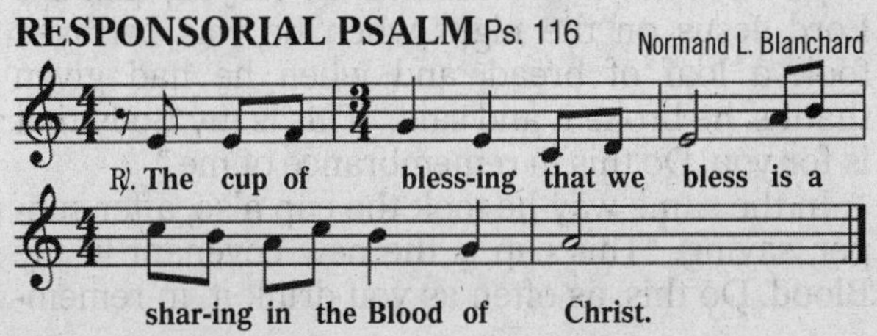
℟. The cup of bless-ing that we bless is a
shar-ing in the Blood of Christ.

What shall I return to the Lord
for all his bounty to me?
I will lift up the cup of salvation
and call on the name of the Lord.
℟. **The cup of blessing that we bless is a sharing in the Blood of Christ.**

Precious in the sight of the Lord
is the death of his faithful ones.
I am your servant, the son of your serving girl.
You have loosed my bonds.—℟.

I will offer to you a thanksgiving sacrifice
and call on the name of the Lord.
I will pay my vows to the Lord
in the presence of all his people.—℟. ↓

SECOND READING 1 Cor. 11.23-26

Paul recounts the events of the Last Supper which were handed down to him. The changing of bread and wine into the Body and Blood of the Lord proclaims again his death. It is a sacrificial meal.

A reading from the first Letter of Saint Paul
to the Corinthians.

BROTHERS and sisters: I received from the Lord what I also handed on to you, that the Lord Jesus on the night when he was betrayed took a loaf of bread, and when he had given thanks, he broke it and said, "This is my Body that is for you. Do this in remembrance of me."

In the same way he took the cup also, after supper, saying, "This cup is the new covenant in my Blood. Do this, as often as you drink it, in remembrance of me." For as often as you eat this bread and drink the cup, you proclaim the Lord's death until he comes. —The word of the Lord. ℟. **Thanks be to God.** ↓

GOSPEL ACCLAMATION Jn. 13.34

℣. Praise to you, Lord Jesus Christ, King of endless glory!*

℟. **Praise to you, Lord Jesus Christ, King of endless glory!**

℣. I give you a new commandment:
love one another as I have loved you.

℟. **Praise to you, Lord Jesus Christ, King of endless glory!** ↓

GOSPEL Jn. 13.1-15

Jesus washes the feet of his disciples to prove to them his sincere love and great humility, which they should imitate.

℣. The Lord be with you. ℟. **And with your spirit.**
✠ A reading from the holy Gospel according to John. ℟. **Glory to you, O Lord.**

BEFORE the festival of the Passover, Jesus knew that his hour had come to depart from this world and go to the Father. Having loved his own who were in the world, he loved them to the end.

The devil had already put it into the heart of Judas, son of Simon Iscariot, to betray him. And during supper Jesus, knowing that the Father had given all things into his hands, and that he

* *See p. 16 for other Gospel Acclamations.*

had come from God and was going to God, got up from the table, took off his outer robe, and tied a towel around himself. Then he poured water into a basin and began to wash the disciples' feet and to wipe them with the towel that was tied around him.

He came to Simon Peter, who said to him, "Lord, are you going to wash my feet?" Jesus answered, "You do not know now what I am doing, but later you will understand." Peter said to him, "You will never wash my feet." Jesus answered, "Unless I wash you, you have no share with me." Simon Peter said to him, "Lord, not my feet only but also my hands and my head!" Jesus said to him, "One who has bathed does not need to wash, except for the feet, but is entirely clean. And you are clean, though not all of you." For he knew who was to betray him; for this reason he said, "Not all of you are clean."

After he had washed their feet, put on his robe, and returned to the table, Jesus said to them, "Do you know what I have done to you? You call me Teacher and Lord—and you are right, for that is what I am. So if I, your Lord and Teacher, have washed your feet, you also ought to wash one another's feet. For I have set you an example, that you also should do as I have done to you."—The Gospel of the Lord.
℟. **Praise to you, Lord Jesus Christ.** ↓

After the proclamation of the Gospel, the Priest gives a homily in which light is shed on the principal mysteries that are commemorated in this Mass, namely, the institution of the Holy Eucharist and of the priestly Order, and the commandment of the Lord concerning fraternal charity.

The Washing of Feet

After the Homily, where a pastoral reason suggests it, the Washing of Feet follows.

Those who are chosen from amongst the people of God are led by the ministers to seats prepared in a suitable place. Then the Priest (removing his chasuble if necessary) goes to each one, and, with the help of the ministers, pours water over each one's feet and then dries them.

Meanwhile some of the following antiphons or other appropriate chants are sung.

ANTIPHON 1 Cf. Jn. 13.4, 5, 15

After the Lord had risen from supper,
he poured water into a basin
and began to wash the feet of his disciples:
he left them this example.

ANTIPHON 2 Cf. Jn. 13.12, 13, 15

The Lord Jesus, after eating supper with his disciples,
washed their feet and said to them:
Do you know what I, your Lord and Master, have done for you?
I have given you an example, that you should do likewise.

ANTIPHON 3 Cf. Jn. 13.6, 7, 8

Lord, are you to wash my feet? Jesus said to him in answer:
If I do not wash your feet, you will have no share with me.
℣. So he came to Simon Peter and Peter said to him:
—Lord ...

℣. What I am doing, you do not know for now,
but later you will come to know.
—Lord ...

ANTIPHON 4 Cf. Jn. 13.14

If I, your Lord and Master, have washed your feet,
how much more should you wash each other's feet?

ANTIPHON 5 Jn. 13.35

This is how all will know that you are my disciples:
if you have love for one another.
℣. Jesus said to his disciples:
—This is how ...

ANTIPHON 6 Jn. 13.34

I give you a new commandment,
that you love one another
as I have loved you, says the Lord.

ANTIPHON 7 1 Cor. 13.13

Let faith, hope and charity, these three, remain among you,
but the greatest of these is charity.
℣. Now faith, hope and charity, these three, remain;
but the greatest of these is charity.
—Let ...

After the Washing of Feet, the Priest washes and dries his hands, puts the chasuble back on, and returns to the chair, and from there he directs the Universal Prayer.

The Creed is not said.

The Liturgy of the Eucharist

At the beginning of the Liturgy of the Eucharist, there may be a procession of the faithful in which gifts for the poor may be presented with the bread and wine.

Meanwhile the following, or another appropriate chant, is sung.

Ant. **Where true charity is dwelling, God is present there.**

℣. **By the love of Christ we have been brought together:**

℣. **let us find in him our gladness and our pleasure;**

℣. **may we love him and revere him, God the living,**

℣. **and in love respect each other with sincere hearts.**

Ant. **Where true charity is dwelling, God is present there.**

℣. **So when we as one are gathered all together,**

℣. **let us strive to keep our minds free of division;**

℣. **may there be an end to malice, strife and quarrels,**

℣. **and let Christ our God be dwelling here among us.**

Ant. **Where true charity is dwelling, God is present there.**

℣. **May your face thus be our vision, bright in glory,**

℣. **Christ our God, with all the blessed Saints in heaven:**

℣. **such delight is pure and faultless, joy unbounded,**

℣. **which endures through countless ages world without end. Amen.** → No. 17, p. 20

PRAYER OVER THE OFFERINGS

Grant us, O Lord, we pray,
that we may participate worthily in these mysteries,
for whenever the memorial of this sacrifice is celebrated
the work of our redemption is accomplished.
Through Christ our Lord.
℟. **Amen.** → No. 21, p. 22 (Pref. 47)

When the Roman Canon is used, this special form of it is said, with proper formulas for the Communicantes (In communion with those), Hanc igitur (Therefore, Lord, we pray), *and* Qui pridie (On the day before he was to suffer).

To you, therefore, most merciful Father,
we make humble prayer and petition
through Jesus Christ, your Son, our Lord:
that you accept
and bless ✠ these gifts, these offerings,
these holy and unblemished sacrifices,
which we offer you firstly
for your holy catholic Church.
Be pleased to grant her peace,
to guard, unite and govern her
throughout the whole world,
together with your servant *N.* our Pope
and *N.* our Bishop,
and all those who, holding to the truth,
and on the catholic and apostolic faith.

the Blood of the new and eternal covenant,
which will be poured out for you and for many
for the forgiveness of sins.

Do this in memory of me.

The rest follows the Roman Canon, pp. 26-29.

COMMUNION ANTIPHON 1 Cor. 11.24-25

This is the Body that will be given up for you; this is the Chalice of the new covenant in my Blood, says the Lord; do this, whenever you receive it, in memory of me. ↓

After the distribution of Communion, a ciborium with hosts for Communion on the following day is left on the altar. The Priest, standing at the chair, says the Prayer after Communion.

PRAYER AFTER COMMUNION

Grant, almighty God,
that, just as we are renewed
by the Supper of your Son in this present age,
so we may enjoy his banquet for all eternity.
Who lives and reigns for ever and ever. ℟. **Amen.**

The Transfer of the Most Blessed Sacrament

After the Prayer after Communion, the Priest puts incense in the thurible while standing, blesses it and then, kneeling, incenses the Blessed Sacrament three times. Then, having put on a white humeral veil, he rises, takes the ciborium, and covers it with the ends of the veil.

A procession is formed in which the Blessed Sacrament, accompanied by torches and incense, is carried through the church to a place of repose prepared in a part of the church or in a chapel suitably decorated. A lay minister with a cross, standing between two other ministers with lighted candles, leads off. Others carrying lighted candles follow. Before the Priest carrying the Blessed Sacrament comes the thurifer with a smoking thurible. Meanwhile, the hymn Pange, lingua *(exclusive of the last two stanzas) or another eucharistic chant is sung.*

When the procession reaches the place of repose, the Priest, with the help of the Deacon if necessary, places the ciborium in the tabernacle, the door of which remains open. Then he puts incense in the thurible and, kneeling, incenses the Blessed Sacrament, while Tantum ergo Sacramentum *or another eucharistic chant is sung. Then the Deacon or the Priest himself places the Sacrament in the tabernacle and closes the door.*

After a period of adoration in silence, the Priest and ministers genuflect and return to the sacristy.

At an appropriate time, the altar is stripped and, if possible, the crosses are removed from the church. It is expedient that any crosses which remain in the church be veiled.

"He bowed his head and gave up his spirit."

MARCH 30

FRIDAY OF THE PASSION OF THE LORD [GOOD FRIDAY]

THE CELEBRATION OF THE PASSION OF THE LORD

This week, on Good Friday and Holy Saturday, the people of God are called to observe a solemn paschal fast. In this way, they are in union with the Christians of every century, and will be ready to receive the joys of the Lord's Resurrection with uplifted and responsive hearts.

The Priest and the Deacon, if a Deacon is present, wearing red vestments as for Mass, go to the altar in silence and, after making a reverence to the altar, prostrate themselves or, if appropriate, kneel and pray in silence for a while. All others kneel.

Then the Priest, with the ministers, goes to the chair where, facing the people, who are standing, he says, with hands extended, one of the following prayers, omitting the invitation Let us pray.

PRAYER

Remember your mercies, O Lord,
and with your eternal protection sanctify your servants,

for whom Christ your Son,
by the shedding of his Blood,
established the Paschal Mystery.
Who lives and reigns for ever and ever. ℟. **Amen.**

OR

O God, who by the Passion of Christ your Son, our Lord,
abolished the death inherited from ancient sin
by every succeeding generation,
grant that just as, being conformed to him,
we have borne by the law of nature
the image of the man of earth,
so by the sanctification of grace
we may bear the image of the Man of heaven.
Through Christ our Lord. ℟. **Amen.**

FIRST PART: THE LITURGY OF THE WORD

FIRST READING Isa. 52.13—53.12

The suffering servant shall be raised up and exalted. The doctrine of expiatory suffering finds supreme expression in these words.

A reading from the book of the Prophet Isaiah.

SEE, my servant shall prosper;
he shall be exalted and lifted up,
and shall be very high.
Just as there were many who were astonished at him
—so marred was his appearance, beyond human semblance,
and his form beyond that of the sons of man—
so he shall startle many nations;
kings shall shut their mouths because of him;

for that which had not been told them they shall see,
and that which they had not heard they shall contemplate.
Who has believed what we have heard?
And to whom has the arm of the Lord been revealed?

For he grew up before the Lord like a young plant,
and like a root out of dry ground;
he had no form or majesty that we should look at him,
nothing in his appearance that we should desire him.
He was despised and rejected by men;
a man of suffering and acquainted with infirmity;
and as one from whom others hide their faces
he was despised,
and we held him of no account.

Surely he has borne our infirmities and carried our diseases;
yet we accounted him stricken,
struck down by God, and afflicted.
But he was wounded for our transgressions,
crushed for our iniquities;
upon him was the punishment that made us whole,
and by his bruises we are healed.

All we like sheep have gone astray;
each has turned to their own way
and the Lord has laid on him
the iniquity of us all.

He was oppressed, and he was afflicted,
yet he did not open his mouth;

like a lamb that is led to the slaughter,
and like a sheep that before its shearers is silent,
so he did not open his mouth.

By a perversion of justice he was taken away.
Who could have imagined his future?
For he was cut off from the land of the living,
stricken for the transgression of my people.
They made his grave with the wicked
and his tomb with the rich,
although he had done no violence,
and there was no deceit in his mouth.

Yet it was the will of the Lord to crush him with pain.
When you make his life an offering for sin,
he shall see his offspring, and shall prolong his days;
through him the will of the Lord shall prosper.
Out of his anguish he shall see light;
he shall find satisfaction through his knowledge.
The righteous one, my servant, shall make many righteous,
and he shall bear their iniquities.

Therefore I will allot him a portion with the great,
and he shall divide the spoil with the strong;
because he poured out himself to death,
and was numbered with the transgressors;
yet he bore the sin of many,
and made intercession for the transgressors.

The word of the Lord. ℟. **Thanks be to God.** ↓

RESPONSORIAL PSALM Ps. 31

Geoffrey Angeles

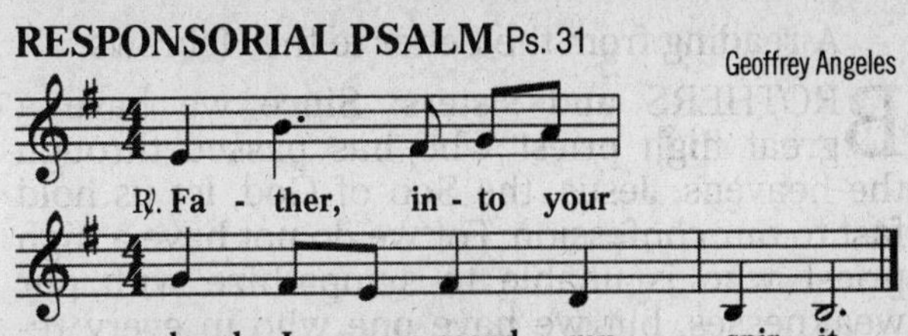
℟. Fa - ther, in - to your
hands I com-mend my spir - it.

In you, O Lord, I seek refuge;
do not let me ever be put to shame;
in your righteousness deliver me.
Into your hand I commit my spirit;
you have redeemed me,
O Lord, faithful God.—℟.

I am the scorn of all my adversaries,
a horror to my neighbours,
an object of dread to my acquaintances.
Those who see me in the street flee from me.
I have passed out of mind like one who is dead;
I have become like a broken vessel.—℟.

But I trust in you, O Lord;
I say, "You are my God."
My times are in your hand;
deliver me from the hand of my enemies and persecutors.—℟.

Let your face shine upon your servant;
save me in your steadfast love.
Be strong, and let your heart take courage,
all you who wait for the Lord.—℟. ↓

SECOND READING Heb. 4.14-16; 5.7-9

The theme of the compassionate high priest appears again in this passage. In him Christians can approach God confidently and without fear.

A reading from the Letter to the Hebrews.

BROTHERS and sisters: Since we have a great high priest who has passed through the heavens, Jesus, the Son of God, let us hold fast to our confession. For we do not have a high priest who is unable to sympathize with our weaknesses, but we have one who in every respect has been tested as we are, yet without sin. Let us therefore approach the throne of grace with boldness, so that we may receive mercy and find grace to help in time of need.

In the days of his flesh, Jesus offered up prayers and supplications, with loud cries and tears, to the one who was able to save him from death, and he was heard because of his reverent submission. Although he was a Son, he learned obedience through what he suffered; and having been made perfect, he became the source of eternal salvation for all who obey him.—The word of the Lord. ℟. **Thanks be to God.** ↓

GOSPEL ACCLAMATION Phil. 2.8-9

℣. Praise and honour to you, Lord Jesus Christ!*
℟. **Praise and honour to you, Lord Jesus Christ!**
℣. Christ became obedient for us to death, even death on a Cross.
Therefore God exalted him and gave him the name above every name.
℟. **Praise and honour to you, Lord Jesus Christ!** ↓

GOSPEL Jn. 18.1—19.42

The Passion is read in the same way as on the preceding Sunday. The narrator is noted by **N.**, *the words of Jesus by a* **J.** *and the words of others by* **S.**

* *See p. 16 for other Gospel Acclamations.*

It is important for us to understand the meaning of Christ's sufferings today. *See the note on p. 270.*

The beginning scene is Christ's agony in the garden. Our Lord knows what is to happen. The Scriptures recount the betrayal, the trial, the condemnation, and the crucifixion of Jesus.

N. THE Passion of our Lord Jesus Christ according to John.

JESUS IS ARRESTED

N. AFTER they had eaten the supper, Jesus went out with his disciples across the Kidron valley to a place where there was a garden, which he and his disciples entered. Now Judas, who betrayed him, also knew the place, because Jesus often met there with his disciples. So Judas brought a detachment of soldiers together with police from the chief priests and the Pharisees, and they came there with lanterns and torches and weapons.

Then Jesus, knowing all that was to happen to him, came forward and asked them, **J.** *"Whom are you looking for?"* **N.** They answered, **S. "Jesus of Nazareth."** [**N.** Jesus replied,] **J.** *"I am he."* **N.** Judas, who betrayed him, was standing with them. When Jesus said to them, "I am he," they stepped back and fell to the ground. Again he asked them, **J.** *"Whom are you looking for?"* [**N.** And they said,] **S. "Jesus of Nazareth."** [**N.** Jesus answered,] **J.** *"I told you that I am he. So if you are looking for me, let these men go."* **N.** This was to fulfill the word that he had spoken, "I did not lose a single one of those whom you gave me."

Then Simon Peter, who had a sword, drew it, struck the high priest's slave, and cut off his right ear. The slave's name was Malchus. Jesus said to Peter, **J.** *"Put your sword back into its sheath. Am I not to drink the cup that the Father has given me?"*

TRIAL BEFORE ANNAS

N. SO the soldiers, their officer, and the Jewish police arrested Jesus and bound him. First they took him to Annas, who was the father-in-law of Caiaphas, the high priest that year. Caiaphas was the one who had advised the Jews that it was better to have one person die for the people.

Simon Peter and another disciple followed Jesus. Since that disciple was known to the high priest, he went with Jesus into the courtyard of the high priest, but Peter was standing outside at the gate. So the other disciple, who was known to the high priest, went out, spoke to the woman who guarded the gate, and brought Peter in. The woman said to Peter, **S. "You are not also one of this man's disciples, are you?" N.** He said, **S. "I am not." N.** Now the slaves and the police had made a charcoal fire because it was cold, and they were standing around it and warming themselves. Peter also was standing with them and warming himself.

Then the high priest questioned Jesus about his disciples and about his teaching. Jesus answered, **J.** *"I have spoken openly to the world; I have always taught in synagogues and in the* *temple, where all the Jews come together. I have said nothing in secret. Why do you ask me? Ask those who heard what I said to them; they know what I said."*

N. When he had said this, one of the police standing nearby struck Jesus on the face, saying, **S. "Is that how you answer the high priest?"** [N. Jesus answered,] **J.** *"If I have spoken wrongly, testify to the wrong. But if I have spoken rightly, why do you strike me?"* **N.** Then Annas sent him bound to Caiaphas the high priest.

PETER DENIES THE LORD JESUS

N. NOW Simon Peter was standing and warming himself. They asked him, **S. "You are not also one of his disciples, are you?"** **N.** He denied it and said, **S. "I am not."** **N.** One of the slaves of the high priest, a relative of the man whose ear Peter had cut off, asked, **S. "Did I not see you in the garden with him?"** **N.** Again Peter denied it, and at that moment the cock crowed.

At this point all may join in singing an acclamation.

TRIAL BEFORE PILATE

N. THEN they took Jesus from Caiaphas to Pilate's headquarters. It was early in the morning. They themselves did not enter the headquarters, so as to avoid ritual defilement and to be able to eat the Passover. So Pilate went out to them and said, **S. "What accusation do you bring against this man?"** **N.** They answered, **S. "If this man were not a criminal, we**

would not have handed him over to you." **N.** Pilate said to them, **S. "Take him yourselves and judge him according to your law."** **N.** They replied, **S. "We are not permitted to put anyone to death."** **N.** (This was to fulfill what Jesus had said when he indicated the kind of death he was to die.)

Then Pilate entered the headquarters again, summoned Jesus, and asked him, **S. "Are you the King of the Jews?"** [**N.** Jesus answered,] **J.** *"Do you ask this on your own, or did others tell you about me?"* [**N.** Pilate replied,] **S. "I am not a Jew, am I? Your own nation and the chief priests have handed you over to me. What have you done?"** [**N.** Jesus answered,] **J.** *"My kingdom is not from this world. If my kingdom were from this world, my followers would be fighting to keep me from being handed over to the Jews. But as it is, my kingdom is not from here."* [**N.** Pilate asked him,] **S. "So you are a king?"** [**N.** Jesus answered,] **J.** *"You say that I am a king. For this I was born, and for this I came into the world, to testify to the truth. Everyone who belongs to the truth listens to my voice."* [**N.** Pilate asked him,] **S. "What is truth?"**

N. After he had said this, Pilate went out to the Jews again and told them, **S. "I find no case against him. But you have a custom that I release someone for you at the Passover. Do you want me to release for you the King of the Jews?"** **N.** They shouted in reply, **S. "Not this man, but Barabbas!"** **N.** Now Barabbas was a bandit.

Then Pilate took Jesus and had him flogged. And the soldiers wove a crown of thorns and put it on his head, and they dressed him in a purple robe. They kept coming up to him, saying, **S. "Hail, King of the Jews!" N.** and they struck him on the face.

Pilate went out again and said to them, **S. "Look, I am bringing him out to you to let you know that I find no case against him." N.** So Jesus came out, wearing the crown of thorns and the purple robe. Pilate said to them, **S. "Here is the man!"**

N. When the chief priests and the police saw him, they shouted, **S. "Crucify him! Crucify him!" N.** Pilate said to them, **S. "Take him yourselves and crucify him; I find no case against him." N.** They answered him, **S. "We have a law, and according to that law he ought to die because he has claimed to be the Son of God."**

N. Now when Pilate heard this, he was more afraid than ever. He entered his headquarters again and asked Jesus, **S. "Where are you from?" N.** But Jesus gave him no answer. Pilate therefore said to him, **S. "Do you refuse to speak to me? Do you not know that I have power to release you, and power to crucify you?"** [**N.** Jesus answered him,] **J.** *"You would have no power over me unless it had been given you from above; therefore the one who handed me over to you is guilty of a greater sin."* **N.** From then on Pilate tried to release him, but the Jews cried out, **S. "If you release this man, you are no friend of the emperor. Everyone**

who claims to be a king sets himself against the emperor." **N.** When Pilate heard these words, he brought Jesus outside and sat on the judge's bench at a place called "The Stone Pavement," or in Hebrew "Gabbatha."

Now it was the day of Preparation for the Passover; and it was about noon. Pilate said to the Jews, **S. "Here is your King!" N.** They cried out, **S. "Away with him! Away with him! Crucify him!" N.** Pilate asked them, **S. "Shall I crucify your King?" N.** The chief priests answered, **S. "We have no king but the emperor." N.** Then Pilate handed Jesus over to them to be crucified.

At this point all may join in singing an appropriate acclamation.

JESUS IS CRUCIFIED AND DIES FOR US

N. SO they took Jesus; and carrying the Cross by himself, he went out to what is called The Place of the Skull, which in Hebrew is called Golgotha. There they crucified him, and with him two others, one on either side, with Jesus between them.

Pilate also had an inscription written and put on the Cross. It read, "Jesus of Nazareth, the King of the Jews." Many of the people read this inscription, because the place where Jesus was crucified was near the city; and it was written in Hebrew, in Latin, and in Greek. Then the chief priests of the Jews said to Pilate, **S. "Do not write, 'The King of the Jews,' but, 'This man said, I am King of the Jews.'" N.** Pilate answered, **S. "What I have written I have written."**

N. When the soldiers had crucified Jesus, they took his clothes and divided them into four parts, one for each soldier. They also took his tunic; now the tunic was seamless, woven in one piece from the top. So they said to one another, **S. "Let us not tear it, but cast lots for it to see who will get it." N.** This was to fulfill what the Scripture says,

"They divided my clothes among themselves,
and for my clothing they cast lots."

And that is what the soldiers did.

Meanwhile, standing near the Cross of Jesus were his mother, and his mother's sister, Mary the wife of Clopas, and Mary Magdalene. When Jesus saw his mother and the disciple whom he loved standing beside her, he said to his mother, **J.** *"Woman, here is your son."* **N.** Then he said to the disciple, **J.** *"Here is your mother."* **N.** And from that hour the disciple took her into his own home.

After this, when Jesus knew that all was now finished, in order to fulfill the Scripture he said, **J.** *"I am thirsty."* **N.** A jar full of sour wine was standing there. So they put a sponge full of the wine on a branch of hyssop and held it to his mouth. When Jesus had received the wine, he said, **J.** *"It is finished."* **N.** Then he bowed his head and gave up his spirit.

Here all kneel and pause for a short time.

EVENTS AFTER JESUS' DEATH

N. SINCE it was the day of Preparation, the Jews did not want the bodies left on the cross during the Sabbath, especially because that Sabbath was a day of great Solemnity. So they asked Pilate to have the legs of the crucified men broken and the bodies removed.

Then the soldiers came and broke the legs of the first and of the other who had been crucified with him. But when they came to Jesus and saw that he was already dead, they did not break his legs. Instead, one of the soldiers pierced his side with a spear, and at once blood and water came out.

(He who saw this has testified so that you also may believe. His testimony is true, and he knows that he tells the truth.) These things occurred so that the Scripture might be fulfilled, "None of his bones shall be broken." And again another passage of Scripture says, "They will look on the one whom they have pierced."

JESUS' BODY IS PLACED IN THE TOMB

N. AFTER these things, Joseph of Arimathea, who was a disciple of Jesus, though a secret one because of his fear of the Jews, asked Pilate to let him take away the body of Jesus. Pilate gave him permission; so he came and removed his body.

Nicodemus, who had at first come to Jesus by night, also came, bringing a mixture of myrrh and aloes, weighing about a hundredweight. They took the body of Jesus and wrapped it with the spices in linen cloths, according to the burial custom of the Jews. Now there was a garden in the place where he was crucified, and in the garden there was a new tomb in which no one had ever been buried. And so, because it was the Jewish day of Preparation, and the tomb was nearby, they laid Jesus there.

After the reading of the Lord's Passion, the Priest gives a brief homily and, at its end, the faithful may be invited to spend a short time in prayer.

THE SOLEMN INTERCESSIONS

The Liturgy of the Word concludes with the Solemn Intercessions, which take place in this way: the Deacon, if a Deacon is present, or if he is not, a lay minister, stands at the ambo, and sings or says the invitation in which the intention is expressed. Then all pray in silence for a while, and afterwards the Priest, standing at the chair or, if appropriate, at the altar, with hands extended, sings or says the prayer.

The faithful may remain either kneeling or standing throughout the entire period of the prayers.

Before the Priest's prayer, in accord with tradition, it is permissible to use the Deacon's invitations Let us kneel — Let us stand, *with all kneeling for silent prayer.*

I. For Holy Church

Let us pray, dearly beloved, for the holy Church of God,
that our God and Lord be pleased to give her peace,
to guard her and to unite her throughout the whole world
and grant that, leading our life in tranquillity and quiet,
we may glorify God the Father almighty.

Prayer in silence. Then the Priest says:

Almighty ever-living God,
who in Christ revealed your glory to all the nations,

watch over the works of your mercy,
that your Church, spread throughout all the world,
may persevere with steadfast faith in confessing your name.
Through Christ our Lord.
℟. **Amen.**

II. For the Pope

Let us pray also for our most Holy Father Pope *N.*,
that our God and Lord,
who chose him for the Order of Bishops,
may keep him safe and unharmed for the Lord's holy Church,
to govern the holy People of God.

Prayer in silence. Then the Priest says:

Almighty ever-living God,
by whose decree all things are founded,
look with favour on our prayers
and in your kindness protect the Pope chosen for us,
that, under him, the Christian people,
governed by you their maker,
may grow in merit by reason of their faith.
Through Christ our Lord.
℟. **Amen.**

III. For all orders and degrees of the faithful

Let us pray also for our Bishop *N.*,
for all Bishops, Priests, and Deacons of the Church
and for the whole of the faithful people.

Prayer in silence. Then the Priest says:

Almighty ever-living God,
by whose Spirit the whole body of the Church
is sanctified and governed,
hear our humble prayer for your ministers,
that, by the gift of your grace,
all may serve you faithfully.
Through Christ our Lord.
℟. **Amen.**

IV. For catechumens

Let us pray also for (our) catechumens,
that our God and Lord
may open wide the ears of their inmost hearts
and unlock the gates of his mercy,
that, having received forgiveness of all their sins
through the waters of rebirth,
they, too, may be one with Christ Jesus our Lord.

Prayer in silence. Then the Priest says:

Almighty ever-living God,
who make your Church ever fruitful with new offspring,
increase the faith and understanding of (our) catechumens,
that, reborn in the font of Baptism,
they may be added to the number of your adopted children.
Through Christ our Lord.
℟. **Amen.**

V. For the unity of Christians

Let us pray also for all our brothers and sisters who believe in Christ,

that our God and Lord may be pleased,
as they live the truth,
to gather them together and keep them in his one Church.

Prayer in silence. Then the Priest says:

Almighty ever-living God,
who gather what is scattered
and keep together what you have gathered,
look kindly on the flock of your Son,
that those whom one Baptism has consecrated
may be joined together by integrity of faith
and united in the bond of charity.
Through Christ our Lord.
℟. **Amen.**

VI. For the Jewish people

Let us pray also for the Jewish people,
to whom the Lord our God spoke first,
that he may grant them to advance in love of his name
and in faithfulness to his covenant.

Prayer in silence. Then the Priest says:

Almighty ever-living God,
who bestowed your promises on Abraham and his descendants,
graciously hear the prayers of your Church,
that the people you first made your own
may attain the fullness of redemption.
Through Christ our Lord.
℟. **Amen.**

VII. For those who do not believe in Christ

Let us pray also for those who do not believe in Christ,
that, enlightened by the Holy Spirit,
they, too, may enter on the way of salvation.

Prayer in silence. Then the Priest says:

Almighty ever-living God,
grant to those who do not confess Christ
that, by walking before you with a sincere heart,
they may find the truth
and that we ourselves, being constant in mutual love
and striving to understand more fully the mystery of your life,
may be made more perfect witnesses to your love in the world.
Through Christ our Lord.
℟. **Amen.**

VIII. For those who do not believe in God

Let us pray also for those who do not acknowledge God,
that, following what is right in sincerity of heart,
they may find the way to God himself.

Prayer in silence. Then the Priest says:

Almighty ever-living God,
who created all people
to seek you always by desiring you
and, by finding you, come to rest,
grant, we pray,
that, despite every harmful obstacle,
all may recognize the signs of your fatherly love

and the witness of the good works
done by those who believe in you,
and so in gladness confess you,
the one true God and Father of our human race.
Through Christ our Lord.
℟. **Amen.**

IX. For those in public office

Let us pray also for those in public office,
that our God and Lord
may direct their minds and hearts according to his will
for the true peace and freedom of all.

Prayer in silence. Then the Priest says:

Almighty ever-living God,
in whose hand lies every human heart
and the rights of peoples,
look with favour, we pray,
on those who govern with authority over us,
that throughout the whole world,
the prosperity of peoples,
the assurance of peace,
and freedom of religion
may through your gift be made secure.
Through Christ our Lord.
℟. **Amen.**

X. For those in tribulation

Let us pray, dearly beloved,
to God the Father almighty,
that he may cleanse the world of all errors,
banish disease, drive out hunger,
unlock prisons, loosen fetters,

granting to travellers safety, to pilgrims return, health to the sick, and salvation to the dying.

Prayer in silence. Then the Priest says:

Almighty ever-living God,
comfort of mourners, strength of all who toil,
may the prayers of those who cry out in any tribulation
come before you,
that all may rejoice,
because in their hour of need
your mercy was at hand.
Through Christ our Lord.
℟. **Amen.**

SECOND PART: THE ADORATION OF THE HOLY CROSS

After the Solemn Intercessions, the solemn Adoration of the Holy Cross takes place. Of the two forms of the showing of the Cross presented here, the more appropriate one, according to pastoral needs, should be chosen.

The Showing of the Holy Cross

First Form

The Deacon accompanied by ministers, or another suitable minister, goes to the sacristy, from which, in procession, accompanied by two ministers with lighted candles, he carries the Cross, covered with a violet veil, through the church to the middle of the sanctuary.

The Priest, standing before the altar and facing the people, receives the Cross, uncovers a little of its upper part and elevates it while beginning the Ecce lignum Crucis (Behold the wood of the Cross)*. He is assisted in singing by the Deacon or, if need be, by the choir. All respond,* Come, let us adore. *At the end of the singing, all kneel and for a brief moment adore in silence, while the Priest stands and holds the Cross raised.*

℣. Behold the wood of the Cross,
on which hung the salvation of the world.

℟. Come, let us a - dore

Then the Priest uncovers the right arm of the Cross and again, raising up the Cross, begins, Behold the wood of the Cross *and everything takes place as above.*

Finally, he uncovers the Cross entirely and, raising it up, he begins the invitation Behold the wood of the Cross *a third time and everything takes place like the first time.*

Second Form

The Priest or the Deacon accompanied by ministers, or another suitable minister, goes to the door of the church, where he receives the unveiled Cross, and the ministers take lighted candles; then the procession sets off through the church to the sanctuary. Near the door, in the middle of the church and before the entrance of the sanctuary, the one who carries the Cross elevates it, singing, Behold the wood of the Cross, *to which all respond,* Come, let us adore. *After each response all kneel and for a brief moment adore in silence, as above.*

The Adoration of the Holy Cross

Then, accompanied by two ministers with lighted candles, the Priest or the Deacon carries the Cross to the entrance of the sanctuary or to another suitable place and there puts it down or hands it over to the ministers to hold. Candles are placed on the right and left sides of the Cross.

For the Adoration of the Cross, first the Priest Celebrant alone approaches, with the chasuble and his shoes removed, if appropriate. Then the clergy, the lay ministers, and the faithful approach, moving as if in procession, and showing reverence to the Cross by a simple genuflection or by some other sign appropriate to the usage of the region, for example, by kissing the Cross.

Only one Cross should be offered for adoration. If, because of the large number of people, it is not possible for all to approach individually, the Priest, after some of the clergy and faithful have adored, takes the Cross and, standing in the middle before the altar, invites the people in a few words to adore the Holy Cross and afterwards holds the Cross elevated higher for a brief time, for the faithful to adore it in silence.

While the adoration of the Holy Cross is taking place, the antiphon Crucem tuam adoramus *(*We adore your Cross, O Lord*), the Reproaches, the hymn* Crux fidelis *(*Faithful Cross*) or other suitable chants are sung, during which all who have already adored the Cross remain seated.*

CHANTS TO BE SUNG DURING THE ADORATION OF THE HOLY CROSS

Antiphon

We adore your Cross, O Lord,
we praise and glorify your holy Resurrection,
for behold, because of the wood of a tree
joy has come to the whole world.

May God have mercy on us and bless us;
may he let his face shed its light upon us
and have mercy on us. Cf. Psalm 66.2

And the antiphon is repeated: **We adore . . .**

The Reproaches

Parts assigned to one of the two choirs separately are indicated by the numbers 1 *(first choir) and* 2 *(second choir); parts sung by both choirs together are marked:* 1 and 2. *Some of the verses may also be sung by two cantors.*

I

1 and 2: **My people, what have I done to you?**
Or how have I grieved you? Answer me!
1: **Because I led you out of the land of Egypt,**
you have prepared a Cross for your Saviour.
1: **Hagios o Theos,**
2: **Holy is God,**
1: **Hagios Ischyros,**
2: **Holy and Mighty,**
1: **Hagios Athanatos, eleison himas.**
2: **Holy and Immortal One, have mercy on us.**

1 and 2: **Because I led you out through the desert forty years**
and fed you with manna and brought you into a land of plenty,
you have prepared a Cross for your Saviour.
1: **Hagios o Theos,**
2: **Holy is God,**
1: **Hagios Ischyros,**
2: **Holy and Mighty,**
1: **Hagios Athanatos, eleison himas.**
2: **Holy and Immortal One, have mercy on us.**

1 and 2: **What more should I have done for you and have not done?**
Indeed, I planted you as my most beautiful chosen vine
and you have turned very bitter for me,
for in my thirst you gave me vinegar to drink
and with a lance you pierced your Saviour's side.

1: **Hagios o Theos,**
2: **Holy is God,**
1: **Hagios Ischyros,**
2: **Holy and Mighty,**
1: **Hagios Athanatos, eleison himas.**
2: **Holy and Immortal One, have mercy on us.**

II

Cantors:
I scourged Egypt for your sake with its firstborn sons,
and you scourged me and handed me over.

1 and 2 repeat:
My people, what have I done to you?
Or how have I grieved you? Answer me!

Cantors:
I led you out from Egypt as Pharoah lay sunk in the Red Sea,
and you handed me over to the chief priests.

1 and 2 repeat:
My people . . .

Cantors:
I opened up the sea before you,
and you opened my side with a lance.

1 and 2 repeat:
My people . . .

Cantors:
I went before you in a pillar of cloud,
and you led me into Pilate's palace.

1 and 2 repeat:
My people . . .

Cantors:
**I fed you with manna in the desert,
and on me you rained blows and lashes.**

1 and 2 repeat:
My people . . .

Cantors:
**I gave you saving water from the rock to drink,
and for drink you gave me gall and vinegar.**

1 and 2 repeat:
My people . . .

Cantors:
**I struck down for you the kings of the Canaanites,
and you struck my head with a reed.**

1 and 2 repeat:
My people . . .

Cantors:
**I put in your hand a royal sceptre,
and you put on my head a crown of thorns.**

1 and 2 repeat:
My people . . .

Cantors:
**I exalted you with great power,
and you hung me on the scaffold of the Cross.**

1 and 2 repeat:
My people . . .

HYMN

All:
Faithful Cross the Saints rely on,
Noble tree beyond compare!
Never was there such a scion,
Never leaf or flower so rare.
Sweet the timber, sweet the iron,
Sweet the burden that they bear!

Cantors:
Sing, my tongue, in exultation
Of our banner and device!
Make a solemn proclamation
Of a triumph and its price:
How the Savior of creation
Conquered by his sacrifice!

All:
Faithful Cross the Saints rely on,
Noble tree beyond compare!
Never was there such a scion,
Never leaf or flower so rare.

Cantors:
For, when Adam first offended,
Eating that forbidden fruit,
Not all hopes of glory ended
With the serpent at the root:
Broken nature would be mended
By a second tree and shoot.

All:
Sweet the timber, sweet the iron,
Sweet the burden that they bear!

Cantors:
Thus the tempter was outwitted
By a wisdom deeper still:
Remedy and ailment fitted,
Means to cure and means to kill;
That the world might be acquitted,
Christ would do his Father's will.

All:
Faithful Cross the Saints rely on,
Noble tree beyond compare!
Never was there such a scion,
Never leaf or flower so rare.

Cantors:
So the Father, out of pity
For our self-inflicted doom,
Sent him from the heavenly city
When the holy time had come:
He, the Son and the Almighty,
Took our flesh in Mary's womb.

All:
Sweet the timber, sweet the iron,
Sweet the burden that they bear!

Cantors:
Hear a tiny baby crying,
Founder of the seas and strands;
See his virgin Mother tying
Cloth around his feet and hands;
Find him in a manger lying
Tightly wrapped in swaddling-bands!

All:
Faithful Cross the Saints rely on,
Noble tree beyond compare!
Never was there such a scion,
Never leaf or flower so rare.

Cantors:
So he came, the long-expected,
Not in glory, not to reign;
Only born to be rejected,

Choosing hunger, toil and pain,
Till the scaffold was erected
And the Paschal Lamb was slain.

All:
Sweet the timber, sweet the iron,
Sweet the burden that they bear!

Cantors:
No disgrace was too abhorrent:
Nailed and mocked and parched he died;
Blood and water, double warrant,
Issue from his wounded side,
Washing in a mighty torrent
Earth and stars and oceantide.

All:
Faithful Cross the Saints rely on,
Noble tree beyond compare!
Never was there such a scion,
Never leaf or flower so rare.

Cantors:
Lofty timber, smooth your roughness,
Flex your boughs for blossoming;
Let your fibers lose their toughness,
Gently let your tendrils cling;
Lay aside your native gruffness,
Clasp the body of your King!

All:
Sweet the timber, sweet the iron,
Sweet the burden that they bear!

Cantors:
Noblest tree of all created,
Richly jewelled and embossed:
Post by Lamb's blood consecrated;
Spar that saves the tempest-tossed;
Scaffold-beam which, elevated,
Carries what the world has cost!

All:
Faithful Cross the Saints rely on,
Noble tree beyond compare!
Never was there such a scion,
Never leaf or flower so rare.

The following conclusion is never to be omitted:

All:
Wisdom, power, and adoration
To the blessed Trinity
For redemption and salvation
Through the Paschal Mystery,
Now, in every generation,
And for all eternity. Amen.

In accordance with local circumstances or popular traditions and if it is pastorally appropriate, the Stabat Mater *may be sung, as found in the Graduale Romanum, or another suitable chant in memory of the compassion of the Blessed Virgin Mary.*

When the adoration has been concluded, the Cross is carried by the Deacon or a minister to its place at the altar. Lighted candles are placed around or on the altar or near the Cross.

THIRD PART: HOLY COMMUNION

A cloth is spread on the altar, and a corporal and the Missal put in place. Meanwhile the Deacon or, if there is no Deacon, the Priest himself, putting on a humeral veil, brings the Blessed Sacrament back from the place of repose to the altar by a shorter route, while all stand in silence. Two ministers with lighted candles accompany the Blessed Sacrament and place their candlesticks around or upon the altar.

When the Deacon, if a Deacon is present, has placed the Blessed Sacrament upon the altar and uncovered the ciborium, the Priest goes to the altar and genuflects.

Then the Priest, with hands joined, says aloud:

At the Saviour's command
and formed by divine teaching,
we dare to say:

The Priest, with hands extended says, and all present continue:

**Our Father, who art in heaven,
hallowed be thy name;
thy kingdom come,
thy will be done
on earth as it is in heaven.
Give us this day our daily bread,
and forgive us our trespasses,
as we forgive those who trespass against us;
and lead us not into temptation,
but deliver us from evil.**

With hands extended, the Priest continues alone:

Deliver us, Lord, we pray, from every evil,
graciously grant peace in our days,
that, by the help of your mercy,
we may be always free from sin
and safe from all distress,
as we await the blessed hope
and the coming of our Saviour, Jesus Christ.

The people conclude the prayer, acclaiming:

For the kingdom, the power and the glory are yours now and for ever.

Then the Priest, with hands joined, says quietly:

May the receiving of your Body and Blood,
Lord Jesus Christ,
not bring me to judgement and condemnation,
but through your loving mercy
be for me protection in mind and body
and a healing remedy.

The Priest then genuflects, takes a particle, and, holding it slightly raised over the ciborium, while facing the people, says aloud:

Behold the Lamb of God,
behold him who takes away the sins of the world.
Blessed are those called to the supper of the Lamb.

And together with the people he adds once:

Lord, I am not worthy
that you should enter under my roof,
but only say the word
and my soul shall be healed.

And facing the altar, he reverently consumes the Body of Christ, saying quietly: May the Body of Christ keep me safe for eternal life.

He then proceeds to distribute Communion to the faithful. During Communion, Psalm 21 or another appropriate chant may be sung.

When the distribution of Communion has been completed, the ciborium is taken by the Deacon or another suitable minister to a place prepared outside the church or, if circumstances so require, it is placed in the tabernacle.

Then the Priest says: Let us pray, *and, after a period of sacred silence, if circumstances so suggest, has been observed, he says the Prayer after Communion.*

Almighty ever-living God,
who have restored us to life
by the blessed Death and Resurrection of your Christ,
preserve in us the work of your mercy,
that, by partaking of this mystery,
we may have a life unceasingly devoted to you.
Through Christ our Lord. ℟. **Amen.** ↓

For the Dismissal the Deacon or, if there is no Deacon, the Priest himself, may say the invitation Bow down for the blessing.

Then the Priest, standing facing the people and extending his hands over them, says this:

PRAYER OVER THE PEOPLE

May abundant blessing, O Lord, we pray,
descend upon your people,
who have honoured the Death of your Son
in the hope of their resurrection:
may pardon come,
comfort be given,
holy faith increase,

and everlasting redemption be made secure.
Through Christ our Lord. ℟. **Amen.** ↓

And all, after genuflecting to the Cross, depart in silence.

After the celebration, the altar is stripped, but the Cross remains on the altar with two or four candlesticks.

MARCH 31

HOLY SATURDAY

On Holy Saturday the Church waits at the Lord's tomb in prayer and fasting, meditating on his Passion and Death and on his Descent into Hell, and awaiting his Resurrection.

The Church abstains from the Sacrifice of the Mass, with the sacred table left bare, until after the solemn Vigil, that is, the anticipation by night of the Resurrection, when the time comes for paschal joys, the abundance of which overflows to occupy fifty days.

"He has been raised; he is not here."

MARCH 31

THE EASTER VIGIL IN THE HOLY NIGHT

By most ancient tradition, this is the night of keeping vigil for the Lord (Ex. 12.42), in which, following the Gospel admonition (Lk. 12.35-37), the faithful, carrying lighted lamps in their hands, should be like those looking for the Lord when he returns, so that at his coming he may find them awake and have them sit at his table.

Of this night's Vigil, which is the greatest and most noble of all solemnities, there is to be only one celebration in each church. It is arranged, moreover, in such a way that after the Lucernarium and Easter Proclamation (which constitutes the first part of this Vigil), Holy Church meditates on the wonders the Lord God has done for his people from the beginning, trusting in his word and promise (the second part, that is, the Liturgy of the Word) until, as day approaches, with new members reborn in Baptism (the third part), the Church is called to the table the Lord has prepared for his people, the memorial of his Death and Resurrection until he comes again (the fourth part).

Candles should be prepared for all who participate in the Vigil. The lights of the church are extinguished.

FIRST PART:
THE SOLEMN BEGINNING OF THE VIGIL OR LUCERNARIUM

THE BLESSING OF THE FIRE AND PREPARATION OF THE CANDLE

A blazing fire is prepared in a suitable place outside the church. When the people are gathered there, the Priest approaches with the ministers, one of whom carries the paschal candle. The processional cross and candles are not carried.

Where, however, a fire cannot be lit outside the church, the rite is carried out as below, p. 333.

The Priest and faithful sign themselves while the Priest says: In the name of the Father, and of the Son, and of the Holy Spirit, *and then he greets the assembled people in the usual way and briefly instructs them about the night vigil in these or similar words:*

Dear brethren (brothers and sisters),
on this most sacred night,
in which our Lord Jesus Christ
passed over from death to life,
the Church calls upon her sons and daughters,
scattered throughout the world,
to come together to watch and pray.
If we keep the memorial
of the Lord's paschal solemnity in this way,
listening to his word and celebrating his mysteries,
then we shall have the sure hope
of sharing his triumph over death
and living with him in God.

Then the Priest blesses the fire, saying with hands extended:

Let us pray.

O God, who through your Son
bestowed upon the faithful the fire of your glory,
sanctify ✠ this new fire, we pray,
and grant that,
by these paschal celebrations,
we may be so inflamed with heavenly desires,
that with minds made pure
we may attain festivities of unending splendour.
Through Christ our Lord.
℟. **Amen.** ↓

After the blessing of the new fire, one of the ministers brings the paschal candle to the Priest, who cuts a cross into the candle with a stylus. Then he makes the Greek letter Alpha above the cross, the letter Omega below, and the four numerals of the current year between the arms of the cross, saying meanwhile:

1. Christ yesterday and today *(he cuts a vertical line);*
2. the Beginning and the End *(he cuts a horizontal line);*
3. the Alpha *(he cuts the letter Alpha above the vertical line);*
4. and the Omega *(he cuts the letter Omega below the vertical line).*
5. All time belongs to him *(he cuts the first numeral of the current year in the upper left corner of the cross);*
6. and all the ages *(he cuts the second numeral of the current year in the upper right corner of the cross).*

7. To him be glory and power *(he cuts the third numeral of the current year in the lower left corner of the cross);*
8. through every age forever. Amen *(he cuts the fourth numeral of the current year in the lower right corner of the cross).*

	A	
2		0
1		8
	Ω	

When the cutting of the cross and of the other signs has been completed, the Priest may insert five grains of incense into the candle in the form of a cross, meanwhile saying:

1. By his holy
2. and glorious wounds,
3. may Christ the Lord
4. guard us
5. and protect us. Amen.

	1	
4	2	5
	3	

Where, because of difficulties that may occur, a fire is not lit, the blessing of fire is adapted to the circumstances. When the people are gathered in the church as on other occasions, the Priest comes to the door of the church, along with the ministers carrying the paschal candle. The people, insofar as it is possible, turn to face the Priest.

The greeting and address take place as above, p. 331; then the fire is blessed and the candle is prepared, as above, pp. 332-333.

The Priest lights the paschal candle from the new fire, saying:

May the light of Christ rising in glory
dispel the darkness of our hearts and minds.

PROCESSION

When the candle has been lit, one of the ministers takes burning coals from the fire and places them in the thuri-

ble, and the Priest puts incense into it in the usual way. The Deacon or, if there is no Deacon, another suitable minister takes the paschal candle and a procession forms. The thurifer with the smoking thurible precedes the Deacon or other minister who carries the paschal candle. After them follows the Priest with the ministers and the people, all holding in their hands unlit candles.

At the door of the church the Deacon, standing and raising up the candle, sings:

The Light of Christ.
Thanks be to God.

And all reply:

The Priest lights his candle from the flame of the paschal candle.

Then the Deacon moves forward to the middle of the church and, standing and raising up the candle, sings a second time:

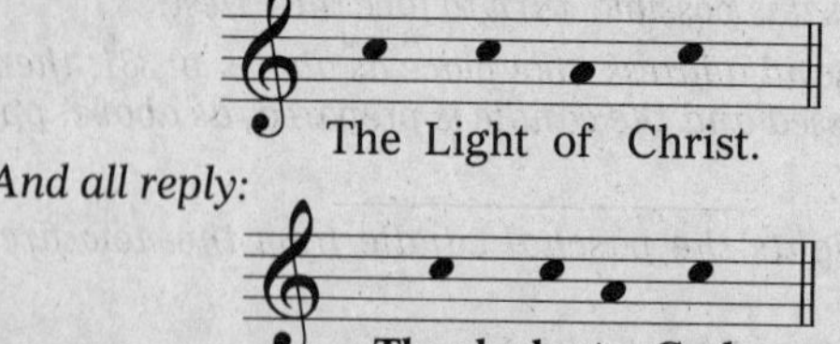
The Light of Christ.
Thanks be to God.

And all reply:

All light their candles from the flame of the paschal candle and continue in procession.

When the Deacon arrives before the altar, he stands facing the people, raises up the candle and sings a third time:

The Light of Christ.
And all reply:
Thanks be to God.

And lights are lit throughout the church, except for the altar candles.

THE EASTER PROCLAMATION (EXSULTET)

Arriving at the altar, the Priest goes to his chair, gives his candle to a minister, puts incense into the thurible and blesses the incense as at the Gospel at Mass. The Deacon goes to the Priest and saying, Your blessing, Father, *asks for and receives a blessing from the Priest, who says in a low voice:*

May the Lord be in your heart and on your lips,
that you may proclaim his paschal praise worthily and well,
in the name of the Father and of the Son, ✠ and of the Holy Spirit.

The Deacon replies: Amen. ↓

This blessing is omitted if the Proclamation is made by someone who is not a Deacon.

The Deacon, after incensing the book and the candle, proclaims the Easter Proclamation (Exsultet) at the ambo or at a lectern, with all standing and holding lighted candles in their hands.

The Easter Proclamation may be made, in the absence of a Deacon, by the Priest himself or by another concelebrating Priest. If, however, because of necessity, a lay cantor sings the Proclamation, the words Therefore, dearest friends *up to the end of the invitation are omitted, along with the greeting* The Lord be with you.

[When the Shorter Form is used, omit the italicized parts.]

Exult, let them exult, the hosts of heaven,
exult, let Angel ministers of God exult,
let the trumpet of salvation
sound aloud our mighty King's triumph!
Be glad, let earth be glad, as glory floods her,
ablaze with light from her eternal King,
let all corners of the earth be glad,
knowing an end to gloom and darkness.
Rejoice, let Mother Church also rejoice,
arrayed with the lightning of his glory,
let this holy building shake with joy,
filled with the mighty voices of the peoples.
(Therefore, dearest friends,
standing in the awesome glory of this holy light,
invoke with me, I ask you,
the mercy of God almighty,
that he, who has been pleased to number me,
though unworthy, among the Levites,
may pour into me his light unshadowed,
that I may sing this candle's perfect praises).

(℣. The Lord be with you. ℟. **And with your spirit.)**
℣. Lift up your hearts. ℟. **We lift them up to the Lord.**
℣. Let us give thanks to the Lord our God. ℟. **It is right and just.**

It is truly right and just,
with ardent love of mind and heart

and with devoted service of our voice,
to acclaim our God invisible, the almighty Father,
and Jesus Christ, our Lord, his Son, his Only Begotten.

Who for our sake paid Adam's debt to the eternal Father,
and, pouring out his own dear Blood,
wiped clean the record of our ancient sinfulness.

These, then, are the feasts of Passover,
in which is slain the Lamb, the one true Lamb,
whose Blood anoints the doorposts of believers.

This is the night,
when once you led our forebears, Israel's children,
from slavery in Egypt
and made them pass dry-shod through the Red Sea.

This is the night
that with a pillar of fire
banished the darkness of sin.

This is the night
that even now, throughout the world,
sets Christian believers apart from worldly vices
and from the gloom of sin,
leading them to grace
and joining them to his holy ones.

This is the night,
when Christ broke the prison-bars of death
and rose victorious from the underworld.

Our birth would have been no gain,
had we not been redeemed.
O wonder of your humble care for us!

O love, O charity beyond all telling,
to ransom a slave you gave away your Son!

O truly necessary sin of Adam,
destroyed completely by the Death of Christ!

O happy fault
that earned so great, so glorious a Redeemer!

O truly blessed night,
worthy alone to know the time and hour
when Christ rose from the underworld!

This is the night
of which it is written:
The night shall be as bright as day,
dazzling is the night for me,
and full of gladness.

The sanctifying power of this night
dispels wickedness, washes faults away,
restores innocence to the fallen, and joy to mourners,
drives out hatred, fosters concord, and brings down the mighty.

On this, your night of grace, O holy Father,
accept this candle, a solemn offering,
the work of bees and of your servants' hands,
an evening sacrifice of praise,
this gift from your most holy Church.

But now we know the praises of this pillar,
which glowing fire ignites for God's honour,
a fire into many flames divided,
yet never dimmed by sharing of its light,
for it is fed by melting wax,
drawn out by mother bees
to build a torch so precious.

O truly blessed night,
when things of heaven are wed to those of earth,
and divine to the human.

Shorter Form only:

On this, your night of grace, O holy Father,
accept this candle, a solemn offering,
the work of bees and of your servants' hands,
an evening sacrifice of praise,
this gift from your most holy Church.

Therefore, O Lord,
we pray you that this candle,
hallowed to the honour of your name,
may persevere undimmed,
to overcome the darkness of this night.
Receive it as a pleasing fragrance,
and let it mingle with the lights of heaven.
May this flame be found still burning
by the Morning Star:
the one Morning Star who never sets,
Christ your Son,
who, coming back from death's domain,
has shed his peaceful light on humanity,
and lives and reigns for ever and ever.

℟. A - men.

SECOND PART:

THE LITURGY OF THE WORD

In this Vigil, the mother of all Vigils, nine readings are provided, namely seven from the Old Testament and two from the New (the Epistle and Gospel), all of which should be read whenever this can be done, so that the character of the Vigil, which demands an extended period of time, may be preserved.

Nevertheless, where more serious pastoral circumstances demand it, the number of readings from the Old Testament may be reduced, always bearing in mind that the reading of the Word of God is a fundamental part of this Easter Vigil. At least three readings should be read from the Old Testament, both from the Law and from the Prophets, and their respective Responsorial Psalms should be sung. Never, moreover, should the reading of chapter 14 of Exodus with its canticle be omitted.

After setting aside their candles, all sit. Before the readings begin, the Priest instructs the people in these or similar words:

Dear brethren (brothers and sisters),
now that we have begun our solemn Vigil,
let us listen with quiet hearts to the Word of God.
Let us meditate on how God in times past saved his people
and in these, the last days, has sent us his Son as our Redeemer.
Let us pray that our God may complete this paschal work of salvation
by the fullness of redemption.

Then the readings follow. A reader goes to the ambo and proclaims the reading. Afterwards a psalmist or a cantor sings or says the Psalm with the people making the response. Then all rise, the Priest says, Let us pray *and, after all have prayed for a while in silence, he says the prayer corresponding to the reading. In place of the Responsorial Psalm a period of sacred silence may be observed, in which case the pause after* Let us pray *is omitted.*

FIRST READING Gen. 1.1—2.2 or 1.1, 26-31a

God created the world and all that is in it, and saw that it was good. This reading from the first book of the Bible shows that God made and loves all that exists.

[If the "Shorter Form" is used, the indented text in brackets is omitted.]

A reading from the book of Genesis.

IN the beginning when God created the heavens and the earth,

[the earth was a formless void and darkness covered the face of the deep, while the spirit of God swept over the face of the waters. Then God said, "Let there be light"; and there was light. And God saw that the light was good; and God separated the light from the darkness. God called the light "Day," and the darkness he called "Night." And there was evening and there was morning, the first day.

And God said, "Let there be a dome in the midst of the waters, and let it separate the waters from the waters." So God made the dome and separated the waters that were under the dome from the waters that were above the dome. And it was so. God called the dome "Sky." And there was evening and there was morning, the second day.

And God said, "Let the waters under the sky be gathered together into one place, and let the dry land appear." And it was so. God called the dry land "Earth," and the waters that were gathered together he called "Seas." And God saw that it was good.

Then God said, "Let the earth put forth vegetation: plants yielding seed, and fruit trees of every kind on earth that bear fruit with the seed in it." And it was so. The earth brought forth vegetation: plants yielding seed of every kind, and trees of every kind bearing fruit with the seed in it. And God saw that it was good. And there was evening and there was morning, the third day.

And God said, "Let there be lights in the dome of the sky to separate the day from the night; and let them be for signs and for seasons and for days and years, and let them be lights in the dome of the sky to give light upon the earth." And it was so.

God made the two great lights—the greater light to rule the day and the lesser light to rule the night—and the stars. God set them in the dome of the sky to give light upon the earth, to rule over the day and over the night, and to separate the light from the darkness. And God saw that it was good. And there was evening and there was morning, the fourth day.

And God said, "Let the waters bring forth swarms of living creatures, and let birds fly above the earth across the dome of the sky." So God created the great sea monsters and every living creature that moves, of every kind, with which the waters swarm, and every winged bird of every kind. And God saw that it was good. God blessed them, saying, "Be fruitful and multiply and fill the waters in the seas, and let birds multiply on the earth." And there was evening and there was morning, the fifth day.

And God said, "Let the earth bring forth living creatures of every kind: cattle and creeping things and wild animals of the earth of every kind." And it was so. God made the wild animals of the earth of every kind, and the cattle of every kind, and everything that creeps upon the ground of every kind. And God saw that it was good.]

[Then] God said, "Let us make man in our image, according to our likeness; and let them have dominion over the fish of the sea, and over the birds of the air, and over the cattle, and over all the wild animals of the earth, and over every creeping thing that creeps upon the earth."

So God created man in his image,
in the image of God he created him;
male and female he created them.

God blessed them, and God said to them, "Be fruitful and multiply, and fill the earth and subdue it; and have dominion over the fish of the sea and over the birds of the air and over every living thing that moves upon the earth." God said, "See, I have given you every plant yielding seed that is upon the face of all the earth, and every tree with seed in its fruit; you shall have them for food. And to every beast of the earth, and to every bird of the air, and to everything that creeps on the earth, everything that has the breath of life, I have given every green plant for food." And it was so. God saw everything that he had made, and indeed, it was very good. And there was evening and there was morning, the sixth day.

[Thus the heavens and the earth were finished, and all their multitude. And on the seventh day God finished the work that he had done, and he rested on the seventh day from all the work that he had done.]

The word of the Lord. ℟. **Thanks be to God.** ↓

RESPONSORIAL PSALM Ps. 104

Geoffrey Angeles

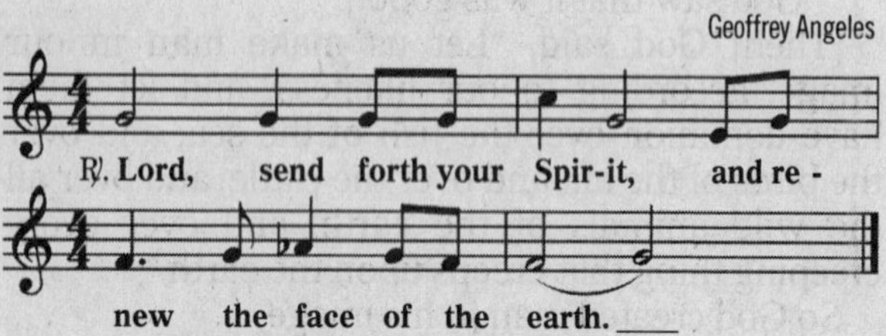
℟. Lord, send forth your Spir-it, and re -
new the face of the earth.

Bless the Lord, O my soul.
O Lord my God, you are very great.
You are clothed with honour and majesty,
wrapped in light as with a garment.—℟.

You set the earth on its foundations,
so that it shall never be shaken.
You cover it with the deep as with a garment;
the waters stood above the mountains.—℟.

You make springs gush forth in the valleys;
they flow between the hills.
By the streams the birds of the air have their habitation;
they sing among the branches.—℟.

From your lofty abode you water the mountains;
the earth is satisfied with the fruit of your work.
You cause the grass to grow for the cattle,
and plants for people to use, to bring forth food
from the earth.—℟.

O Lord, how manifold are your works!
In wisdom you have made them all;
the earth is full of your creatures.
Bless the Lord, O my soul.—℟. ↓

OR

RESPONSORIAL PSALM Ps. 33

Leo Marchildon

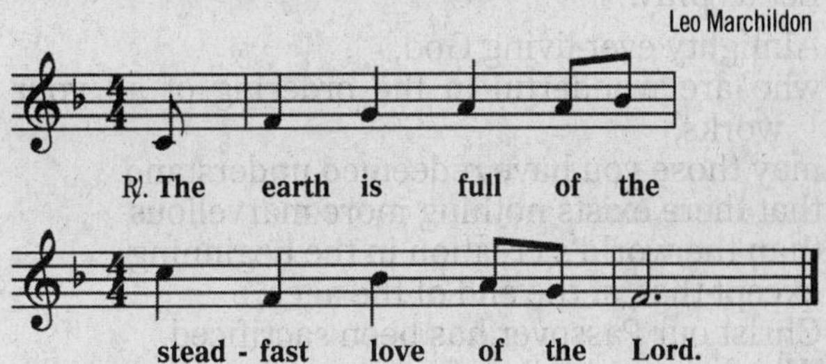
℟. The earth is full of the
stead - fast love of the Lord.

The word of the Lord is upright,
and all his work is done in faithfulness.
He loves righteousness and justice;
the earth is full of the steadfast love of the Lord.
—℟.

By the word of the Lord the heavens were made,
and all their host by the breath of his mouth.
He gathered the waters of the sea as in a bottle;
he put the deeps in storehouses.—℟.

Blessed is the nation whose God is the Lord,
the people whom he has chosen as his heritage.
The Lord looks down from heaven;
he sees all human beings.
℟. **The earth is full of the steadfast love of the Lord.**

Our soul waits for the Lord;
he is our help and shield.
Let your steadfast love, O Lord, be upon us,
even as we hope in you.—℟. ↓

PRAYER

Let us pray.

Almighty ever-living God,
who are wonderful in the ordering of all your works,
may those you have redeemed understand
that there exists nothing more marvellous
than the world's creation in the beginning
except that, at the end of the ages,
Christ our Passover has been sacrificed.
Who lives and reigns for ever and ever.
℟. **Amen.** ↓

OR

PRAYER (On the creation of man)

O God, who wonderfully created human nature
and still more wonderfully redeemed it,
grant us, we pray,
to set our minds against the enticements of sin,
that we may merit to attain eternal joys.

Through Christ our Lord.
℟. **Amen.** ↓

SECOND READING Gen. 22.1-18 or 22.1-2, 9-13, 15-18

Abraham is obedient to the will of God. Because God asks him, without hesitation he prepares to sacrifice his son, Isaac. In the new order, God sends the only Son to redeem us by his death on the cross.

[If the "Shorter Form" is used, the indented text in brackets is omitted.]

A reading from the book of Genesis.

GOD tested Abraham. He said to him, "Abraham!" And Abraham said, "Here I am." God said, "Take your son, your only son Isaac, whom you love, and go to the land of Moriah, and offer him there as a burnt offering on one of the mountains that I shall show you."

[So Abraham rose early in the morning, saddled his donkey, and took two of his young men with him, and his son Isaac; he cut the wood for the burnt offering, and set out and went to the place in the distance that God had shown him.

On the third day Abraham looked up and saw the place far away. Then Abraham said to his young men, "Stay here with the donkey; the boy and I will go over there; we will worship, and then we will come back to you." Abraham took the wood of the burnt offering and laid it on his son Isaac, and he himself carried the fire and the knife. So the two of them walked on together.

Isaac said to his father Abraham, "Father!" And Abraham said, "Here I am, my son." Isaac said, "The fire and the wood are here, but where is the lamb for a burnt offering?" Abraham said, "God himself will provide the lamb for a burnt offering, my son." So the two of them walked on together.]

When Abraham and Isaac came to the place that God had shown him, Abraham built an altar there and laid the wood in order. He bound his son Isaac, and laid him on the altar, on top of the wood. Then Abraham reached out his hand and took the knife to kill his son.

But the Angel of the Lord called to him from heaven, and said, "Abraham, Abraham!" And he said, "Here I am." The Angel said, "Do not lay your hand on the boy or do anything to him; for now I know that you fear God, since you have not withheld your son, your only son, from me." And Abraham looked up and saw a ram, caught in a thicket by its horns. Abraham went and took the ram and offered it up as a burnt offering instead of his son.

[So Abraham called that place "The Lord will provide"; as it is said to this day, "On the mount of the Lord it shall be provided."]

The Angel of the Lord called to Abraham a second time from heaven, and said, "By myself I have sworn, says the Lord: Because you have done this, and have not withheld your son, your only son, I will indeed bless you, and I will make your offspring as numerous as the stars of heaven, and as the sand that is on the seashore. And your offspring shall possess the gate of their enemies, and by your offspring shall all the nations of the earth gain blessing for themselves, because you have obeyed my voice."—The word of the Lord. ℟. **Thanks be to God.** ↓

RESPONSORIAL PSALM Ps. 16

David McIsaac

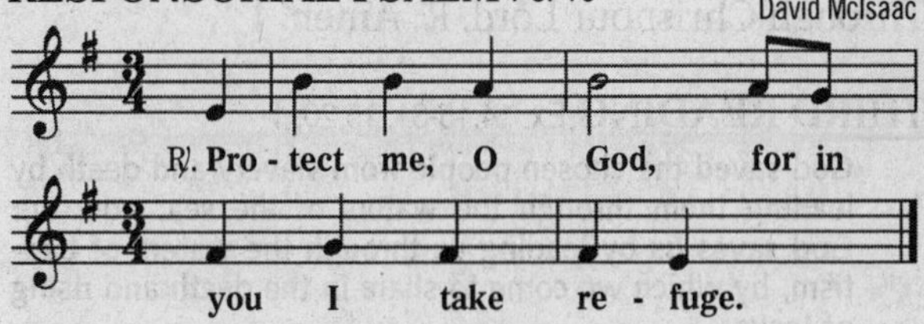
℟. Pro - tect me, O God, for in
you I take re - fuge.

The Lord is my chosen portion and my cup;
you hold my lot.
I keep the Lord always before me;
because he is at my right hand, I shall not be moved.—℟.

Therefore my heart is glad, and my soul rejoices;
my body also rests secure.
For you do not give me up to Sheol,
or let your faithful one see the Pit.—℟.

You show me the path of life.
In your presence there is fullness of joy;
in your right hand are pleasures
forevermore.—℟. ↓

PRAYER

Let us pray.

O God, supreme Father of the faithful,
who increase the children of your promise
by pouring out the grace of adoption

throughout the whole world
and who through the Paschal Mystery
make your servant Abraham father of nations,
as once you swore,
grant, we pray,
that your peoples may enter worthily
into the grace to which you call them.
Through Christ our Lord. ℟. **Amen.** ↓

THIRD READING Ex. 14.15-31; 15.20, 1

God saved the chosen people from slavery and death by leading them through the waters of the sea; now our God saves us by leading us through the waters of baptism, by which we come to share in the death and rising of Jesus.

A reading from the book of Exodus.

THE Lord said to Moses, "Why do you cry out to me? Tell the children of Israel to go forward. But you, lift up your staff, and stretch out your hand over the sea and divide it, that the children of Israel may go into the sea on dry ground. Then I will harden the hearts of the Egyptians so that they will go in after them; and so I will gain glory for myself over Pharaoh and all his army, his chariots, and his chariot drivers. And the Egyptians shall know that I am the Lord, when I have gained glory for myself over Pharaoh, his chariots, and his chariot drivers."

The Angel of God who was going before the Israelite army moved and went behind them; and the pillar of cloud moved from in front of them and took its place behind them. It came between the army of Egypt and the army of Israel. And so the cloud was there with the darkness, and it lit up the night; one did not come near the other all night.

Then Moses stretched out his hand over the sea. The Lord drove the sea back by a strong east wind all night, and turned the sea into dry land; and the waters were divided. The children of Israel went into the sea on dry ground, the waters forming a wall for them on their right and on their left.

The Egyptians pursued, and went into the sea after them, all of Pharaoh's horses, chariots, and chariot drivers. At the morning watch, the Lord in the pillar of fire and cloud looked down upon the Egyptian army, and threw the Egyptian army into panic. He clogged their chariot wheels so that they turned with difficulty. The Egyptians said, "Let us flee from the children of Israel, for the Lord is fighting for them against Egypt."

Then the Lord said to Moses, "Stretch out your hand over the sea, so that the water may come back upon the Egyptians, upon their chariots and chariot drivers." So Moses stretched out his hand over the sea, and at dawn the sea returned to its normal depth. As the Egyptians fled before it, the Lord tossed the Egyptians into the sea. The waters returned and covered the chariots and the chariot drivers, the entire army of Pharaoh that had followed them into the sea; not one of them remained.

But the children of Israel walked on dry ground through the sea, the waters forming a wall for them on their right and on their left. Thus the Lord saved Israel that day from the Egyptians; and

Israel saw the Egyptians dead on the seashore. Israel saw the great work that the Lord did against the Egyptians. So the people feared the Lord and believed in the Lord and in his servant Moses.

The Prophet Miriam, Aaron's sister, took a tambourine in her hand; and all the women went out after her with tambourines and with dancing. Moses and the children of Israel sang this song to the Lord: ↓

RESPONSORIAL PSALM Ex. 15

Geoffrey Angeles

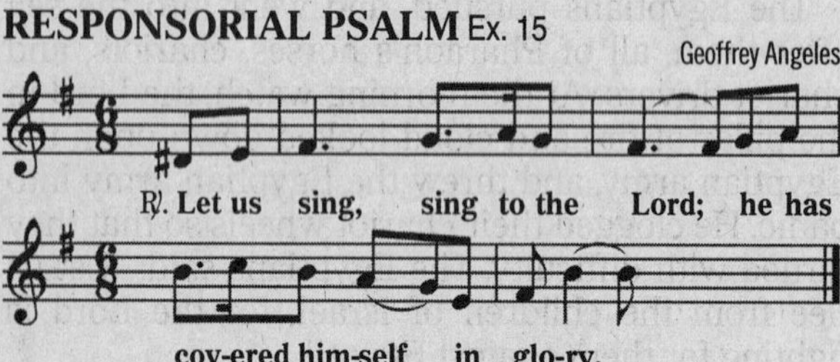
℟. Let us sing, sing to the Lord; he has
cov-ered him-self in glo-ry.

I will sing to the Lord, for he has triumphed gloriously;
horse and rider he has thrown into the sea.
The Lord is my strength and my might,
and he has become my salvation;
this is my God, and I will praise him,
my father's God, and I will exalt him.—℟.

The Lord is a warrior;
the Lord is his name.
Pharaoh's chariots and his army he cast into the sea;
his picked officers were sunk in the Red Sea.
The floods covered them;
they went down into the depths like a stone.—℟.

Your right hand, O Lord, glorious in power;
your right hand, O Lord, shattered the enemy.
In the greatness of your majesty
you overthrew your adversaries;
you sent out your fury,
it consumed them like stubble.—℟.

You brought your people in
and planted them
on the mountain of your own possession,
the place, O Lord, that you made your abode,
the sanctuary, O Lord, that your hands have established.
The Lord will reign forever and ever.—℟. ↓

PRAYER

Let us pray.

O God, whose ancient wonders
remain undimmed in splendour even in our day,
for what you once bestowed on a single people,
freeing them from Pharaoh's persecution
by the power of your right hand,
now you bring about as the salvation of the nations
through the waters of rebirth,
grant, we pray, that the whole world
may become children of Abraham
and inherit the dignity of Israel's birthright.
Through Christ our Lord.
℟. **Amen.** ↓

OR

PRAYER

O God, who by the light of the New Testament
have unlocked the meaning
of wonders worked in former times,
so that the Red Sea prefigures the sacred font
and the nation delivered from slavery
foreshadows the Christian people,
grant, we pray, that all nations,
obtaining the privilege of Israel by merit of faith,
may be reborn by partaking of your Spirit.
Through Christ our Lord.
℟. **Amen.** ↓

FOURTH READING Isa. 54.5-14

For a time, God hid from the chosen people, but God's love for this people is everlasting. God takes pity on them and promises them prosperity.

A reading from the book of the Prophet Isaiah.

THUS says the Lord, the God of hosts.
Your Maker is your husband,
the Lord of hosts is his name;
the Holy One of Israel is your Redeemer,
the God of the whole earth he is called.
For the Lord has called you
like a wife forsaken and grieved in spirit,
like the wife of a man's youth when she is cast off,
says your God.

For a brief moment I abandoned you,
but with great compassion I will gather you.

In overflowing wrath for a moment
I hid my face from you,
but with everlasting love I will have compassion on you,
says the Lord, your Redeemer.

This is like the days of Noah to me:
Just as I swore that the waters of Noah
would never again go over the earth,
so I have sworn that I will not be angry with you
and will not rebuke you.
For the mountains may depart
and the hills be removed,
but my steadfast love shall not depart from you,
and my covenant of peace shall not be removed,
says the Lord, who has compassion on you.

O afflicted one, storm-tossed, and not comforted,
I am about to set your stones in antimony,
and lay your foundations with sapphires.
I will make your pinnacles of rubies,
your gates of jewels,
and all your walls of precious stones.

All your children shall be taught by the Lord,
and great shall be the prosperity of your children.
In righteousness you shall be established;
you shall be far from oppression, for you shall not fear;
and from terror, for it shall not come near you.

The word of the Lord. ℟. **Thanks be to God.** ↓

RESPONSORIAL PSALM Ps. 30

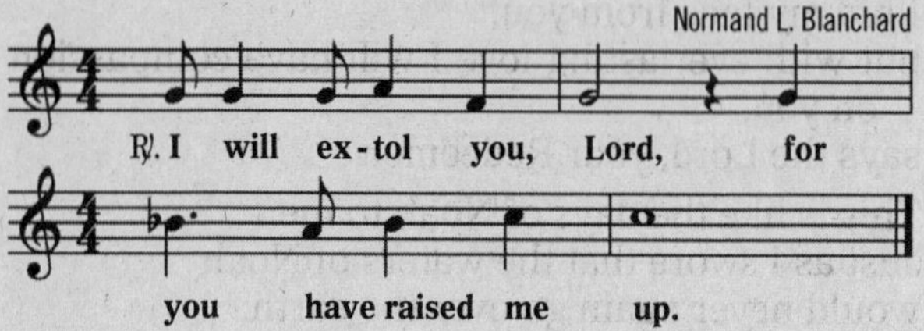
Normand L. Blanchard
℟. I will ex-tol you, Lord, for
you have raised me up.

I will extol you, O Lord, for you have drawn me up,
and did not let my foes rejoice over me.
O Lord, you brought up my soul from Sheol,
restored me to life from among those gone down to the Pit.—℟.

Sing praises to the Lord, O you his faithful ones,
and give thanks to his holy name.
For his anger is but for a moment;
his favour is for a lifetime.
Weeping may linger for the night,
but joy comes with the morning.—℟.

Hear, O Lord, and be gracious to me!
O Lord, be my helper!
You have turned my mourning into dancing.
O Lord my God, I will give thanks to you forever. —℟. ↓

PRAYER

Let us pray.

Almighty ever-living God,
surpass, for the honour of your name,
what you pledged to the Patriarchs by reason of their faith,

and through sacred adoption increase the children of your promise,
so that what the Saints of old never doubted would come to pass
your Church may now see in great part fulfilled.
Through Christ our Lord. ℟. **Amen.** ↓

Alternatively, other prayers may be used from among those which follow the readings that have been omitted.

FIFTH READING Isa. 55.1-11

God is a loving Father, calling all people to come back. Our God promises an everlasting covenant with them. God is merciful, generous, and forgiving.

A reading from the book of the Prophet Isaiah.

THUS says the Lord:
"Everyone who thirsts,
come to the waters;
and you that have no money,
come, buy and eat!
Come, buy wine and milk
without money and without price.
Why do you spend your money for that which is not bread,
and your labour for that which does not satisfy?
Listen carefully to me, and eat what is good,
and delight yourselves in rich food.
Incline your ear, and come to me;
listen, so that you may live.
I will make with you an everlasting covenant,
my steadfast, sure love for David.
See, I made him a witness to the peoples,
a leader and commander for the peoples.

See, you shall call nations that you do not know,
and nations that do not know you shall run to you,
because of the Lord your God, the Holy One of Israel,
for he has glorified you.

Seek the Lord while he may be found,
call upon him while he is near;
let the wicked person forsake their way,
and the unrighteous person their thoughts;
let that person return to the Lord that he may have mercy on them,
and to our God, for he will abundantly pardon.

For my thoughts are not your thoughts,
nor are your ways my ways, says the Lord.
For as the heavens are higher than the earth,
so are my ways higher than your ways
and my thoughts than your thoughts.

For as the rain and the snow come down from heaven,
and do not return there until they have watered the earth,
making it bring forth and sprout,
giving seed to the sower and bread to the one who eats,
so shall my word be that goes out from my mouth;
it shall not return to me empty,
but it shall accomplish that which I purpose,
and succeed in the thing for which I sent it."

The word of the Lord.

℟. **Thanks be to God.** ↓

RESPONSORIAL PSALM Isa. 12

Normand L. Blanchard

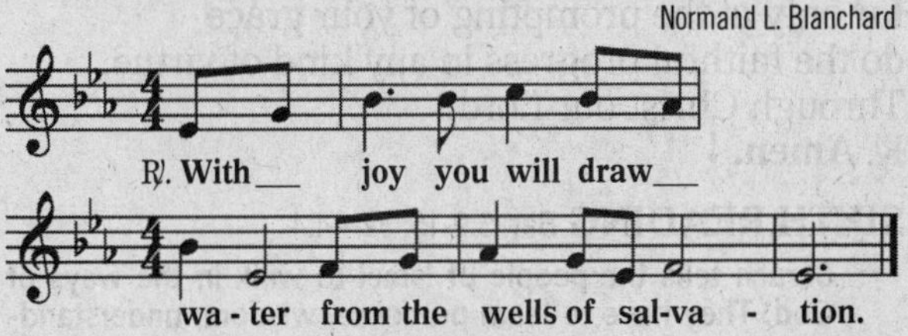
℟. With___ joy you will draw___
wa - ter from the wells of sal-va - tion.

Surely God is my salvation;
I will trust, and will not be afraid,
for the Lord God is my strength and my might;
he has become my salvation.
With joy you will draw water
from the wells of salvation.—℟.

Give thanks to the Lord,
call on his name;
make known his deeds among the nations;
proclaim that his name is exalted.—℟.

Sing praises to the Lord,
for he has done gloriously;
let this be known in all the earth.
Shout aloud and sing for joy, O royal Zion,
for great in your midst
is the Holy One of Israel.—℟. ↓

PRAYER

Let us pray.

Almighty ever-living God,
sole hope of the world,
who by the preaching of your Prophets
unveiled the mysteries of this present age,

graciously increase the longing of your people,
for only at the prompting of your grace
do the faithful progress in any kind of virtue.
Through Christ our Lord.
℟. **Amen.** ↓

SIXTH READING Bar. 3.9-15, 32—4.4

Baruch tells the people of Israel to walk in the ways of God. They have to learn prudence, wisdom, understanding. Then they will have peace forever.

A reading from the book of the Prophet Baruch.

HEAR the commandments of life, O Israel;
give ear, and learn wisdom!
Why is it, O Israel,
why is it that you are in the land of your enemies,
that you are growing old in a foreign country,
that you are defiled with the dead,
that you are counted among those in Hades?
You have forsaken the fountain of wisdom.
If you had walked in the way of God,
you would be living in peace forever.

Learn where there is wisdom,
where there is strength,
where there is understanding,
so that you may at the same time discern
where there is length of days, and life,
where there is light for the eyes, and peace.
Who has found her place?
And who has entered her storehouses?

But the one who knows all things knows her,
he found her by his understanding.
The one who prepared the earth for all time
filled it with four-footed creatures;

the one who sends forth the light, and it goes;
he called it, and it obeyed him, trembling;
the stars shone in their watches, and were glad;
he called them, and they said, "Here we are!"
They shone with gladness for him who made them.

This is our God;
no other can be compared to him.
He found the whole way to knowledge,
and gave her to his servant Jacob
and to Israel, whom he loved.
Afterward she appeared on earth
and lived with humanity.

She is the book of the commandments of God,
the law that endures forever.
All who hold her fast will live,
and those who forsake her will die.

Turn, O Jacob, and take her;
walk toward the shining of her light.
Do not give your glory to another,
or your advantages to an alien people.
Happy are we, O Israel,
for we know what is pleasing to God.

The word of the Lord. ℟. **Thanks be to God.** ↓

RESPONSORIAL PSALM Ps. 19

Frank Lynch

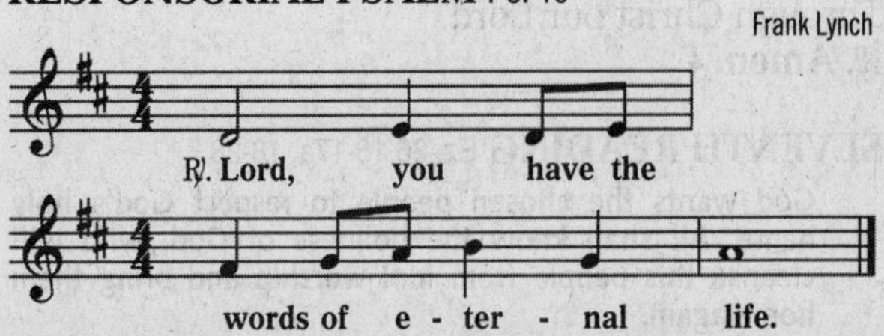
℟. Lord, you have the
words of e - ter - nal life.

The law of the Lord is perfect,
reviving the soul;
the decrees of the Lord are sure,
making wise the simple.
℟. **Lord, you have the words of eternal life.**

The precepts of the Lord are right,
rejoicing the heart;
the commandment of the Lord is clear,
enlightening the eyes.—℟.

The fear of the Lord is pure,
enduring forever;
the ordinances of the Lord are true
and righteous altogether.—℟.

More to be desired are they than gold,
even much fine gold;
sweeter also than honey,
and drippings of the honeycomb.—℟. ↓

PRAYER

Let us pray.

O God, who constantly increase your Church
by your call to the nations,
graciously grant
to those you wash clean in the waters of Baptism
the assurance of your unfailing protection.
Through Christ our Lord.
℟. **Amen.** ↓

SEVENTH READING Ez. 36.16-17a, 18-28

God wants the chosen people to respect God's holy name. All shall know the holiness of God, who will cleanse this people from idol worship and bring them home again.

A reading from the book of the Prophet Ezekiel.

THE word of the Lord came to me: Son of man, when the house of Israel lived on their own soil, they defiled it with their ways and their deeds; their conduct in my sight was unclean. So I poured out my wrath upon them for the blood that they had shed upon the land, and for the idols with which they had defiled it. I scattered them among the nations, and they were dispersed through the countries; in accordance with their conduct and their deeds I judged them.

But when they came to the nations, wherever they came, they profaned my holy name, in that it was said of them, "These are the people of the Lord, and yet they had to go out of his land."

But I had concern for my holy name, which the house of Israel had profaned among the nations to which they came. Therefore say to the house of Israel, Thus says the Lord God: It is not for your sake, O house of Israel, that I am about to act, but for the sake of my holy name, which you have profaned among the nations to which you came.

I will sanctify my great name, which has been profaned among the nations, and which you have profaned among them; and the nations shall know that I am the Lord, says the Lord God, when through you I display my holiness before their eyes.

I will take you from the nations, and gather you from all the countries, and bring you into your own land.

I will sprinkle clean water upon you, and you shall be clean from all your uncleanness, and from all your idols I will cleanse you.

A new heart I will give you, and a new spirit I will put within you; and I will remove from your body the heart of stone and give you a heart of flesh. I will put my spirit within you, and make you follow my statutes and be careful to observe my ordinances. Then you shall live in the land that I gave to your ancestors; and you shall be my people, and I will be your God.—The word of the Lord. ℟. **Thanks be to God.** ↓

When Baptism is celebrated, the following Responsorial Psalm is used.

RESPONSORIAL PSALM Ps. 42

Michel Guimont

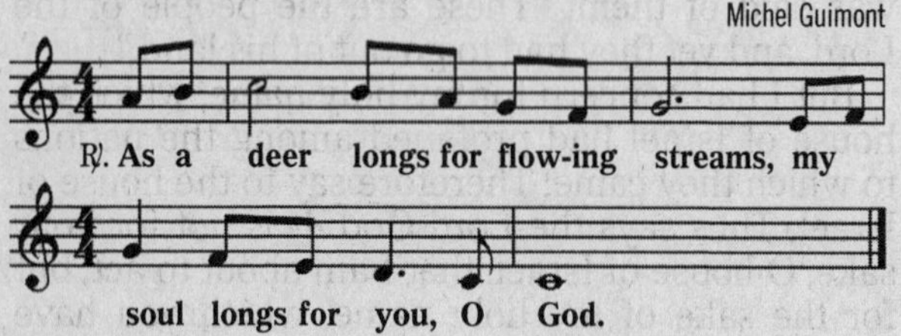
℟. As a deer longs for flow-ing streams, my
soul longs for you, O God.

My soul thirsts for God, for the living God.
When shall I come and behold the face of God?
—℟.

I went with the throng,
and led them in procession to the house of God,
with glad shouts and songs of thanksgiving,
a multitude keeping festival.—℟.

O send out your light and your truth;
let them lead me;
let them bring me to your holy mountain
and to your dwelling.—℟.

Then I will go to the altar of God,
to God my exceeding joy;
and I will praise you with the harp,
O God, my God.—℟. ↓

OR

When Baptism is not celebrated, the Responsorial Psalm after the Fifth Reading (Isa. 12) as above, p. 359, may be used; or the following:

RESPONSORIAL PSALM Ps. 51

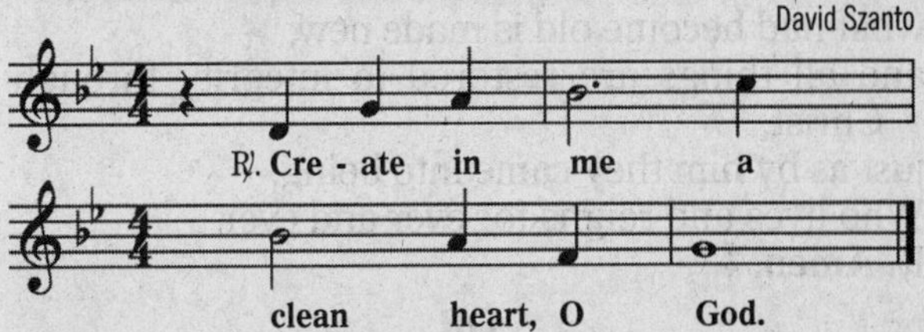
David Szanto
℟. Cre - ate in me a
clean heart, O God.

Create in me a clean heart, O God,
and put a new and right spirit within me.
Do not cast me away from your presence,
and do not take your holy spirit from me.—℟.

Restore to me the joy of your salvation,
and sustain in me a willing spirit.
Then I will teach transgressors your ways,
and sinners will return to you.—℟.

For you have no delight in sacrifice;
if I were to give a burnt offering, you would not be pleased.
The sacrifice acceptable to God
is a broken spirit;
a broken and contrite heart, O God,
you will not despise.—℟. ↓

PRAYER

Let us pray.

O God of unchanging power and eternal light,
look with favour on the wondrous mystery of the whole Church
and serenely accomplish the work of human salvation,
which you planned from all eternity;
may the whole world know and see
that what was cast down is raised up,
what had become old is made new,
and all things are restored to integrity through Christ,
just as by him they came into being.
Who lives and reigns for ever and ever.
℟. **Amen.** ↓

OR

PRAYER

O God, who by the pages of both Testaments
instruct and prepare us to celebrate the Paschal Mystery,
grant that we may comprehend your mercy,
so that the gifts we receive from you this night
may confirm our hope of the gifts to come.
Through Christ our Lord. ℟. **Amen.** ↓

After the last reading from the Old Testament with its Responsorial Psalm and its prayer, the altar candles are lit, and the Priest intones the hymn Gloria in excelsis Deo *(*Glory to God in the highest*), which is taken up by all, while bells are rung, according to local custom.*

When the hymn is concluded, the Priest says the Collect in the usual way.

COLLECT

Let us pray.

O God, who make this most sacred night radiant
with the glory of the Lord's Resurrection,
stir up in your Church a spirit of adoption,
so that, renewed in body and mind,
we may render you undivided service.
Through our Lord Jesus Christ, your Son,
who lives and reigns with you in the unity of the
Holy Spirit,
one God, for ever and ever. ℟. **Amen.** ↓

Then the reader proclaims the reading from the Apostle.

EPISTLE Rom. 6.3-11

In baptism we are united to Christ, and we begin to be formed in him. Christ has died; we will die. Christ is risen; we will rise.

A reading from the Letter of Saint Paul
to the Romans.

BROTHERS and sisters: Do you not know that all of us who have been baptized into Christ Jesus were baptized into his death? Therefore we have been buried with him by baptism into death, so that, just as Christ was raised from the dead by the glory of the Father, so we too might walk in newness of life. For if we have been united with him in a death like his, we will certainly be united with him in a resurrection like his.

We know that our old self was crucified with him so that the body of sin might be destroyed, and we might no longer be enslaved to sin. For whoever has died is freed from sin. But if we have died with Christ, we believe that we will also live with him.

We know that Christ, being raised from the dead, will never die again; death no longer has dominion over him. The death he died, he died to sin, once for all; but the life he lives, he lives to God. So you also must consider yourselves dead to sin and alive to God in Christ Jesus.—The word of the Lord. ℟. **Thanks be to God.** ↓

After the Epistle has been read, all rise, then the Priest solemnly intones the Alleluia *three times, raising his voice by a step each time, with all repeating it. If necessary, the psalmist intones the* Alleluia.

RESPONSORIAL PSALM – SOLEMN ALLELUIA Ps. 118

Geoffrey Angeles

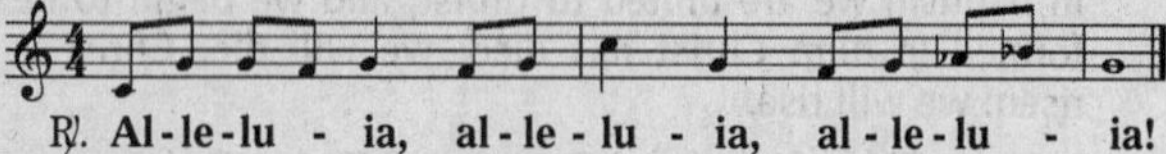
℟. Al - le - lu - ia, al - le - lu - ia, al - le - lu - ia!

O give thanks to the Lord, for he is good;
his steadfast love endures forever.
Let Israel say,
"His steadfast love endures forever."—℟.

"The right hand of the Lord is exalted;
the right hand of the Lord does valiantly."
I shall not die, but I shall live,
and recount the deeds of the Lord.—℟.

The stone that the builders rejected
has become the chief cornerstone.
This is the Lord's doing;
it is marvellous in our eyes.—℟. ↓

GOSPEL Mk. 16.1-8

On Easter morning, Mary Magdalene, Mary the mother of James, and Salome go to anoint the body of Jesus. An angel

announces to them the amazing news that Jesus of Nazareth is risen as he had said and is on his way to Galilee: Alleluia!

℣. The Lord be with you. ℟. **And with your spirit.**
✠ A reading from the holy Gospel according to Mark. ℟. **Glory to you, O Lord.**

WHEN the Sabbath was over, Mary Magdalene, and Mary the Mother of James, and Salome bought spices, so that they might go and anoint Jesus. And very early on the first day of the week, when the sun had risen, they went to the tomb. They had been saying to one another, "Who will roll away the stone for us from the entrance to the tomb?" When they looked up, they saw that the stone, which was very large, had already been rolled back.

As they entered the tomb, they saw a young man, dressed in a white robe, sitting on the right side; and they were alarmed. But he said to them, "Do not be alarmed; you are looking for Jesus of Nazareth, who was crucified. He has been raised; he is not here. Look, there is the place they laid him.

But go, tell his disciples and Peter that he is going ahead of you to Galilee; there you will see him, just as he told you." So they went out and fled from the tomb, for terror and amazement had seized them; and they said nothing to anyone, for they were afraid.—The Gospel of the Lord. ℟. **Praise to you, Lord Jesus Christ.**

After the Gospel, the Homily, even if brief, is not to be omitted.

Then the Liturgy of the Sacraments of Initiation begins.

THIRD PART:
THE LITURGY OF THE SACRAMENTS OF INITIATION

The following is adapted from the Rite of Christian Initiation of Adults.

Celebration of Baptism

PRESENTATION OF THE CANDIDATES

An assisting Deacon or other minister calls the candidates for Baptism forward and their godparents present them. The Invitation to Prayer and the Litany of the Saints follow.

INVITATION TO PRAYER

The Priest addresses the following or a similar invitation for the assembly to join in prayer for the candidates for Baptism.

Dearly beloved,
with one heart and one soul, let us by our prayers
come to the aid of these our brothers and sisters
in their blessed hope,
so that, as they approach the font of rebirth,
the almighty Father may bestow on them
all his merciful help.

LITANY OF THE SAINTS

The singing of the Litany of the Saints is led by cantors and may include, at the proper place, names of other Saints (for example, the Titular Saint of the church, the Patron Saints of the place or of those to be baptized) or petitions suitable to the occasion.

℣. Lord, have mer-cy. ℟. **Lord, have mer-cy.**
℣. Christ, have mer-cy. ℟. **Christ, have mer-cy.**
℣. Lord, have mer-cy. ℟. **Lord, have mer-cy.**
Holy Mary, Mother of God, [ ] ℟. **Pray for us.**

Saint Michael,*
Holy Angels of God,
Saint John the Baptist,
Saint Joseph,
Saint Peter and Saint Paul,
Saint Andrew,
Saint John,
Saint Mary Magdalene,
Saint Stephen,
Saint Ignatius of Antioch,
Saint Lawrence,
Saint Perpetua and Saint Felicity,
Saint Agnes,
Saint Gregory,
Saint Augustine,
Saint Athanasius,
Saint Basil,
Saint Martin,
Saint Benedict,
Saint Francis and Saint Dominic,
Saint Francis Xavier,

* *Repeat* Pray for us *after each invocation.*

Saint John Vianney,
Saint Catherine of Siena,
Saint Teresa of Jesus,
All holy men and women, Saints of God,

Lord, be mer-ci-ful, ℟. **Lord, de-liv-er us, we pray.**

From all evil,*
From every sin,
From everlasting death,
By your Incarnation,
By your Death and Resurrection,
By the outpouring of the Holy Spirit,

Be merciful to us sin-ners, ℟. **Lord, we ask you, hear our prayer.**

Bring these chosen ones to new birth through the grace of Baptism, **Lord, we ask you, hear our prayer.**

Jesus, Son of the living God, **Lord, we ask you, hear our prayer.**

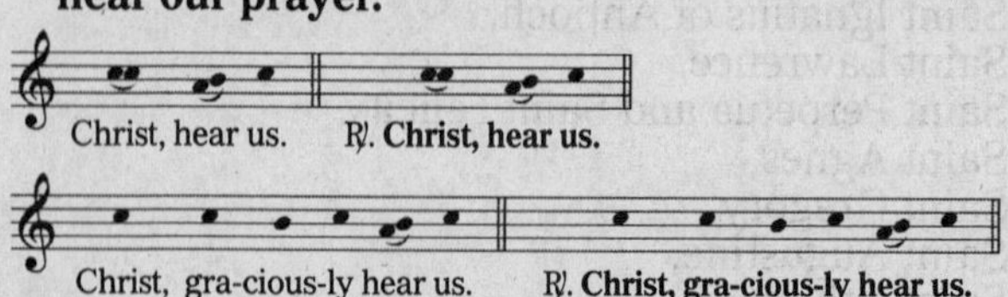
Christ, hear us. ℟. **Christ, hear us.**
Christ, gra-cious-ly hear us. ℟. **Christ, gra-cious-ly hear us.**

BLESSING OF BAPTISMAL WATER

The Priest then blesses the baptismal water, saying the following prayer with hands extended:

---

* *Repeat* Lord, deliver us, we pray *after each invocation.*

O God, who by invisible power
accomplish a wondrous effect
through sacramental signs
and who in many ways have prepared water, your creation,
to show forth the grace of Baptism;

O God, whose Spirit
in the first moments of the world's creation
hovered over the waters,
so that the very substance of water
would even then take to itself the power to sanctify;

O God, who by the outpouring of the flood
foreshadowed regeneration,
so that from the mystery of one and the same element of water
would come an end to vice and a beginning of virtue;

O God, who caused the children of Abraham
to pass dry-shod through the Red Sea,
so that the chosen people,
set free from slavery to Pharaoh,
would prefigure the people of the baptized;

O God, whose Son,
baptized by John in the waters of the Jordan,
was anointed with the Holy Spirit,
and, as he hung upon the Cross,
gave forth water from his side along with blood,
and after his Resurrection, commanded his disciples:
"Go forth, teach all nations, baptizing them

in the name of the Father and of the Son and of the Holy Spirit,"
look now, we pray, upon the face of your Church
and graciously unseal for her the fountain of Baptism.

May this water receive by the Holy Spirit
the grace of your Only Begotten Son,
so that human nature, created in your image
and washed clean through the Sacrament of Baptism
from all the squalor of the life of old,
may be found worthy to rise to the life of newborn children
through water and the Holy Spirit.

And, if appropriate, lowering the paschal candle into the water either once or three times, he continues:

May the power of the Holy Spirit,
O Lord, we pray,
come down through your Son
into the fullness of this font,

and, holding the candle in the water, he continues:

so that all who have been buried with Christ
by Baptism into death
may rise again to life with him.
Who lives and reigns with you in the unity of the Holy Spirit,
one God, for ever and ever.

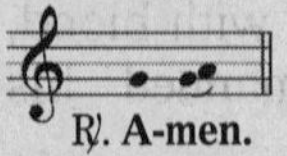
℟. A-men.

Then the candle is lifted out of the water, as the people acclaim:

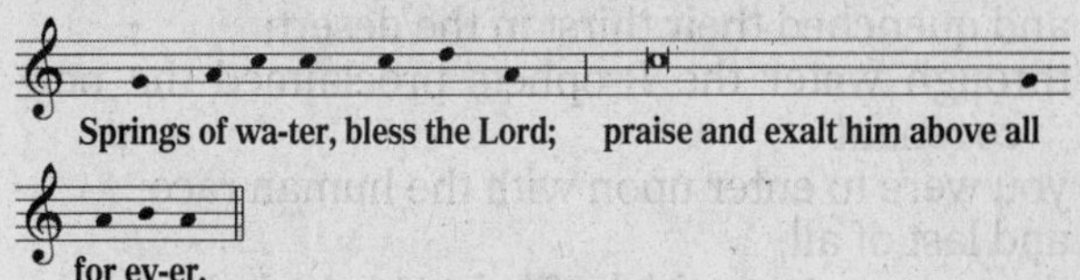
Springs of wa-ter, bless the Lord; praise and exalt him above all
for ev-er.

THE BLESSING OF WATER

If no one present is to be baptized and the font is not to be blessed, the Priest introduces the faithful to the blessing of water, saying:

Dear brothers and sisters,
let us humbly beseech the Lord our God
to bless this water he has created,
which will be sprinkled upon us
as a memorial of our Baptism.
May he graciously renew us,
that we may remain faithful to the Spirit
whom we have received.

And after a brief pause in silence, he proclaims the following prayer, with hands extended:

Lord our God,
in your mercy be present to your people
who keep vigil on this most sacred night,
and, for us who recall the wondrous work of our creation
and the still greater work of our redemption,
graciously bless this water.
For you created water to make the fields fruitful
and to refresh and cleanse our bodies.
You also made water the instrument of your mercy:
for through water you freed your people from slavery

and quenched their thirst in the desert;
through water the Prophets proclaimed the new covenant
you were to enter upon with the human race;
and last of all,
through water, which Christ made holy in the Jordan,
you have renewed our corrupted nature
in the bath of regeneration.

Therefore, may this water be for us
a memorial of the Baptism we have received,
and grant that we may share
in the gladness of our brothers and sisters,
who at Easter have received their Baptism.
Through Christ our Lord.
℟. **Amen.**

RENUNCIATION OF SIN AND PROFESSION OF FAITH

If there are baptismal candidates, the Priest, in a series of questions to which the candidates reply, **I do**, *asks the candidates to renounce sin and profess their faith.*

BAPTISM

The Priest baptizes each candidate either by immersion or by the pouring of water.

N., I baptize you in the name of the Father, and of the Son, and of the Holy Spirit.

EXPLANATORY RITES

The celebration of Baptism continues with the explanatory rites, after which the celebration of Confirmation normally follows.

ANOINTING AFTER BAPTISM

If the Confirmation of those baptized is separated from their Baptism, the Priest anoints them with chrism immediately after Baptism.

The God of power and Father of our Lord Jesus Christ
has freed you from sin
and brought you to new life
through water and the Holy Spirit.

He now anoints you with the chrism of salvation,
so that, united with his people,
you may remain for ever a member of Christ
who is Priest, Prophet, and King.

Newly baptized: **Amen.**

In silence each of the newly baptized is anointed with chrism on the crown of the head.

CLOTHING WITH A BAPTISMAL GARMENT

The garment used in this Rite may be white or of a colour that conforms to local custom. If circumstances suggest, this Rite may be omitted.

N. and *N.*, you have become a new creation
and have clothed yourselves in Christ.
Receive this baptismal garment
and bring it unstained to the judgment seat of our Lord Jesus Christ,
so that you may have everlasting life.

Newly baptized: **Amen.**

PRESENTATION OF A LIGHTED CANDLE

The Priest takes the Easter candle in his hands or touches it, saying:

Godparents, please come forward to give to the newly baptized the light of Christ.

A godparent of each of the newly baptized goes to the Priest, lights a candle from the Easter candle, then presents it to the newly baptized.

You have been enlightened by Christ.
Walk always as children of the light
and keep the flame of faith alive in your hearts.
When the Lord comes, may you go out to meet him
with all the saints in the heavenly kingdom.

Newly baptized: **Amen.**

The Renewal of Baptismal Promises

INVITATION

After the celebration of Baptism, the Priest addresses the community, in order to invite those present to the renewal of their baptismal promises; the candidates for reception into full communion join the rest of the community in this renunciation of sin and profession of faith. All stand and hold lighted candles.

The Priest addresses the faithful in these or similar words.

Dear brethren (brothers and sisters), through the Paschal Mystery
we have been buried with Christ in Baptism,
so that we may walk with him in newness of life.
And so, now that our Lenten observance is concluded,
let us renew the promises of Holy Baptism,
by which we once renounced Satan and his works
and promised to serve God in the holy Catholic Church.
And so I ask you:

A

Priest: Do you renounce Satan?

All: **I do.**

Priest: And all his works?

All: **I do.**

Priest: And all his empty show?

All: **I do.**

B

Priest: Do you renounce sin,
so as to live in the freedom of the children of God?

All: **I do.**

Priest: Do you renounce the lure of evil,
so that sin may have no mastery over you?

All: **I do.**

Priest: Do you renounce Satan,
the author and prince of sin?

All: **I do.**

PROFESSION OF FAITH

Then the Priest continues:

Priest: Do you believe in God,
the Father almighty,
Creator of heaven and earth?

All: **I do.**

Priest: Do you believe in Jesus Christ, his only Son, our Lord,
who was born of the Virgin Mary,
suffered death and was buried,
rose again from the dead
and is seated at the right hand of the Father?

All: **I do.**

Priest: Do you believe in the Holy Spirit,
the holy catholic Church,
the communion of saints,
the forgiveness of sins,
the resurrection of the body,
and life everlasting?

All: **I do.**

And the Priest concludes:

And may almighty God, the Father of our Lord Jesus Christ,
who has given us new birth by water and the Holy Spirit
and bestowed on us forgiveness of our sins,
keep us by his grace,
in Christ Jesus our Lord,
for eternal life.
All: **Amen.**

SPRINKLING WITH BAPTISMAL WATER

The Priest sprinkles all the people with the blessed baptismal water, while all sing the following song or any other that is baptismal in character.

ANTIPHON

**I saw water flowing from the Temple,
from its right-hand side, alleluia;
and all to whom this water came were saved
and shall say: Alleluia, alleluia.**

Celebration of Reception

INVITATION

If Baptism has been celebrated at the font, the Priest, the assisting ministers, and the newly baptized with their godparents proceed to the sanctuary. As they do so the assembly may sing a suitable song.

Then in the following or similar words the Priest invites the candidates for reception, along with their sponsors, to come into the sanctuary and before the community to make a profession of faith.

N. and *N.*, of your own free will you have asked to be received into the full communion of the Catholic Church. You have made your decision after careful thought under the guidance of the Holy Spirit. I now invite you to come forward with your sponsors and in the presence of this community to profess the Catholic faith. In this faith you will be one with us for the first time at the eucharistic table of the Lord Jesus, the sign of the Church's unity.

PROFESSION BY THE CANDIDATES

When the candidates for reception and their sponsors have taken their places in the sanctuary, the Priest asks the candidates to make the following profession of faith. The candidates say:

I believe and profess all that the holy Catholic Church believes, teaches, and proclaims to be revealed by God.

ACT OF RECEPTION

Then the candidates with their sponsors go individually to the Priest, who says to each candidate (laying his right hand on the head of any candidate who is not to receive Confirmation):

N., the Lord receives you into the Catholic Church.
His loving kindness has led you here,
so that in the unity of the Holy Spirit
you may have full communion with us
in the faith that you have professed in the presence of his family.

Celebration of Confirmation

INVITATION

The newly baptized with their godparents and, if they have not received the Sacrament of Confirmation, the newly received with their sponsors, stand before the Priest. He first speaks briefly to the newly baptized and the newly received in these or similar words.

My dear candidates for Confirmation, by your Baptism you have been born again in Christ and you have become members of Christ and of his priestly people. Now you are to share in the outpouring of the Holy Spirit among us, the Spirit sent by the Lord upon his apostles at Pentecost and given by them and their successors to the baptized.

The promised strength of the Holy Spirit, which you are to receive, will make you more like Christ and help you to be witnesses to his suffering, death, and resurrection. It will strengthen you to be active members of the Church and to build up the Body of Christ in faith and love.

My dear friends, let us pray to God our Father, that he will pour out the Holy Spirit on these candidates for Confirmation to strengthen them with his gifts and anoint them to be more like Christ, the Son of God.

All pray briefly in silence.

LAYING ON OF HANDS

The Priest holds his hands outstretched over the entire group of those to be confirmed and says the following prayer.

Almighty God, Father of our Lord Jesus Christ,
Who brought these your servants to new birth
by water and the Holy Spirit,
freeing them from sin:
send upon them, O Lord, the Holy Spirit, the Paraclete;
give them the spirit of wisdom and understanding,
the spirit of counsel and fortitude,
the spirit of knowledge and piety;
fill them with the spirit of the fear of the Lord.
Through Christ our Lord.
℟. **Amen.**

ANOINTING WITH CHRISM

Either or both godparents and sponsors place the right hand on the shoulder of the candidate; and a godparent or a sponsor of the candidate gives the candidate's name to the minister of the sacrament. During the conferral of the sacrament an appropriate song may be sung.

The minister of the sacrament dips his right thumb in the chrism and makes the Sign of the Cross on the forehead of the one to be confirmed as he says:

N., be sealed with the Gift of the Holy Spirit.
Newly confirmed: **Amen.**

Minister: Peace be with you.
Newly confirmed: **And with your spirit.**

After all have received the sacrament, the newly confirmed as well as the godparents and sponsors are led to their places in the assembly.

[Since the Profession of Faith is not said, the Universal Prayer (no. 16, p. 19) begins immediately and for the first time the neophytes take part in it.]

FOURTH PART:
THE LITURGY OF THE EUCHARIST

The Priest goes to the altar and begins the Liturgy of the Eucharist in the usual way.

It is desirable that the bread and wine be brought forward by the newly baptized or, if they are children, by their parents or godparents.

PRAYER OVER THE OFFERINGS

Accept, we ask, O Lord,
the prayers of your people
with the sacrificial offerings,
that what has begun in the paschal mysteries
may, by the working of your power,
bring us to the healing of eternity.
Through Christ our Lord.
℟. **Amen.**

→ No. 21, p. 22 (Pref. 21: on this night above all)

In the Eucharistic Prayer, a commemoration is made of the baptized and their godparents in accord with the formulas which are found in the Roman Missal and Roman Ritual for each of the Eucharistic Prayers.

COMMUNION ANTIPHON 1 Cor. 5:7-8

Christ our Passover has been sacrificed; therefore let us keep the feast with the unleavened bread of purity and truth, alleluia. ↓

Psalm 117 may appropriately be sung.

PRAYER AFTER COMMUNION

Pour out on us, O Lord, the Spirit of your love,
and in your kindness make those you have nourished
by this paschal Sacrament
one in mind and heart.
Through Christ our Lord. ℟. **Amen.** ↓

SOLEMN BLESSING

May almighty God bless you
through today's Easter Solemnity
and, in his compassion,
defend you from every assault of sin.
℟. **Amen.**

And may he, who restores you to eternal life
in the Resurrection of his Only Begotten,
endow you with the prize of immortality.
℟. **Amen.**

Now that the days of the Lord's Passion have drawn to a close,
may you who celebrate the gladness of the Paschal Feast
come with Christ's help, and exulting in spirit,
to those feasts that are celebrated in eternal joy.
℟. **Amen.**

And may the blessing of almighty God,
the Father, and the Son, ✠ and the Holy Spirit,

come down on you and remain with you for ever.
℟. **Amen.**

The final blessing formula from the Rite of Baptism of Adults or of Children may also be used, according to circumstances.

To dismiss the people the Deacon or, if there is no Deacon, the Priest himself sings or says:

Go forth, the Mass is ended, alleluia, alleluia.

OR

Go in peace, alleluia, alleluia.

℟. **Thanks be to God, al-le-lu-ia, al-le - lu - ia.**

This practice is observed throughout the Octave of Easter.

"I have risen, and I am with you still."

APRIL 1

THE RESURRECTION OF THE LORD: EASTER SUNDAY

ENTRANCE ANTIPHON Cf. Ps. 138.18, 5-6

I have risen, and I am with you still, alleluia. You have laid your hand upon me, alleluia. Too wonderful for me, this knowledge, alleluia, alleluia.

→ No. 2, p. 10

OR Lk. 24.34; cf. Rev. 1.6

The Lord is truly risen, alleluia. To him be glory and power for all the ages of eternity, alleluia, alleluia. → No. 2, p. 10

COLLECT

O God, who on this day,
through your Only Begotten Son,
have conquered death
and unlocked for us the path to eternity,
grant, we pray, that we who keep
the solemnity of the Lord's Resurrection

may, through the renewal brought by your Spirit,
rise up in the light of life.
Through our Lord Jesus Christ, your Son,
who lives and reigns with you in the unity of the
Holy Spirit,
one God, for ever and ever. ℟. **Amen.** ↓

FIRST READING Acts 10.34a, 37-43

In his sermon Peter sums up the good news, the Gospel. Salvation comes through Christ, the beloved Son of the Father, and the anointed of the Holy Spirit.

A reading from the Acts of the Apostles.

PETER began to speak: "You know the message that spread throughout Judea, beginning in Galilee after the baptism that John announced: how God anointed Jesus of Nazareth with the Holy Spirit and with power; how he went about doing good and healing all who were oppressed by the devil, for God was with him.

We are witnesses to all that he did both in Judea and in Jerusalem. They put him to death by hanging him on a tree; but God raised him on the third day and allowed him to appear, not to all the people but to us who were chosen by God as witnesses, and who ate and drank with him after he rose from the dead.

He commanded us to preach to the people and to testify that he is the one ordained by God as judge of the living and the dead. All the Prophets testify about him that everyone who believes in him receives forgiveness of sins through his name."—The word of the Lord. ℟. **Thanks be to God.** ↓

RESPONSONSORIAL PSALM Ps. 118

Michel Guimont
℟. This is the day the Lord__ has made;
let us re - joice and be glad.

Or: ℟. **Alleluia! Alleluia! Alleluia!**

O give thanks to the Lord, for he is good;
his steadfast love endures forever.
Let Israel say,
"His steadfast love endures forever."—℟.

"The right hand of the Lord is exalted;
the right hand of the Lord does valiantly."
I shall not die, but I shall live,
and recount the deeds of the Lord.—℟.

The stone that the builders rejected
has become the chief cornerstone.
This is the Lord's doing;
it is marvellous in our eyes.—℟. ↓

One of the following texts may be chosen as the Second Reading.

SECOND READING Col. 3.1-4

Look to the glory of Christ in which we share because our lives are hidden in him through baptism, and we are destined to share in his glory.

A reading from the Letter of Saint Paul
to the Colossians.

BROTHERS and sisters: If you have been raised with Christ, seek the things that are above, where Christ is, seated at the right hand of God. Set your minds on things that are above, not on things that are on earth, for you have died, and your life is hidden with Christ in God. When Christ who is your life is revealed, then you also will be revealed with him in glory.—The word of the Lord. ℟. **Thanks be to God.** ↓

OR

SECOND READING 1 Cor. 5.6b-8

Turn away from your old ways, from sin. Have a change of heart; be virtuous.

A reading from the first Letter of Saint Paul to the Corinthians.

DO you not know that a little yeast leavens the whole batch of dough? Clean out the old yeast so that you may be a new batch, as you really are unleavened. For our paschal lamb, Christ, has been sacrificed. Therefore, let us celebrate the festival, not with the old yeast, the yeast of malice and evil, but with the unleavened bread of sincerity and truth.—The word of the Lord. ℟. **Thanks be to God.** ↓

SEQUENCE *(Victimae paschali laudes)*

1. Christians, praise the paschal victim!
Offer thankful sacrifice!

2. Christ the Lamb has saved the sheep,
Christ the just one paid the price,
Reconciling sinners to the Father.

3. Death and life fought bitterly
For this wondrous victory;
The Lord of life who died reigns glorified!

4. "O Mary, come and say
what you saw at break of day."

5. "The empty tomb of my living Lord!
I saw Christ Jesus risen and adored!

6. "Bright angels testified,
Shroud and grave clothes side by side!

7. "Yes, Christ my hope rose gloriously.
He goes before you into Galilee."

8. Share the Good News, sing joyfully:
His death is victory!
Lord Jesus, Victor King, show us mercy. ↓

GOSPEL ACCLAMATION 1 Cor. 5.7-8

℣. Alleluia. ℟. **Alleluia.**

℣. Christ, our Paschal Lamb, has been sacrificed; let us feast with joy in the Lord.

℟. **Alleluia.** ↓

(FOR MORNING MASS)

GOSPEL Jn. 20.1-18 or 20.1-9

Let us ponder this mystery of Christ's rising, and like Christ's first followers be strengthened in our faith.

[If the "Shorter Form" is used, the indented text in brackets is omitted.]

℣. The Lord be with you. ℟. **And with your spirit.**

✠ A reading from the holy Gospel according to John. ℟. **Glory to you, O Lord.**

EARLY on the first day of the week, while it was still dark, Mary Magdalene came to the tomb and saw that the stone had been removed from the tomb. So she ran and went to Simon Peter and the other disciple, the one whom

Jesus loved, and said to them, "They have taken the Lord out of the tomb, and we do not know where they have laid him."

Then Peter and the other disciple set out and went toward the tomb. The two were running together, but the other disciple outran Peter and reached the tomb first. He bent down to look in and saw the linen wrappings lying there, but he did not go in.

Then Simon Peter came, following him, and went into the tomb. He saw the linen wrappings lying there, and the cloth that had been on Jesus' head, not lying with the linen wrappings but rolled up in a place by itself. Then the other disciple, who reached the tomb first, also went in, and he saw and believed; for as yet they did not understand the Scripture, that he must rise from the dead.

> [Then the disciples returned to their homes. But Mary Magdalene stood weeping outside the tomb. As she wept, she bent over to look into the tomb; and she saw two Angels in white, sitting where the body of Jesus had been lying, one at the head and the other at the feet. They said to her, "Woman, why are you weeping?" She said to them, "They have taken away my Lord, and I do not know where they have laid him."
>
> When she had said this, she turned around and saw Jesus standing there, but she did not know that it was Jesus. Jesus said to her, "Woman, why are you weeping? Whom are you looking for?" Supposing him to be the

gardener, she said to him, "Sir, if you have carried him away, tell me where you have laid him, and I will take him away."

Jesus said to her, "Mary!" She turned and said to him in Hebrew, "Rabbouni!" which means Teacher. Jesus said to her, "Do not hold on to me, because I have not yet ascended to the Father. But go to my brothers and say to them, 'I am ascending to my Father and your Father, to my God and your God.'"

Mary Magdalene went and announced to the disciples, "I have seen the Lord," and she told them that he had said these things to her.]

The Gospel of the Lord. ℟. **Praise to you, Lord Jesus Christ.** → No. 15, p. 18

In Easter Sunday Masses which are celebrated with a congregation, the rite of the renewal of baptismal promises may take place after the Homily, according to the text used at the Easter Vigil (p. 378). In that case the Creed is omitted.

OR

(The Gospel from the Easter Vigil noted below may be used.)

GOSPEL Mk. 16.1-8

See p. 369.

(FOR AN AFTERNOON OR EVENING MASS)

GOSPEL Lk. 24.13-35

Let us accept the testimony of these two witnesses that our hearts may burn with the fire of faith.

℣. The Lord be with you. ℟. **And with your spirit.**

✠ A reading from the holy Gospel according to Luke. ℟. **Glory to you, O Lord.**

ON the first day of the week, two of the disciples were going to a village called Emmaus, about eleven kilometres from Jerusalem, and talking with each other about all these things that had happened. While they were talking and discussing, Jesus himself came near and went with them, but their eyes were kept from recognizing him.

And he said to them, "What are you discussing with each other while you walk along?" They stood still, looking sad. Then one of them, whose name was Cleopas, answered him, "Are you the only stranger in Jerusalem who does not know the things that have taken place there in these days?"

He asked them, "What things?" They replied, "The things about Jesus of Nazareth, who was a Prophet mighty in deed and word before God and all the people, and how our chief priests and leaders handed him over to be condemned to death and crucified him. But we had hoped that he was the one to redeem Israel. Yes, and besides all this, it is now the third day since these things took place. Moreover, some women of our group astounded us. They were at the tomb early this morning, and when they did not find his body there, they came back and told us that they had indeed seen a vision of Angels who said that he was alive. Some of those who were with us went to the tomb and found it just as the women had said; but they did not see him."

Then he said to them, "Oh, how foolish you are, and how slow of heart to believe all that the Prophets have declared! Was it not necessary that the Christ should suffer these things and then enter into his glory?"

Then beginning with Moses and all the Prophets, he interpreted to them the things about himself in all the Scriptures. As they came near the village to which they were going, he walked ahead as if he were going on. But they urged him strongly, saying, "Stay with us, because it is almost evening and the day is now nearly over." So he went in to stay with them.

When he was at the table with them, he took bread, blessed and broke it, and gave it to them. Then their eyes were opened, and they recognized him; and he vanished from their sight.

They said to each other, "Were not our hearts burning within us while he was talking to us on the road, while he was opening the Scriptures to us?"

That same hour they got up and returned to Jerusalem; and they found the eleven and their companions gathered together. These were saying, "The Lord has risen indeed, and he has appeared to Simon!"

Then they told what had happened on the road, and how he had been made known to them in the breaking of the bread.—The Gospel of the Lord. ℟. **Praise to you, Lord Jesus Christ.**

→ No. 15, p. 18

However, in Easter Sunday Masses which are celebrated with a congregation, the rite of the renewal of baptismal promises may take place after the Homily, according to the text used at the Easter Vigil (p. 378). In that case the Creed is omitted.

PRAYER OVER THE OFFERINGS

Exultant with paschal gladness, O Lord,
we offer the sacrifice
by which your Church
is wondrously reborn and nourished.
Through Christ our Lord.
℟. **Amen.**

→ No. 21, p. 22 (Pref. 21: on this day above all)

When the Roman Canon is used, the proper forms of the Communicantes *(*In communion with those*) and* Hanc igitur *(*Therefore, Lord, we pray*) are said.*

COMMUNION ANTIPHON 1 Cor. 5.7-8

Christ our Passover has been sacrificed, alleluia; therefore let us keep the feast with the unleavened bread of purity and truth, alleluia, alleluia. ↓

PRAYER AFTER COMMUNION

Look upon your Church, O God,
with unfailing love and favour,
so that, renewed by the paschal mysteries,
she may come to the glory of the resurrection.
Through Christ our Lord. ℟. **Amen.** → No. 30, p. 77

To impart the blessing at the end of Mass, the Priest may appropriately use the formula of Solemn Blessing for the Mass of the Easter Vigil, p. 385.

Dismissal: see p. 386.

"Thomas answered him, 'My Lord and my God!'"

APRIL 8

2nd SUNDAY OF EASTER
(or of DIVINE MERCY)

ENTRANCE ANTIPHON 1 Pet. 2.2

Like newborn infants, you must long for the pure, spiritual milk, that in him you may grow to salvation, alleluia. → No. 2, p. 10

OR 4 Esdr 2.36-37

Receive the joy of your glory, giving thanks to God, who has called you into the heavenly Kingdom, alleluia. → No. 2, p. 10

COLLECT

God of everlasting mercy,
who in the very recurrence of the paschal feast
kindle the faith of the people you have made your own,
increase, we pray, the grace you have bestowed,
that all may grasp and rightly understand
in what font they have been washed,

by whose Spirit they have been reborn,
by whose Blood they have been redeemed.
Through our Lord Jesus Christ, your Son,
who lives and reigns with you in the unity of the Holy Spirit,
one God, for ever and ever. ℟. **Amen.** ↓

FIRST READING Acts 4.32-35

The faithful lived a common life, sharing all their goods. They prayed together and broke bread. Daily their numbers increased.

A reading from the Acts of the Apostles.

THE whole group of those who believed were of one heart and soul, and no one claimed private ownership of any possessions, but everything they owned was held in common.

With great power the Apostles gave their testimony to the resurrection of the Lord Jesus, and great grace was upon them all.

There was not a needy person among them, for as many as owned lands or houses sold them and brought the proceeds of what was sold. They laid it at the Apostles' feet, and it was distributed to each as any had need.—The word of the Lord. ℟. **Thanks be to God.** ↓

RESPONSORIAL PSALM Ps. 118

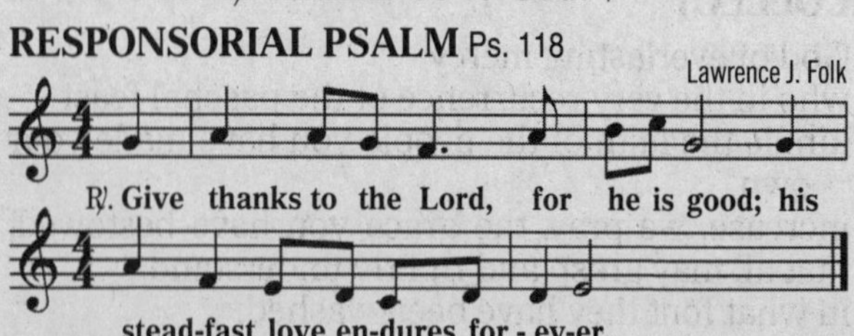
Lawrence J. Folk
℟. Give thanks to the Lord, for he is good; his
stead-fast love en-dures for - ev-er.

Or: ℟. **Alleluia!**

Let Israel say,
"His steadfast love endures forever."
Let the house of Aaron say,
"His steadfast love endures forever."
Let those who fear the Lord say,
"His steadfast love endures forever."—℟.

"The right hand of the Lord is exalted;
the right hand of the Lord does valiantly."
I shall not die, but I shall live,
and recount the deeds of the Lord.
The Lord has punished me severely,
but he did not give me over to death.—℟.

The stone that the builders rejected
has become the chief cornerstone.
This is the Lord's doing;
it is marvellous in our eyes.
This is the day that the Lord has made;
let us rejoice and be glad in it.—℟. ↓

SECOND READING 1 Jn. 5.1-6

Our faith comes from God. The proof of loving God is our observing the commandments. The Spirit, the Spirit of truth, will testify to this.

A reading from the first Letter of Saint John.

BELOVED: Everyone who believes that Jesus is the Christ has been born of God, and everyone who loves the parent loves the child.

By this we know that we love the children of God, when we love God and obey his commandments. For the love of God is this, that we obey his commandments. And his commandments are not burdensome, for whatever is born of God conquers the world. And this is the victory that conquers the world, our faith.

Who is it that conquers the world but the one who believes that Jesus is the Son of God? This is the one who came by water and blood, Jesus Christ, not with the water only but with the water and the blood. And the Spirit is the one that testifies, for the Spirit is the truth.—The word of the Lord. ℟. **Thanks be to God.** ↓

GOSPEL ACCLAMATION See Jn. 20.29

℣. Alleluia. ℟. **Alleluia.**

℣. You believed, Thomas, because you have seen me;
blessed are those who have not seen and yet believe.

℟. **Alleluia.** ↓

GOSPEL Jn. 20.19-31

Jesus appears to the disciples, coming through locked doors. He shows them his hands and side. He greets them in peace and gives them the power to forgive sin. A week later Jesus appears again directly to Thomas, who now professes his belief.

℣. The Lord be with you. ℟. **And with your spirit.**
✠ A reading from the holy Gospel according to John. ℟. **Glory to you, O Lord.**

IT was evening on the day Jesus rose from the dead, the first day of the week, and the doors of the house where the disciples had met were locked for fear of the Jews. Jesus came and stood among them and said, "Peace be with you." After he said this, he showed them his hands and his side. Then the disciples rejoiced when they saw the Lord.

Jesus said to them again, "Peace be with you. As the Father has sent me, so I send you." When he had said this, he breathed on them and said to them, "Receive the Holy Spirit. If you forgive the sins of any, they are forgiven them; if you retain the sins of any, they are retained."

But Thomas, who was called the Twin, one of the twelve, was not with them when Jesus came. So the other disciples told him, "We have seen the Lord." But he said to them, "Unless I see the mark of the nails in his hands, and put my finger in the mark of the nails and my hand in his side, I will not believe."

After eight days his disciples were again in the house, and Thomas was with them. Although the doors were shut, Jesus came and stood among them and said, "Peace be with you." Then he said to Thomas, "Put your finger here and see my hands. Reach out your hand and put it in my side. Do not doubt but believe." Thomas answered him, "My Lord and my God!"

Jesus said to him, "Have you believed because you have seen me? Blessed are those who have not seen and yet have come to believe."

Now Jesus did many other signs in the presence of his disciples, which are not written in this book. But these are written so that you may come to believe that Jesus is the Christ, the Son of God, and that through believing you may have life in his name.—The Gospel of the Lord. ℟. **Praise to you, Lord Jesus Christ.** → No. 15, p. 18

PRAYER OVER THE OFFERINGS

Accept, O Lord, we pray,
the oblations of your people
(and of those you have brought to new birth),
that, renewed by confession of your name and by
 Baptism,
they may attain unending happiness.
Through Christ our Lord.
℟. **Amen.**

→ No. 21, p. 22 (Pref. 21: on this day above all)

When the Roman Canon is used, the proper forms of the Communicantes *(*In communion with those*) and* Hanc igitur *(*Therefore, Lord, we pray*) are said.*

COMMUNION ANTIPHON Cf. Jn. 20.27

Bring your hand and feel the place of the nails, and do not be unbelieving but believing, alleluia. ↓

PRAYER AFTER COMMUNION

Grant, we pray, almighty God,
that our reception of this paschal Sacrament
may have a continuing effect
in our minds and hearts.
Through Christ our Lord.
℟. **Amen.** → No. 30, p. 77

Optional Solemn Blessings, p. 97, and Prayers over the People, p. 105

Dismissal: see p. 386.

"Thus it is written, that the Christ is to suffer and to rise from the dead."

APRIL 15

3rd SUNDAY OF EASTER

ENTRANCE ANTIPHON Cf. Ps. 65.1-2

Cry out with joy to God, all the earth; O sing to the glory of his name. O render him glorious praise, alleluia. → No. 2, p. 10

COLLECT

May your people exult for ever, O God,
in renewed youthfulness of spirit,
so that, rejoicing now in the restored glory of our adoption,
we may look forward in confident hope
to the rejoicing of the day of resurrection.
Through our Lord Jesus Christ, your Son,
who lives and reigns with you in the unity of the Holy Spirit,
one God, for ever and ever. ℟. **Amen.** ↓

FIRST READING Acts 3.13-15, 17-19

Peter teaches how God glorified his Son, but the people crucified him. They acted out of ignorance, however. Now they are to reform and ask God for forgiveness.

A reading from the Acts of the Apostles.

AT the temple gate, Peter addressed the people: "The God of Abraham, the God of Isaac, and the God of Jacob, the God of our fathers has glorified his servant Jesus, whom you handed over and rejected in the presence of Pilate, though he had decided to release him.

But you rejected the Holy and Righteous One and asked to have a murderer given to you, and you killed the Author of life, whom God raised from the dead. To this we are witnesses.

And now, brothers and sisters, I know that you acted in ignorance, as did also your rulers. In this way God fulfilled what he had foretold through all the Prophets, that his Christ would suffer.

Repent therefore, and turn to God so that your sins may be wiped out."—The word of the Lord.
℟. **Thanks be to God.** ↓

RESPONSORIAL PSALM Ps. 4

Normand L. Blanchard

℟. Let the light of your face
shine on us, O Lord.

Or: ℟. **Alleluia!**

gave him a piece of broiled fish, and he took it and ate in their presence.

Then he said to them, "These are my words that I spoke to you while I was still with you—that everything written about me in the Law of Moses, the Prophets, and the Psalms must be fulfilled." Then he opened their minds to understand the Scriptures, and he said to them, "Thus it is written, that the Christ is to suffer and to rise from the dead on the third day, and that repentance and forgiveness of sins is to be proclaimed in his name to all nations, beginning from Jerusalem. You are witnesses of these things."—The Gospel of the Lord. ℟. **Praise to you, Lord Jesus Christ.** → No. 15, p. 18

PRAYER OVER THE OFFERINGS

Receive, O Lord, we pray,
these offerings of your exultant Church,
and, as you have given her cause for such great
 gladness,
grant also that the gifts we bring
may bear fruit in perpetual happiness.
Through Christ our Lord.
℟. **Amen.** → No. 21, p. 22 (Pref. 21-25)

COMMUNION ANTIPHON Cf. Lk. 24.35

The disciples recognized the Lord Jesus in the breaking of the bread, alleluia. ↓

OR Lk. 24.46-47

The Christ had to suffer and on the third day rise from the dead; in his name repentance and

remission of sins must be preached to all the nations, alleluia. ↓

PRAYER AFTER COMMUNION

Look with kindness upon your people, O Lord,
and grant, we pray,
that those you were pleased to renew by eternal mysteries
may attain in their flesh
the incorruptible glory of the resurrection.
Through Christ our Lord.
℟. **Amen.** → No. 30, p. 77

Optional Solemn Blessings, p. 97, and Prayers over the People, p. 105

"I am the good shepherd."

APRIL 22

4th SUNDAY OF EASTER

ENTRANCE ANTIPHON Cf. Ps. 32.5-6

The merciful love of the Lord fills the earth; by the word of the Lord the heavens were made, alleluia. → No. 2, p. 10

COLLECT

Almighty ever-living God,
lead us to a share in the joys of heaven,
so that the humble flock may reach
where the brave Shepherd has gone before.
Who lives and reigns with you in the unity of the
Holy Spirit,
one God, for ever and ever.
℟. **Amen.** ↓

FIRST READING Acts 4.7-12

Peter explains the cure of the cripple. It was a miracle performed in the name of Jesus, whom the people had rejected. There is no salvation except in Jesus.

A reading from the Acts of the Apostles.

WHILE Peter and John were speaking to the people about the resurrection of Jesus, the captain of the temple arrested them and placed them in custody.

The next day the rulers, elders and scribes assembled. When they had made the prisoners stand in their midst, they inquired, "By what power or by what name did you do this?" Then Peter, filled with the Holy Spirit, said to them, "Rulers of the people and elders, if we are questioned today because of a good deed done to someone who was sick and are asked how this man has been healed, let it be known to all of you, and to all the people of Israel, that this man is standing before you in good health by the name of Jesus Christ of Nazareth, whom you crucified, whom God raised from the dead.

This Jesus is
'the stone that was rejected by you, the builders;
it has become the cornerstone.'
There is salvation in no one else, for there is no other name under heaven given among human beings by which we must be saved."—The word of the Lord. ℟. **Thanks be to God.** ↓

RESPONSORIAL PSALM Ps. 118

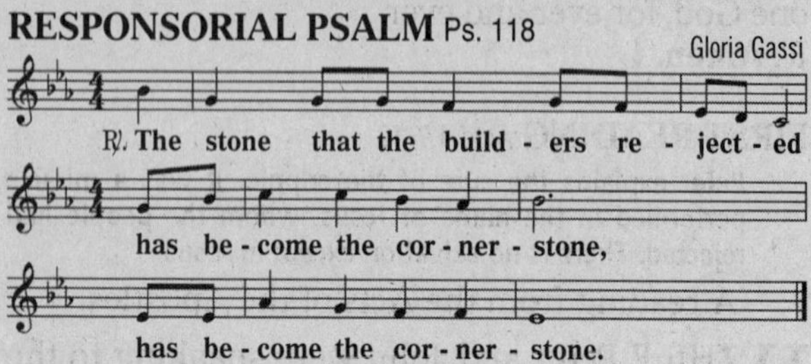
Gloria Gassi
℟. The stone that the build - ers re - ject - ed
has be - come the cor - ner - stone,
has be - come the cor - ner - stone.

Or: ℟. **Alleluia!**

O give thanks to the Lord, for he is good;
his steadfast love endures forever!
It is better to take refuge in the Lord
than to put confidence in humans.
It is better to take refuge in the Lord
than to put confidence in princes.—℟.

I thank you that you have answered me
and have become my salvation.
The stone that the builders rejected
has become the chief cornerstone.
This is the Lord's doing;
it is marvellous in our eyes.—℟.

Blessed is the one who comes in the name of the Lord.
We bless you from the house of the Lord.
You are my God, and I will give thanks to you;

you are my God, I will extol you.
O give thanks to the Lord, for he is good,
for his steadfast love endures forever.—℟. ↓

SECOND READING 1 Jn. 3.1-2

The Father shows his love for human beings by calling them his children. The world does not recognize the follower of Christ because it did not recognize Christ himself.

A reading from the first Letter of Saint John.

BELOVED: See what love the Father has given us, that we should be called children of God; and that is what we are. The reason the world does not know us is that it did not know him.

Beloved, we are God's children now; what we will be has not yet been revealed. What we do know is this: when he is revealed, we will be like him, for we will see him as he is.—The word of the Lord. ℟. **Thanks be to God.** ↓

GOSPEL ACCLAMATION Jn. 10.14

℣. Alleluia. ℟. **Alleluia.**
℣. I am the good shepherd, says the Lord;
I know my own, and my own know me.
℟. **Alleluia.** ↓

GOSPEL Jn. 10.11-18

Jesus calls himself the good shepherd. A shepherd cares for his sheep, lives and dies for them if necessary. There is to be one flock and one shepherd.

℣. The Lord be with you. ℟. **And with your spirit.**
✠ A reading from the holy Gospel according to John. ℟. **Glory to you, O Lord.**

JESUS said: "I am the good shepherd. The good shepherd lays down his life for the sheep. The hired hand, who is not the shepherd and does not own the sheep, sees the wolf coming and leaves the sheep and runs away—and the wolf snatches them and scatters them. The hired hand runs away because a hired hand does not care for the sheep.

I am the good shepherd. I know my own and my own know me, just as the Father knows me and I know the Father. And I lay down my life for the sheep. I have other sheep that do not belong to this fold. I must bring them also, and they will listen to my voice. So there will be one flock, one shepherd.

For this reason the Father loves me, because I lay down my life in order to take it up again. No one takes it from me, but I lay it down of my own accord. I have power to lay it down, and I have power to take it up again. I have received this command from my Father."—The Gospel of the Lord. ℟. **Praise to you, Lord Jesus Christ.**

→ No. 15, p. 18

PRAYER OVER THE OFFERINGS

Grant, we pray, O Lord,
that we may always find delight in these paschal mysteries,
so that the renewal constantly at work within us
may be the cause of our unending joy.
Through Christ our Lord.
℟. **Amen.** → No. 21, p. 22 (Pref. 21-25)

COMMUNION ANTIPHON

The Good Shepherd has risen, who laid down his life for his sheep and willingly died for his flock, alleluia. ↓

PRAYER AFTER COMMUNION

Look upon your flock, kind Shepherd,
and be pleased to settle in eternal pastures
the sheep you have redeemed
by the Precious Blood of your Son.
Who lives and reigns for ever and ever.
℟. **Amen.** → No. 30, p. 77

Optional Solemn Blessings, p. 97, and Prayers over the People, p. 105

"I am the true vine, and my Father is the vinegrower."

APRIL 29

5th SUNDAY OF EASTER

ENTRANCE ANTIPHON Cf. Ps. 97.1-2

O sing a new song to the Lord, for he has worked wonders; in the sight of the nations he has shown his deliverance, alleluia. → No. 2, p. 10

COLLECT

Almighty ever-living God,
constantly accomplish the Paschal Mystery within us,
that those you were pleased to make new in Holy Baptism
may, under your protective care, bear much fruit
and come to the joys of life eternal.
Through our Lord Jesus Christ, your Son,
who lives and reigns with you in the unity of the Holy Spirit,
one God, for ever and ever.
℟. **Amen.** ↓

FIRST READING Acts 9.26-31

Because of Paul's earlier reputation, the Christians were fearful of him. He explained his conversion to them. He was then accepted and began to spread the message of the gospel.

A reading from the Acts of the Apostles.

WHEN Saul had come to Jerusalem, he attempted to join the disciples; and they were all afraid of him, for they did not believe that he was a disciple. But Barnabas took him, brought him to the Apostles, and described for them how on the road he had seen the Lord, who had spoken to him, and how in Damascus Saul had spoken boldly in the name of Jesus.

So Saul went in and out among them in Jerusalem, speaking boldly in the name of the Lord. He spoke and argued with the Hellenists; but they were attempting to kill him. When the believers learned of it, they brought Saul down to Caesarea and sent him off to Tarsus.

Meanwhile the Church throughout Judea, Galilee, and Samaria had peace and was built up. Living in the fear of the Lord and in the comfort of the Holy Spirit, it increased in numbers.—The word of the Lord. ℟. **Thanks be to God.** ↓

RESPONSORIAL PSALM Ps. 22

Frank Lynch

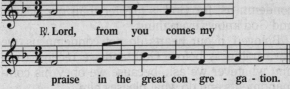

℟. Lord, from you comes my praise in the great con - gre - ga - tion.

Or: ℟. **Alleluia!**

My vows I will pay before those who fear him.
The poor shall eat and be satisfied;
those who seek him shall praise the Lord.
May your hearts live forever.—℟.

All the ends of the earth shall remember and turn to the Lord;
and all the families of the nations shall worship before him.
To him, indeed, shall all who sleep in the earth bow down;
before him shall bow all who go down to the dust.—℟.

I shall live for him.
Posterity will serve him;
future generations will be told about the Lord,
and proclaim his deliverance to a people yet unborn,
saying that he has done it.—℟. ↓

SECOND READING 1 Jn. 3.18-24

Christians are to love in deed and in truth. A clear conscience is proof of God's favour. To keep the commandments is to please God.

A reading from the first Letter of Saint John.

LITTLE children, let us love, not in word or speech, but in truth and action. And by this we will know that we are from the truth and will reassure our hearts before him whenever our hearts condemn us; for God is greater than our hearts, and God knows everything.

Beloved, if our hearts do not condemn us, we have boldness before God; and we receive from him whatever we ask, because we obey his commandments and do what pleases him.

And this is his commandment, that we should believe in the name of his Son Jesus Christ and love one another, just as he has commanded us. Whoever obeys his commandments abides in him, and he abides in them. And by this we know that he abides in us, by the Spirit that he has given us.—The word of the Lord. ℟. **Thanks be to God.** ↓

GOSPEL ACCLAMATION Jn. 15.4, 5

℣. Alleluia. ℟. **Alleluia.**

℣. Abide in me as I abide in you, says the Lord; my branches bear much fruit.

℟. **Alleluia.** ↓

GOSPEL Jn. 15.1-8

Jesus compares himself to the vine and the branches. Whoever is united to Jesus will do good and be re-

warded. But anyone who does not live in Jesus will wither like a cut-off vine.

℣. The Lord be with you. ℟. **And with your spirit.**
✠ A reading from the holy Gospel according to John. ℟. **Glory to you, O Lord.**

JESUS said to his disciples: "I am the true vine, and my Father is the vinegrower. He removes every branch in me that bears no fruit. Every branch that bears fruit he prunes to make it bear more fruit. You have already been cleansed by the word that I have spoken to you.

Abide in me as I abide in you. Just as the branch cannot bear fruit by itself unless it abides in the vine, neither can you unless you abide in me. I am the vine, you are the branches. Whoever abides in me and I in them bears much fruit, because apart from me you can do nothing.

Whoever does not abide in me is thrown away like a branch and withers; such branches are gathered, thrown into the fire, and burned.

If you abide in me, and my words abide in you, ask for whatever you wish, and it will be done for you. My Father is glorified by this, that you bear much fruit and become my disciples."—The Gospel of the Lord. ℟. **Praise to you, Lord Jesus Christ.** → No. 15, p. 18

PRAYER OVER THE OFFERINGS

O God, who by the wonderful exchange effected
in this sacrifice
have made us partakers of the one supreme
Godhead,

grant, we pray,
that, as we have come to know your truth,
we may make it ours by a worthy way of life.
Through Christ our Lord.
℟. **Amen.** → No. 21, p. 22 (Pref. 21-25)

COMMUNION ANTIPHON Cf. Jn. 15.1, 5

I am the true vine and you are the branches, says the Lord. Whoever remains in me, and I in him, bears fruit in plenty, alleluia. ↓

PRAYER AFTER COMMUNION

Graciously be present to your people, we pray, O Lord,
and lead those you have imbued with heavenly mysteries
to pass from former ways to newness of life.
Through Christ our Lord.
℟. **Amen.** → No. 30, p. 77

Optional Solemn Blessings, p. 97, and Prayers over the People, p. 105

"This is my commandment, that you love one another."

MAY 6

6th SUNDAY OF EASTER

ENTRANCE ANTIPHON Cf. Isa. 48.20

Proclaim a joyful sound and let it be heard; proclaim to the ends of the earth: The Lord has freed his people, alleluia. → No. 2, p. 10

COLLECT

Grant, almighty God,
that we may celebrate with heartfelt devotion
these days of joy,
which we keep in honour of the risen Lord,
and that what we relive in remembrance
we may always hold to in what we do.
Through our Lord Jesus Christ, your Son,
who lives and reigns with you in the unity of the
Holy Spirit,
one God, for ever and ever.
℟. **Amen.** ↓

FIRST READING Acts 10.25-26, 34-35, 44-48

Peter visits Cornelius and his family. God will favour anyone who acts uprightly, Jews and Gentiles alike. Peter gives orders that all who believe should be baptized.

A reading from the Acts of the Apostles.

ON Peter's arrival, Cornelius, a centurion of the Italian cohort, met him, and falling at his feet, worshipped him. But Peter made him get up, saying, "Stand up; I am only a man."

Then Peter began to speak, "I truly understand that God shows no partiality, but in every nation anyone who fears him and does what is right is acceptable to him."

While Peter was still speaking, the Holy Spirit fell upon all who heard the word. The circumcised believers who had come with Peter were astounded that the gift of the Holy Spirit had been poured out even on the Gentiles, for they heard them speaking in tongues and extolling God. Then Peter said, "Can anyone withhold the water for baptizing these people who have received the Holy Spirit just as we have?" So he ordered them to be baptized in the name of Jesus Christ. Then they invited him to stay for several days.—The word of the Lord. ℟. **Thanks be to God.** ↓

RESPONSORIAL PSALM Ps. 98

Mary Richard

℟. The Lord has re - vealed his vic-to-ry in the
sight of the na - tions.

Or: ℟. **Alleluia!**

O sing to the Lord a new song,
for he has done marvellous things.
His right hand and his holy arm
have brought him victory.—℟.

The Lord has made known his victory;
he has revealed his vindication in the sight of the nations.
He has remembered his steadfast love
and faithfulness to the house of Israel.—℟.

All the ends of the earth have seen
the victory of our God.
Make a joyful noise to the Lord, all the earth;
break forth into joyous song and sing praises.
—℟. ↓

SECOND READING 1 Jn. 4.7-10

Christians should love one another, for God is love. A person without love does not know God. In love, God has sent the Son as an offering for our sins.

A reading from the first Letter of Saint John.

BELOVED, let us love one another, because love is from God; everyone who loves is born of God and knows God. Whoever does not love does not know God, for God is love.

God's love was revealed among us in this way: God sent his only-begotten Son into the world so that we might live through him. In this is love, not that we loved God but that he loved us and sent his Son to be the atoning sacrifice for our sins.—The word of the Lord. ℟. **Thanks be to God.** ↓

GOSPEL ACCLAMATION Jn. 14.23

℣. Alleluia. ℟. **Alleluia.**
℣. Those who love me will keep my word,
and my Father will love them, and we will come to them.
℟. **Alleluia.** ↓

GOSPEL Jn. 15.9-17

Jesus admonishes his disciples to continue the love he has shown to them. The keeping of the commandments will prove this. "Love one another."

℣. The Lord be with you. ℟. **And with your spirit.**
✠ A reading from the holy Gospel according to John. ℟. **Glory to you, O Lord.**

JESUS said to his disciples: "As the Father has loved me, so I have loved you; abide in my love. If you keep my commandments, you will abide in my love, just as I have kept my Father's commandments and abide in his love.

I have said these things to you so that my joy may be in you, and that your joy may be complete. This is my commandment, that you love one another as I have loved you. No one has greater love than this, to lay down one's life for one's friends.

You are my friends if you do what I command you. I do not call you servants any longer, because the servant does not know what the master is doing; but I have called you friends, because I have made known to you everything that I have heard from my Father.

You did not choose me but I chose you. And I appointed you to go and bear fruit, fruit that will last, so that the Father will give you whatever you ask him in my name. I am giving you these commands so that you may love one another."—The Gospel of the Lord. ℟. **Praise to you, Lord Jesus Christ.** → No. 15, p. 18

PRAYER OVER THE OFFERINGS

May our prayers rise up to you, O Lord,
together with the sacrificial offerings,
so that, purified by your graciousness,
we may be conformed to the mysteries of your mighty love.
Through Christ our Lord.
℟. **Amen.** → No. 21, p. 22 (Pref. 21-25)

COMMUNION ANTIPHON Jn. 14.15-16

If you love me, keep my commandments, says the Lord, and I will ask the Father and he will send you another Paraclete, to abide with you for ever, alleluia. ↓

PRAYER AFTER COMMUNION

Almighty ever-living God,
who restore us to eternal life in the Resurrection of Christ,
increase in us, we pray, the fruits of this paschal Sacrament
and pour into our hearts the strength of this saving food.
Through Christ our Lord.
℟. **Amen.** → No. 30, p. 77

Optional Solemn Blessings, p. 97, and Prayers over the People, p. 105

"Go into all the world and proclaim the good news to the whole creation."

MAY 13

THE ASCENSION OF THE LORD

Solemnity

AT THE VIGIL MASS (May 12)

ENTRANCE ANTIPHON Ps. 67.33, 35

You kingdoms of the earth, sing to God; praise the Lord, who ascends above the highest heavens; his majesty and might are in the skies, alleluia.

→ No. 2, p. 10

COLLECT

O God, whose Son today ascended to the heavens
as the Apostles looked on,
grant, we pray, that, in accordance with his promise,
we may be worthy for him to live with us always on earth,
and we with him in heaven.

Who lives and reigns with you in the unity of the Holy Spirit,
one God, for ever and ever. ℟. **Amen.** ↓

The readings for this Mass can be found beginning on p. 426.

PRAYER OVER THE OFFERINGS

O God, whose Only Begotten Son, our High Priest,
is seated ever-living at your right hand to intercede for us,
grant that we may approach with confidence the throne of grace
and there obtain your mercy.
Through Christ our Lord.
℟. **Amen.** → No. 21, p. 22 (Pref. 26-27)

When the Roman Canon is used, the proper form of the Communicantes (In communion with those) *is said.*

COMMUNION ANTIPHON Cf. Heb. 10.12

Christ, offering a single sacrifice for sins, is seated for ever at God's right hand, alleluia. ↓

PRAYER AFTER COMMUNION

May the gifts we have received from your altar, Lord,
kindle in our hearts a longing for the heavenly homeland
and cause us to press forward, following in the Saviour's footsteps,
to the place where for our sake he entered before us.
Who lives and reigns for ever and ever.
℟. **Amen.** → No. 30, p. 77

Optional Solemn Blessings, p. 97, and Prayers over the People, p. 105

AT THE MASS DURING THE DAY

ENTRANCE ANTIPHON Acts 1.11

Men of Galilee, why gaze in wonder at the heavens? This Jesus whom you saw ascending into heaven will return as you saw him go, alleluia.

→ No. 2, p. 10

COLLECT

Gladden us with holy joys, almighty God,
and make us rejoice with devout thanksgiving,
for the Ascension of Christ your Son
is our exaltation,
and, where the Head has gone before in glory,
the Body is called to follow in hope.
Through our Lord Jesus Christ, your Son,
who lives and reigns with you in the unity of the Holy Spirit,
one God, for ever and ever. ℟. **Amen.** ↓

OR

Grant, we pray, almighty God,
that we, who believe that your Only Begotten Son, our Redeemer,
ascended this day to the heavens,
may in spirit dwell already in heavenly realms.
Who lives and reigns with you in the unity of the Holy Spirit,
one God, for ever and ever. ℟. **Amen.** ↓

FIRST READING Acts 1.1-11

Christ is divine! He will come again! Our faith affirms this for us. We live in the era of the Holy Spirit.

A reading from the Acts of the Apostles.

IN the first book, Theophilus, I wrote about all that Jesus did and taught from the beginning until the day when he was taken up to heaven, after giving instructions through the Holy Spirit to the Apostles whom he had chosen. After his suffering he presented himself alive to them by many convincing proofs, appearing to them during forty days and speaking about the kingdom of God.

While staying with them, he ordered them not to leave Jerusalem, but to wait there for the promise of the Father. "This," he said, "is what you have heard from me; for John baptized with water, but you will be baptized with the Holy Spirit not many days from now."

So when they had come together, they asked him, "Lord, is this the time when you will restore the kingdom to Israel?" He replied, "It is not for you to know the times or periods that the Father has set by his own authority. But you will receive power when the Holy Spirit has come upon you; and you will be my witnesses in Jerusalem, in all Judea and Samaria, and to the ends of the earth."

When he had said this, as they were watching, he was lifted up, and a cloud took him out of their sight. While he was going and they were gazing up toward heaven, suddenly two men in white robes stood by them. They said, "Men of Galilee, why do you stand looking up toward heaven? This Jesus, who has been taken up from you into heaven, will come in the same way as you saw him go into heaven."—The word of the Lord. ℟. **Thanks be to God.** ↓

RESPONSORIAL PSALM Ps. 47

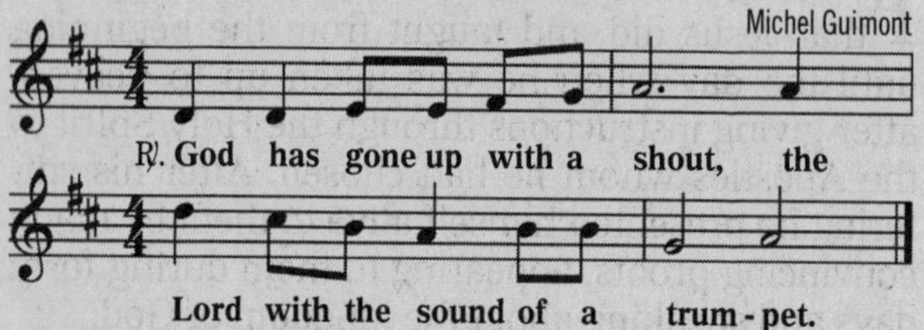
Michel Guimont
℟. God has gone up with a shout, the
Lord with the sound of a trum - pet.

Or: ℟. **Alleluia!**

Clap your hands, all you peoples;
shout to God with loud songs of joy.
For the Lord, the Most High, is awesome,
a great king over all the earth.—℟.

God has gone up with a shout,
the Lord with the sound of a trumpet.
Sing praises to God, sing praises;
sing praises to our King, sing praises.—℟.

For God is the king of all the earth;
sing praises with a Psalm.
God is king over the nations;
God sits on his holy throne.—℟. ↓

SECOND READING Eph. 1.17-23

Paul speaks of the Father of glory who wills to grant wisdom and knowledge as we come to know him.

A reading from the Letter of Saint Paul
to the Ephesians.

BROTHERS and sisters: I pray that the God of our Lord Jesus Christ, the Father of glory, may give you a spirit of wisdom and revelation as you come to know him, so that, with the eyes of your heart enlightened, you may know what is the hope to which he has called you, what are the riches of his glorious inheritance among the saints, and what is the immeasurable greatness of his power for us who believe, according to the working of his great power. God put this power to work in Christ when he raised him from the dead and seated him at his right hand in the heavenly places, far above all rule and authority and power and dominion, and above every name that is named, not only in this age but also in the age to come. And he has put all things under his feet and has made him the head over all things for the Church, which is his body, the fullness of him who fills all in all.—The word of the Lord. ℟. **Thanks be to God.** ↓

OR Eph. 4.1-13 or 4.1-7, 11-13

Our hope is in God, our strength. With Christ our head, we his people will receive the gift of wisdom and insight.

[If the "Shorter Form" is used, the indented text in brackets is omitted.]

A reading from the Letter of Saint Paul to the Ephesians.

BROTHERS and sisters: I, the prisoner in the Lord, beg you to lead a life worthy of the calling to which you have been called, with all humility and gentleness, with patience, bearing with one another in love, making every effort to maintain the unity of the Spirit in the bond of peace.

There is one body and one Spirit, just as you were called to the one hope of your calling, one Lord, one faith, one baptism, one God and Father of all, who is above all and through all and in all.

But each of us was given grace according to the measure of Christ's gift.

[Therefore it is said, "When he ascended on high he made captivity itself a captive; he gave gifts to his people."

When it says, "He ascended," what does it mean but that he had also descended into the lower parts of the earth?

He who descended is the same one who ascended far above all the heavens, so that he might fill all things.]

The gifts he gave were that some would be Apostles, some Prophets, some evangelists, some pastors and teachers, to equip the saints for the work of ministry, for building up the body of Christ, until all of us come to the unity of the faith and of the knowledge of the Son of God, to maturity, to the measure of the full stature of Christ.—The word of the Lord. ℟. **Thanks be to God.** ↓

GOSPEL ACCLAMATION Mt. 28.19, 20

℣. Alleluia. ℟. **Alleluia.**
℣. Go make disciples of all nations.
I am with you always, to the end of the age.
℟. **Alleluia.** ↓

GOSPEL Mk. 16.15-20

Jesus makes his disciples apostles to preach the good news. He promises them special signs of protection on earth. Then Jesus is taken up into heaven.

℣. The Lord be with you. ℟. **And with your spirit.**
✠ A reading from the holy Gospel according to Mark. ℟. **Glory to you, O Lord.**

JESUS appeared to the eleven, and he said to them, "Go into all the world and proclaim the good news to the whole creation. The one who believes and is baptized will be saved; but the one who does not believe will be condemned. And these signs will accompany those who believe: by using my name they will cast out demons; they will speak in new tongues; they will pick up snakes in their hands, and if they drink any deadly thing, it will not hurt them; they will lay their hands on the sick, and they will recover."

So then the Lord Jesus, after he had spoken to them, was taken up into heaven and sat down at the right hand of God. And they went out and proclaimed the good news everywhere, while the Lord worked with them and confirmed the message by the signs that accompanied it.—The Gospel of the Lord. ℟. **Praise to you, Lord Jesus Christ.** → No. 15, p. 18

PRAYER OVER THE OFFERINGS

We offer sacrifice now in supplication, O Lord,
to honour the wondrous Ascension of your Son:
grant, we pray,
that through this most holy exchange
we, too, may rise up to the heavenly realms.
Through Christ our Lord.
℟. **Amen.** → No. 21, p. 22 (Pref. 26-27)

When the Roman Canon is used, the proper form of the Communicantes (In communion with those) *is said.*

COMMUNION ANTIPHON Mt. 28.20

Behold, I am with you always, even to the end of the age, alleluia. ↓

PRAYER AFTER COMMUNION

Almighty ever-living God,
who allow those on earth to celebrate divine mysteries,
grant, we pray,
that Christian hope may draw us onward
to where our nature is united with you.
Through Christ our Lord.
℟. **Amen.** → No. 30, p. 77

Optional Solemn Blessings, p. 97, and Prayers over the People, p. 105

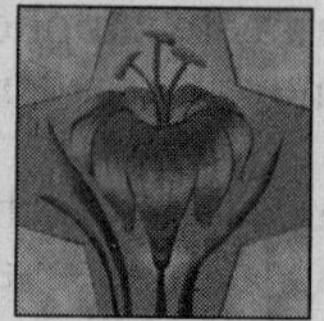

"All of them were filled with the Holy Spirit."

MAY 20

PENTECOST SUNDAY

Solemnity

AT THE VIGIL MASS (Simple Form) (May 19)

ENTRANCE ANTIPHON Rom. 5.5; cf. 8.11

The love of God has been poured into our hearts through the Spirit of God dwelling within us, alleluia. → No. 2, p. 10

COLLECT

Almighty ever-living God,
who willed the Paschal Mystery
to be encompassed as a sign in fifty days,
grant that from out of the scattered nations
the confusion of many tongues
may be gathered by heavenly grace
into one great confession of your name.
Through our Lord Jesus Christ, your Son,

who lives and reigns with you in the unity of the
Holy Spirit,
one God, for ever and ever. ℟. **Amen.** ↓

OR

Grant, we pray, almighty God,
that the splendor of your glory
may shine forth upon us
and that, by the bright rays of the Holy Spirit,
the light of your light may confirm the hearts
of those born again by your grace.
Through our Lord Jesus Christ, your Son,
who lives and reigns with you in the unity of the
Holy Spirit,
one God, for ever and ever. ℟. **Amen.** ↓

FIRST READING

A Gen. 11.1-9

Those who put their trust in pride and human ability are bound to fail.

A reading from the book of Genesis.

NOW the whole earth had one language and the same words. And as people migrated from the east, they came upon a plain in the land of Shinar and settled there. And they said to one another, "Come, let us make bricks, and burn them thoroughly." And they had brick for stone, and bitumen for mortar. Then they said, "Come, let us build ourselves a city, and a tower with its top in the heavens, and let us make a name for ourselves; otherwise we shall be scattered abroad upon the face of the whole earth." The Lord came down to see the city and the tower, which the children of Adam had built. And the Lord said, "Look, they are one people, and they have all one language; and this is only the beginning of what they will do; nothing that they propose to do will now be impossible for them. Come, let us go down, and confuse their language there, so that they will not understand one another's speech." So the Lord scattered them abroad from there over the face of all the earth, and they left off building the city. Therefore it was called Babel, because there the Lord confused the language of all the earth; and from there the Lord scattered them abroad over the face of all the earth.—The word of the Lord. ℟. **Thanks be to God.** ↓

OR

B Ex. 19.3-8a, 16-20

The Lord God covenants with the Israelites—they are to be a holy nation, a princely kingdom.

A reading from the book of Exodus.

MOSES went up to God; the Lord called to him from the mountain, saying, "Thus you shall say to the house of Jacob, and tell the children of Israel: 'You have seen what I did to the Egyptians, and how I bore you on eagles' wings and brought you to myself. Now therefore, if you obey my voice and keep my covenant, you shall be my treasured possession out of all the peoples. Indeed, the whole earth is mine, but you shall be for me a priestly kingdom and a holy nation.' These are the words that you shall speak to the children of Israel." So Moses came, summoned the elders of the people, and set before them all these words that the Lord had commanded him. The people all answered as one: "Everything that the Lord has spoken we will do."

On the morning of the third day there was thunder and lightning, as well as a thick cloud on the mountain, and a blast of a trumpet so loud that all the people who were in the camp trembled. Moses brought the people out of the camp to meet God. They took their stand at the foot of the mountain. Now Mount Sinai was wrapped in smoke, because the Lord had descended upon it in fire; the smoke went up like the smoke of a kiln, while the whole mountain shook violently. As the blast of the trumpet grew louder and louder, Moses would speak and God would answer him in thunder. When the Lord descended upon Mount Sinai, to the top of the mountain, the Lord summoned Moses to the top of the mountain, and Moses went up.—The word of the Lord. ℟. **Thanks be to God.** ↓

OR

C Ez. 37.1-14

The prophet, in a vision, sees the power of God—the band of the living and the dead, as he describes the resurrection of the dead.

A reading from the book of the Prophet Ezekiel.

THE hand of the Lord came upon me, and he brought me out by the spirit of the Lord and set me down in the middle of a valley; it was full of bones. He led me all around them; there were very many lying in the valley, and they were very dry. He said to me, "Son of man, can these bones live?" I answered, "O Lord God, you know." Then he said to me, "Prophesy to these bones, and say to them: O dry bones, hear the word of the Lord. Thus says the Lord God to these bones: I will cause breath to enter you, and you shall live. I will lay sinews on you, and will cause flesh to come upon you, and cover you with skin, and put breath in you, and you shall live; and you shall know that I am the Lord." So I prophesied as I had been commanded; and as I prophesied, suddenly there was a noise, a rattling, and the bones came together, bone to its bone. I looked, and there were sinews on them, and flesh had come upon them, and skin had covered them; but there was no breath in them. Then he said to me, "Prophesy to the breath, prophesy, son of man, and say to the breath: Thus says the Lord God: Come from the four winds, and breathe upon these slain, that they may live." I prophesied as he commanded me, and the breath came into them, and they lived, and stood on their feet, a vast multitude. Then he said to me, "Son of man, these bones are the whole house of Israel. They say, 'Our bones are dried up, and our hope is lost; we are cut off completely.' Therefore prophesy, and say to them, Thus says the Lord God: I am going to open your graves, and bring you up from your graves, O my people; and I will bring you back to the land of Israel. And you shall know that I am the Lord, when I open your graves, and bring you up from your graves, O my people. I will put my spirit within you, and you shall live, and I will place you on your own soil; then you shall know that I, the

Lord, have spoken and will act," says the Lord.— The word of the Lord. ℟. **Thanks be to God.** ↓

OR

D Joel 2.28-32

At the end of time, the Day of the Lord, Judgment Day, those who persevere in faith will be saved.

A reading from the book of the Prophet Joel.

THUS says the Lord:
I will pour out my spirit on all flesh;
your sons and your daughters shall prophesy,
your elders shall dream dreams,
and your young people shall see visions.
Even on the male and female slaves,
in those days, I will pour out my spirit.
I will show portents in the heavens and on the earth,
blood and fire and columns of smoke.
The sun shall be turned to darkness,
and the moon to blood,
before the great and terrible day of the Lord comes.
Then everyone who calls on the name of the Lord shall be saved;
for in Mount Zion and in Jerusalem
there shall be those who escape, as the Lord has said,
and among the survivors shall be those whom the Lord calls.

The word of the Lord. ℟. **Thanks be to God.** ↓

RESPONSORIAL PSALM Ps. 104 Normand L. Blanchard

℟. Lord, send forth your Spir-it, and re - new the face of the earth.

Or: ℟. **Alleluia!**

Bless the Lord, O my soul.
O Lord my God, you are very great.
You are clothed with honour and majesty,
wrapped in light as with a garment.—℟.

O Lord, how manifold are your works!
In wisdom you have made them all;
the earth is full of your creatures,
living things both small and great.—℟.

These all look to you
to give them their food in due season;
when you give to them, they gather it up;
when you open your hand, they are filled with good things.—℟.

When you take away their breath,
they die and return to their dust.
When you send forth your spirit, they are created;
and you renew the face of the earth.—℟. ↓

SECOND READING Rom. 8.22-27

Be patient and have hope. The Spirit intercedes for us.

A reading from the Letter of Saint Paul to the Romans.

BROTHERS and sisters: we know that the whole creation has been groaning in labour pains until now; and not only the creation, but we ourselves, who have the first fruits of the Spirit, groan inwardly while we wait for adoption to sonship, the redemption of our bodies. For in hope we were saved. Now hope that is seen is not hope. For who hopes for what is seen? But if we hope for what we do not see, we wait for it with patience. Likewise the Spirit helps us in our weakness; for we do not know how to pray as we ought, but that very Spirit intercedes with sighs too deep for words. And God, who searches the heart, knows what is the mind of the Spirit, because the Spirit intercedes for the saints according to the will of God.—The word of the Lord. ℟. **Thanks be to God.** ↓

GOSPEL ACCLAMATION

℣. Alleluia. ℟. **Alleluia.**
℣. Come, Holy Spirit, fill the hearts of your faithful and kindle in them the fire of your love.
℟. **Alleluia.** ↓

GOSPEL Jn. 7.37-39

Jesus indicates that the Holy Spirit will bear witness to the good news. He will guide Christians to the truth and teach about things to come.

℣. The Lord be with you. ℟. **And with your spirit.**
✠ A reading from the holy Gospel according to John. ℟. **Glory to you, O Lord.**

ON the last day of the festival, the great day, while Jesus was standing in the temple, he cried out, "Let anyone who is thirsty come to me and drink. As the Scripture has said, 'Out of the heart of the one who believes in me shall flow rivers of living water.' " Now he said this about the Spirit, which believers in him were to receive; for as yet there was no Spirit, because Jesus was not yet glorified.—The Gospel of the Lord. ℟. **Praise to you, Lord Jesus Christ.**

→ No. 15, p. 18

PRAYER OVER THE OFFERINGS

Pour out upon these gifts the blessing of your Spirit,
we pray, O Lord,
so that through them your Church may be imbued with such love
that the truth of your saving mystery
may shine forth for the whole world.
Through Christ our Lord.
℟. **Amen.** → Pref. 28, p. 449

When the Roman Canon is used, the proper form of the Communicantes *(*In communion with those*) is said.*

COMMUNION ANTIPHON Jn. 7.37

On the last day of the festival, Jesus stood and cried out: If anyone is thirsty, let him come to me and drink, alleluia. ↓

PRAYER AFTER COMMUNION

May these gifts we have consumed
benefit us, O Lord,
that we may always be aflame with the same Spirit,

whom you wondrously poured out on your Apostles.
Through Christ our Lord.
℟. **Amen.** → No. 30, p. 77

Optional Solemn Blessings, p. 97, and Prayers over the People, p. 105

(At the end of the Dismissal, the people respond: **"Thanks be to God, alleluia, alleluia."***)*

AT THE MASS DURING THE DAY

ENTRANCE ANTIPHON Wis. 1.7

The Spirit of the Lord has filled the whole world and that which contains all things understands what is said, alleluia. → No. 2, p. 10

OR Rom. 5.5; cf. 8.11

The love of God has been poured into our hearts through the Spirit of God dwelling within us, alleluia. → No. 2, p. 10

COLLECT

O God, who by the mystery of today's great feast
sanctify your whole Church in every people and nation,
pour out, we pray, the gifts of the Holy Spirit
across the face of the earth
and, with the divine grace that was at work
when the Gospel was first proclaimed,
fill now once more the hearts of believers.
Through our Lord Jesus Christ, your Son,
who lives and reigns with you in the unity of the Holy Spirit,
one God, for ever and ever. ℟. **Amen.** ↓

FIRST READING Acts 2.1-11

On this day the Holy Spirit in fiery tongues descended upon the apostles and the Mother of Jesus. Today the law of grace and purification from sin was announced. Three thousand were baptized.

A reading from the Acts of the Apostles.

WHEN the day of Pentecost had come, they were all together in one place. And suddenly from heaven there came a sound like the rush of a violent wind, and it filled the entire house where they were sitting. Divided tongues, as of fire, appeared among them, and a tongue rested on each of them. All of them were filled with the Holy Spirit and began to speak in other languages, as the Spirit gave them ability.

Now there were devout Jews from every nation under heaven living in Jerusalem. And at this sound the crowd gathered and was bewildered, because each one heard them speaking in their own language. Amazed and astonished, they asked, "Are not all these who are speaking Galileans? And how is it that we hear, each of us, in our own language? Parthians, Medes, Elamites, and residents of Mesopotamia, Judea and Cappadocia, Pontus and Asia, Phrygia and Pamphylia, Egypt and the parts of Libya belonging to Cyrene, and visitors from Rome, both Jews and converts, Cretans and Arabs—in our own languages we hear them speaking about God's deeds of power."—The word of the Lord.

℟. **Thanks be to God.** ↓

RESPONSORIAL PSALM Ps. 104

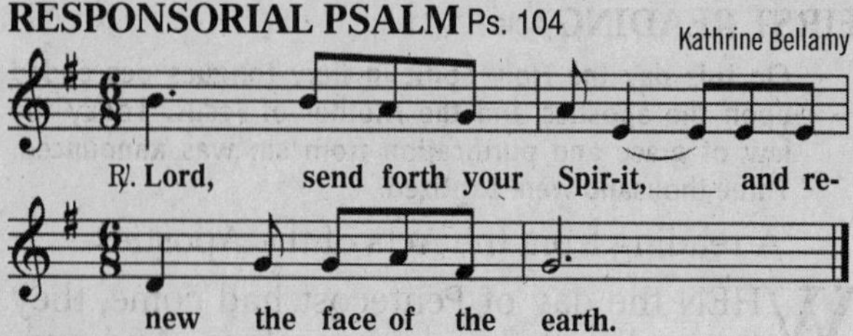
Kathrine Bellamy
℟. Lord, send forth your Spir-it, and re-
new the face of the earth.

Or: ℟. **Alleluia!**

Bless the Lord, O my soul.
O Lord my God, you are very great.
O Lord, how manifold are your works!
the earth is full of your creatures.—℟.

When you take away their breath,
they die and return to their dust.
When you send forth your spirit, they are created;
and you renew the face of the earth.—℟.

May the glory of the Lord endure forever;
may the Lord rejoice in his works.
May my meditation be pleasing to him,
for I rejoice in the Lord.—℟. ↓

SECOND READING 1 Cor. 12.3b-7, 12-13

No one can confess the divinity and sovereignty of Jesus unless inspired by the Holy Spirit. Different gifts and ministries are given, but all for the one body with Jesus.

A reading from the first Letter of Saint Paul to the Corinthians.

BROTHERS and sisters: No one can say "Jesus is Lord" except by the Holy Spirit.

Now there are varieties of gifts, but the same Spirit; and there are varieties of services, but the same Lord; and there are varieties of activities, but it is the same God who activates all of them in everyone. To each is given the manifestation of the Spirit for the common good.

For just as the body is one and has many members, and all the members of the body, though many, are one body, so it is with Christ. For in the one Spirit we were all baptized into one body—Jews or Greeks, slaves or free—and we were all made to drink of one Spirit.—The word of the Lord. ℟. **Thanks be to God.** ↓

OR

SECOND READING Gal. 5.16-25

Paul's concrete advice illustrates the love which he stresses. "Good deeds" are not to be excluded from Christian life. There is no law against such virtuous actions.

A reading from the Letter of Saint Paul to the Galatians.

BROTHERS and sisters: Live by the Spirit, I say, and do not gratify the desires of the flesh. For what the flesh desires is opposed to the Spirit, and what the Spirit desires is opposed to the flesh; for these are opposed to each other, to prevent you from doing what you want.

But if you are led by the Spirit, you are not subject to the law. Now the works of the flesh are obvious: fornication, impurity, licentiousness, idolatry, sorcery, enmities, strife, jealousy, anger, quarrels, dissensions, factions, envy, drunkenness, carousing, and things like these. I am warning you, as I warned you before: those who do such things will not inherit the kingdom of God.

By contrast, the fruit of the Spirit is love, joy, peace, patience, kindness, generosity, faithfulness, gentleness, and self-control. There is no law against such things. And those who belong to Christ Jesus have crucified the flesh with its passions and desires. If we live by the Spirit, let us also be guided by the Spirit.—The word of the Lord. ℟. **Thanks be to God.** ↓

SEQUENCE *(Veni, Sancte Spiritus)*

1. Holy Spirit, Lord divine,
Come, from heights of heav'n and shine,
Come with blessed radiance bright!

2. Come, O Father of the poor,
Come, whose treasured gifts ensure,
Come, our heart's unfailing light!

3. Of consolers, wisest, best,
And our soul's most welcome guest,
Sweet refreshment, sweet repose.

4. In our labour rest most sweet,
Pleasant coolness in the heat,
Consolation in our woes.

5. Light most blessed, shine with grace
In our heart's most secret place,
Fill your faithful through and through.

6. Left without your presence here,
Life itself would disappear,
Nothing thrives apart from you!

7. Cleanse our soiled hearts of sin,
Arid souls refresh within,
Wounded lives to health restore.

8. Bend the stubborn heart and will,
Melt the frozen, warm the chill,
Guide the wayward home once more!

9. On the faithful who are true
And profess their faith in you,
In your sev'nfold gift descend!

10. Give us virtue's sure reward,
Give us your salvation, Lord,
Give us joys that never end! ↓

GOSPEL ACCLAMATION

℣. Alleluia. ℟. **Alleluia.**
℣. Come, Holy Spirit, fill the hearts of your faithful and kindle in them the fire of your love.
℟. **Alleluia.** ↓

GOSPEL Jn. 20.19-23

Jesus breathes on the disciples to indicate the conferring of the Holy Spirit. Here we see the origin of power over sin, the Sacrament of Penance. This shows the power of the Holy Spirit in the hearts of human beings.

℣. The Lord be with you. ℟. **And with your spirit.**
✠ A reading from the holy Gospel according to John. ℟. **Glory to you, O Lord.**

IT was evening on the day Jesus rose from the dead, the first day of the week, and the doors of the house where the disciples had met were locked for fear of the Jews. Jesus came and stood among them and said, "Peace be with you." After he said this, he showed them his hands and his side. Then the disciples rejoiced when they saw the Lord. Jesus said to them again, "Peace be with you. As the Father has sent me, so I send you." When he had said this, he breathed on them and said to them, "Receive the Holy Spirit. If you forgive the sins of any, they are forgiven them; if you retain the sins of any, they are retained."—The Gospel of the Lord. ℟. **Praise to you, Lord Jesus Christ.** → No. 15, p. 18

OR

GOSPEL Jn. 15.26-27; 16.12-15

Jesus indicates that the Holy Spirit will bear witness to the good news. He will guide Christians to the truth and teach about things to come.

℣. The Lord be with you. ℟. **And with your spirit.**
✠ A reading from the holy Gospel according to John. ℟. **Glory to you, O Lord.**

JESUS said to the disciples: "When the Advocate comes, whom I will send to you from the Father, the Spirit of truth who comes from the Father, he will testify on my behalf. You also are to testify because you have been with me from the beginning.

I still have many things to say to you, but you cannot bear them now. When the Spirit of truth comes, he will guide you into all the truth; for he will not speak on his own, but will speak whatever he hears, and he will declare to you the things that are to come. He will glorify me, because he will take what is mine and declare it to you.

All that the Father has is mine. For this reason I said that he will take what is mine and declare it to you."—The Gospel of the Lord. ℟. **Praise to you, Lord Jesus Christ.** → No. 15, p. 18

PRAYER OVER THE OFFERINGS

Grant, we pray, O Lord,
that, as promised by your Son,
the Holy Spirit may reveal to us more abundantly
the hidden mystery of this sacrifice
and graciously lead us into all truth.
Through Christ our Lord. ℟. **Amen.** ↓

PREFACE (28)

℣. The Lord be with you. ℟. **And with your spirit.** ℣. Lift up your hearts. ℟. **We lift them up to the Lord.** ℣. Let us give thanks to the Lord our God. ℟. **It is right and just.**

It is truly right and just, our duty and our salvation,
always and everywhere to give you thanks,
Lord, holy Father, almighty and eternal God.

For, bringing your Paschal Mystery to completion,
you bestowed the Holy Spirit today
on those you made your adopted children
by uniting them to your Only Begotten Son.
This same Spirit, as the Church came to birth,
opened to all peoples the knowledge of God
and brought together the many languages of the earth
in profession of the one faith.

Therefore, overcome with paschal joy,
every land, every people exults in your praise
and even the heavenly Powers, with the angelic hosts,
sing together the unending hymn of your glory,
as they acclaim: → No. 23, p. 23

When the Roman Canon is used, the proper form of the Communicantes *(*In communion with those*) is said.*

COMMUNION ANTIPHON Acts 2.4, 11

They were all filled with the Holy Spirit and spoke of the marvels of God, alleluia. ↓

PRAYER AFTER COMMUNION

O God, who bestow heavenly gifts upon your Church,

safeguard, we pray, the grace you have given,
that the gift of the Holy Spirit poured out upon her
may retain all its force
and that this spiritual food
may gain her abundance of eternal redemption.
Through Christ our Lord.
℟. **Amen.** → No. 30, p. 77

Optional Solemn Blessings, p. 97, and Prayers over the People, p. 105

(At the end of the Dismissal, the people respond: **"Thanks be to God, alleluia, alleluia."***)*

AΩ

"Glory to the Father, the Son, and the Holy Spirit."

MAY 27

THE MOST HOLY TRINITY

Solemnity

ENTRANCE ANTIPHON

Blest be God the Father, and the Only Begotten Son of God, and also the Holy Spirit, for he has shown us his merciful love. → No. 2, p. 10

COLLECT

God our Father, who by sending into the world
the Word of truth and the Spirit of sanctification
made known to the human race your wondrous mystery,
grant us, we pray, that in professing the true faith,
we may acknowledge the Trinity of eternal glory
and adore your Unity, powerful in majesty.
Through our Lord Jesus Christ, your Son,
who lives and reigns with you in the unity of the Holy Spirit,
one God, for ever and ever. ℟. **Amen.** ↓

FIRST READING Deut. 4.32-34, 39-40

Moses asks the people to reflect on what has happened and whether or not God was their sole Creator and protector. For this reason God's laws and commandments must be obeyed.

A reading from the book of Deuteronomy.

MOSES spoke to the people saying, "Ask now about former ages, long before your own, ever since the day that God created man on the earth; ask from one end of heaven to the other: 'Has anything so great as this ever happened or has its like ever been heard of?'

Has any people ever heard the voice of a god speaking out of a fire, as you have heard, and lived? Or has any god ever attempted to go and take a nation for himself from the midst of another nation, by trials, by signs and wonders, by war, by a mighty hand and an outstretched arm, and by terrifying displays of power, as the Lord your God did for you in Egypt before your very eyes?

So acknowledge today and take to heart that the Lord is God in heaven above and on the earth beneath; there is no other. Keep his statutes and his commandments, which I am commanding you today for your own well-being and that of your descendants after you, so that you may long remain in the land that the Lord your God is giving you for all time."—The word of the Lord. ℟. **Thanks be to God.** ↓

RESPONSORIAL PSALM Ps. 33

Normand L. Blanchard

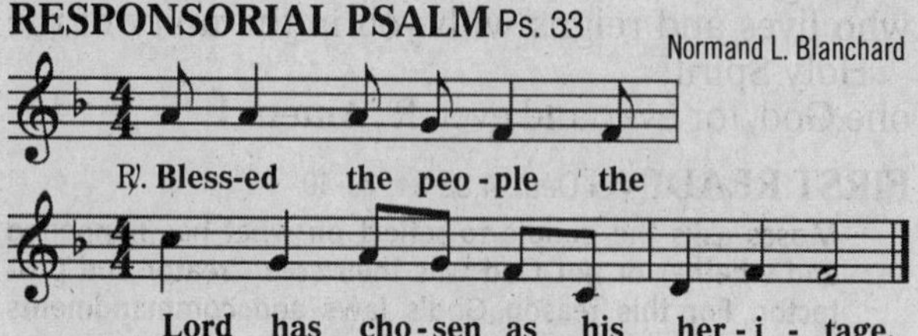
℟. Bless-ed the peo-ple the
Lord has cho-sen as his her-i-tage.

The word of the Lord is upright,
and all his work is done in faithfulness.
He loves righteousness and justice;
the earth is full of the steadfast love of the Lord.—℟.

By the word of the Lord the heavens were made,
and all their host by the breath of his mouth.
For he spoke, and it came to be;
he commanded, and it stood firm.—℟.

Truly the eye of the Lord is on those who fear him,
on those who hope in his steadfast love,
to deliver their souls from death,
and to keep them alive in famine.—℟.

Our soul waits for the Lord;
he is our help and shield.
Let your steadfast love, O Lord, be upon us,
even as we hope in you.—℟. ↓

SECOND READING Rom. 8.14-17

The Spirit of God makes Christians adopted sons and daughters of God. They become at the same time heirs of God with Christ.

A reading from the Letter of Saint Paul to the Romans.

BROTHERS and sisters: All who are led by the Spirit of God are sons and daughters of God. For you did not receive a spirit of slavery to fall back into fear, but you have received a spirit of adoption to sonship. When we cry, "Abba! Father!" it is that very Spirit bearing witness with our spirit that we are children of God, and if children, then heirs, heirs of God and joint heirs with Christ if in fact, we suffer with him so that we may also be glorified with him.—The word of the Lord. ℟. **Thanks be to God.** ↓

GOSPEL ACCLAMATION See Rev. 1.8

℣. Alleluia. ℟. **Alleluia.**
℣. Glory to the Father, the Son, and the Holy Spirit:
to God who is, who was, and who is to come.
℟. **Alleluia.** ↓

GOSPEL Mt. 28.16-20

At Jesus' request the Eleven assemble and fall down in homage. Jesus gives them the all-pervading command to preach to all people and baptize them. He also promises to be with them to the end of time.

℣. The Lord be with you. ℟. **And with your spirit.**
✠ A reading from the holy Gospel according to Matthew. ℟. **Glory to you, O Lord.**

THE eleven disciples went to Galilee, to the mountain to which Jesus had directed them. When they saw him, they worshipped him; but some doubted.

And Jesus came and said to them, "All authority in heaven and on earth has been given to me. Go therefore and make disciples of all nations, baptizing them in the name of the Father and of the Son and of the Holy Spirit, and teaching them to obey everything that I have commanded you. And remember, I am with you always, to the end of the age."—The Gospel of the Lord. ℟. **Praise to you, Lord Jesus Christ.** → No. 15, p. 18

PRAYER OVER THE OFFERINGS

Sanctify by the invocation of your name,
we pray, O Lord our God,
this oblation of our service,
and by it make of us an eternal offering to you.
Through Christ our Lord. ℟. **Amen.** ↓

PREFACE (43)

℣. The Lord be with you. ℟. **And with your spirit.** ℣. Lift up your hearts. ℟. **We lift them up to the Lord.** ℣. Let us give thanks to the Lord our God. ℟. **It is right and just.**

It is truly right and just, our duty and our salvation,
always and everywhere to give you thanks,
Lord, holy Father, almighty and eternal God.

For with your Only Begotten Son and the Holy Spirit
you are one God, one Lord:

not in the unity of a single person,
but in a Trinity of one substance.

For what you have revealed to us of your glory
we believe equally of your Son
and of the Holy Spirit,
so that, in the confessing of the true and eternal Godhead,
you might be adored in what is proper to each Person,
their unity in substance,
and their equality in majesty.

For this is praised by Angels and Archangels,
Cherubim, too, and Seraphim,
who never cease to cry out each day,
as with one voice they acclaim: → No. 23, p. 23

COMMUNION ANTIPHON Gal. 4.6

Since you are children of God, God has sent into your hearts the Spirit of his Son, the Spirit who cries out: Abba, Father. ↓

PRAYER AFTER COMMUNION

May receiving this Sacrament, O Lord our God,
bring us health of body and soul,
as we confess your eternal holy Trinity and undivided Unity.
Through Christ our Lord.
℟. **Amen.** → No. 30, p. 77

Optional Solemn Blessings, p. 97, and Prayers over the People, p. 105

"This is my body. . . ."

JUNE 3

THE MOST HOLY BODY AND BLOOD OF CHRIST

(CORPUS CHRISTI)

Solemnity

ENTRANCE ANTIPHON Cf. Ps. 80.17

He fed them with the finest wheat and satisfied them with honey from the rock. → No. 2, p. 10

COLLECT

O God, who in this wonderful Sacrament
have left us a memorial of your Passion,
grant us, we pray,
so to revere the sacred mysteries of your Body and Blood
that we may always experience in ourselves
the fruits of your redemption.
Who live and reign with God the Father

in the unity of the Holy Spirit,
one God, for ever and ever. ℟. **Amen.** ↓

FIRST READING Ex. 24.3-8

The Israelites promised to observe all the prescriptions of the Lord as related by Moses. To seal this promise Moses offered a sacrifice to the Lord and sprinkled the people with the blood offering.

A reading from the book of Exodus.

MOSES came and told the people all the words of the Lord and all the ordinances; and all the people answered with one voice, and said, "All the words that the Lord has spoken we will do."

And Moses wrote down all the words of the Lord. He rose early in the morning, and built an altar at the foot of the mountain, and set up twelve pillars, corresponding to the twelve tribes of Israel. He sent young men of the children of Israel, who offered burnt offerings and sacrificed oxen as offerings of well-being to the Lord. Moses took half of the blood and put it in basins, and half of the blood he dashed against the altar.

Then he took the book of the covenant, and read it in the hearing of the people; and they said, "All that the Lord has spoken we will do, and we will be obedient."

Moses took the blood and dashed it on the people, and said, "See the blood of the covenant that the Lord has made with you in accordance with all these words."—The word of the Lord. ℟. **Thanks be to God.** ↓

RESPONSORIAL PSALM Ps. 116

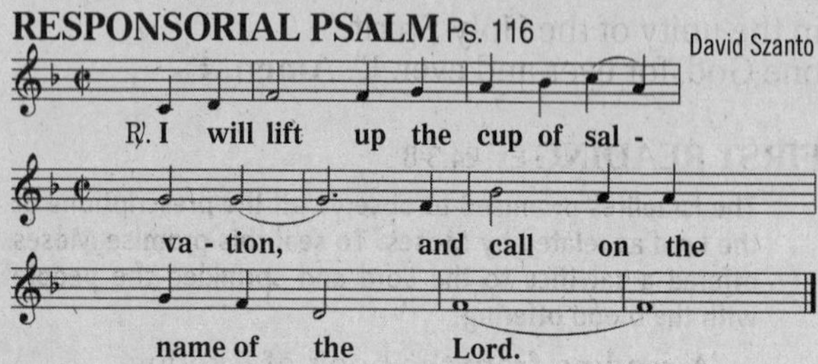
David Szanto
℟. I will lift up the cup of sal - va - tion, and call on the name of the Lord.

Or: ℟. **Alleluia!**

What shall I return to the Lord
for all his bounty to me?
I will lift up the cup of salvation
and call on the name of the Lord.—℟.

Precious in the sight of the Lord
is the death of his faithful ones.
O Lord, I am your servant, the son of your serving girl.
You have loosed my bonds.—℟.

I will offer to you a thanksgiving sacrifice
and call on the name of the Lord.
I will pay my vows to the Lord
in the presence of all his people.—℟. ↓

SECOND READING Heb. 9.11-15

Jesus came as high priest, not offering the blood of animals but his own Blood, to redeem us forever.

A reading from the Letter to the Hebrews.

BROTHERS and sisters: When Christ came as a high priest of the good things that have come, then through the greater and perfect tent—not made with hands, that is, not of this creation—he entered once for all into the Holy Place, not with the blood of goats and calves, but with his own blood, thus obtaining eternal redemption.

For if the blood of goats and bulls, with the sprinkling of the ashes of a heifer, sanctifies those who have been defiled so that their flesh is purified, how much more will the blood of Christ, who through the eternal Spirit offered himself without blemish to God, purify our conscience from dead works to worship the living God!

For this reason Christ is the mediator of a new covenant, so that those who are called may receive the promised eternal inheritance, because a death has occurred that redeems them from the transgressions under the first covenant.—The word of the Lord. ℟. **Thanks be to God.** ↓

SEQUENCE *(Lauda Sion)*

The optional sequence is intended to be sung; otherwise it is better omitted. The shorter version begins at the asterisk.

1. Laud, O Sion, your salvation,
laud with hymns of exultation
Christ, your King and Shepherd true:
Bring him all the praise you know,
He is more than you bestow;
never can you reach his due.

2. Wondrous theme for glad thanksgiving
is the living and life-giving
Bread today before you set,
from his hands of old partaken,
As we know, by faith unshaken,
where the Twelve at supper met.

3. Full and clear ring out your chanting,
let not joy nor grace be wanting.
From your heart let praises burst.
For this day the Feast is holden,
When the institution olden
of that Supper was rehearsed.

4. Here the new law's new oblation,
by the new King's revelation,
Ends the forms of ancient rite.
Now the new the old effaces,
Substance now the shadow chases,
light of day dispels the night.

5. What he did at supper seated,
Christ ordained to be repeated,
His remembrance not to cease.
And his rule for guidance taking,
Bread and wine we hallow, making,
thus, our sacrifice of peace.
6. This the truth each Christian learns:
bread into his own flesh Christ turns,
To his precious Blood the wine.
Sight must fail, no thought conceives,
But a steadfast faith believes,
resting on a power divine.
7. Here beneath these signs are hidden
priceless things to sense forbidden.
Signs alone, not things, we see:
Blood and flesh as wine, bread broken;
Yet beneath each wondrous token,
Christ entire we know to be.
8. All who of this great food partake,
they sever not the Lord, nor break:
Christ is whole to all that taste.
Be one or be a thousand fed
They eat alike that living Bread,
eat of him who cannot waste.
9. Good and guilty likewise sharing,
though their different ends preparing:
timeless death, or blessed life.
Life to these, to those damnation,
Even like participation
is with unlike outcomes rife.
10. When the sacrament is broken,
doubt not, but believe as spoken,
That each severed outward token
does the very whole contain.
None that precious gift divides,
breaking but the sign betides.
Jesus still the same abides,
still unbroken he remains.
*11. Hail, the food of Angels given
to the pilgrim who has striven,
to the child as bread from heaven,
food alone for spirit meant:
Now the former types fulfilling—
Isaac bound, a victim willing,
Paschal Lamb, its life-blood spilling,
manna to the ancients sent.
12. Bread yourself, good Shepherd, tend us;
Jesus, with your love befriend us.
You refresh us and defend us;
to your lasting goodness send us
That the land of life we see.
Lord, who all things both rule and know,
who on this earth such food bestow,
Grant that with your saints we follow
to that banquet ever hallow,
With them heirs and guests to be. ↓

GOSPEL ACCLAMATION Jn. 6.51-52

℣. Alleluia. ℟. **Alleluia.**

℣. I am the living bread that came down from heaven, says the Lord;

whoever eats of this bread will live forever.

℟. **Alleluia.** ↓

GOSPEL Mk. 14.12-16, 22-26

Jesus gave instructions for the Passover supper. At this meal he took bread and wine and changed it into his Body and Blood and gave this Eucharist to his disciples. They all ate and drank at Jesus' request.

℣. The Lord be with you. ℟. **And with your spirit.**
✠ A reading from the holy Gospel according to Mark. ℟. **Glory to you, O Lord.**

ON the first day of Unleavened Bread, when the Passover lamb is sacrificed, the disciples said to Jesus, "Where do you want us to go and make the preparations for you to eat the Passover?"

So he sent two of his disciples, saying to them, "Go into the city, and a man carrying a jar of water will meet you; follow him, and wherever he enters, say to the owner of the house, 'The Teacher asks, "Where is my guest room where I may eat the Passover with my disciples?"' He will show you a large room upstairs, furnished and ready. Make preparations for us there."

So the disciples set out and went to the city, and found everything as he had told them; and they prepared the Passover meal.

While they were eating, he took a loaf of bread, and after blessing it he broke it, gave it to them, and said, "Take; this is my Body." Then he took a cup, and after giving thanks he gave it to them, and all of them drank from it. He said to them, "This is my Blood of the covenant, which is poured out for many. Truly I tell you, I will never again drink of the fruit of the vine until that day when I drink it new in the kingdom of God."

When they had sung the hymn, they went out to the Mount of Olives.—The Gospel of the Lord.
℟. **Praise to you, Lord Jesus Christ.** → No. 15, p. 18

PRAYER OVER THE OFFERINGS

Grant your Church, O Lord, we pray,
the gifts of unity and peace,
whose signs are to be seen in mystery
in the offerings we here present.
Through Christ our Lord.
℟. **Amen.** → No. 21, p. 22 (Pref. 47-48)

COMMUNION ANTIPHON Jn. 6.57

Whoever eats my flesh and drinks my blood remains in me and I in him, says the Lord. ↓

PRAYER AFTER COMMUNION

Grant, O Lord, we pray,
that we may delight for all eternity
in that share in your divine life,
which is foreshadowed in the present age
by our reception of your precious Body and Blood.
Who live and reign for ever and ever.
℟. **Amen.** → No. 30, p. 77

Optional Solemn Blessings, p. 97, and Prayers over the People, p. 105

"Whoever does the will of God is my brother and sister and mother."

JUNE 10

10th SUNDAY IN ORDINARY TIME

ENTRANCE ANTIPHON Cf. Ps. 26.1-2

The Lord is my light and my salvation; whom shall I fear? The Lord is the stronghold of my life; whom should I dread? When those who do evil draw near, they stumble and fall. → No. 2, p. 10

COLLECT

O God, from whom all good things come,
grant that we, who call on you in our need,
may at your prompting discern what is right,
and by your guidance do it.
Through our Lord Jesus Christ, your Son,
who lives and reigns with you in the unity of the Holy Spirit,
one God, for ever and ever. ℟. **Amen.** ↓

FIRST READING Gen. 3:8-15

Notice the promise of a Redeemer, who will overcome evil by striking at its head. The sacred writer is convinced that God will intervene.

A reading from the book of Genesis.

AFTER the woman and the man had eaten from the tree, they heard the sound of the Lord God walking in the garden at the time of the evening breeze, and the man and his wife hid themselves from the presence of the Lord God among the trees of the garden. But the Lord God called to the man, and said to him, "Where are you?" He said, "I heard the sound of you in the garden, and I was afraid, because I was naked; and I hid myself."

God said, "Who told you that you were naked? Have you eaten from the tree of which I commanded you not to eat?"

The man said, "The woman whom you gave to be with me, she gave me fruit from the tree, and I ate."

Then the Lord God said to the woman, "What is this that you have done?" The woman said, "The serpent tricked me, and I ate." The Lord God said to the serpent, "Because you have done this, cursed are you among all animals and among all wild creatures; upon your belly you shall go, and dust you shall eat all the days of your life. I will put enmity between you and the woman, and between your offspring and hers; he will strike your head, and you will strike his heel."—The word of the Lord. ℟. **Thanks be to God.** ↓

RESPONSORIAL PSALM Ps. 130

Frank Lynch

℟. With the Lord there is stead-fast
love, and great pow-er to re - deem.

Out of the depths I cry to you, O Lord.
Lord, hear my voice!
Let your ears be attentive
to the voice of my supplications!—℟.

If you, O Lord, should mark iniquities,
Lord, who could stand?
But there is forgiveness with you,
so that you may be revered.—℟.

I wait for the Lord,
my soul waits, and in his word I hope;
my soul waits for the Lord
more than watchmen for the morning.—℟.

For with the Lord there is steadfast love,
and with him is great power to redeem.
It is he who will redeem Israel
from all its iniquities.—℟. ↓

SECOND READING 2 Cor. 4.13—5.1

Paul makes a few beautiful statements that may encourage those of us who are getting on in years. He says: "We do not lose heart. Even though our outer self is wasting away, our inner self is being renewed day by day."

A reading from the second letter of Saint Paul to the Corinthians.

BROTHERS and sisters: Just as we have the same spirit of faith that is in accordance with Scripture—"I believe, and so I spoke"—we also believe, and so we speak, because we know that the one who raised the Lord Jesus will raise us also with Jesus, and will bring us with you into his presence. Yes, everything is for your sake, so that grace, as it extends to more and more people, may increase thanksgiving, to the glory of God.

So we do not lose heart. Even though our outer self is wasting away, our inner self is being renewed day by day. For this slight momentary affliction is preparing us for an eternal weight of glory beyond all measure, because we look not at what can be seen but at what cannot be seen; for what can be seen is temporary, but what cannot be seen is eternal.

For we know that if the earthly tent we live in is destroyed, we have a building from God, a house not made with hands, eternal in the heavens.—The word of the Lord. ℟. **Thanks be to God.** ↓

GOSPEL ACCLAMATION Jn. 12.31-32

℣. Alleluia. ℟. **Alleluia.**
℣. Now the ruler of this world will be driven out,
and when I am lifted up from the earth, I will draw all people to myself.
℟. **Alleluia.** ↓

GOSPEL Mk. 3.20-35

The gist of today's Gospel is the ongoing battle between good and evil. Jesus expels demons and indicates that the final defeat of evil, promised for the world to come, has been initiated in our history.

℣. The Lord be with you. ℟. **And with your spirit.**
✠ A reading from the holy Gospel according to Mark. ℟. **Glory to you, O Lord.**

JESUS went home and the crowd came together again, so that they could not even eat. When his family heard it, they went out to restrain him, for people were saying, "He has gone out of his mind."

And the scribes who came down from Jerusalem said, "He has Beelzebul, and by the ruler of the demons he casts out demons."

And Jesus called them to him, and spoke to them in parables, "How can Satan cast out Satan? If a kingdom is divided against itself, that kingdom cannot stand. And if a house is divided against itself, that house will not be able to stand. And if Satan has risen up against himself and is divided, he cannot stand, but his end has come. But no one can enter a strong man's house and plunder his property without first tying up the strong man; then indeed the house can be plundered.

Truly I tell you, people will be forgiven for their sins and whatever blasphemies they utter; but whoever blasphemes against the Holy Spirit can never have forgiveness, but is guilty of an eternal sin"—for they had said, "He has an unclean spirit."

Then his mother and his brothers came; and standing outside, they sent to him and called him.

A crowd was sitting around him; and they said to him, "Your mother and your brothers and sisters are outside, asking for you."

And Jesus replied, "Who are my mother and my brothers?" And looking at those who sat around him, he said, "Here are my mother and my brothers! Whoever does the will of God is my brother and sister and mother."—The Gospel of the Lord.
℟. **Praise to you, Lord Jesus Christ.** → No. 15, p. 18

PRAYER OVER THE OFFERINGS

Look kindly upon our service, O Lord, we pray,
that what we offer
may be an acceptable oblation to you
and lead us to grow in charity.
Through Christ our Lord.
℟. **Amen.** → No. 21, p. 22 (Pref. 29-36)

COMMUNION ANTIPHON Ps. 17.3

The Lord is my rock, my fortress, and my deliverer; my God is my saving strength. ↓

OR 1 Jn. 4.16

God is love, and whoever abides in love abides in God, and God in him. ↓

PRAYER AFTER COMMUNION

May your healing work, O Lord,
free us, we pray, from doing evil
and lead us to what is right.
Through Christ our Lord.
℟. **Amen.** → No. 30, p. 77

Optional Solemn Blessings, p. 97, and Prayers over the People, p. 105

"The kingdom of God . . . is like a mustard seed."

JUNE 17

11th SUNDAY IN ORDINARY TIME

ENTRANCE ANTIPHON Cf. Ps. 26.7, 9

O Lord, hear my voice, for I have called to you; be my help. Do not abandon or forsake me, O God, my Saviour! → No. 2, p. 10

COLLECT

O God, strength of those who hope in you,
graciously hear our pleas,
and, since without you mortal frailty can do nothing,
grant us always the help of your grace,
that in following your commands
we may please you by our resolve and our deeds.
Through our Lord Jesus Christ, your Son,
who lives and reigns with you in the unity of the Holy Spirit,
one God, for ever and ever. ℟. **Amen.** ↓

FIRST READING Ez. 17.22-24

The restoration of Israel will be a kind of resurrection. From the modest beginnings of the Church, the good news will spread to all humanity.

A reading from the book of the Prophet Ezekiel.

THUS says the Lord God:
"I myself will take a sprig
from the lofty top of a cedar;
I will set it out.
I will break off a tender one
from the topmost of its young twigs;
I myself will plant it
on a high and lofty mountain.

On the mountain height of Israel
I will plant it,
in order that it may produce boughs and bear fruit,
and become a noble cedar.
Under it every kind of bird will live;
in the shade of its branches will nest
winged creatures of every kind.

All the trees of the field shall know
that I am the Lord.
I bring low the high tree,
I make high the low tree;
I dry up the green tree
and make the dry tree flourish.
I the Lord have spoken;
I will accomplish it."

The word of the Lord. ℟. **Thanks be to God.** ↓

RESPONSORIAL PSALM Ps. 92

Normand L. Blanchard

℟. Lord, it is good to give thanks to ___ you.

It is good to give thanks to the Lord,
to sing praises to your name, O Most High;
to declare your steadfast love in the morning,
and your faithfulness by night.—℟.

The righteous flourish like the palm tree,
and grow like a cedar in Lebanon.
They are planted in the house of the Lord;
they flourish in the courts of our God.—℟.

In old age they still produce fruit;
they are always green and full of sap,
showing that the Lord is upright;
he is my rock, and there is no unrighteousness in him.—℟. ↓

SECOND READING 2 Cor. 5.6-10

While we wait for the Lord, we should please him in all things. Then we will be found without reproach when we appear before him in judgment.

A reading from the second Letter of Saint Paul to the Corinthians.

BROTHERS and sisters, we are always confident, even though we know that while we are at home in the body we are away from the Lord—for we walk by faith, not by sight. Yes, we do have confidence, and we would rather be away from the body and at home with the Lord.

So whether we are at home or away, we make it our aim to please him. For all of us must appear before the judgment seat of Christ, so that each may receive recompense for what he or she has done in the body, whether good or evil.—The word of the Lord. ℟. **Thanks be to God.** ↓

GOSPEL ACCLAMATION

℣. Alleluia. ℟. **Alleluia.**
℣. The seed is the word of God, Christ is the sower;
all who come to him will live for ever.
℟. **Alleluia.** ↓

GOSPEL Mk. 4.26-34

From small beginnings the Church of Christ has arisen for the salvation of all peoples. Through Christ's preaching, God the Father revealed all that he had to say to us.

℣. The Lord be with you. ℟. **And with your spirit.**
✠ A reading from the holy Gospel according to Mark. ℟. **Glory to you, O Lord.**

SUCH a large crowd gathered around Jesus that he got into a boat and began to teach them using many parables.

Jesus said: "The kingdom of God is as if a man would scatter seed on the ground, and would sleep and rise night and day, and the seed would sprout and grow, without his knowing how. The earth produces of itself, first the stalk, then the head, then the full grain in the head. But when the grain is ripe, at once he goes in with the sickle, because the harvest has come."

Jesus also said, "With what can we compare the kingdom of God, or what parable will we use for it? It is like a mustard seed, which, when sown upon the ground, is the smallest of all the seeds on earth; yet when it is sown it grows up and becomes the greatest of all shrubs, and puts forth large branches, so that the birds of the air can make nests in its shade."

With many such parables Jesus spoke the word to them, as they were able to hear it; he did not speak to them except in parables, but he explained everything in private to his disciples.—The Gospel of the Lord. ℟. **Praise to you, Lord Jesus Christ.** → No. 15, p. 18

PRAYER OVER THE OFFERINGS

O God, who in the offerings presented here
provide for the twofold needs of human nature,
nourishing us with food
and renewing us with your Sacrament,
grant, we pray,
that the sustenance they provide
may not fail us in body or in spirit.
Through Christ our Lord.
℟. **Amen.** → No. 21, p. 22 (Pref. 29-36)

COMMUNION ANTIPHON Ps. 26.4

There is one thing I ask of the Lord, only this do I seek: to live in the house of the Lord all the days of my life. ↓

OR Jn. 17.11

Holy Father, keep in your name those you have given me, that they may be one as we are one, says the Lord. ↓

PRAYER AFTER COMMUNION

As this reception of your Holy Communion,
O Lord,
foreshadows the union of the faithful in you,
so may it bring about unity in your Church.
Through Christ our Lord. ℟. **Amen.** → No. 30, p. 77

Optional Solemn Blessings, p. 97, and Prayers over the People, p. 105

John "was in the wilderness until the day he appeared publicly to Israel."

JUNE 24

THE NATIVITY OF ST. JOHN THE BAPTIST

Solemnity

AT THE VIGIL MASS (June 23)

ENTRANCE ANTIPHON Lk. 1.15, 14

He will be great in the sight of the Lord and will be filled with the Holy Spirit, even from his

mother's womb; and many will rejoice at his birth. → No. 2, p. 10

COLLECT

Grant, we pray, almighty God,
that your family may walk in the way of salvation
and, attentive to what Saint John the Precursor urged,
may come safely to the One he foretold,
our Lord Jesus Christ.
Who lives and reigns with you in the unity of the Holy Spirit,
one God, for ever and ever. ℟. **Amen.** ↓

FIRST READING Jer. 1.4-10

In poetic language, Jeremiah describes his call as a prophet. He was afraid to accept it and tried to avoid it. Jeremiah's greatness is that he finally accepted and was faithful to his call.

A reading from the book of the Prophet Jeremiah.

THE word of the Lord came to me saying,
"Before I formed you in the womb I knew you,
and before you were born I consecrated you;
I appointed you a Prophet to the nations."

Then I said, "Ah, Lord God! Truly I do not know how to speak, for I am only a boy." But the Lord said to me,

"Do not say, 'I am only a boy';
for you shall go to all to whom I send you,
and you shall speak whatever I command you.
Do not be afraid of them,
for I am with you to deliver you,
says the Lord."

Then the Lord put out his hand and touched my mouth; and the Lord said to me,

"Now I have put my words in your mouth.
See, today I appoint you over nations and over kingdoms,
to pluck up and to pull down,
to destroy and to overthrow,
to build and to plant."

The word of the Lord. ℟. **Thanks be to God.** ↓

RESPONSORIAL PSALM Ps. 71

Michel Guimont

℟. From my moth-er's womb, you have been my strength.

In you, O Lord, I take refuge;
let me never be put to shame.
In your righteousness deliver me and rescue me;
incline your ear to me and save me.—℟.

Be to me a rock of refuge,
a strong fortress, to save me,
for you are my rock and my fortress.
Rescue me, O my God, from the hand of the wicked.—℟.

For you, O Lord, are my hope,
my trust, O Lord, from my youth.
Upon you I have leaned from my birth;
from my mother's womb you have been my strength.—℟.

My mouth will tell of your righteous acts,
of your deeds of salvation all day long.
O God, from my youth you have taught me,
and I still proclaim your wondrous deeds.—℟. ↓

SECOND READING 1 Pet. 1.8-12

The author refers to the prophets of the Old Testament (of whom John the Baptist was the last), and declares that God's Spirit was guiding them. These prophets foresaw a Messiah to come. He would have to suffer in order to gain victory.

A reading from the first Letter of Saint Peter.

BELOVED: Although you have not seen Jesus Christ, you love him; and even though you do not see him now, you believe in him and rejoice with an indescribable and glorious joy, for you are receiving the outcome of your faith, the salvation of your souls.

The Prophets who prophesied of the grace that was to be yours concerning this salvation made careful search and inquiry, inquiring about the person or time that the Spirit of Christ within them indicated when he testified in advance to the sufferings and the subsequent glory destined for Christ.

It was revealed to the Prophets that they were serving not themselves but you, in regard to the things that have now been announced to you through those who brought you good news by the Holy Spirit sent from heaven—things into which Angels long to look!

Therefore prepare your minds for action; discipline yourselves; set all your hope on the grace that Jesus Christ will bring you when he is revealed.—The word of the Lord. ℟. **Thanks be to God.** ↓

GOSPEL ACCLAMATION Jn. 1.7; Lk. 1.17

℣. Alleluia. ℟. **Alleluia.**
℣. He came as a witness to testify to the light,

to make ready a people prepared for the Lord.
℟. **Alleluia.** ↓

GOSPEL Lk. 1.5-17

The infancy narratives of both the forerunner and the Messiah himself are very similar. They already indicate "Gospel," which means "good tidings." Luke wants to teach that John will be great and dedicated to a magnificent task in life, namely, "to make ready a people prepared for the Lord."

℣. The Lord be with you. ℟. **And with your spirit.**
✠ A reading from the holy Gospel according to Luke. ℟. **Glory to you, O Lord.**

IN the days of King Herod of Judea, there was a priest named Zechariah, who belonged to the priestly order of Abijah. His wife was a descendant of Aaron, and her name was Elizabeth. Both of them were righteous before God, living blamelessly according to all the commandments and regulations of the Lord. But they had no children, because Elizabeth was barren, and both were getting on in years.

Once when Zechariah was serving as priest before God and his section was on duty, he was chosen by lot, according to the custom of the priesthood, to enter the sanctuary of the Lord and offer incense. Now at the time of the incense offering, the whole assembly of the people was praying outside.

Then there appeared to him an Angel of the Lord, standing at the right side of the altar of incense. When Zechariah saw him, he was terrified; and fear overwhelmed him.

But the Angel said to him, "Do not be afraid, Zechariah, for your prayer has been heard. Your wife Elizabeth will bear you a son, and you will name him John.

You will have joy and gladness, and many will rejoice at his birth, for he will be great in the sight of the Lord. He must never drink wine or strong drink; even before his birth he will be filled with the Holy Spirit.

He will turn many of the people of Israel to the Lord their God. With the spirit and power of Elijah he will go before him, to turn the hearts of parents to their children, and the disobedient to the wisdom of the righteous, to make ready a people prepared for the Lord."—The Gospel of the Lord.
℟. **Praise to you, Lord Jesus Christ.** → No. 15, p. 18

PRAYER OVER THE OFFERINGS

Look with favour, O Lord,
upon the offerings made by your people
on the Solemnity of Saint John the Baptist,
and grant that what we celebrate in mystery
we may follow with deeds of devoted service.
Through Christ our Lord. ℟. **Amen.** → Pref. 61, p. 484

COMMUNION ANTIPHON Lk. 1.68

Blessed be the Lord, the God of Israel! He has visited his people and redeemed them. ↓

PRAYER AFTER COMMUNION

May the marvellous prayer of Saint John the Baptist
accompany us who have eaten our fill
at this sacrificial feast, O Lord,
and, since Saint John proclaimed your Son
to be the Lamb who would take away our sins,

may he implore now for us your favour.
Through Christ our Lord.
℟. **Amen.** → No. 30, p. 77

Optional Solemn Blessings, p. 97, and Prayers over the People, p. 105

AT THE MASS DURING THE DAY

ENTRANCE ANTIPHON Jn. 1.6-7; Lk. 1.17

A man was sent from God, whose name was John. He came to testify to the light, to prepare a people fit for the Lord. → No. 2, p. 10

COLLECT

O God, who raised up Saint John the Baptist
to make ready a nation fit for Christ the Lord,
give your people, we pray,
the grace of spiritual joys
and direct the hearts of all the faithful
into the way of salvation and peace.
Through our Lord Jesus Christ, your Son,
who lives and reigns with you in the unity of the Holy Spirit,
one God, for ever and ever. ℟. **Amen.** ↓

FIRST READING Isa. 49.1-6

This passage marks the beginning of the Second Song of the Suffering Servant of Yahweh. He has a mission as a prophet. He is disappointed about the success of his preaching, yet, in faith, he knows that his "reward [is] with my God."

A reading from the book of the Prophet Isaiah.

LISTEN to me, O coastlands,
pay attention, you peoples from far away!

The Lord called me before I was born,
while I was in my mother's womb he named me.

He made my mouth like a sharp sword,
in the shadow of his hand he hid me;
he made me a polished arrow,
in his quiver he hid me away.

And the Lord said to me,
"You are my servant, Israel, in whom I will be glorified."
But I said, "I have laboured in vain,
I have spent my strength for nothing and vanity;
yet surely my cause is with the Lord,
and my reward with my God."

And now the Lord says,
who formed me in the womb to be his servant,
to bring Jacob back to him,
and that Israel might be gathered to him,
for I am honoured in the sight of the Lord,
and my God has become my strength.

He says,
"It is too small a thing that you should be my servant
to raise up the tribes of Jacob
and to restore the survivors of Israel;
I will give you as a light to the nations,
that my salvation may reach to the end of the earth."
The word of the Lord. ℟. **Thanks be to God.** ↓

RESPONSORIAL PSALM Ps. 139

Normand L. Blanchard

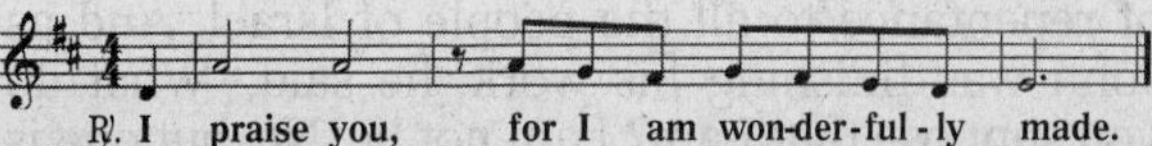
℟. I praise you, for I am won-der-ful-ly made.

O Lord, you have searched me and known me.
You know when I sit down and when I rise up;
you discern my thoughts from far away.
You search out my path and my lying down,
and are acquainted with all my ways.
℟. **I praise you, for I am wonderfully made.**

For it was you who formed my inward parts;
you knit me together in my mother's womb.
I praise you,
for I am fearfully and wonderfully made.—℟.

Wonderful are your works; that I know very well.
My frame was not hidden from you,
when I was being made in secret,
intricately woven in the depths of the earth.—℟. ↓

SECOND READING Acts 13.22-26

Paul sees King David both as a type of Jesus and as his ancestor. According to Hebrew thinking, the Messiah would re-establish God's kingdom on earth; he would be another David. The New Testament authors see Jesus Christ as that new King David, with John the Baptist as his herald.

A reading from the Acts of the Apostles.

IN those days, Paul said: "God made David king of our ancestors. In his testimony about him God said, 'I have found David, son of Jesse, to be a man after my heart, who will carry out all my wishes.'

Of this man's posterity God has brought to Israel a Saviour, Jesus, as he promised; before his coming John had already proclaimed a baptism of repentance to all the people of Israel. And as John was finishing his work, he said, 'What do you suppose that I am? I am not he. No, but one is coming after me; I am not worthy to untie the thong of the sandals on his feet.'

You descendants of Abraham's family, and others who fear God, to us the message of this salvation has been sent."—The word of the Lord. ℟. **Thanks be to God.** ↓

GOSPEL ACCLAMATION Lk. 1.76

℣. Alleluia. ℟. **Alleluia.**
℣. You, child, will be called the Prophet of the Most High;
for you will go before the Lord to prepare his ways.
℟. **Alleluia.** ↓

GOSPEL Lk. 1.57-66, 80

Like the other great men of the Bible, John got his name from God. "John" means "God is gracious," and it indicates his call. John preached to sinners that God is gracious, provided that they turn to God.

℣. The Lord be with you. ℟. **And with your spirit.**
✠ A reading from the holy Gospel according to Luke. ℟. **Glory to you, O Lord.**

THE time came for Elizabeth to give birth, and she bore a son. Her neighbours and relatives heard that the Lord had shown his great mercy to her, and they rejoiced with her.

On the eighth day they came to circumcise the child, and they were going to name him Zechariah after his father. But his mother said, "No; he is to be called John." They said to her, "None of your relatives has this name." Then they began motioning to his father to find out what name he wanted to give him.

He asked for a writing tablet and wrote, "His name is John." And all of them were amazed. Immediately his mouth was opened and his tongue freed, and he began to speak, praising God.

Fear came over all their neighbours, and all these things were talked about throughout the entire hill country of Judea. All who heard them pondered them and said, "What then will this child become?" For, indeed, the hand of the Lord was with him.

The child grew and became strong in spirit, and he was in the wilderness until the day he appeared publicly to Israel.—The Gospel of the Lord. ℟. **Praise to you, Lord Jesus Christ.**

→ No. 15, p. 18

PRAYER OVER THE OFFERINGS

We place these offerings on your altar, O Lord,
to celebrate with fitting honour the nativity of him
who both foretold the coming of the world's Saviour
and pointed him out when he came.
Who lives and reigns for ever and ever.
℟. **Amen.** ↓

PREFACE (61)

℣. The Lord be with you. ℟. **And with your spirit.** ℣. Lift up your hearts. ℟. **We lift them up to the Lord.** ℣. Let us give thanks to the Lord our God. ℟. **It is right and just.**

It is truly right and just, our duty and our salvation,
always and everywhere to give you thanks,
Lord, holy Father, almighty and eternal God,
through Christ our Lord.

In his Precursor, Saint John the Baptist,
we praise your great glory,
for you consecrated him for a singular honour
among those born of women.

His birth brought great rejoicing;
even in the womb he leapt for joy
at the coming of human salvation.
He alone of all the prophets
pointed out the Lamb of redemption.

And to make holy the flowing waters,
he baptized the very author of Baptism
and was privileged to bear him supreme witness
by the shedding of his blood.

And so, with the Powers of heaven,
we worship you constantly on earth,
and before your majesty
without end we acclaim: → No. 23, p. 23

COMMUNION ANTIPHON Cf. Lk. 1.78

Through the tender mercy of our God, the Dawn from on high will visit us. ↓

PRAYER AFTER COMMUNION

Having feasted at the banquet of the heavenly Lamb,
we pray, O Lord,
that, finding joy in the nativity of Saint John the Baptist,
your Church may know as the author of her rebirth
the Christ whose coming John foretold.
Who lives and reigns for ever and ever.
℟. **Amen.** → No. 30, p. 77

Optional Solemn Blessings, p. 97, and Prayers over the People, p. 105

"He took her by the hand and said to her, . . . 'Little girl, get up!' "

JULY 1

13th SUNDAY IN ORDINARY TIME

ENTRANCE ANTIPHON Ps. 46.2

All peoples, clap your hands. Cry to God with shouts of joy! → No. 2, p. 10

COLLECT

O God, who through the grace of adoption
chose us to be children of light,
grant, we pray,
that we may not be wrapped in the darkness of error
but always be seen to stand in the bright light of truth.
Through our Lord Jesus Christ, your Son,
who lives and reigns with you in the unity of the Holy Spirit,
one God, for ever and ever.
℟. **Amen.** ↓

FIRST READING Wis. 1.13-15; 2.23-24

God does not rejoice in the destruction of the living. Rather, God formed us to be imperishable. If we practise justice we will live forever.

A reading from the book of Wisdom.

GOD did not make death,
and he does not delight in the death of the living.
For he created all things so that they might exist;
the generative forces of the world are wholesome,
and there is no destructive poison in them,
and the dominion of Hades is not on earth.
For righteousness is immortal.

For God created man for incorruption,
and made him in the image of his own eternity,
but through the devil's envy death entered the world,
and those who belong to his company experience it.

The word of the Lord. ℟. **Thanks be to God.** ↓

RESPONSORIAL PSALM Ps. 30

Normand L. Blanchard

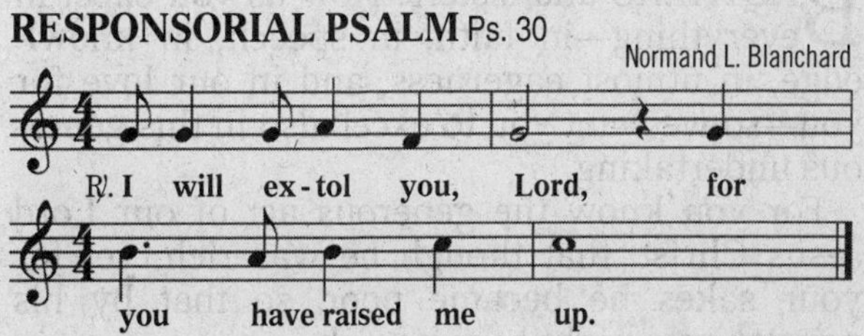
℟. I will ex - tol you, Lord, for
you have raised me up.

I will extol you, O Lord, for you have drawn me up,
and did not let my foes rejoice over me.
O Lord, you brought up my soul from Sheol,

restored me to life from among those gone down to
the Pit.

℟. **I will extol you, Lord, for you have raised me up.**

Sing praises to the Lord, O you his faithful ones,
and give thanks to his holy name.
For his anger is but for a moment;
his favour is for a lifetime.
Weeping may linger for the night,
but joy comes with the morning.—℟.

Hear, O Lord, and be gracious to me!
O Lord, be my helper!
You have turned my mourning into dancing.
O Lord my God, I will give thanks to you forever.
—℟. ↓

SECOND READING 2 Cor. 8.7, 9, 13-15

Christians should be generous to others in imitation of the total liberality of Christ, who gave his life for the salvation of all.

A reading from the second Letter of Saint Paul to the Corinthians.

BROTHERS and sisters: Now as you excel in everything—in faith, in speech, in knowledge, in utmost eagerness, and in our love for you—so we want you to excel also in this generous undertaking.

For you know the generous act of our Lord Jesus Christ, that though he was rich, yet for your sakes he became poor, so that by his poverty you might become rich.

I do not mean that there should be relief for others and pressure on you, but it is a question of a fair balance between your present abundance and their need, so that their abundance may be for your need, in order that there may be a fair balance.

As it is written,

"The one who had much did not have too much,
and the one who had little did not have too little."

The word of the Lord. ℟. **Thanks be to God.** ↓

GOSPEL ACCLAMATION 2 Tim. 1.10

℣. Alleluia. ℟. **Alleluia.**
℣. Our Saviour Jesus Christ has abolished death and has brought us life through the Gospel.
℟. **Alleluia.** ↓

GOSPEL Mk. 5.21-43 or 5.21-24, 35-43

Jesus overcomes the death of Jairus' daughter and the ailment of the woman with the hemorrhage. He thus prefigures his victory over the death of alienation from God. Jesus is the Prophet of the end time who has come to bring us life by restoring our relationship of love with God.

[If the "Shorter Form" is used, the indented text in brackets is omitted.]

℣. The Lord be with you. ℟. **And with your spirit.**
✠ A reading from the holy Gospel according to Mark. ℟. **Glory to you, O Lord.**

WHEN Jesus had crossed in the boat to the other side, a great crowd gathered around him; and he was by the sea. Then one of the synagogue leaders named Jairus came and, when he saw Jesus, fell at his feet and begged him repeatedly, "My little daughter is at the point of death. Come and lay your hands on her, so that she may be made well, and live." So Jesus went with him.

And a large crowd followed him and pressed in on him.

[Now there was a woman who had been suffering from hemorrhages for twelve years. She had endured much under many physicians, and had spent all that she had; and she was no better, but rather grew worse. She had heard about Jesus, and came up behind him in the crowd and touched his cloak, for she said, "If I but touch his clothes, I will be made well." Immediately her hemorrhage stopped; and she felt in her body that she was healed of her disease.

Immediately aware that power had gone forth from him, Jesus turned about in the crowd and said, "Who touched my clothes?" And his disciples said to him, "You see the crowd pressing in on you; how can you say, 'Who touched me'?"

He looked all around to see who had done it. But the woman, knowing what had happened to her, came in fear and trembling, fell down before him, and told him the whole truth. Jesus said to her, "Daughter, your faith has made you well; go in peace, and be healed of your disease."]

[While Jesus was still speaking,] some people came from the leader's house to say, "Your daughter is dead. Why trouble the teacher any further?" But overhearing what they said, Jesus said to the leader of the synagogue, "Do not fear, only believe."

Jesus allowed no one to follow him. When they came to the house of the leader of the synagogue, he saw a commotion, people weeping and wailing loudly. When he had entered, he said to them, "Why do you make a commotion and weep? The child is not dead but sleeping." And they laughed at him.

Then Jesus put them all outside, and took the child's father and mother and those who were with him, and went in where the child was. He took her by the hand and said to her, "Talitha cum," which means, "Little girl, get up!" And immediately the girl got up and began to walk about for she was twelve years of age. At this they were overcome with amazement.

He strictly ordered them that no one should know this, and told them to give her something to eat.—The Gospel of the Lord. ℟. **Praise to you, Lord Jesus Christ.** → No. 15, p. 18

PRAYER OVER THE OFFERINGS

O God, who graciously accomplish
the effects of your mysteries,
grant, we pray,
that the deeds by which we serve you
may be worthy of these sacred gifts.
Through Christ our Lord.
℟. **Amen.** → No. 21, p. 22 (Pref. 29-36)

COMMUNION ANTIPHON Cf. Ps. 102.1

Bless the Lord, O my soul, and all within me, his holy name. ↓

OR Jn. 17.20-21

O Father, I pray for them, that they may be one in us, that the world may believe that you have sent me, says the Lord. ↓

PRAYER AFTER COMMUNION

May this divine sacrifice we have offered and received
fill us with life, O Lord, we pray,
so that, bound to you in lasting charity,
we may bear fruit that lasts for ever.
Through Christ our Lord.
℟. **Amen.** → No. 30, p. 77

Optional Solemn Blessings, p. 97, and Prayers over the People, p. 105

"A Prophet is not without honour, except in his hometown."

JULY 8

14th SUNDAY IN ORDINARY TIME

ENTRANCE ANTIPHON Cf. Ps. 47.10-11

Your merciful love, O God, we have received in the midst of your temple. Your praise, O God, like your name, reaches the ends of the earth; your right hand is filled with saving justice.

→ No. 2, p. 10

COLLECT

O God, who in the abasement of your Son
have raised up a fallen world,
fill your faithful with holy joy,
for on those you have rescued from slavery to sin
you bestow eternal gladness.
Through our Lord Jesus Christ, your Son,
who lives and reigns with you in the unity of the
  Holy Spirit,
one God, for ever and ever.
℟. **Amen.** ↓

FIRST READING Ez. 2.3-5

Ezekiel is selected by God to be a prophet and messenger to the Israelites. When resisted, Ezekiel is to say: "Thus says the Lord God." This will show that he is a prophet.

A reading from the book of the Prophet Ezekiel.

A SPIRIT entered into me and set me on my feet; and I heard one speaking to me: "Son of man, I am sending you to the children of Israel, to a nation of rebels who have rebelled against me; they and their ancestors have transgressed against me to this very day. The descendants are impudent and stubborn. I am sending you to them, and you shall say to them, 'Thus says the Lord God.' Whether they hear or refuse to hear (for they are a rebellious house), they shall know that there has been a Prophet among them."—The word of the Lord. ℟. **Thanks be to God.** ↓

RESPONSORIAL PSALM Ps. 123

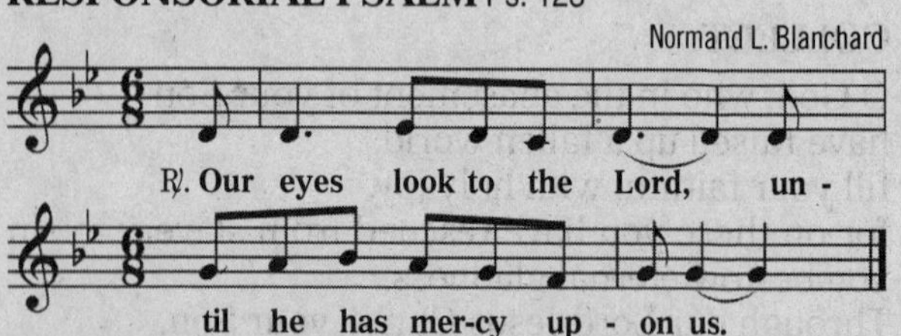
Normand L. Blanchard
℟. Our eyes look to the Lord, un -
til he has mer-cy up - on us.

To you I lift up my eyes—
O you who are enthroned in the heavens—
as the eyes of servants
look to the hand of their master.—℟.

As the eyes of a maid
to the hand of her mistress,

and day by day bring our conduct
closer to the life of heaven.
Through Christ our Lord.
℟. **Amen.** → No. 21, p. 22 (Pref. 29-36)

COMMUNION ANTIPHON Ps. 33.9

Taste and see that the Lord is good; blessed the man who seeks refuge in him. ↓

OR Mt. 11.28

Come to me, all who labour and are burdened, and I will refresh you, says the Lord. ↓

PRAYER AFTER COMMUNION

Grant, we pray, O Lord,
that, having been replenished by such great gifts,
we may gain the prize of salvation
and never cease to praise you.
Through Christ our Lord.
℟. **Amen.** → No. 30, p. 77

Optional Solemn Blessings, p. 97, and Prayers over the People, p. 105

"Jesus . . . began to send them out two by two."

JULY 15

15th SUNDAY IN ORDINARY TIME

ENTRANCE ANTIPHON Cf. Ps. 16.15

As for me, in justice I shall behold your face; I shall be filled with the vision of your glory.

→ No. 2, p. 10

COLLECT

O God, who show the light of your truth
to those who go astray,
so that they may return to the right path,
give all who for the faith they profess
are accounted Christians
the grace to reject whatever is contrary to the name of Christ
and to strive after all that does it honour.
Through our Lord Jesus Christ, your Son,
who lives and reigns with you in the unity of the Holy Spirit,
one God, for ever and ever. ℟. **Amen.** ↓

FIRST READING Amos 7.12-15

Amos writes how he was chosen by God to go out and prophesy to the people of Israel.

A reading from the book of the Prophet Amos.

AMAZIAH, the priest of Bethel, said to Amos, "O seer, go, flee away to the land of Judah, earn your bread there, and prophesy there; but never again prophesy at Bethel, for it is the king's sanctuary, and it is a temple of the kingdom."

Then Amos answered Amaziah, "I am no Prophet, nor a Prophet's son; but I am a herdsman, and a dresser of sycamore trees, and the Lord took me from following the flock, and the Lord said to me, 'Go, prophesy to my people Israel.'"—The word of the Lord. ℟. **Thanks be to God.** ↓

RESPONSORIAL PSALM Ps. 85

Gloria Gassi

℟. Show us your stead-fast love, O
Lord, and grant us your sal - va - tion.

Let me hear what God the Lord will speak,
for he will speak peace to his people.
Surely his salvation is at hand for those who fear him,
that his glory may dwell in our land.—℟.

Steadfast love and faithfulness will meet;
righteousness and peace will kiss each other.
Faithfulness will spring up from the ground,
and righteousness will look down from the sky.—℟.

The Lord will give what is good,
and our land will yield its increase.
Righteousness will go before him,
and will make a path for his steps.
℟. **Show us your steadfast love, O Lord, and grant us your salvation.** ↓

SECOND READING Eph. 1.3-14 or 1.3-10

God chose his followers to be holy, blameless, and filled with love—to be his adopted children in Jesus. In Jesus and through the seal of the Holy Spirit, full redemption shall come to humankind.

[If the "Shorter Form" is used, the indented text in brackets is omitted.]

A reading from the Letter of Saint Paul
to the Ephesians.

BLESSED be the God and Father of our Lord Jesus Christ, who has blessed us in Christ with every spiritual blessing in the heavenly places, just as he chose us in Christ before the foundation of the world to be holy and blameless before him in love.

He destined us for adoption to sonship as his own through Jesus Christ, according to the good pleasure of his will, to the praise of his glorious grace that he freely bestowed on us in the Beloved.

In Christ we have redemption through his blood, the forgiveness of our trespasses, according to the riches of his grace that he lavished on us. With all wisdom and insight God has made known to us the mystery of his will, according to his good pleasure that he set forth in Christ, as a plan for the fullness of time, to gather up all things in Christ, things in heaven and things on earth.

[In Christ we have also obtained an inheritance, having been destined according to the purpose of him who accomplishes all things according to his counsel and will, so that we, who were the first to set our hope on Christ, might live for the praise of his glory.

In him you also, when you had heard the word of truth, the Gospel of your salvation, and had believed in him, were marked with the seal of the promised Holy Spirit.

This is the pledge of our inheritance toward redemption as God's own people, to the praise of his glory.]

The word of the Lord. ℟. **Thanks be to God.** ↓

GOSPEL ACCLAMATION See Eph. 1.17-18

℣. Alleluia. ℟. **Alleluia.**

℣. May the Father of our Lord Jesus Christ enlighten the eyes of our heart
that we may know the hope to which we are called.

℟. **Alleluia.** ↓

GOSPEL Mk. 6.7-13

Jesus sent out the Twelve, instructing them to take only a staff and to preach the gospel. If they were refused a listening ear, they should leave the locality. They cured many sick people.

℣. The Lord be with you. ℟. **And with your spirit.**
✠ A reading from the holy Gospel according to Mark. ℟. **Glory to you, O Lord.**

JESUS called the twelve and began to send them out two by two, and gave them authority over the unclean spirits. He ordered them to take nothing for their journey except a staff, no bread, no bag, no money in their belts; but to wear sandals and not to put on two tunics.

Jesus said to them, "Wherever you enter a house, stay there until you leave the place. If any place will not welcome you and they refuse to hear you, as you leave, shake off the dust that is on your feet as a testimony against them."

So the twelve went out and proclaimed that all should repent. They cast out many demons, and anointed with oil many who were sick and cured them.—The Gospel of the Lord. ℟. **Praise to you, Lord Jesus Christ.** → No. 15, p. 18

PRAYER OVER THE OFFERINGS

Look upon the offerings of the Church, O Lord,
as she makes her prayer to you,
and grant that, when consumed by those who believe,
they may bring ever greater holiness.
Through Christ our Lord.
℟. **Amen.** → No. 21, p. 22 (Pref. 29-36)

COMMUNION ANTIPHON Cf. Ps. 83.4-5

The sparrow finds a home, and the swallow a nest for her young: by your altars, O Lord of hosts, my King and my God. Blessed are they

who dwell in your house, for ever singing your praise. ↓

OR Jn. 6.57

Whoever eats my flesh and drinks my blood remains in me and I in him, says the Lord. ↓

PRAYER AFTER COMMUNION

Having consumed these gifts, we pray, O Lord,
that, by our participation in this mystery,
its saving effects upon us may grow.
Through Christ our Lord.
℟. **Amen.** → No. 30, p. 77

Optional Solemn Blessings, p. 97, and Prayers over the People, p. 105

"They went away in the boat . . . by themselves."

JULY 22

16th SUNDAY IN ORDINARY TIME

ENTRANCE ANTIPHON Ps. 53.6, 8

See, I have God for my help. The Lord sustains

my soul. I will sacrifice to you with willing heart, and praise your name, O Lord, for it is good.

→ No. 2, p. 10

COLLECT

Show favour, O Lord, to your servants
and mercifully increase the gifts of your grace,
that, made fervent in hope, faith and charity,
they may be ever watchful in keeping your commands.
Through our Lord Jesus Christ, your Son,
who lives and reigns with you in the unity of the Holy Spirit,
one God, for ever and ever. ℟. **Amen.** ↓

FIRST READING Jer. 23.1-6

Woe to those who sow evil. Their evil deeds will be punished. Good shepherds will be appointed. A righteous Branch for David will come, and Judah will be saved.

A reading from the book of the Prophet Jeremiah.

"WOE to the shepherds who destroy and scatter the sheep of my pasture!" says the Lord. Therefore, thus says the Lord, the God of Israel, concerning the shepherds who shepherd my people: It is you who have scattered my flock, and have driven them away, and you have not attended to them.

"So I will attend to you for your evil doings," says the Lord. "Then I myself will gather the remnant of my flock out of all the lands where I have driven them, and I will bring them back to their fold, and they shall be fruitful and multiply. I will raise up shepherds over them who will shepherd them, and they shall not fear any longer, or be dismayed, nor shall any be missing," says the Lord.

"The days are surely coming," says the Lord, "when I will raise up for David a righteous Branch, and he shall reign as king and deal wisely, and shall execute justice and righteousness in the land. In his days Judah will be saved and Israel will live in safety. And this is the name by which he will be called: 'The Lord is our righteousness.'"—The word of the Lord. ℟. **Thanks be to God.** ↓

RESPONSORIAL PSALM Ps. 23

Michel Guimont

℟. The Lord is my
shep - herd; I shall not want.

The Lord is my shepherd, I shall not want.
He makes me lie down in green pastures;
he leads me beside still waters;
he restores my soul.—℟.

He leads me in right paths for his name's sake.
Even though I walk through the darkest valley,
I fear no evil;
for you are with me;
your rod and your staff—they comfort me.—℟.

You prepare a table before me
in the presence of my enemies;
you anoint my head with oil;
my cup overflows.—℟.

Surely goodness and mercy shall follow me
all the days of my life,
and I shall dwell in the house of the Lord
my whole life long.
℟. **The Lord is my shepherd; I shall not want.** ↓

SECOND READING Eph. 2.13-18

Paul tells the Ephesians that Jesus has brought them together, bringing peace and reconciliation through his cross.

A reading from the Letter of Saint Paul
to the Ephesians.

BROTHERS and sisters: Now in Christ Jesus you who once were far off have been brought near by the blood of Christ. For he is our peace; in his flesh he has made both Jews and Gentiles into one and has broken down the dividing wall, that is, the hostility between us.

He has abolished the law with its commandments and ordinances, that he might create in himself one New Man in place of the two, thus making peace, and might reconcile both groups to God in one body through the Cross, thus putting to death that hostility through it.

So Christ Jesus came and proclaimed peace to you who were far off and peace to those who were near; for through him both of us have access in one Spirit to the Father.—The word of the Lord. ℟. **Thanks be to God.** ↓

GOSPEL ACCLAMATION Jn. 10.27

℣. Alleluia. ℟. **Alleluia.**
℣. My sheep hear my voice, says the Lord;

I know them, and they follow me.
℟. **Alleluia.** ↓

GOSPEL Mk. 6.30-34

When Jesus called the apostles aside to rest, the people followed them, even to a deserted place.

℣. The Lord be with you. ℟. **And with your spirit.**
✠ A reading from the holy Gospel according to Mark. ℟. **Glory to you, O Lord.**

THE Apostles returned from their mission. They gathered around Jesus, and told him all that they had done and taught.

He said to them, "Come away to a deserted place all by yourselves and rest a while." For many were coming and going, and they had no leisure even to eat. And they went away in the boat to a deserted place by themselves.

Now many saw them going and recognized them, and they hurried there on foot from all the towns and arrived ahead of them. As Jesus went ashore, he saw a great crowd; and he had compassion for them, because they were like sheep without a shepherd; and he began to teach them many things.—The Gospel of the Lord. ℟. **Praise to you, Lord Jesus Christ.** → No. 15, p. 18

PRAYER OVER THE OFFERINGS

O God, who in the one perfect sacrifice
brought to completion varied offerings of the law,
accept, we pray, this sacrifice from your faithful servants
and make it holy, as you blessed the gifts of Abel,
so that what each has offered to the honour of your majesty

may benefit the salvation of all.
Through Christ our Lord.
℟. **Amen.** → No. 21, p. 22 (Pref. 29-36)

COMMUNION ANTIPHON Ps. 110.4-5

The Lord, the gracious, the merciful, has made a memorial of his wonders; he gives food to those who fear him. ↓

OR Rev. 3.20

Behold, I stand at the door and knock, says the Lord. If anyone hears my voice and opens the door to me, I will enter his house and dine with him, and he with me. ↓

PRAYER AFTER COMMUNION

Graciously be present to your people, we pray,
O Lord,
and lead those you have imbued with heavenly
mysteries
to pass from former ways to newness of life.
Through Christ our Lord.
℟. **Amen.** → No. 30, p. 77

Optional Solemn Blessings, p. 97, and Prayers over the People, p. 105

"Jesus took the loaves, and . . . he distributed them. . . ."

JULY 29

17th SUNDAY IN ORDINARY TIME

ENTRANCE ANTIPHON Cf. Ps. 67.6-7, 36

God is in his holy place, God who unites those who dwell in his house; he himself gives might and strength to his people. → No. 2, p. 10

COLLECT

O God, protector of those who hope in you,
without whom nothing has firm foundation,
nothing is holy,
bestow in abundance your mercy upon us
and grant that, with you as our ruler and guide,
we may use the good things that pass
in such a way as to hold fast even now
to those that ever endure.
Through our Lord Jesus Christ, your Son,
who lives and reigns with you in the unity of the
Holy Spirit,
one God, for ever and ever. ℟. **Amen.** ↓

FIRST READING 2 Kgs. 4.42-44

At the command from Elisha, the man of God, the barley bread was placed before the people, indicating that this comes from the Lord. Even though a hundred ate the bread, some was left over.

A reading from the second book of Kings.

A MAN came bringing food from the first fruits to Elisha, the man of God: twenty loaves of barley and fresh ears of grain in his sack. Elisha said, "Give it to the people and let them eat."

But his servant said, "How can I set this before a hundred people?" So Elisha repeated, "Give it to the people and let them eat, for thus says the Lord, 'They shall eat and have some left.'"

The servant set it before them, they ate, and had some left, according to the word of the Lord.—The word of the Lord. ℟. **Thanks be to God.** ↓

RESPONSORIAL PSALM Ps. 145

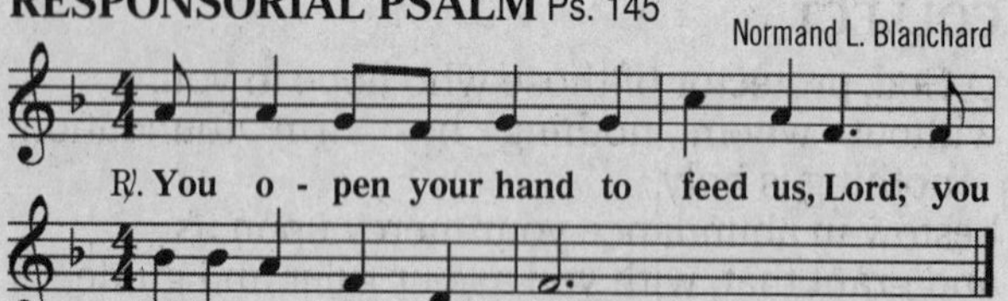
Normand L. Blanchard
℟. You o - pen your hand to feed us, Lord; you
sat-is-fy all our needs.

All your works shall give thanks to you, O Lord,
and all your faithful shall bless you.
They shall speak of the glory of your kingdom,
and tell of your power.—℟.

The eyes of all look to you,
and you give them their food in due season.

You open your hand,
satisfying the desire of every living thing.—℟.

The Lord is just in all his ways,
and kind in all his doings.
The Lord is near to all who call on him,
to all who call on him in truth.—℟. ↓

SECOND READING Eph. 4.1-6

A life worthy of the Lord consists of humility, gentleness, patience, and bearing with one another in love.

A reading from the Letter of Saint Paul
to the Ephesians.

BROTHERS and sisters: I, the prisoner in the Lord, beg you to lead a life worthy of the calling to which you have been called, with all humility and gentleness, with patience, bearing with one another in love, making every effort to maintain the unity of the Spirit in the bond of peace. There is one body and one Spirit, just as you were called to the one hope of your calling, one Lord, one faith, one baptism, one God and Father of all, who is above all and through all and in all.—The word of the Lord. ℟. **Thanks be to God.** ↓

GOSPEL ACCLAMATION Lk. 7.16

℣. Alleluia. ℟. **Alleluia.**
℣. A great Prophet has risen among us;
God has looked favourably on his people.
℟. **Alleluia.** ↓

GOSPEL Jn. 6.1-15

Jesus told the five thousand to sit down. He took the five barley loaves and a couple of fish, gave thanks, and told the disciples to pass out the food to all.

℣. The Lord be with you. ℟. **And with your spirit.**
✠ A reading from the holy Gospel according to John. ℟. **Glory to you, O Lord.**

JESUS went to the other side of the Sea of Galilee, also called the Sea of Tiberias. A large crowd kept following him, because they saw the signs that he was doing for the sick. Jesus went up the mountain and sat down there with his disciples. Now the Passover, the festival of the Jews, was near.

When he looked up and saw a large crowd coming toward him, Jesus said to Philip, "Where are we to buy bread for these people to eat?" He said this to test him, for he himself knew what he was going to do. Philip answered him, "Six months' wages would not buy enough bread for each of them to get a little."

One of his disciples, Andrew, Simon Peter's brother, said to Jesus, "There is a boy here who has five barley loaves and two fish. But what are they among so many people?" Jesus said, "Make the people sit down." Now there was a great deal of grass in the place; so they sat down, about five thousand in all.

Then Jesus took the loaves, and when he had given thanks, he distributed them to those who were seated; so also the fish, as much as they wanted.

When they were satisfied, he told his disciples, "Gather up the fragments left over, so that nothing may be lost." So they gathered them up, and from the fragments of the five barley loaves, left by those who had eaten, they filled twelve baskets.

When the people saw the sign that he had done, they began to say, "This is indeed the Prophet who is to come into the world." When Jesus realized that they were about to come and take him by force to make him king, he withdrew again to the mountain by himself.—The Gospel of the Lord.
℟. **Praise to you, Lord Jesus Christ.** → No. 15, p. 18

PRAYER OVER THE OFFERINGS

Accept, O Lord, we pray, the offerings
which we bring from the abundance of your gifts,
that through the powerful working of your grace
these most sacred mysteries may sanctify our
present way of life
and lead us to eternal gladness.
Through Christ our Lord.
℟. **Amen.** → No. 21, p. 22 (Pref. 29-36)

COMMUNION ANT. Ps. 102.2

Bless the Lord, O my soul, and never forget all his benefits. ↓

OR Mt. 5.7-8

Blessed are the merciful, for they shall receive mercy. Blessed are the clean of heart, for they shall see God. ↓

PRAYER AFTER COMMUNION

We have consumed, O Lord, this divine Sacrament,
the perpetual memorial of the Passion of your Son;
grant, we pray, that this gift,
which he himself gave us with love beyond all telling,
may profit us for salvation.
Through Christ our Lord.
℟. **Amen.** → No. 30, p. 77

Optional Solemn Blessings, p. 97, and Prayers over the People, p. 105

JHS

"The bread of God is that which comes down from heaven and gives life to the world."

AUGUST 5

18th SUNDAY IN ORDINARY TIME

ENTRANCE ANTIPHON Ps. 69.2, 6

O God, come to my assistance; O Lord, make haste to help me! You are my rescuer, my help; O Lord, do not delay. → No. 2, p. 10

COLLECT

Draw near to your servants, O Lord,
and answer their prayers with unceasing kindness,
that, for those who glory in you as their Creator
and guide,
you may restore what you have created
and keep safe what you have restored.
Through our Lord Jesus Christ, your Son,
who lives and reigns with you in the unity of the
Holy Spirit,
one God, for ever and ever. ℟. **Amen.** ↓

FIRST READING Ex. 16.2-4, 12-15, 31a

The Israelites begin to grumble, and the Lord promises to rain down bread from heaven and give them quail to eat at twilight. By this they will know that the Lord is God.

A reading from the book of Exodus.

THE whole congregation of the children of Israel complained against Moses and Aaron in the wilderness. The children of Israel said to them, "If only we had died by the hand of the Lord in the land of Egypt, when we sat by the fleshpots and ate our fill of bread; for you have brought us out into this wilderness to kill this whole assembly with hunger."

Then the Lord said to Moses, "I am going to rain bread from heaven for you, and each day the people shall go out and gather enough for that day. In that way I will test them, whether they will follow my instruction or not.

I have heard the complaining of the children of Israel; say to them, 'At twilight you shall eat meat, and in the morning you shall have your fill of bread; then you shall know that I am the Lord your God.'"

In the evening quails came up and covered the camp; and in the morning there was a layer of dew around the camp.

When the layer of dew lifted, there on the surface of the wilderness was a fine flaky substance, as fine as frost on the ground. When the children of Israel saw it, they said to one another, "What is it?" For they did not know what it was. Moses said to them, "It is the bread that the Lord has given you to eat."

The house of Israel called it manna.—The word of the Lord. ℟. **Thanks be to God.** ↓

RESPONSORIAL PSALM Ps. 78

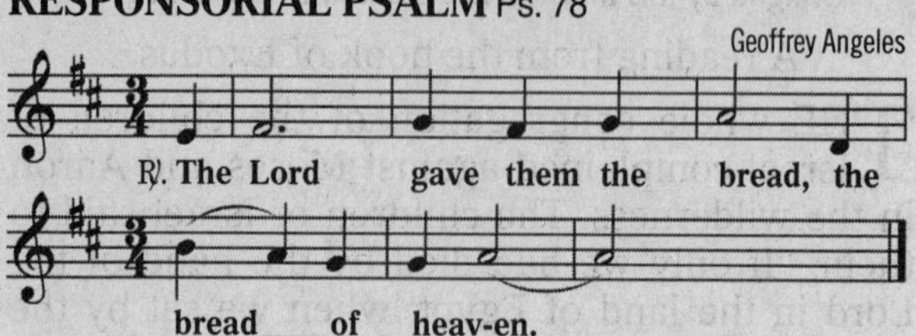
Geoffrey Angeles
℟. The Lord gave them the bread, the
bread ___ of heav-en.

Things that we have heard and known,
that our ancestors have told us, we will not hide;
we will tell to the coming generation
the glorious deeds of the Lord, and his might.
and the wonders that he has done.—℟.

He commanded the skies above,
and opened the doors of heaven;
he rained down on them manna to eat,
and gave them the bread of heaven.—℟.

Man ate of the bread of Angels;
he sent them food in abundance.
And he brought them to his holy hill,
to the mountain that his right hand had won.—℟. ↓

SECOND READING Eph. 4.17, 20-24

Paul tells the Ephesians that they must abandon their old pagan ways and acquire a fresh, spiritual way of living—to become new people created according to the likeness of God.

A reading from the Letter of Saint Paul to the Ephesians.

BROTHERS and sisters: Now this I affirm and insist on in the Lord: you must no longer live as the Gentiles live, in the futility of their minds.

That is not the way you learned Christ! For surely you have heard about him and were taught in him, as truth is in Jesus.

You were taught to put away your former way of life, your old self, corrupt and deluded by its lusts, and to be renewed in the spirit of your minds, and to clothe yourselves with the New Man, created according to the likeness of God in true righteousness and holiness.—The word of the Lord. ℟. **Thanks be to God.** ↓

GOSPEL ACCLAMATION Mt. 4.4

℣. Alleluia. ℟. **Alleluia.**
℣. Man does not live by bread alone,

but by every word that comes from the mouth of God.
℟. **Alleluia.** ↓

GOSPEL Jn. 6.24-35

After feeding the multitude, Jesus and his disciples went across the lake. The people found them, and Jesus cautioned them that they were looking only for signs and food. Jesus says that he is the bread of life. God demands faith in the one he sent.

℣. The Lord be with you. ℟. **And with your spirit.**
✠ A reading from the holy Gospel according to John. ℟. **Glory to you, O Lord.**

WHEN the crowd saw that neither Jesus nor his disciples were at the place where Jesus had given the bread, they themselves got into the boats and went to Capernaum looking for Jesus.

When they found him on the other side of the sea, they said to him, "Rabbi, when did you come here?" Jesus answered them, "Very truly, I tell you, you are looking for me, not because you saw signs, but because you ate your fill of the loaves. Do not work for the food that perishes, but for the food that endures for eternal life, which the Son of Man will give you. For it is on him that God the Father has set his seal." Then they said to Jesus, "What must we do to perform the works of God?"

Jesus answered them, "This is the work of God, that you believe in him whom he has sent." So they said to him, "What sign are you going to give us then, so that we may see it and believe you? What work are you performing? Our ancestors ate the manna in the wilderness; as it is written, 'He gave them bread from heaven to eat.'"

Then Jesus said to them, "Very truly, I tell you, it was not Moses who gave you the bread from heaven, but it is my Father who gives you the true bread from heaven. For the bread of God is that which comes down from heaven and gives life to the world."

They said to him, "Sir, give us this bread always." Jesus said to them, "I am the bread of life. Whoever comes to me will never be hungry, and whoever believes in me will never be thirsty."—The Gospel of the Lord. ℟. **Praise to you, Lord Jesus Christ.** → No. 15, p. 18

PRAYER OVER THE OFFERINGS

Graciously sanctify these gifts, O Lord, we pray,
and, accepting the oblation of this spiritual sacrifice,
make of us an eternal offering to you.
Through Christ our Lord.
℟. **Amen.** → No. 21, p. 22 (Pref. 29-36)

COMMUNION ANTIPHON Wis. 16.20

You have given us, O Lord, bread from heaven, endowed with all delights and sweetness in every taste. ↓

OR Jn. 6.35

I am the bread of life, says the Lord; whoever comes to me will not hunger and whoever believes in me will not thirst. ↓

PRAYER AFTER COMMUNION

Accompany with constant protection, O Lord,
those you renew with these heavenly gifts
and, in your never-failing care for them,
make them worthy of eternal redemption.
Through Christ our Lord.
℟. **Amen.** → No. 30, p. 77

Optional Solemn Blessings, p. 97, and Prayers over the People, p. 105

"I am the bread of life."

AUGUST 12

19th SUNDAY IN ORDINARY TIME

ENTRANCE ANTIPHON Cf. Ps. 73.20, 19, 22, 23

Look to your covenant, O Lord, and forget not the life of your poor ones for ever. Arise, O God, and defend your cause, and forget not the cries of those who seek you. → No. 2, p. 10

COLLECT

Almighty ever-living God,
whom, taught by the Holy Spirit,
we dare to call our Father,
bring, we pray, to perfection in our hearts
the spirit of adoption as your sons and daughters,
that we may merit to enter into the inheritance
which you have promised.
Through our Lord Jesus Christ, your Son,
who lives and reigns with you in the unity of the
Holy Spirit,
one God, for ever and ever. ℟. **Amen.** ↓

FIRST READING 1 Kgs. 19.4-8

Elijah, being discouraged, prayed for death. Twice an Angel came to him and supplied him with food. Strengthened by this food and by the word of God, Elijah got up and continued his journey to the mountain of God, Horeb.

A reading from the first book of Kings.

ELIJAH went a day's journey into the wilderness, and came and sat down under a solitary broom tree. He asked that he might die: "It is enough; now, O Lord, take away my life, for I am no better than my ancestors."

Then Elijah lay down under the broom tree and fell asleep. Suddenly an Angel touched him and said to him, "Get up and eat." He looked, and there at his head was a cake baked on hot stones, and a jar of water. He ate and drank, and lay down again.

The Angel of the Lord came a second time, touched him, and said, "Get up and eat, otherwise the journey will be too much for you." Elijah got up, and ate and drank; then he went in the strength of that food forty days and forty nights to Horeb the mountain of God.—The word of the Lord. ℟. **Thanks be to God.** ↓

RESPONSORIAL PSALM Ps. 34

Paul K. McKay

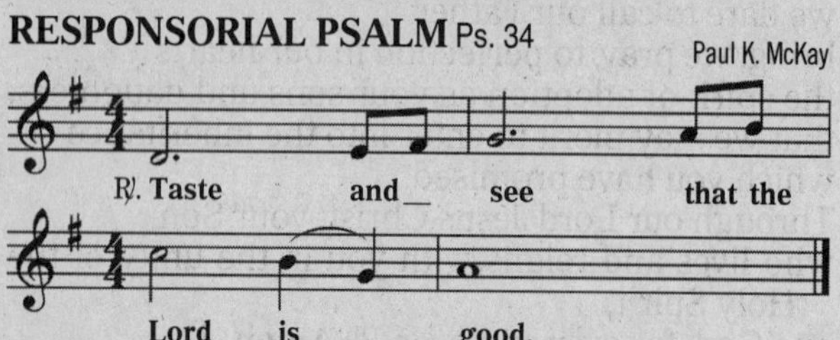
℟. Taste and see that the
Lord is good.

I will bless the Lord at all times;
his praise shall continually be in my mouth.
My soul makes its boast in the Lord;
let the humble hear and be glad.—℟.

O magnify the Lord with me,
and let us exalt his name together.
I sought the Lord, and he answered me,
and delivered me from all my fears.—℟.

Look to him, and be radiant;
so your faces shall never be ashamed.
The poor one called, and the Lord heard,
and saved that person from every trouble.—℟.

The Angel of the Lord encamps
around those who fear him, and delivers them.
O taste and see that the Lord is good;
blessed is the one who takes refuge in him.—℟. ↓

SECOND READING Eph. 4.30—5.2

Paul directs the Ephesians to be kind, tenderhearted, and forgiving. They are to imitate God as beloved children, and follow the way of love as Christ loved us.

A reading from the Letter of Saint Paul to the Ephesians.

BROTHERS and sisters: Do not grieve the Holy Spirit of God, with which you were marked with a seal for the day of redemption. Put away from you all bitterness and wrath and anger and wrangling and slander, together with all malice, and be kind to one another, tender-hearted, forgiving one another, as God in Christ has forgiven you.

Therefore be imitators of God, as beloved children, and live in love, as Christ loved us and gave himself up for us, a fragrant offering and sacrifice to God.—The word of the Lord. ℟. **Thanks be to God.** ↓

GOSPEL ACCLAMATION Jn. 6.51

℣. Alleluia. ℟. **Alleluia.**
℣. I am the living bread that came down from heaven, says the Lord;
whoever eats of this bread will live for ever.
℟. **Alleluia.** ↓

GOSPEL Jn. 6.41-51

The people question Jesus' origin, and Jesus tells them that no one can come to him unless drawn by the Father. Those who believe will have eternal life.

℣. The Lord be with you. ℟. **And with your spirit.**
✠ A reading from the holy Gospel according to John. ℟. **Glory to you, O Lord.**

THE people began to complain about Jesus because he said, "I am the bread that came down from heaven." They were saying, "Is not this Jesus, the son of Joseph, whose father and mother we know? How can he now say, 'I have come down from heaven'?"

Jesus answered them, "Do not complain among yourselves. No one can come to me unless the Father who sent me draw them; and I will raise that person up on the last day. It is written in the Prophets, 'And they shall all be taught by God.' Everyone who has heard and learned from the Father comes to me. Not that anyone has seen the Father except the one who is from God; he has seen the Father. Very truly, I tell you, whoever believes has eternal life.

I am the bread of life. Your ancestors ate the manna in the wilderness, and they died. This is the bread that comes down from heaven, so that one may eat of it and not die. I am the living bread that came down from heaven. Whoever eats of this bread will live forever; and the bread that I will give for the life of the world is my flesh."—The Gospel of the Lord. ℟. **Praise to you, Lord Jesus Christ.** → No. 15, p. 18

PRAYER OVER THE OFFERINGS

Be pleased, O Lord, to accept the offerings of your Church,
for in your mercy you have given them to be offered
and by your power you transform them
into the mystery of our salvation.
Through Christ our Lord.
℟. **Amen.** → No. 21, p. 22 (Pref. 29-36)

COMMUNION ANTIPHON Ps. 146.12, 14

O Jerusalem, glorify the Lord, who gives you your fill of finest wheat. ↓

OR Cf. Jn. 6.51

The bread that I will give, says the Lord, is my flesh for the life of the world. ↓

PRAYER AFTER COMMUNION

May the communion in your Sacrament
that we have consumed, save us, O Lord,
and confirm us in the light of your truth.
Through Christ our Lord.
℟. **Amen.** → No. 30, p. 77

Optional Solemn Blessings, p. 97, and Prayers over the People, p. 105

"The bread that I will give
for the life of the world is my flesh."

AUGUST 19

20th SUNDAY IN ORDINARY TIME

ENTRANCE ANTIPHON Ps. 83.10-11

Turn your eyes, O God, our shield; and look on the face of your anointed one; one day within your courts is better than a thousand elsewhere.

→ No. 2, p. 10

COLLECT

O God, who have prepared for those who love you
good things which no eye can see,
fill our hearts, we pray, with the warmth of your love,
so that, loving you in all things and above all things,
we may attain your promises,
which surpass every human desire.
Through our Lord Jesus Christ, your Son,

who lives and reigns with you in the unity of the
Holy Spirit,
one God, for ever and ever. ℟. **Amen.** ↓

FIRST READING Prov. 9.1-6

Proverbs directing attention to young men who were to take their places in the royal court speak of food and drink. A diet of wisdom, however, will lead to prudent living, religious wisdom, vision, and moderation.

A reading from the book of Proverbs.

WISDOM has built her house,
she has hewn her seven pillars.
She has slaughtered her animals,
she has mixed her wine,
she has also set her table.
She has sent out her servant girls,
she calls from the highest places in the town,
"You that are simple, turn in here!"

To those without sense she says,
"Come, eat of my bread
and drink of the wine I have mixed.
Lay aside immaturity, and live,
and walk in the way of insight."

The word of the Lord. ℟. **Thanks be to God.** ↓

RESPONSORIAL PSALM Ps. 34

Normand L. Blanchard

℟. Taste and see that the
Lord is good.

I will bless the Lord at all times;
his praise shall continually be in my mouth.
My soul makes its boast in the Lord;
let the humble hear and be glad.
℟. **Taste and see that the Lord is good.**

O fear the Lord, you his holy ones,
for those who fear him have no want.
The young lions suffer want and hunger,
but those who seek the Lord lack no good thing.—℟.

Come, O children, listen to me;
I will teach you the fear of the Lord.
Which of you desires life,
and covets many days to enjoy good?—℟.

Keep your tongue from evil,
and your lips from speaking deceit.
Depart from evil, and do good;
seek peace, and pursue it.—℟. ↓

SECOND READING Eph. 5.15-20

Christians should be careful to live according to the will of the Lord. They should avoid carefree living and are to give praise and worship to God in the name of Jesus.

A reading from the Letter of Saint Paul to the Ephesians.

BROTHERS and sisters, be careful how you live, not as unwise people but as wise, making the most of the time, because the days are evil. So do not be foolish, but understand what the will of the Lord is.

Do not get drunk with wine, for that is debauchery; but be filled with the Spirit, as you sing Psalms and hymns and spiritual songs among yourselves, singing and making music to the Lord in your hearts, giving thanks to God the Father at all times and for everything in the name of our Lord Jesus Christ.—The word of the Lord. ℟. **Thanks be to God.** ↓

GOSPEL ACCLAMATION Jn. 6.56

℣. Alleluia. ℟. **Alleluia.**
℣. Whoever eats my flesh and drinks my blood abides in me,
and I in them, says the Lord.
℟. **Alleluia.** ↓

GOSPEL Jn. 6.51-58

Jesus proclaims that he is the living bread from heaven. Whoever eats of it shall live forever. When the people quarrel about this teaching, Jesus repeats it without any qualification.

℣. The Lord be with you. ℟. **And with your spirit.**
✠ A reading from the holy Gospel according to John. ℟. **Glory to you, O Lord.**

JESUS said to the people: "I am the living bread that came down from heaven. Whoever eats of this bread will live forever; and the bread that I will give for the life of the world is my flesh."

The people then disputed among themselves, saying, "How can this man give us his flesh to eat?"

So Jesus said to them, "Very truly, I tell you, unless you eat the flesh of the Son of Man and drink his blood, you have no life in you. Whoever eats my flesh and drinks my blood has eternal life, and I will raise them up on the last day; for my flesh is true food and my blood is true drink. Whoever eats my flesh and drinks my blood abides in me, and I in them.

Just as the living Father sent me, and I live because of the Father, so whoever eats me will live because of me. This is the bread that came down from heaven, not like that which your ancestors ate, and they died. But the one who eats this bread will live forever."—The Gospel of the Lord.
℟. **Praise to you, Lord Jesus Christ.** → No. 15, p. 18

PRAYER OVER THE OFFERINGS

Receive our oblation, O Lord,
by which is brought about a glorious exchange,
that, by offering what you have given,
we may merit to receive your very self.
Through Christ our Lord.
℟. **Amen.** → No. 21, p. 22 (Pref. 29-36)

COMMUNION ANTIPHON Ps. 129.7

With the Lord there is mercy; in him is plentiful redemption. ↓

OR Jn. 6.51

I am the living bread that came down from heaven, says the Lord. Whoever eats of this bread will live for ever. ↓

PRAYER AFTER COMMUNION

Made partakers of Christ through these Sacraments,
we humbly implore your mercy, Lord,
that, conformed to his image on earth,
we may merit also to be his co-heirs in heaven.
Who lives and reigns for ever and ever.
℟. **Amen.** → No. 30, p. 77

Optional Solemn Blessings, p. 97, and Prayers over the People, p. 105

"No one can come to me unless it is granted them by my Father."

AUGUST 26

21st SUNDAY IN ORDINARY TIME

ENTRANCE ANTIPHON Cf. Ps. 85.1-3

Turn your ear, O Lord, and answer me; save the servant who trusts in you, my God. Have mercy on me, O Lord, for I cry to you all the day long.

→ No. 2, p. 10

COLLECT

O God, who cause the minds of the faithful
to unite in a single purpose,
grant your people to love what you command
and to desire what you promise,
that, amid the uncertainties of this world,
our hearts may be fixed on that place
where true gladness is found.
Through our Lord Jesus Christ, your Son,
who lives and reigns with you in the unity of the
Holy Spirit,
one God, for ever and ever. ℟. **Amen.↓**

FIRST READING Jos. 24.1-2a, 15-17, 18b

Joshua admonished the Israelites to decide their allegiance to God. They answered that they would serve the God of their ancestors, who delivered them from slavery and protected them.

A reading from the book of Joshua.

JOSHUA gathered all the tribes of Israel to Shechem, and summoned the elders, the heads, the judges, and the officers of Israel; and they presented themselves before God.

And Joshua said to all the people, "If you are unwilling to serve the Lord, choose this day whom you will serve, whether the gods your ancestors served in the region beyond the River or the gods of the Amorites in whose land you are living. As for me and my household, we will serve the Lord."

Then the people answered, "Far be it from us that we should forsake the Lord to serve other gods; for it is the Lord our God who brought us and our ancestors up from the land of Egypt, out of the house of slavery, and who did those great signs in our sight. He protected us along all the way that we went, and among all the peoples through whom we passed. Therefore we also will serve the Lord, for he is our God."—The word of the Lord. ℟. **Thanks be to God.** ↓

RESPONSORIAL PSALM Ps. 34

Michel Guimont
℟. Taste and see that the

Lord is good.

I will bless the Lord at all times;
his praise shall continually be in my mouth.
My soul makes its boast in the Lord;
let the humble hear and be glad.—℟.

The eyes of the Lord are on the righteous,
and his ears are open to their cry.
The face of the Lord is against evil-doers,
to cut off the remembrance of them from the earth.—℟.

When the righteous cry for help, the Lord hears,
and rescues them from all their troubles.
The Lord is near to the brokenhearted,
and saves the crushed in spirit.—℟.

Many are the afflictions of the righteous one,
but the Lord rescues him from them all.
He keeps all his bones;
not one of them will be broken.—℟.

Evil brings death to the wicked,
and those who hate the righteous will be condemned.
The Lord redeems the life of his servants;
none of those who take refuge in him will be condemned.—℟. ↓

SECOND READING Eph. 4.32—5.1-2, 21-32

Paul gives specific directives to wives and husbands. Wives are to be submissive to their husbands as the Church submits to Christ. Husbands must love their

wives as their own bodies. They are to be ever faithful to each other.

A reading from the Letter of Saint Paul to the Ephesians.

BROTHERS and sisters: Be kind to one another, tenderhearted, forgiving one another, as God in Christ has forgiven you. Therefore be imitators of God, as beloved children, and live in love, as Christ loved us and gave himself up for us, a fragrant offering and sacrifice to God. Be subject to one another out of reverence for Christ.

Wives, be subject to your husbands as you are to the Lord. For the husband is the head of the wife just as Christ is the head of the Church, the body of which he is the Saviour. Just as the Church is subject to Christ, so also wives ought to be, in everything, to their husbands.

Husbands, love your wives, just as Christ loved the Church and gave himself up for her, in order to make her holy by cleansing her with the washing of water by the word, so as to present the Church to himself in splendour, without a spot or wrinkle or anything of the kind—yes, so that she may be holy and without blemish.

In the same way, husbands should love their wives as they do their own bodies. He who loves his wife loves himself. For no one ever hates his own body, but he nourishes and tenderly cares for it, just as Christ does for the Church, because we are members of his body.

"For this reason a man will leave his father and mother and be joined to his wife, and the two will become one flesh." This is a great mystery, and I am applying it to Christ and the Church.—The word of the Lord. ℟. **Thanks be to God.** ↓

GOSPEL ACCLAMATION Jn. 6.63, 68

℣. Alleluia. ℟. **Alleluia.**
℣. Your words, Lord, are spirit and life;
you have the words of eternal life.
℟. **Alleluia.** ↓

GOSPEL Jn. 6.53, 60-69

Jesus emphasizes that to believe in him demands faith—a gift from his Father. Many left Jesus, but Peter, speaking for the Twelve, turned and said, "Lord, to whom can we go? You have the words of eternal life."

℣. The Lord be with you. ℟. **And with your spirit.**
✠ A reading from the holy Gospel according to John. ℟. **Glory to you, O Lord.**

JESUS said to the people: "Very truly, I tell you, unless you eat the flesh of the Son of Man and drink his blood, you have no life in you."

When many of his disciples heard this, they said: "This teaching is difficult; who can accept it?"

But Jesus, being aware that his disciples were complaining about it, said to them, "Does this offend you? Then what if you were to see the Son of Man ascending to where he was before? It is the spirit that gives life; the flesh is useless. The words that I have spoken to you are spirit and life. But among you there are some who do not believe." For Jesus knew from the first who were the ones that did not believe, and who was the one that would betray him.

And he said, "For this reason I have told you that no one can come to me unless it is granted them by my Father."

Because of this many of his disciples turned back, and no longer went about with him. So Jesus asked the twelve, "Do you also wish to go away?"

Simon Peter answered him, "Lord, to whom can we go? You have the words of eternal life. We have come to believe and know that you are the Holy One of God."—The Gospel of the Lord.
℟. **Praise to you, Lord Jesus Christ.** → No. 15, p. 18

PRAYER OVER THE OFFERINGS

O Lord, who gained for yourself a people by adoption
through the one sacrifice offered once for all,
bestow graciously on us, we pray,
the gifts of unity and peace in your Church.
Through Christ our Lord.
℟. **Amen.** → No. 21, p. 22 (Pref. 29-36)

COMMUNION ANTIPHON Cf. Ps. 103.13-15

The earth is replete with the fruits of your work, O Lord; you bring forth bread from the earth and wine to cheer the heart. ↓

OR Cf. Jn. 6.54

Whoever eats my flesh and drinks my blood has eternal life, says the Lord, and I will raise him up on the last day. ↓

PRAYER AFTER COMMUNION

Complete within us, O Lord, we pray,
the healing work of your mercy

and graciously perfect and sustain us,
so that in all things we may please you.
Through Christ our Lord.
℟. **Amen.** → No. 30, p. 77

Optional Solemn Blessings, p. 97, and Prayers over the People, p. 105

"There is nothing outside a person that by going in can defile them."

SEPTEMBER 2

22nd SUNDAY IN ORDINARY TIME

ENTRANCE ANTIPHON Cf. Ps. 85.3, 5

Have mercy on me, O Lord, for I cry to you all the day long. O Lord, you are good and forgiving, full of mercy to all who call to you. → No. 2, p. 10

COLLECT

God of might, giver of every good gift,
put into our hearts the love of your name,
so that, by deepening our sense of reverence,

you may nurture in us what is good
and, by your watchful care,
keep safe what you have nurtured.
Through our Lord Jesus Christ, your Son,
who lives and reigns with you in the unity of the
Holy Spirit,
one God, for ever and ever. ℟. **Amen.** ↓

FIRST READING Deut. 4.1-2, 6-8

Moses warns the people that they are not to add or subtract from the statutes and decrees of the Lord. God is looking after them directly.

A reading from the book of Deuteronomy.

"NOW, Israel, give heed to the statutes and ordinances that I am teaching you to observe, so that you may live to enter and occupy the land that the Lord, the God of your fathers, is giving you. You must neither add anything to what I command you nor take away anything from it, but keep the commandments of the Lord your God with which I am charging you.

You must observe them diligently, for this will show your wisdom and discernment to the peoples, who, when they hear all these statutes, will say, 'Surely this great nation is a wise and discerning people!' For what other great nation has a god so near to it as the Lord our God is whenever we call to him? And what other great nation has statutes and ordinances as just as this entire law that I am setting before you today?"—The word of the Lord. ℟. **Thanks be to God.** ↓

RESPONSORIAL PSALM Ps. 15

Geoffrey Angeles

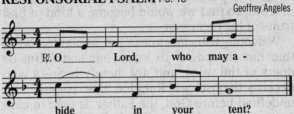

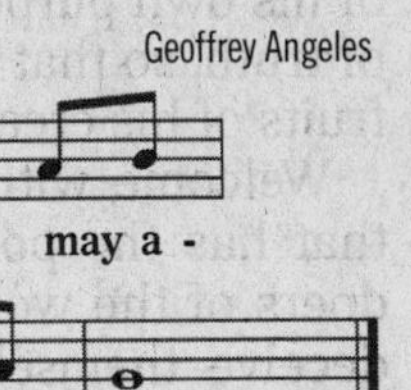
℟. O Lord, who may a - bide in your tent?

Whoever walks blamelessly, and does what is right,
and speaks the truth from their heart;
whoever does not slander with their tongue.—℟.

Whoever does no evil to a friend,
nor takes up a reproach against a neighbour;
in whose eyes the wicked one is despised,
but who honours those who fear the Lord.—℟.

Whoever stands by their oath even to their hurt;
who does not lend money at interest,
and does not take a bribe against the innocent.
One who does these things shall never be moved.—℟. ↓

SECOND READING Jas. 1.17-18, 21-22, 27

Everything worthwhile comes from God. Christians should welcome God's word, listen to it, and act upon it. They should care for widows and orphans.

A reading from the Letter of Saint James.

EVERY generous act of giving, with every perfect gift, is from above, coming down from the Father of lights, with whom there is no variation or shadow due to change. In fulfilment of his own purpose he gave us birth by the word of truth, so that we would become a kind of first fruits of his creatures.

Welcome with meekness the implanted word that has the power to save your souls. But be doers of the word, and not merely hearers who deceive themselves. Religion that is pure and undefiled before God, the Father, is this: to care for orphans and widows in their distress, and to keep oneself unstained by the world.—The word of the Lord. ℟. **Thanks be to God.** ↓

GOSPEL ACCLAMATION Jas. 1.18

℣. Alleluia. ℟. **Alleluia.**
℣. The Father gave us birth by the word of truth, that we would become first fruits of his creation.
℟. **Alleluia.** ↓

GOSPEL Mk. 7.1-8, 14-15, 21-23

The Pharisees questioned Jesus because his followers were lax in observing the prescribed ritual washings. In answer, Jesus condemned lip service. It is wicked thoughts from the heart that make a person impure.

℣. The Lord be with you. ℟. **And with your spirit.**
✠ A reading from the holy Gospel according to Mark. ℟. **Glory to you, O Lord.**

WHEN the Pharisees and some of the scribes who had come from Jerusalem gathered around Jesus, they noticed that some of his disciples were eating with defiled hands, that is, without washing them. For the Pharisees, and all the Jews, do not eat unless they thoroughly wash their hands, thus observing the tradition of the elders; and they do not eat anything from the market unless they wash it; and there are also many other traditions that they observe, the washing of cups, pots, and bronze kettles. So the Pharisees and the scribes asked him, "Why do your disciples not live according to the tradition of the elders, but eat with defiled hands?"

Jesus said to them, "Isaiah prophesied rightly about you hypocrites, as it is written,

'This people honours me with their lips,
  but their hearts are far from me;
in vain do they worship me,
  teaching human precepts as doctrines.'

You abandon the commandment of God and hold to human tradition."

Then Jesus called the crowd again and said to them, "Listen to me, all of you, and understand: there is nothing outside a person that by going in can defile them, but the things that come out of a person are what defile them.

For it is from within, from the human heart, that evil intentions come: fornication, theft, murder, adultery, avarice, wickedness, deceit, licentiousness, envy, slander, pride, folly.

All these evil things come from within, and they defile a person."—The Gospel of the Lord.

℟. **Praise to you, Lord Jesus Christ.** → No. 15, p. 18

PRAYER OVER THE OFFERINGS

May this sacred offering, O Lord,
confer on us always the blessing of salvation,
that what it celebrates in mystery

it may accomplish in power.
Through Christ our Lord.
℟. **Amen.** → No. 21, p. 22 (Pref. 29-36)

COMMUNION ANTIPHON Ps. 30.20

How great is the goodness, Lord, that you keep for those who fear you. ↓

OR Mt. 5.9-10

Blessed are the peacemakers, for they shall be called children of God. Blessed are they who are persecuted for the sake of righteousness, for theirs is the Kingdom of Heaven. ↓

PRAYER AFTER COMMUNION

Renewed by this bread from the heavenly table,
we beseech you, Lord,
that, being the food of charity,
it may confirm our hearts
and stir us to serve you in our neighbour.
Through Christ our Lord.
℟. **Amen.** → No. 30, p. 77

Optional Solemn Blessings, p. 97, and Prayers over the People, p. 105

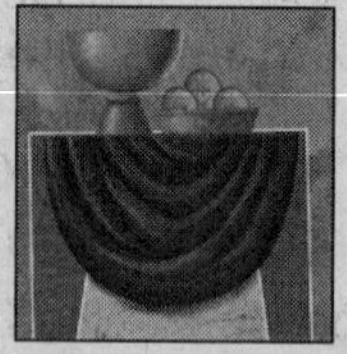

"Ephphatha," that is, "Be opened."

SEPTEMBER 9

23rd SUNDAY IN ORDINARY TIME

ENTRANCE ANTIPHON Ps. 118.137, 124

You are just, O Lord, and your judgment is right; treat your servant in accord with your merciful love. → No. 2, p. 10

COLLECT

O God, by whom we are redeemed and receive
adoption,
look graciously upon your beloved sons and
daughters,
that those who believe in Christ
may receive true freedom
and an everlasting inheritance.
Through our Lord Jesus Christ, your Son,
who lives and reigns with you in the unity of the
Holy Spirit,
one God, for ever and ever. ℟. **Amen.** ↓

FIRST READING Isa. 35.4-7

Isaiah speaks of the Messiah's coming. At that time God will come to save the people and bring many blessings to them.

A reading from the book of the Prophet Isaiah.

SAY to those who are of a fearful heart,
"Be strong, do not fear!
Here is your God.
He will come with vengeance,
with terrible recompense.
He will come and save you."

Then the eyes of the blind shall be opened,
and the ears of the deaf unstopped;
then the lame shall leap like a deer,
and the tongue of the mute sing for joy.

For waters shall break forth in the wilderness,
and streams in the desert;
the burning sand shall become a pool,
and the thirsty ground springs of water.

The word of the Lord. ℟. **Thanks be to God.** ↓

RESPONSORIAL PSALM Ps. 146

Normand L. Blanchard

℟. Praise ___ the Lord, ___ O my soul!

Or: ℟. **Alleluia!**

It is the Lord who keeps faith forever,
who executes justice for the oppressed;
who gives food to the hungry.
The Lord sets the prisoners free.—℟.

The Lord opens the eyes of the blind
and lifts up those who are bowed down;

the Lord loves the righteous
and watches over the strangers.—℟.

The Lord upholds the orphan and the widow,
but the way of the wicked he brings to ruin.
The Lord will reign forever,
your God, O Zion, for all generations.—℟. ↓

SECOND READING Jas. 2.1-5

James warns the Christians about showing favouritism to the rich. No one is in a position to judge. God chose those who were poor according to worldly standards in order to make them rich in faith.

A reading from the Letter of Saint James.

MY brothers and sisters, do you with your acts of favouritism really believe in our glorious Lord Jesus Christ? For if a man with gold rings and in fine clothes comes into your assembly, and if a poor person in dirty clothes also comes in, and if you take notice of the one wearing the fine clothes and say, "Have a seat here, please," while to the one who is poor you say, "Stand there," or, "Sit at my feet," have you not made distinctions among yourselves, and become judges with evil thoughts?

Listen, my beloved brothers and sisters. Has not God chosen the poor in the world to be rich in faith and to be heirs of the kingdom that he has promised to those who love him?—The word of the Lord. ℟. **Thanks be to God.** ↓

GOSPEL ACCLAMATION Mt. 4.23

℣. Alleluia. ℟. **Alleluia.**

℣. Jesus proclaimed the good news of the kingdom
and cured every sickness among the people.
℟. **Alleluia.** ↓

GOSPEL Mk. 7.31-37

The people brought to Jesus a deaf man to be cured. Taking him aside, Jesus cured him, asking him to keep this a secret. But the man proclaimed the cure all the more. The people were amazed at Jesus' power.

℣. The Lord be with you. ℟. **And with your spirit.**
✠ A reading from the holy Gospel according to Mark. ℟. **Glory to you, O Lord.**

RETURNING from the region of Tyre, Jesus went by way of Sidon towards the Sea of Galilee, in the region of the Decapolis.

They brought to him a man who was deaf and who had an impediment in his speech; and they begged him to lay his hand on him. Jesus took him aside in private, away from the crowd, and put his fingers into his ears, and he spat and touched his tongue. Then looking up to heaven, he sighed and said to him, "Ephphatha," that is, "Be opened." And immediately the man's ears were opened, his tongue was released, and he spoke plainly.

Then Jesus ordered them to tell no one; but the more he ordered them, the more zealously they proclaimed it. They were astounded beyond measure, saying, "He has done everything well; he even makes the deaf to hear and the mute to speak."—The Gospel of the Lord.
℟. **Praise to you, Lord Jesus Christ.** → No. 15, p. 18

PRAYER OVER THE OFFERINGS

O God, who give us the gift of true prayer and of peace,
graciously grant that, through this offering,
we may do fitting homage to your divine majesty
and, by partaking of the sacred mystery,
we may be faithfully united in mind and heart.
Through Christ our Lord.
℟. **Amen.** → No. 21, p. 22 (Pref. 29-36)

COMMUNION ANTIPHON Cf. Ps. 41.2-3

Like the deer that yearns for running streams, so my soul is yearning for you, my God; my soul is thirsting for God, the living God. ↓

OR Jn. 8.12

I am the light of the world, says the Lord; whoever follows me will not walk in darkness, but will have the light of life. ↓

PRAYER AFTER COMMUNION

Grant that your faithful, O Lord,
whom you nourish and endow with life
through the food of your Word and heavenly Sacrament,
may so benefit from your beloved Son's great gifts
that we may merit an eternal share in his life.
Who lives and reigns for ever and ever.
℟. **Amen.** → No. 30, p. 77

Optional Solemn Blessings, p. 97, and Prayers over the People, p. 105

"Whoever wants to become my follower, let him deny himself and take up his cross and follow me."

SEPTEMBER 16

24th SUNDAY IN ORDINARY TIME

ENTRANCE ANTIPHON Cf. Sir. 36.18

Give peace, O Lord, to those who wait for you, that your prophets be found true. Hear the prayers of your servant, and of your people Israel.

→ No. 2, p. 10

COLLECT

Look upon us, O God,
Creator and ruler of all things,
and, that we may feel the working of your mercy,
grant that we may serve you with all our heart.
Through our Lord Jesus Christ, your Son,
who lives and reigns with you in the unity of the
Holy Spirit,
one God, for ever and ever.
℟. **Amen.** ↓

FIRST READING Isa. 50.5-9

Isaiah speaks of his sufferings, but God is his help and upholds him in misery.

A reading from the book of the Prophet Isaiah.

THE Lord God has opened my ear,
and I was not rebellious,
I did not turn backward.
I gave my back to those who struck me,
and my cheeks to those who pulled out the beard;
I did not hide my face
from insult and spitting.

The Lord God helps me;
therefore I have not been disgraced;
therefore I have set my face like flint,
and I know that I shall not be put to shame;
he who vindicates me is near.

Who will contend with me?
Let us stand up together.
Who are my adversaries?
Let them confront me.
It is the Lord God who helps me;
who will declare me guilty?

The word of the Lord. ℟. **Thanks be to God.** ↓

RESPONSONSORIAL PSALM Ps. 116

Frank Lynch

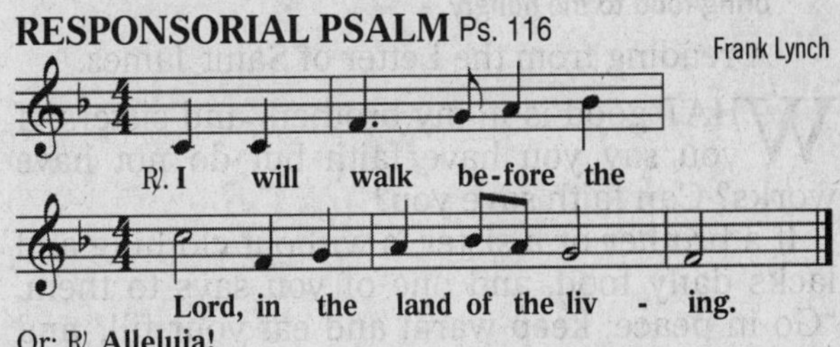
℟. I will walk be-fore the
Lord, in the land of the liv - ing.

Or: ℟. **Alleluia!**

I love the Lord, because he has heard
my voice and my supplications.
Because he inclined his ear to me,
therefore I will call on him as long as I live.
℟. **I will walk before the Lord, in the land of the living.**

Or: ℟. **Alleluia!**

The snares of death encompassed me;
the pangs of Sheol laid hold on me;
I suffered distress and anguish.
Then I called on the name of the Lord:
"O Lord, I pray, save my life!"—℟.

Gracious is the Lord, and righteous;
our God is merciful.
The Lord protects the simple;
when I was brought low, he saved me.—℟.

For you have delivered my soul from death,
my eyes from tears, my feet from stumbling.
I will walk before the Lord
in the land of the living.—℟. ↓

SECOND READING Jas. 2.14-18

Faith expressed only in words is dead; it must be carried into action. Words alone will not cover the naked nor bring food to the hungry.

A reading from the Letter of Saint James.

WHAT good is it, my brothers and sisters, if you say you have faith but do not have works? Can faith save you?

If a brother or a sister is without clothing and lacks daily food, and one of you says to them, "Go in peace; keep warm and eat your fill," and yet you do not supply their bodily needs, what is the good of that? So faith by itself, if it has no works, is dead.

But someone will say, "You have faith and I have works." Show me your faith apart from your works, and I by my works will show you my faith. —The word of the Lord. ℟. **Thanks be to God.** ↓

GOSPEL ACCLAMATION Gal. 6.14

℣. Alleluia. ℟. **Alleluia.**

℣. May I never boast of anything except the Cross of the Lord,
by which the world has been crucified to me, and I to the world.

℟. **Alleluia.** ↓

GOSPEL Mk. 8.27-35

In answer to Jesus' question, Peter acknowledges that Jesus is the Messiah. Jesus then tells of his future sufferings, death, and resurrection. To follow him, we must take up our cross.

℣. The Lord be with you. ℟. **And with your spirit.**
✠ A reading from the holy Gospel according to Mark. ℟. **Glory to you, O Lord.**

JESUS went on with his disciples to the villages of Caesarea Philippi; and on the way he asked his disciples, "Who do people say that I am?" And they answered him, "John the Baptist; and others, Elijah; and still others, one of the Prophets."

Jesus asked them, "But who do you say that I am?" Peter answered him, "You are the Christ." And he sternly ordered them not to tell anyone about him.

Then he began to teach them that the Son of Man must undergo great suffering, and be rejected by the elders, the chief priests, and the scribes, and be killed, and after three days rise again. He said all this quite openly.

And Peter took Jesus aside and began to rebuke him. But turning and looking at his disciples, he rebuked Peter and said, "Get behind me, Satan! For you are thinking not as God does, but as humans do."

Jesus called the crowd with his disciples, and said to them, "Whoever wants to become my follower, let him deny himself and take up his cross and follow me. For whoever wants to save their life will lose it, and whoever loses their life for my sake, and for the sake of the Gospel, will save it."—The Gospel of the Lord. ℟. **Praise to you, Lord Jesus Christ.** → No. 15, p. 18

PRAYER OVER THE OFFERINGS

Look with favour on our supplications, O Lord,
and in your kindness accept these, your servants' offerings,
that what each has offered to the honour of your name
may serve the salvation of all.
Through Christ our Lord.
℟. **Amen.** → No. 21, p. 22 (Pref. 29-36)

COMMUNION ANTIPHON Cf. Ps. 35.8

How precious is your mercy, O God! The children of men seek shelter in the shadow of your wings. ↓

OR Cf. 1 Cor. 10.16

The chalice of blessing that we bless is a communion in the Blood of Christ; and the bread that we break is a sharing in the Body of the Lord. ↓

PRAYER AFTER COMMUNION

May the working of this heavenly gift, O Lord, we pray,
take possession of our minds and bodies,
so that its effects, and not our own desires,
may always prevail in us.
Through Christ our Lord. ℟. **Amen.** → No. 30, p. 77

Optional Solemn Blessings, p. 97, and Prayers over the People, p. 105

"Whoever welcomes one such child . . . welcomes me."

SEPTEMBER 23

25th SUNDAY IN ORDINARY TIME

ENTRANCE ANTIPHON

I am the salvation of the people, says the Lord. Should they cry to me in any distress, I will hear them, and I will be their Lord for ever.

→ No. 2, p. 10

COLLECT

O God, who founded all the commands of your sacred Law
upon love of you and of our neighbour,
grant that, by keeping your precepts,
we may merit to attain eternal life.
Through our Lord Jesus Christ, your Son,
who lives and reigns with you in the unity of the Holy Spirit,
one God, for ever and ever. ℟. **Amen.** ↓

FIRST READING Wis. 2.12, 17-20

The godless detest the righteous one because the man of God disturbs their conscience. They are anxious to do away with the good.

A reading from the book of Wisdom.

THE godless say:
"Let us lie in wait for the righteous one,
who makes life inconvenient to us and opposes our actions;
who reproaches us for sins against the law,
and accuses us of sins against our training.

Let us see if his words are true,
and let us test what will happen at the end of his life;
for if the righteous one is God's son, God will help him,
and will deliver him from the hand of his adversaries.

Let us test him with insult and torture,
so that we may find out how gentle he is,
and make trial of his forbearance.
Let us condemn him to a shameful death,

for, according to what he says, he will be protected."

The word of the Lord. ℟. **Thanks be to God.** ↓

RESPONSORIAL PSALM Ps. 54

David Szanto

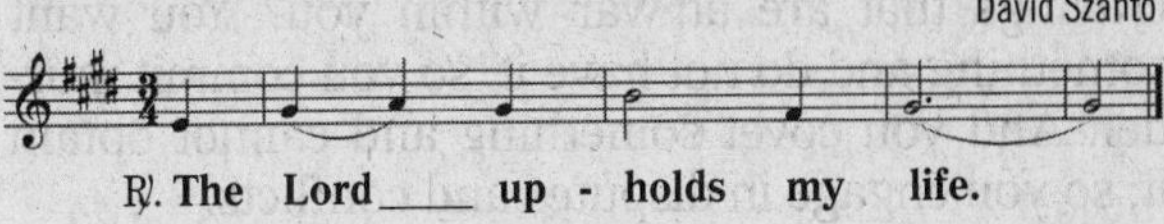
℟. The Lord ___ up - holds my life.

Save me, O God, by your name,
and vindicate me by your might.
Hear my prayer, O God;
give ear to the words of my mouth.—℟.

For the insolent have risen against me,
the ruthless seek my life;
they do not set God before them.—℟.

But surely, God is my helper;
the Lord is the upholder of my life.
With a freewill offering I will sacrifice to you;
I will give thanks to your name, for it is good.—℟. ↓

SECOND READING Jas. 3.16—4.3

Wisdom begets innocence. It is peace-loving, kind, docile, impartial, and sincere. The inner cravings of humans lead to murder, envy, and squandering.

A reading from the Letter of Saint James.

BELOVED: Where there is envy and selfish ambition, there will also be disorder and wickedness of every kind. But the wisdom from above is first pure, then peaceable, gentle, willing to yield, full of mercy and good fruits, without a trace of partiality or hypocrisy. And a harvest of righteousness is sown in peace for those who make peace.

Those conflicts and disputes among you, where do they come from? Do they not come from your cravings that are at war within you? You want something and do not have it; so you commit murder. And you covet something and cannot obtain it; so you engage in disputes and conflicts.

You do not have, because you do not ask. You ask and do not receive, because you ask wrongly, in order to spend what you get on your pleasures.—The word of the Lord. ℟. **Thanks be to God.** ↓

GOSPEL ACCLAMATION 2 Thess. 2.14

℣. Alleluia. ℟. **Alleluia.**
℣. God has called us through the good news,
to obtain the glory of our Lord Jesus Christ.
℟. **Alleluia.** ↓

GOSPEL Mk. 9.30-37

> **Jesus tells his trusted disciples of his forthcoming sufferings, death, and Resurrection. Then he tells the Twelve about humility.**

℣. The Lord be with you. ℟. **And with your spirit.**
✠ A reading from the holy Gospel according to Mark. ℟. **Glory to you, O Lord.**

AFTER leaving the mountain Jesus and his disciples went on from there and passed through Galilee. He did not want anyone to know it; for he was teaching his disciples, saying to them, "The Son of Man is to be betrayed into the hands of men, and they will kill him, and three days after being killed, he will rise again." But they did not understand what he was saying and were afraid to ask him.

Then they came to Capernaum; and when he was in the house Jesus asked them, "What were you arguing about on the way?" But they were silent, for on the way they had argued with one another who was the greatest.

Jesus sat down, called the twelve, and said to them, "Whoever wants to be first must be last of all and servant of all."

Then he took a little child and put it among them; and taking it in his arms, he said to them, "Whoever welcomes one such child in my name welcomes me, and whoever welcomes me welcomes not me but the one who sent me."—The Gospel of the Lord. ℟. **Praise to you, Lord Jesus Christ.** → No. 15, p. 18

PRAYER OVER THE OFFERINGS

Receive with favour, O Lord, we pray,
the offerings of your people,
that what they profess with devotion and faith
may be theirs through these heavenly mysteries.
Through Christ our Lord.
℟. **Amen.** → No. 21, p. 22 (Pref. 29-36)

COMMUNION ANTIPHON Ps. 118.4-5

You have laid down your precepts to be carefully kept; may my ways be firm in keeping your statutes. ↓

OR Jn. 10.14

I am the Good Shepherd, says the Lord; I know my sheep, and mine know me. ↓

PRAYER AFTER COMMUNION

Graciously raise up, O Lord,
those you renew with this Sacrament,
that we may come to possess your redemption
both in mystery and in the manner of our life.
Through Christ our Lord.
℟. **Amen.** → No. 30, p. 77

Optional Solemn Blessings, p. 97, and Prayers over the People, p. 105

"Whoever is not against us is for us."

SEPTEMBER 30

26th SUNDAY IN ORDINARY TIME

ENTRANCE ANTIPHON Dan. 3.31, 29, 30, 43, 42

All that you have done to us, O Lord, you have done with true judgement, for we have sinned

against you and not obeyed your commandments. But give glory to your name and deal with us according to the bounty of your mercy.

→ No. 2, p. 10

COLLECT

O God, who manifest your almighty power
above all by pardoning and showing mercy,
bestow, we pray, your grace abundantly upon us
and make those hastening to attain your promises
heirs to the treasures of heaven.
Through our Lord Jesus Christ, your Son,
who lives and reigns with you in the unity of the
Holy Spirit,
one God, for ever and ever. ℟. **Amen.** ↓

FIRST READING Num. 11.25-29

The Lord empowered seventy elders with the gift of prophecy. Some complained, but Moses replied that it would be even more wonderful if all the people were prophets.

A reading from the book of Numbers.

THE Lord came down in the cloud, took some of the spirit that was on Moses and put it on the seventy elders. When the spirit rested upon them, they prophesied. But they did not do so again.

Two men remained in the camp, one named Eldad, and the other named Medad, and the spirit rested on them; they were among those registered, but they had not gone out to the tent, and so they prophesied in the camp. A young man ran and told Moses, "Eldad and Medad are prophesying in the camp."

Joshua son of Nun, the assistant of Moses, one of his chosen men, said, "My lord Moses, stop them!" But Moses said to him, "Are you jealous for my sake? Would that all the Lord's people were Prophets, and that the Lord would put his spirit on them!"—The word of the Lord. ℟. **Thanks be to God.** ↓

RESPONSORIAL PSALM Ps. 19

Geoffrey Angeles, David Szanto

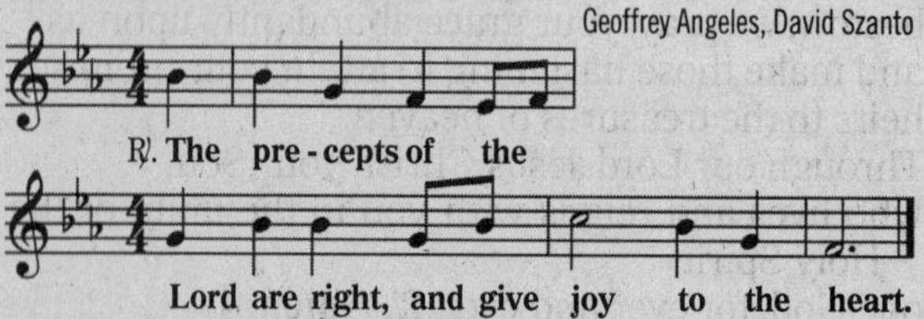
℟. The pre - cepts of the
Lord are right, and give joy to the heart.

The law of the Lord is perfect,
reviving the soul;
the decrees of the Lord are sure,
making wise the simple.—℟.

The fear of the Lord is pure,
enduring forever;
the ordinances of the Lord are true
and righteous altogether.—℟.

By them is your servant warned;
in keeping them there is great reward.
But who can detect unmindful errors?
Clear me from hidden faults.—℟.

Keep back your servant also from the insolent;
do not let them have dominion over me.
Then I shall be blameless,
and innocent of great transgression.—℟. ↓

SECOND READING Jas. 5.1-6

James deplores the injustice committed by the rich. He speaks of their pending miseries, their wanton luxury, wages withheld from workers. All these witness to their sin.

A reading from the Letter of Saint James.

COME now, you rich people, weep and wail for the miseries that are coming to you. Your riches have rotted, and your clothes are moth-eaten. Your gold and silver have rusted, and their rust will be evidence against you, and it will eat your flesh like fire.

You have laid up treasure for the last days. Listen! The wages of the labourers who mowed your fields, which you kept back by fraud, cry out, and the cries of the harvesters have reached the ears of the Lord of hosts.

You have lived on the earth in luxury and in pleasure; you have fattened your hearts in a day of slaughter. You have condemned and murdered the righteous one, who does not resist you.—The word of the Lord. ℟. **Thanks be to God.** ↓

GOSPEL ACCLAMATION Jn. 17.17b

℣. Alleluia. ℟. **Alleluia.**
℣. Your word, O Lord, is truth;
sanctify us in the truth.
℟. **Alleluia.** ↓

GOSPEL Mk. 9.38-43, 45, 47-48

Jesus reminds his followers that nothing done in his name will go unrewarded. But anyone who deceives a simple believer will be severely punished.

℣. The Lord be with you. ℟. **And with your spirit.**
✠ A reading from the holy Gospel according to Mark. ℟. **Glory to you, O Lord.**

AFTER Jesus had finished teaching the disciples, John said to him, "Teacher, we saw someone casting out demons in your name, and we tried to stop him, because he was not following us." But Jesus said, "Do not stop him; for no one who does a deed of power in my name will be able soon afterward to speak evil of me. Whoever is not against us is for us.

For truly I tell you, whoever gives you a cup of water to drink because you bear the name of Christ will by no means lose the reward. If any of you put a stumbling block before one of these little ones who believe in me, it would be better for you if a great millstone were hung around your neck and you were thrown into the sea.

If your hand causes you to stumble, cut it off; it is better for you to enter life maimed than to have two hands and to go to hell, to the unquenchable fire. And if your foot causes you to stumble, cut it off; it is better for you to enter life lame than to have two feet and to be thrown into hell. And if your eye causes you to stumble, tear it out; it is better for you to enter the kingdom of God with one eye than to have two eyes and to be thrown into hell, where their worm never dies, and the fire is never quenched."—The Gospel of the Lord. ℟. **Praise to you, Lord Jesus Christ.** → No. 15, p. 18

PRAYER OVER THE OFFERINGS

Grant us, O merciful God,
that this our offering may find acceptance with you
and that through it the wellspring of all blessing

may be laid open before us.
Through Christ our Lord.
℟. **Amen.** → No. 21, p. 22 (Pref. 29-36)

COMMUNION ANTIPHON Cf. Ps. 118.49-50

Remember your word to your servant, O Lord, by which you have given me hope. This is my comfort when I am brought low. ↓

OR 1 Jn. 3.16

By this we came to know the love of God: that Christ laid down his life for us; so we ought to lay down our lives for one another. ↓

PRAYER AFTER COMMUNION

May this heavenly mystery, O Lord,
restore us in mind and body,
that we may be co-heirs in glory with Christ,
to whose suffering we are united
whenever we proclaim his Death.
Who lives and reigns for ever and ever.
℟. **Amen.** → No. 30, p. 77

Optional Solemn Blessings, p. 97, and Prayers over the People, p. 105

"A man shall leave his father and mother . . . and the two shall become one flesh."

OCTOBER 7

27th SUNDAY IN ORDINARY TIME

ENTRANCE ANTIPHON Cf. Est. 4.17

Within your will, O Lord, all things are established, and there is none that can resist your will. For you have made all things, the heaven and the earth, and all that is held within the circle of heaven; you are the Lord of all. → No. 2, p. 10

COLLECT

Almighty ever-living God,
who in the abundance of your kindness
surpass the merits and the desires of those who entreat you,
pour out your mercy upon us
to pardon what conscience dreads
and to give what prayer does not dare to ask.
Through our Lord Jesus Christ, your Son,

who lives and reigns with you in the unity of the
Holy Spirit,
one God, for ever and ever. ℟. **Amen.** ↓

FIRST READING Gen. 2.7ab, 15, 18-24

God, knowing that a man needs companionship, created animals and birds and finally placed Adam in a deep sleep and took one of his ribs, forming a woman. This is why a man leaves his mother and father to become one with his wife.

A reading from the book of Genesis.

THE Lord God formed man from the dust of the ground, and breathed into his nostrils the breath of life, and put him in the garden of Eden to till it and keep it.

Then the Lord God said, "It is not good that the man should be alone; I will make him a helper as his partner." So out of the ground the Lord God formed every animal of the field and every bird of the air, and brought them to the man to see what he would call them; and whatever the man called every living creature, that was its name. The man gave names to all cattle, and to the birds of the air, and to every animal of the field; but for the man there was not found a helper as his partner.

So the Lord God caused a deep sleep to fall upon the man, and he slept; then he took one of his ribs and closed up its place with flesh. And the rib that the Lord God had taken from the man he made into a woman and brought her to the man.

Then the man said,
"This at last is bone of my bones
and flesh of my flesh;

this one shall be called Woman,
for out of Man this one was taken."

Therefore a man leaves his father and his mother and clings to his wife, and they become one flesh.—The word of the Lord. ℟. **Thanks be to God.** ↓

RESPONSORIAL PSALM Ps. 128

Lester Frederick Delgado

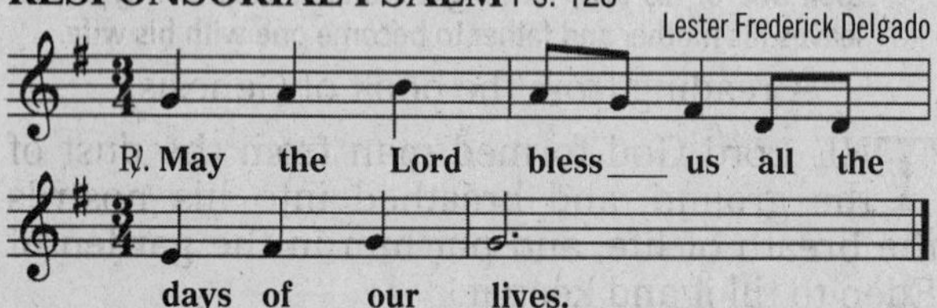
℟. May the Lord bless___ us all the
days of our lives.

Blessed is everyone who fears the Lord,
who walks in his ways.
You shall eat the fruit of the labour of your hands;
you shall be happy, and it shall go well with you.—℟.

Your wife will be like a fruitful vine
within your house;
your children will be like olive shoots
around your table.—℟.

Thus shall the man be blessed who fears the Lord.
The Lord bless you from Zion.
May you see the prosperity of Jerusalem
all the days of your life.—℟. ↓

SECOND READING Heb. 2.9-11

To suffer, Jesus took a human body. In this way God made our leader perfect through suffering, bringing us salvation. All who are consecrated have a common Father.

A reading from the Letter to the Hebrews.

WE do indeed see Jesus, who for a little while was made lower than the Angels, now crowned with glory and honour because of the suffering of death, so that by the grace of God he might taste death for everyone.

It was fitting that God, for whom and through whom all things exist, in bringing many sons and daughters to glory should make the pioneer of their salvation perfect through sufferings. For the one who sanctifies and those who are sanctified are all from one.

For this reason he is not ashamed to call them brothers and sisters.—The word of the Lord. ℟. **Thanks be to God.** ↓

GOSPEL ACCLAMATION 1 Jn. 4.12

℣. Alleluia. ℟. **Alleluia.**
℣. If we love one another,
God will live in us in perfect love.
℟. **Alleluia.** ↓

GOSPEL Mk. 10.2-16 or 10.2-12

The Pharisees, knowing the permission of Moses about divorce, test Jesus, but he recalls the reason for the command and reminds them of God's intention for the unity of marriage. Divorce followed by remarriage is adultery. Jesus then speaks about his love for little children.

[If the "Shorter Form" is used, the indented text in brackets is omitted.]

℣. The Lord be with you. ℟. **And with your spirit.**
✠ A reading from the holy Gospel according to Mark. ℟. **Glory to you, O Lord.**

SOME Pharisees came, and to test Jesus they asked, "Is it lawful for a man to divorce his wife?" Jesus answered them, "What did Moses command you?" They said, "Moses allowed a man to write a certificate of dismissal and to divorce her."

But Jesus said to them, "Because of your hardness of heart he wrote this commandment for you. But from the beginning of creation, 'God made them male and female.' 'For this reason a man shall leave his father and mother and be joined to his wife, and the two shall become one flesh.' So they are no longer two, but one flesh. Therefore what God has joined together, let no one separate."

Then in the house the disciples asked him again about this matter. Jesus said to them, "Whoever divorces his wife and marries another commits adultery against her; and if she divorces her husband and marries another, she commits adultery."

[People were bringing little children to him in order that Jesus might touch them; and the disciples spoke sternly to them. But when Jesus saw this, he was indignant and said to them, "Let the little children come to me; do not stop them: for it is to such as these that the kingdom of God belongs. Truly I tell you, whoever does not receive the kingdom of God as a little child will never enter it."

And Jesus took them up in his arms, laid his hands on them, and blessed them.]

The Gospel of the Lord. ℟. **Praise to you, Lord Jesus Christ.** → No. 15, p. 18

PRAYER OVER THE OFFERINGS

Accept, O Lord, we pray,
the sacrifices instituted by your commands
and, through the sacred mysteries,
which we celebrate with dutiful service,
graciously complete the sanctifying work
by which you are pleased to redeem us.
Through Christ our Lord.
℟. **Amen.** → No. 21, p. 22 (Pref. 29-36)

COMMUNION ANTIPHON Lam. 3.25

The Lord is good to those who hope in him, to the soul that seeks him. ↓

OR Cf. 1 Cor. 10.17

Though many, we are one bread, one body, for we all partake of the one Bread and one Chalice. ↓

PRAYER AFTER COMMUNION

Grant us, almighty God,
that we may be refreshed and nourished
by the Sacrament which we have received,
so as to be transformed into what we consume.
Through Christ our Lord.
℟. **Amen.** → No. 30, p. 77

Optional Solemn Blessings, p. 97, and Prayers over the People, p. 105

"Sell what you own, and give the money to the poor . . . ; then come, follow me."

OCTOBER 14

28th SUNDAY IN ORDINARY TIME

ENTRANCE ANTIPHON Ps. 129.3-4

If you, O Lord, should mark iniquities, Lord, who could stand? But with you is found forgiveness, O God of Israel. → No. 2, p. 10

COLLECT

May your grace, O Lord, we pray,
at all times go before us and follow after
and make us always determined
to carry out good works.
Through our Lord Jesus Christ, your Son,
who lives and reigns with you in the unity of the
  Holy Spirit,
one God, for ever and ever.
℟. **Amen.** ↓

FIRST READING Wis. 7.7-11

To what can Wisdom be compared in value? It is above all desires because in it all good things are found.

A reading from the book of Wisdom.

I PRAYED, and understanding was given me;
I called on God, and the spirit of wisdom came to me.

I preferred her to sceptres and thrones,
and I accounted wealth as nothing in comparison with her.
Neither did I liken to her any priceless gem,
because all gold is but a little sand in her sight,
and silver will be accounted as clay before her.

I loved her more than health and beauty,
and I chose to have her rather than light,
because her radiance never ceases.
All good things came to me along with her,
and in her hands uncounted wealth.

The word of the Lord. ℟. **Thanks be to God.** ↓

RESPONSORIAL PSALM Ps. 90

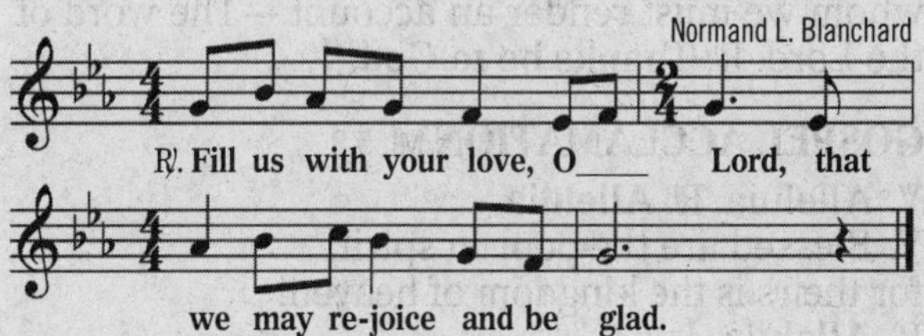
Normand L. Blanchard
℟. Fill us with your love, O Lord, that
we may re-joice and be glad.

Teach us to count our days
that we may gain a wise heart.
Turn, O Lord! How long?
Have compassion on your servants!—℟.

Satisfy us in the morning with your steadfast love,
so that we may rejoice and be glad all our days.
Make us glad as many days as you have afflicted us,
and as many years as we have seen evil.
℟. **Fill us with your love, O Lord, that we may rejoice and be glad.**

Let your work be manifest to your servants,
and your glorious power to their children.
Let the favour of the Lord our God be upon us,
and prosper for us the work of our hands.—℟. ↓

SECOND READING Heb. 4.12-13

God's word is penetrating and sharp. Nothing is hidden from God, to whom all must render an account.

A reading from the Letter to the Hebrews.

THE word of God is living and active, sharper than any two-edged sword, piercing until it divides soul from spirit, joints from marrow; it is able to judge the thoughts and intentions of the heart.

And before God no creature is hidden, but all are naked and laid bare to the eyes of the one to whom we must render an account.—The word of the Lord. ℟. **Thanks be to God.** ↓

GOSPEL ACCLAMATION Mt. 5.3

℣. Alleluia. ℟. **Alleluia.**
℣. Blessed are the poor in spirit;
for theirs is the kingdom of heaven!
℟. **Alleluia.** ↓

GOSPEL Mk. 10.17-30 or 10.17-27

A rich man asks Jesus what he must do to be saved. Jesus answers: keep the commandments. The man says that he

does. One thing more, then, Jesus lovingly continues: sell what you have and give to the poor. The man left. Jesus added how hard it is for a rich person to get to heaven.

[If the "Shorter Form" is used, the indented text in brackets is omitted.]

℣. The Lord be with you. ℟. **And with your spirit.**
✠ A reading from the holy Gospel according to Mark. ℟. **Glory to you, O Lord.**

AS Jesus was setting out on a journey, a man ran up and knelt before him, and asked him, "Good Teacher, what must I do to inherit eternal life?"

Jesus said to him, "Why do you call me good? No one is good but God alone. You know the commandments: 'You shall not murder; You shall not commit adultery; You shall not steal; You shall not bear false witness; You shall not defraud; Honour your father and mother.'"

He said to Jesus, "Teacher, I have kept all these since my youth." Jesus, looking at him, loved him and said, "You lack one thing; go, sell what you own, and give the money to the poor, and you will have treasure in heaven; then come, follow me." When the man heard this, he was shocked and went away grieving, for he had many possessions.

Then Jesus looked around and said to his disciples, "How hard it will be for those who have wealth to enter the kingdom of God!" And the disciples were perplexed at these words. But Jesus said to them again, "Children, how hard it is to enter the kingdom of God! It is easier for a camel to go through the eye of a needle than for someone who is rich to enter the kingdom of God."

They were greatly astounded and said to one another, "Then who can be saved?" Jesus looked at them and said, "For humans it is impossible, but not for God; for God all things are possible."

[Peter began to say to him, "Look, we have left everything and followed you." Jesus said, "Truly I tell you, there is no one who has left house or brothers or sisters or mother or father or children or fields, for my sake and for the sake of the good news, who will not receive a hundredfold now in this age—houses, brothers and sisters, mothers and children, and fields—but with persecutions—and in the age to come, eternal life."]

The Gospel of the Lord. ℟. **Praise to you, Lord Jesus Christ.** → No. 15, p. 18

PRAYER OVER THE OFFERINGS

Accept, O Lord, the prayers of your faithful
with the sacrificial offerings,
that, through these acts of devotedness,
we may pass over to the glory of heaven.
Through Christ our Lord.
℟. **Amen.** → No. 21, p. 22 (Pref. 29-36)

COMMUNION ANTIPHON Cf. Ps. 33.11

The rich suffer want and go hungry, but those who seek the Lord lack no blessing. ↓

OR 1 Jn. 3.2

When the Lord appears, we shall be like him, for we shall see him as he is. ↓

PRAYER AFTER COMMUNION

We entreat your majesty most humbly, O Lord,
that, as you feed us with the nourishment
which comes from the most holy Body and Blood
of your Son,
so you may make us sharers of his divine nature.
Who lives and reigns for ever and ever.
℟. **Amen.** → No. 30, p. 77

Optional Solemn Blessings, p. 97, and Prayers over the People, p. 105

"To sit at my right hand or at my left
is not mine to grant."

OCTOBER 21

29th SUNDAY IN ORDINARY TIME

ENTRANCE ANTIPHON Cf. Ps. 16.6, 8

To you I call; for you will surely heed me, O God; turn your ear to me; hear my words. Guard me as the apple of your eye; in the shadow of your wings protect me. → No. 2, p. 10

COLLECT

Almighty ever-living God,
grant that we may always conform our will to yours
and serve your majesty in sincerity of heart.
Through our Lord Jesus Christ, your Son,
who lives and reigns with you in the unity of the Holy Spirit,
one God, for ever and ever. ℟. **Amen.** ↓

FIRST READING Isa. 53.10-11

The suffering servant speaks of his life as a sin offering that his people may prosper and enjoy a long life. Through his suffering, he will bear the guilt of many.

A reading from the book of the Prophet Isaiah.

IT was the will of the Lord to crush him with pain.
When you make his life an offering for sin,
he shall see his offspring, and shall prolong his days;
through him the will of the Lord shall prosper.
Out of his anguish he shall see light;
he shall find satisfaction through his knowledge.
The righteous one, my servant, shall make many righteous,
and he shall bear their iniquities.

The word of the Lord. ℟. **Thanks be to God.** ↓

RESPONSORIAL PSALM Ps. 33

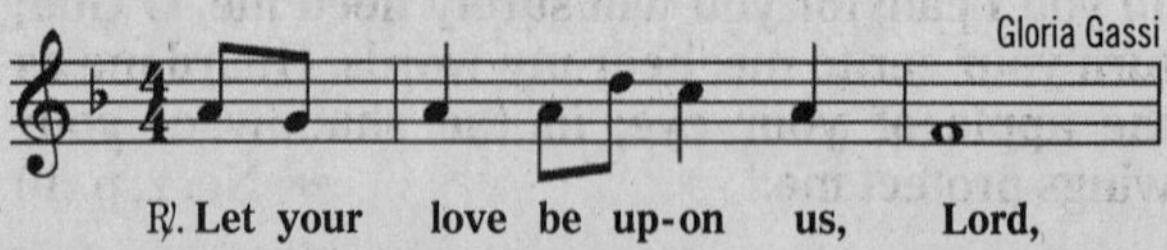
Gloria Gassi
℟. Let your love be up-on us, Lord,

ev - en as we hope in you.

The word of the Lord is upright,
and all his work is done in faithfulness.
He loves righteousness and justice;
the earth is full of the steadfast love of the Lord.—℟.

Truly the eye of the Lord is on those who fear him,
on those who hope in his steadfast love,
to deliver their soul from death,
and to keep them alive in famine.—℟.

Our soul waits for the Lord;
he is our help and shield.
Let your steadfast love, O Lord, be upon us,
even as we hope in you.—℟. ↓

SECOND READING Heb. 4.14-16

Jesus Christ, the Son of God, is the high priest who shares all our weaknesses, except sin. His mercy comes to all who seek it.

A reading from the Letter to the Hebrews.

BROTHERS and sisters: Since we have a great high priest who has passed through the heavens, Jesus, the Son of God, let us hold fast to our confession. For we do not have a high priest who is unable to sympathize with our weaknesses, but we have one who in every respect has been tested as we are, yet without sin.

Let us therefore approach the throne of grace with boldness, so that we may receive mercy and find grace to help in time of need.—The word of the Lord. ℟. **Thanks be to God.** ↓

GOSPEL ACCLAMATION Mk. 10.45

℣. Alleluia. ℟. **Alleluia.**
℣. The Son of Man came to serve
and to give his life as a ransom for many.
℟. **Alleluia.** ↓

GOSPEL Mk. 10.35-45 or 10.42-45

James and John request a special honour in the kingdom of heaven. Jesus reminds them and the other ten that anyone who aspires to greatness must be prepared to serve first. The Son of Man has come to serve.

[If the "Shorter Form" is used, the indented text in brackets is omitted.]

℣. The Lord be with you. ℟. **And with your spirit.**
✠ A reading from the holy Gospel according to Mark. ℟. **Glory to you, O Lord.**

[JAMES and John, the sons of Zebedee, came forward to Jesus and said to him, "Teacher, we want you to do for us whatever we ask of you." And Jesus said to them, "What is it you want me to do for you?" And they said to him, "Grant us to sit, one at your right hand and one at your left, in your glory."

But Jesus said to them, "You do not know what you are asking. Are you able to drink the cup that I drink, or be baptized with the baptism that I am baptized with?" They replied, "We are able." Then Jesus said to them, "The cup that I drink you will drink; and with the baptism with which I am baptized, you will be baptized; but to sit at my right hand or at my left is not mine to grant, but it is for those for whom it has been prepared."

When the ten heard this, they began to be angry with James and John.]

So Jesus called them and said to them, "You know that among the Gentiles those whom they recognize as their rulers lord it over them, and their great ones are tyrants over them. But it is not so among you; whoever wishes to become great among you must be your servant, and whoever wishes to be first among you must be slave of all. For the Son of Man came not to be served but to serve, and to give his life as a ransom for many."—The Gospel of the Lord.
℟. **Praise to you, Lord Jesus Christ.**

→ No. 15, p. 18

PRAYER OVER THE OFFERINGS

Grant us, Lord, we pray,
a sincere respect for your gifts,
that, through the purifying action of your grace,
we may be cleansed by the very mysteries we serve.
Through Christ our Lord.
℟. **Amen.** → No. 21, p. 22 (Pref. 29-36)

COMMUNION ANTIPHON Cf. Ps. 32.18-19

Behold, the eyes of the Lord are on those who fear him, who hope in his merciful love, to rescue their souls from death, to keep them alive in famine. ↓

OR Mk. 10.45

The Son of Man has come to give his life as a ransom for many. ↓

PRAYER AFTER COMMUNION

Grant, O Lord, we pray,
that, benefiting from participation in heavenly things,
we may be helped by what you give in this present age
and prepared for the gifts that are eternal.
Through Christ our Lord.
℟. **Amen.** → No. 30, p. 77

Optional Solemn Blessings, p. 97, and Prayers over the People, p. 105

IHS

"Jesus, Son of David, have mercy on me!"

OCTOBER 28

30th SUNDAY IN ORDINARY TIME

ENTRANCE ANTIPHON Cf. Ps. 104.3-4

Let the hearts that seek the Lord rejoice; turn to the Lord and his strength; constantly seek his face. → No. 2, p. 10

COLLECT

Almighty ever-living God,
increase our faith, hope and charity,
and make us love what you command,
so that we may merit what you promise.
Through our Lord Jesus Christ, your Son,
who lives and reigns with you in the unity of the
Holy Spirit,
one God, for ever and ever. ℟. **Amen.** ↓

FIRST READING Jer. 31.7-9

Jeremiah's hymn opens with joy. God has bestowed salvation on the people.

A reading from the book of the Prophet Jeremiah.

THUS says the Lord:
"Sing aloud with gladness for Jacob,
and raise shouts for the chief of the nations;
proclaim, give praise, and say,
'Save, O Lord, your people,
the remnant of Israel.'

See, I am going to bring them from the land of the north,
and gather them from the farthest parts of the earth,
among them those who are blind and those who are lame,
those with child and those in labour, together;
a great company, they shall return here.

With weeping they shall come,
and with consolations I will lead them back,
I will let them walk by brooks of water,
in a straight path in which they shall not stumble;
for I have become a father to Israel,
and Ephraim is my firstborn."

The word of the Lord. ℟. **Thanks be to God.** ↓

RESPONSORIAL PSALM Ps. 126

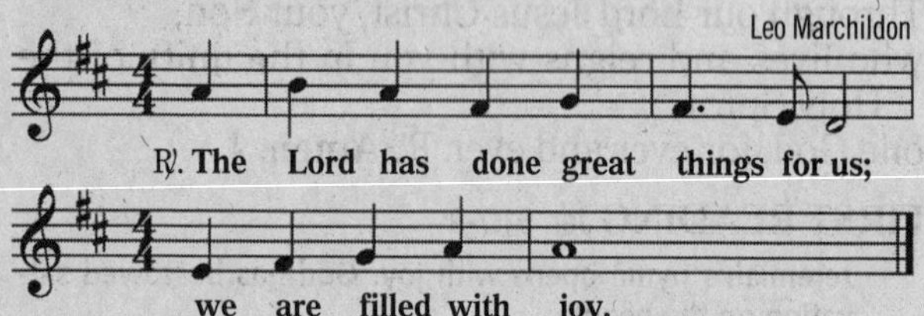
Leo Marchildon
℟. The Lord has done great things for us;
we are filled with joy.

When the Lord restored the fortunes of Zion,
we were like those who dream.

Then our mouth was filled with laughter,
and our tongue with shouts of joy.—R̸.

Then it was said among the nations,
"The Lord has done great things for them."
The Lord has done great things for us,
and we rejoiced.—R̸.

Restore our fortunes, O Lord,
like the watercourses in the desert of the Negev.
May those who sow in tears
reap with shouts of joy.—R̸.

Those who go out weeping,
bearing the seed for sowing,
shall come home with shouts of joy,
carrying their sheaves.—R̸. ↓

SECOND READING Heb. 5.1-6

Every high priest is designated by God. He is selected from among the people to be their mediator with God. No one takes this honour by himself.

A reading from the Letter to the Hebrews.

EVERY high priest chosen from among men is put in charge of things pertaining to God on their behalf, to offer gifts and sacrifices for sins. He is able to deal gently with the ignorant and wayward, since he himself is subject to weakness; and because of this he must offer sacrifice for his own sins as well as for those of the people. And one does not presume to take this honour, but takes it only when called by God, just as Aaron was.

So also Christ did not glorify himself in becoming a high priest, but was appointed by the one who said to him,

"You are my Son,
today I have begotten you";
as he says also in another place,
"You are a priest forever,
according to the order of Melchizedek."
The word of the Lord. ℟. **Thanks be to God.** ↓

GOSPEL ACCLAMATION 2 Tim. 1.10

℣. Alleluia. ℟. **Alleluia.**
℣. Our Saviour Jesus Christ has abolished death and brought us life through the Gospel.
℟. **Alleluia.** ↓

GOSPEL Mk. 10.46-52

Bartimaeus, a blind man, hearing Jesus, called out loudly; "Jesus, Son of David, have mercy on me!" Jesus summoned him and, seeing his faith, cured him. Bartimaeus followed Jesus.

℣. The Lord be with you. ℟. **And with your spirit.**
✠ A reading from the holy Gospel according to Mark. ℟. **Glory to you, O Lord.**

AS Jesus and his disciples and a large crowd were leaving Jericho, Bartimaeus son of Timaeus, a blind beggar, was sitting by the roadside. When he heard that it was Jesus of Nazareth, he began to shout out and say, "Jesus, Son of David, have mercy on me!" Many sternly ordered him to be quiet, but he cried out even more loudly, "Son of David, have mercy on me!"

Jesus stood still and said, "Call him here." And they called the blind man, saying to him, "Take heart; get up, he is calling you." So throwing off his cloak, he sprang up and came to Jesus.

Then Jesus said to him, "What do you want me to do for you?" The blind man said to him, "My teacher, let me see again." Jesus said to him, "Go; your faith has made you well." Immediately the man regained his sight and followed Jesus on the way.—The Gospel of the Lord.
℟. **Praise to you, Lord Jesus Christ.** → No. 15, p. 18

PRAYER OVER THE OFFERINGS

Look, we pray, O Lord,
on the offerings we make to your majesty,
that whatever is done by us in your service
may be directed above all to your glory.
Through Christ our Lord.
℟. **Amen.** → No. 21, p. 22 (Pref. 29-36)

COMMUNION ANTIPHON Cf. Ps. 19.6

We will ring out our joy at your saving help and exult in the name of our God. ↓

OR Eph. 5.2

Christ loved us and gave himself up for us, as a fragrant offering to God. ↓

PRAYER AFTER COMMUNION

May your Sacraments, O Lord, we pray,
perfect in us what lies within them,
that what we now celebrate in signs
we may one day possess in truth.
Through Christ our Lord.
℟. **Amen.** → No. 30, p. 77

Optional Solemn Blessings, p. 97, and Prayers over the People, p. 105

"You shall love your neighbour as yourself."

NOVEMBER 4

31st SUNDAY IN ORDINARY TIME

ENTRANCE ANTIPHON Cf. Ps 37.22-23

Forsake me not, O Lord, my God; be not far from me! Make haste and come to my help, O Lord, my strong salvation! → No. 2, p. 10

COLLECT

Almighty and merciful God,
by whose gift your faithful offer you
right and praiseworthy service,
grant, we pray,
that we may hasten without stumbling
to receive the things you have promised.
Through our Lord Jesus Christ, your Son,
who lives and reigns with you in the unity of the
Holy Spirit,
one God, for ever and ever. ℟. **Amen.** ↓

FIRST READING Deut. 6.2-6

Moses instructs the people to hold fast to the commandments of the Lord. In this way they shall love God and they will prosper in the Lord's favour.

A reading from the book of Deuteronomy.

MOSES spoke to the people: "May you and your children and your children's children fear the Lord your God all the days of your life, and keep all his decrees and his commandments that I am commanding you, so that your days may be long.

Hear therefore, O Israel, and observe them diligently, so that it may go well with you, and so that you may multiply greatly in a land flowing with milk and honey, as the Lord, the God of your Fathers, has promised you.

Hear, O Israel: The Lord is our God, the Lord alone. You shall love the Lord your God with all your heart, and with all your soul, and with all your might. Keep these words that I am commanding you today in your heart."—The word of the Lord. ℟. **Thanks be to God.** ↓

RESPONSORIAL PSALM Ps. 18

Normand L. Blanchard

℟. I love you, O Lord, my___ strength.

I love you, O Lord, my strength.
The Lord is my rock, my fortress, and my deliverer.
My God, my rock in whom I take refuge,

my shield, and the source of my salvation, my stronghold.
℟. **I love you, O Lord, my strength.**

I call upon the Lord, who is worthy to be praised,
so I shall be saved from my enemies.
From his temple he heard my voice,
and my cry to him reached his ears.—℟.

The Lord lives! Blessed be my rock,
and exalted be the God of my salvation.
Great triumphs he gives to his king,
and shows steadfast love to his anointed.—℟. ↓

SECOND READING Heb. 7.23-28

Jesus has a priesthood that will not pass away. He is "a high priest, holy, blameless, undefiled, separated from sinners, and exalted above the heavens." He offered one sacrifice for sin.

A reading from the Letter to the Hebrews.

THE priests of the first covenant were many in number, because they were prevented by death from continuing in office; but Jesus holds his priesthood permanently, because he continues forever. Consequently he is able for all time to save those who approach God through him, since he always lives to make intercession for them.

For it was fitting that we should have such a high priest, holy, blameless, undefiled, separated from sinners, and exalted above the heavens. Unlike the other high priests, he has no need to offer sacrifices day after day, first for his own sins, and then for those of the people; this he did once for all when he offered himself.

For the law appoints as high priests those who are subject to weakness, but the word of the oath, which came later than the law, appoints a Son who has been made perfect forever.—The word of the Lord. ℟. **Thanks be to God.** ↓

GOSPEL ACCLAMATION Jn. 14.23

℣. Alleluia. ℟. **Alleluia.**
℣. Whoever loves me will keep my word,
and my Father will love him, and we will come to him.
℟. **Alleluia.** ↓

GOSPEL Mk. 12.28-34

Jesus describes the first commandment—total love for God—and the second—love for neighbour.

℣. The Lord be with you. ℟. **And with your spirit.**
✠ A reading from the holy Gospel according to Mark. ℟. **Glory to you, O Lord.**

ONE of the scribes came near and heard the religious authorities disputing with one another, and seeing that Jesus answered them well, he asked him, "Which commandment is the first of all?"

Jesus answered, "The first is, 'Hear, O Israel: the Lord our God, the Lord is one; you shall love the Lord your God with all your heart, and with all your soul, and with all your mind, and with all your strength.'

The second is this, 'You shall love your neighbour as yourself.' There is no other commandment greater than these."

Then the scribe said to him, "You are right, Teacher; you have truly said that 'he is one, and besides him there is no other'; and 'to love him with all the heart, and with all the understanding, and with all the strength,' and 'to love one's neighbour as oneself,'—this is much more important than all whole burnt offerings and sacrifices."

When Jesus saw that the scribe answered wisely, he said to him, "You are not far from the kingdom of God." After that no one dared to ask Jesus any question.—The Gospel of the Lord.
℟. **Praise to you, Lord Jesus Christ.**

→ No. 15, p. 18

PRAYER OVER THE OFFERINGS

May these sacrificial offerings, O Lord,
become for you a pure oblation,
and for us a holy outpouring of your mercy.
Through Christ our Lord.
℟. **Amen.** → No. 21, p. 22 (Pref. 29-36)

COMMUNION ANTIPHON Cf. Ps. 15.11

You will show me the path of life, the fullness of joy in your presence, O Lord. ↓

OR Jn. 6.58

Just as the living Father sent me and I have life because of the Father, so whoever feeds on me shall have life because of me, says the Lord. ↓

PRAYER AFTER COMMUNION

May the working of your power, O Lord,
increase in us, we pray,
so that, renewed by these heavenly Sacraments,

we may be prepared by your gift
for receiving what they promise.
Through Christ our Lord.
℟. **Amen.** → No. 30, p. 77

Optional Solemn Blessings, p. 97, and Prayers over the People, p. 105

"She out of her poverty has put in everything she had, all she had to live on."

NOVEMBER 11

32nd SUNDAY IN ORDINARY TIME

ENTRANCE ANTIPHON Cf. Ps. 87.3

Let my prayer come into your presence. Incline your ear to my cry for help, O Lord. → No. 2, p. 10

COLLECT

Almighty and merciful God,
graciously keep from us all adversity,
so that, unhindered in mind and body alike,
we may pursue in freedom of heart
the things that are yours.

Through our Lord Jesus Christ, your Son,
who lives and reigns with you in the unity of the
Holy Spirit,
one God, for ever and ever.
℟. **Amen.** ↓

FIRST READING 1 Kgs. 17.10-16

Elijah asked a poor widow for food and water. Regardless of her dire want, she baked a cake for him. The Lord rewarded her and her son with oil and food for many days.

A reading from the first book of Kings.

ELIJAH, the Prophet, set out and went to Zarephath. When he came to the gate of the town, a widow was there gathering sticks; he called to her and said, "Bring me a little water in a vessel, so that I may drink." As she was going to bring it, he called to her and said, "Bring me a morsel of bread in your hand."

But she said, "As the Lord your God lives, I have nothing baked, only a handful of meal in a jar, and a little oil in a jug; I am now gathering a couple of sticks, so that I may go home and prepare it for myself and my son, that we may eat it, and die."

Elijah said to her, "Do not be afraid; go and do as you have said; but first make me a little cake of it and bring it to me, and afterwards make something for yourself and your son. For thus says the Lord the God of Israel: 'The jar of meal will not be emptied and the jug of oil will not fail until the day that the Lord sends rain on the earth.'"

She went and did as Elijah said, so that she as well as he and her household ate for many days.

The jar of meal was not emptied, neither did the jug of oil fail, according to the word of the Lord that he spoke by Elijah.—The word of the Lord. ℟. **Thanks be to God.** ↓

RESPONSORIAL PSALM Ps. 146

Leo Marchildon

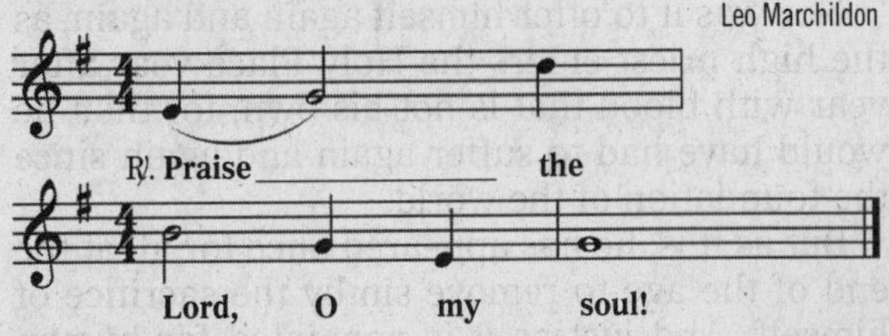
℟. Praise ___ the
Lord, O my soul!

Or: ℟. **Alleluia!**

It is the Lord who keeps faith forever,
who executes justice for the oppressed;
who gives food to the hungry.
The Lord sets the prisoners free.—℟.

The Lord opens the eyes of the blind
and lifts up those who are bowed down;
the Lord loves the righteous
and watches over the strangers.—℟.

The Lord upholds the orphan and the widow,
but the way of the wicked he brings to ruin.
The Lord will reign forever,
your God, O Zion, for all generations.—℟. ↓

SECOND READING Heb. 9.24-28

Christ entered into heaven to appear before God, not for sacrifice again, but to take away sin by his sacrifice. Christ will not die again, but he will come to bring about salvation for those who wait for him.

A reading from the Letter to the Hebrews.

CHRIST did not enter a sanctuary made by human hands, a mere copy of the true one, but he entered into heaven itself, now to appear in the presence of God on our behalf.

Nor was it to offer himself again and again, as the high priest enters the Holy Place year after year with blood that is not his own; for then he would have had to suffer again and again since the foundation of the world.

But as it is, he has appeared once for all at the end of the age to remove sin by the sacrifice of himself. And just as it is appointed for human beings to die once, and after that comes the judgment, so Christ, having been offered once to bear the sins of many, will appear a second time, not to deal with sin, but to save those who are eagerly waiting for him.—The word of the Lord. ℟. **Thanks be to God.** ↓

GOSPEL ACCLAMATION Mt. 5.3

℣. Alleluia. ℟. **Alleluia.**
℣. Blessed are the poor in spirit;
for theirs is the kingdom of heaven!
℟. **Alleluia.** ↓

GOSPEL Mk. 12.38-44 or 12.41-44

Jesus exposes the scribes who have betrayed their office. The wealthy contribute much to the collection from their surplus, but the two coins from the widow are of more value before God.

[If the "Shorter Form" is used, the indented text in brackets is omitted.]

℣. The Lord be with you. ℟. **And with your spirit.**
✠ A reading from the holy Gospel according to Mark. ℟. **Glory to you, O Lord.**

> [JESUS was teaching in the temple, and a large crowd was listening to him. He said, "Beware of the scribes, who like to walk around in long robes, and to be greeted with respect in the marketplaces, and to have the best seats in the synagogues and places of honour at banquets! They devour widows' houses and for the sake of appearance say long prayers. They will receive the greater condemnation."]

Jesus sat down opposite the treasury, and watched the crowd putting money into the treasury. Many rich people put in large sums. A poor widow came and put in two small copper coins, which are worth a penny. Then he called his disciples and said to them, "Truly I tell you, this poor widow has put in more than all those who are contributing to the treasury. For all of them have contributed out of their abundance; but she out of her poverty has put in everything she had, all she had to live on."—The Gospel of the Lord. ℟. **Praise to you, Lord Jesus Christ.**

→ No. 15, p. 18

PRAYER OVER THE OFFERINGS

Look with favour, we pray, O Lord,
upon the sacrificial gifts offered here,

that, celebrating in mystery the Passion of your Son,
we may honour it with loving devotion.
Through Christ our Lord.
℟. **Amen.** → No. 21, p. 22 (Pref. 29-36)

COMMUNION ANTIPHON Cf. Ps. 22.1-2

The Lord is my shepherd; there is nothing I shall want. Fresh and green are the pastures where he gives me repose, near restful waters he leads me. ↓

OR Cf. Lk. 24.35

The disciples recognized the Lord Jesus in the breaking of bread. ↓

PRAYER AFTER COMMUNION

Nourished by this sacred gift, O Lord,
we give you thanks and beseech your mercy,
that, by the pouring forth of your Spirit,
the grace of integrity may endure
in those your heavenly power has entered.
Through Christ our Lord.
℟. **Amen.** → No. 30, p. 77

Optional Solemn Blessings, p. 97, and Prayers over the People, p. 105

"The Son of Man . . . will send out the Angels, and gather his elect from the four winds."

NOVEMBER 18

33rd SUNDAY IN ORDINARY TIME

ENTRANCE ANTIPHON Jer. 29.11, 12, 14

The Lord said: I think thoughts of peace and not of affliction. You will call upon me, and I will answer you, and I will lead back your captives from every place. → No. 2, p. 10

COLLECT

Grant us, we pray, O Lord our God,
the constant gladness of being devoted to you,
for it is full and lasting happiness
to serve with constancy
the author of all that is good.
Through our Lord Jesus Christ, your Son,
who lives and reigns with you in the unity of the
  Holy Spirit,
one God, for ever and ever.
℟. **Amen.** ↓

FIRST READING Dan. 12.1-3

Daniel describes events that will occur at the end of the world. It will be a time of distress, but the just will live forever in glory while others shall endure disgrace.

A reading from the book of the Prophet Daniel.

AT that time Michael, the great prince, the protector of your people, shall arise. There shall be a time of anguish, such as has never occurred since nations first came into existence. But at that time your people shall be delivered, everyone who is found written in the book. Many of those who sleep in the dust of the earth shall awake, some to everlasting life, and some to shame and everlasting contempt.

Those who are wise shall shine like the brightness of the sky, and those who lead many to righteousness, like the stars forever and ever.—The word of the Lord. ℟. **Thanks be to God.** ↓

RESPONSORIAL PSALM Ps. 16

David MacIsaac

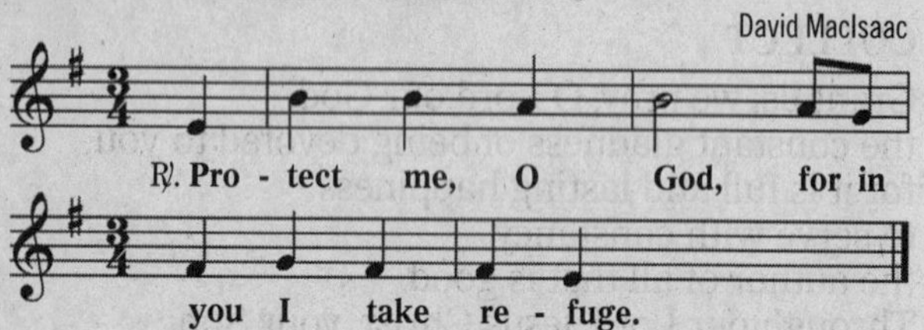
℟. Pro - tect me, O God, for in
you I take re - fuge.

The Lord is my chosen portion and my cup;
you hold my lot.
I keep the Lord always before me;
because he is at my right hand, I shall not be moved.—℟.

Therefore my heart is glad, and my soul rejoices;
my body also rests secure.
For you do not give me up to Sheol,
or let your faithful one see the Pit.—℟.

You show me the path of life.
In your presence there is fullness of joy;
in your right hand are pleasures
forevermore.—℟. ↓

SECOND READING Heb. 10.11-14, 18

Unlike the other priests, Jesus offered only one sacrifice for sin and took his place forever at God's right hand. He has perfected those who are being sanctified.

A reading from the Letter to the Hebrews.

EVERY priest stands day after day at his service, offering again and again the same sacrifices that can never take away sins.

But when Christ had offered for all time a single sacrifice for sins, "he sat down at the right hand of God," and since then has been waiting "until his enemies would be made a footstool for his feet." For by a single offering he has perfected for all time those who are sanctified.

Where there is forgiveness of sin and lawless deeds, there is no longer any offering for sin.—The word of the Lord. ℟. **Thanks be to God.** ↓

GOSPEL ACCLAMATION Lk. 21.36

℣. Alleluia. ℟. **Alleluia.**
℣. Be alert at all times,
praying that you may be able to stand before the Son of Man.
℟. **Alleluia.** ↓

GOSPEL Mk. 13.24-32

Jesus tells about the end of the world—the darkening of the sun, moon, and stars. Then the Son of Man will come in glory. Learn from the signs of the fig tree. No one knows the exact time of this happening.

℣. The Lord be with you. ℟. **And with your spirit.**
✠ A reading from the holy Gospel according to Mark. ℟. **Glory to you, O Lord.**

JESUS spoke to his disciples about the end which is to come:

"In those days, after the time of suffering,
the sun will be darkened,
and the moon will not give its light,
and the stars will be falling from heaven,
and the powers in the heavens will be shaken.

Then they will see 'the Son of Man coming in clouds' with great power and glory. Then he will send out the Angels, and gather his elect from the four winds, from the ends of the earth to the ends of heaven.

From the fig tree learn its lesson: as soon as its branch becomes tender and puts forth its leaves, you know that summer is near. So also, when you see these things taking place, you know that he is near, at the very gates.

Truly I tell you, this generation will not pass away until all these things have taken place. Heaven and earth will pass away, but my words will not pass away.

But about that day or hour no one knows, neither the Angels in heaven, nor the Son, but only the Father."—The Gospel of the Lord. ℟. **Praise to you, Lord Jesus Christ.** → No. 15, p. 18

PRAYER OVER THE OFFERINGS

Grant, O Lord, we pray,
that what we offer in the sight of your majesty
may obtain for us the grace of being devoted to you
and gain us the prize of everlasting happiness.
Through Christ our Lord.
℟. **Amen.** → No. 21, p. 22 (Pref. 29-36)

COMMUNION ANTIPHON Ps. 72.28

To be near God is my happiness, to place my hope in God the Lord. ↓

OR Mk. 11.23, 24

Amen, I say to you: Whatever you ask in prayer, believe that you will receive, and it shall be given to you, says the Lord. ↓

PRAYER AFTER COMMUNION

We have partaken of the gifts of this sacred mystery,
humbly imploring, O Lord,
that what your Son commanded us to do
in memory of him
may bring us growth in charity.
Through Christ our Lord.
℟. **Amen.** → No. 30, p. 77

Optional Solemn Blessings, p. 97, and Prayers over the People, p. 105

"My kingdom is not from this world."

NOVEMBER 25

OUR LORD JESUS CHRIST, KING OF THE UNIVERSE

(34th Sunday in Ordinary Time)

Solemnity

ENTRANCE ANTIPHON Rev. 5.12; 1.6

How worthy is the Lamb who was slain, to receive power and divinity, and wisdom and strength and honour. To him belong glory and power for ever and ever. → No. 2, p. 10

COLLECT

Almighty ever-living God,
whose will is to restore all things
in your beloved Son, the King of the universe,
grant, we pray,
that the whole creation, set free from slavery,
may render your majesty service
and ceaselessly proclaim your praise.
Through our Lord Jesus Christ, your Son,

who lives and reigns with you in the unity of the
Holy Spirit,
one God, for ever and ever. ℟. **Amen.** ↓

FIRST READING Dan. 7.13-14

Daniel foresees the coming of the Son of Man. He receives all honour and glory. All peoples of every nation serve him. His kingship shall last forever.

A reading from the book of the Prophet Daniel.

I HAD a dream and visions as I lay in bed.
As I watched in the night visions,
I saw one like a son of man coming with the clouds of heaven.
And he came to the One who is Ancient of Days
and was presented before him.
To him was given dominion and glory and kingship,
that all peoples, nations and languages should serve him.
His dominion is an everlasting dominion
that shall not pass away,
and his kingship is one that shall never be destroyed.

The word of the Lord. ℟. **Thanks be to God.** ↓

RESPONSORIAL PSALM Ps. 93

Paul K. McKay

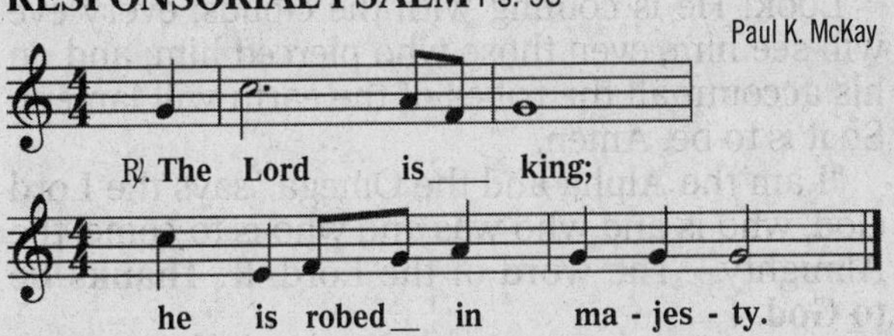
℟. The Lord is king;
he is robed in ma - jes - ty.

The Lord is king, he is robed in majesty;
the Lord is robed,
he is girded with strength.
℟. **The Lord is king; he is robed in majesty.**

He has established the world; it shall never be moved;
your throne is established from of old;
you are from everlasting.—℟.

Your decrees are very sure;
holiness befits your house,
O Lord, forevermore.—℟. ↓

SECOND READING Rev. 1.5-8

By the shedding of his Blood, Jesus has made us a royal nation of priests to serve God. The Lord God is the Alpha and the Omega—the beginning and the end. He is the Almighty.

A reading from the book of Revelation.

JESUS Christ is the faithful witness, the firstborn of the dead, and the ruler of the kings of the earth. To him who loves us and freed us from our sins by his blood, and made us to be a kingdom, priests serving his God and Father, to him be glory and dominion forever and ever. Amen.

Look! He is coming with the clouds; every eye will see him, even those who pierced him; and on his account all the tribes of the earth will lament. So it is to be. Amen.

"I am the Alpha and the Omega," says the Lord God, who is and who was and who is to come, the Almighty.—The word of the Lord. ℟. **Thanks be to God.** ↓

GOSPEL ACCLAMATION Mk. 11.9-10

℣. Alleluia. ℟. **Alleluia.**
℣. Blessed is the coming kingdom of our father David;
blessed is the one who comes in the name of the Lord!
℟. **Alleluia.** ↓

GOSPEL Jn. 18.33b-37

Before Pilate, Jesus states that he is a king but that his kingdom is not of this world. Jesus says that he came into the world to bear witness to the truth.

℣. The Lord be with you. ℟. **And with your spirit.**
✠ A reading from the holy Gospel according to John. ℟. **Glory to you, O Lord.**

PILATE asked Jesus, "Are you the King of the Jews?" Jesus answered, "Do you ask this on your own, or did others tell you about me?" Pilate replied, "I am not a Jew, am I? Your own nation and the chief priests have handed you over to me. What have you done?"

Jesus answered, "My kingdom is not from this world. If my kingdom were from this world, my followers would be fighting to keep me from being handed over to the Jews. But as it is, my kingdom is not from here."

Pilate asked him, "So you are a king?" Jesus answered, "You say that I am a king. For this I was born, and for this I came into the world, to testify to the truth. Everyone who belongs to the truth listens to my voice."—The Gospel of the Lord. ℟. **Praise to you, Lord Jesus Christ.**

→ No. 15, p. 18

PRAYER OVER THE OFFERINGS

As we offer you, O Lord, the sacrifice
by which the human race is reconciled to you,
we humbly pray
that your Son himself may bestow on all nations
the gifts of unity and peace.
Through Christ our Lord. ℟. **Amen.** ↓

PREFACE (51)

℣. The Lord be with you. ℟. **And with your spirit.**
℣. Lift up your hearts. ℟. **We lift them up to the Lord.**
℣. Let us give thanks to the Lord our God.
℟. **It is right and just.**

It is truly right and just, our duty and our salvation,
always and everywhere to give you thanks,
Lord, holy Father, almighty and eternal God.

For you anointed your Only Begotten Son,
our Lord Jesus Christ, with the oil of gladness
as eternal Priest and King of all creation,
so that, by offering himself on the altar of the Cross
as a spotless sacrifice to bring us peace,
he might accomplish the mysteries of human redemption
and, making all created things subject to his rule,
he might present to the immensity of your majesty
an eternal and universal kingdom,
a kingdom of truth and life,

a kingdom of holiness and grace,
a kingdom of justice, love and peace.

And so, with Angels and Archangels,
with Thrones and Dominions,
and with all the hosts and Powers of heaven,
we sing the hymn of your glory,
as without end we acclaim: → No. 23, p. 23

COMMUNION ANTIPHON Ps. 28.10-11

The Lord sits as King for ever. The Lord will bless his people with peace. ↓

PRAYER AFTER COMMUNION

Having received the food of immortality,
we ask, O Lord,
that, glorying in obedience
to the commands of Christ, the King of the universe,
we may live with him eternally in his heavenly Kingdom.
Who lives and reigns for ever and ever.
℟. **Amen.** → No. 30, p. 77

Optional Solemn Blessings, p. 97, and Prayers over the People, p. 105

HYMNAL

1 O Come, O Come, Emmanuel

Tr. J. M. Neale, 1816-66
and others

Veni Emmanuel
Melody adapted by
T. Helmore, 1811-90

1. O come, O come, Em - man - u - el, And ran -
2. O come, thou rod of Jes - se, free Thine own
3. O come, thou day-spring, come and cheer Our spir -
4. O come, thou key of Da - vid, come, And o -
5. O come, O come, thou Lord of might, Who to

1. som cap - tive Is - ra - el, That mourns in
2. from Sa - tan's tyr - an - ny; From depths of
3. its by thine ad - vent here; Dis - perse the
4. pen wide our heav'n - ly home; Make safe the
5. thy tribes, from Si - nai's height, In an - cient

1. low - ly ex - ile here, Un - til the Son of
2. hell thy peo - ple save, And give them vic - t'ry
3. gloom -y clouds of night, And death's dark shad-ows
4. way that leads on high, And close the path to
5. times didst give the law In cloud, in ma - jes -

Refrain:

1. God ap-pear.
2. o'er the grave.
3. put to flight. Re - joice! Re-joice! O Is -
4. mis - er - y.
5. ty, and awe.

ra - el. To thee shall come Em - man - u - el.

Hark, a Mystic Voice Is Sounding 2

Tr. E. Caswall, 1849

En Clara Vox
R.L. de Pearsall, 1795-1856

1.
Hark, a mystic voice is sounding;
"Christ is nigh," It seems to say;
"Cast away the dreams of darkness,
O ye children of the day."

2.
Startled at the solemn warning,
Let the earthbound soul arise;
Christ her sun, all sloth dispelling,
Shines upon the morning skies.

3.
Lo, the Lamb so long expected
Comes with pardon down from heav'n;
Let us haste, with tears of sorrow,
One and all, to be forgiv'n.

The Coming of Our God 3

1.
The coming of our Lord
Our thought must now employ;
Then let us meet him on the road.
With song of holy joy.

2.
The co-eternal Son
A maiden's offspring see;
A servant's form Christ putteth on;
To set his people free.

3.
Daughter of Sion, rise
To greet thine Infant King;
Not let thy thankless heart despise
The pardon he doth bring.

O Come, Divine Messiah 4

Anne Pellegrin, 1663-1745
Sr. St. Mary of St. Philip

Venez Divin Messie
16th Century French
Harm. G. Ridout, 1971

O come, divine Messiah!
The world in silence waits the day
When hope shall sing its triumph,
And sadness flee away.

Chorus: Sweet Saviour, haste,
Come, come to earth:
Dispel the night, and show thy face,
And bid us hail the dawn of grace.
O come, divine Messiah,
The world in silence waits the day
When hope shall sing its triumph,
And sadness flee away.

5

Hark! The Herald Angels Sing

1. Hark! The herald angels sing,
"Glory to the newborn King.
Peace on earth, and mercy mild,
God and sinners reconciled."
Joyful, all ye nations, rise,
Join the triumph of the skies.
With th'angelic host proclaim,
"Christ is born in Bethlehem."

—*Refrain.* Hark! The herald angels sing,
"Glory to the newborn King."

2. Christ, by highest heav'n adored,
Christ, the everlasting Lord.
Late in time behold him come,
Offspring of a virgin's womb.
Veiled in flesh, the Godhead see;
Hail th'incarnate Deity!
Pleased as Man with men to appear,
Jesus, our Emmanuel. —*Refrain*

6

Silent Night

Silent night, holy night!
All is calm, all is bright.
'Round yon Virgin Mother and Child.
Holy Infant so tender and mild:
Sleep in heavenly peace,
Sleep in heavenly peace!

Silent night, holy night!
Shepherds quake at the sight!
Glories stream from heaven afar.
Heav'nly hosts sing Alleluia:
Christ, the Saviour is born,
Christ, the Saviour is born!

7

We Three Kings

1. We three kings of Orient are
Bearing gifts we traverse afar,
Field and fountain, moor and mountain,
Following yonder Star.

Refrain: O Star of wonder, Star of night,
Star with royal beauty bright,
Westward leading, still proceeding,
Guide us to thy perfect light.

2. Born a king on Bethlehem's plain,
Gold I bring to crown Him again,
King forever, ceasing never,
Over us all to reign. —*Refrain*

O Come, All Ye Faithful

8

1. O come, all ye faithful, joyful and triumphant,
O come ye, O come ye to Bethlehem;
Come and behold him born the King of angels.

—*Refrain:* O come, let us adore him,
O come, let us adore him,
O come, let us adore him, Christ the Lord.

2. Sing choirs of angels, Sing in exultation,
Sing all ye citizens of Heav'n above;
Glory to God in the highest. —*Refrain*

3. See how the shepherd summoned to his cradle,
Leaving their flocks draw nigh with lowly fear;
We too will thither bend our joyful footsteps. —*Refrain*

The First Noel

9

1. The first Noel the angel did say,
Was to certain poor shepherds in fields as they lay;
In fields where they lay keeping their sheep
On a cold winter's night that was so deep.

—*Refrain:* Noel, Noel, Noel, Noel,
Born is the King of Israel.

2. They looked up and saw a star,
Shining in the east, beyond them far,
And to the earth it gave great light,
And so it continued both day and night. —*Refrain*

3. This star drew nigh to the northwest,
O'er Bethlehem it took its rest,
And there it did both stop and stay,
Right over the place where Jesus lay. —*Refrain*

4. Then entered in those wise men three,
Full reverently upon their knee,
And offered there in his presence,
Their gold and myrrh and frankincense. —*Refrain*

10 Angels We Have Heard on High

1. Angels we have heard on high,
Sweetly singing o'er the plain,
And the mountains in reply
Echoing their joyous strain.

Refrain: Gloria in excelsis Deo. (Repeat)

2. Shepherds, why this jubilee,
Why your joyous strains prolong?
Say, what may the tidings be
Which inspire your heav'nly song? *—Refrain*

3. Come to Bethlehem and see
Him whose birth the angels sing;
Come, adore on bended knee
Christ the Lord, the newborn King. *—Refrain*

11 Joy to the World

1.
Joy to the world! The Lord is come;
Let earth receive her King;
Let every heart prepare him room,
And heav'n and nature sing,
And heav'n and nature sing,
And heaven, and heaven and nature sing.

2.
Joy to the world! the Saviour reigns;
Let men their songs employ,
While fields and floods,
Rocks, hills, and plains,
Repeat the sounding joy,
Repeat the sounding joy,
Repeat, repeat the sounding joy.

12 O Sing a Joyous Carol

1. O sing a joyous carol
Unto the Holy Child,
And praise with gladsome voices
His mother undefiled.
Our gladsome voices greeting
Shall hail our Infant King;
And our sweet Lady listens
When joyful voices sing.

2. Who is there meekly lying
In yonder stable poor?
Dear children, it is Jesus;
He bids you now adore.
Who is there kneeling by him?
In Virgin beauty fair?
It is our Mother Mary,
She bids you all draw near.

Lord, Who throughout These 40 Days 13

1. Lord, Who throughout these forty days
   For us did fast and pray,
   Teach us to overcome our sins
   And close by you to stay.

2. As you with Satan did contend
   And did the vic'try win,
   O give us strength in you to fight,
   In you to conquer sin.

3. As you did hunger and did thirst,
   So teach us, gracious Lord,
   To die to self and so to live
   By your most holy word.

O Faithful Cross 14

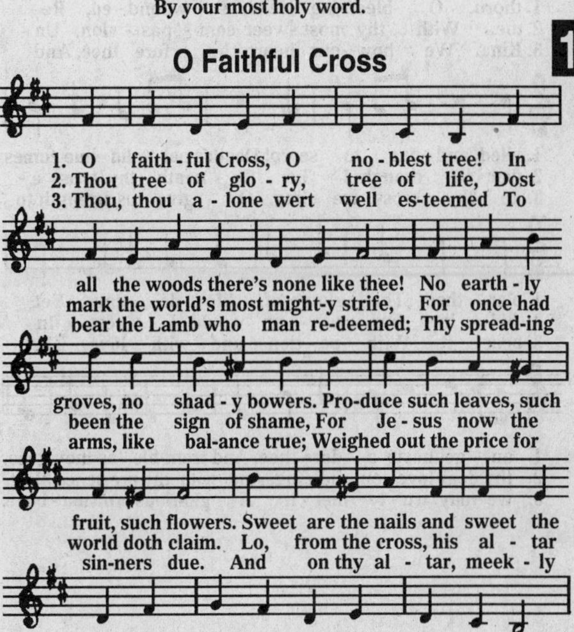
1. O faith - ful Cross, O no - blest tree! In
2. Thou tree of glo - ry, tree of life, Dost
3. Thou, thou a - lone wert well es-teemed To
all the woods there's none like thee! No earth - ly
mark the world's most might-y strife, For once had
bear the Lamb who man re-deemed; Thy spread-ing
groves, no shad - y bowers. Pro-duce such leaves, such
been the sign of shame, For Je - sus now the
arms, like bal-ance true; Weighed out the price for
fruit, such flowers. Sweet are the nails and sweet the
world doth claim. Lo, from the cross, his al - tar
sin-ners due. And on thy al - tar, meek - ly
wood That bears a load so sweet, so good!
throne, He gent - ly draws and rules his own.
laid, The lamb of God a - tone - ment made.

15 O Sacred Head, Surrounded

H.W. Baker, 1861
A.T. Russell, 1851, alt.

Passion Chorale
H. L. Hassler, 1601
Adapted, J.S. Bach, 1685-1750

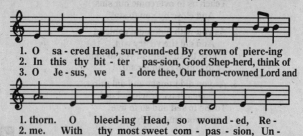

1. O sa - cred Head, sur-round-ed By crown of pierc-ing
2. In this thy bit - ter pas-sion, Good Shep-herd, think of
3. O Je - sus, we a - dore thee, Our thorn-crowned Lord and

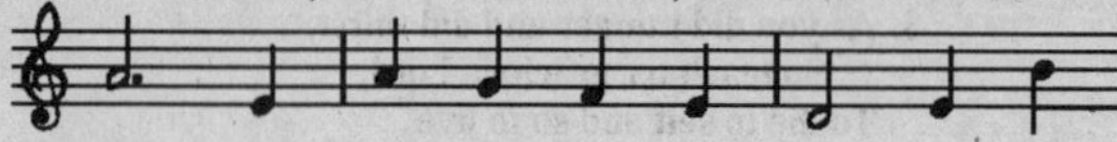

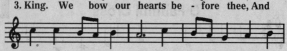

1. thorn. O bleed-ing Head, so wound - ed, Re -
2. me. With thy most sweet com - pas - sion, Un -
3. King. We bow our hearts be - fore thee, And

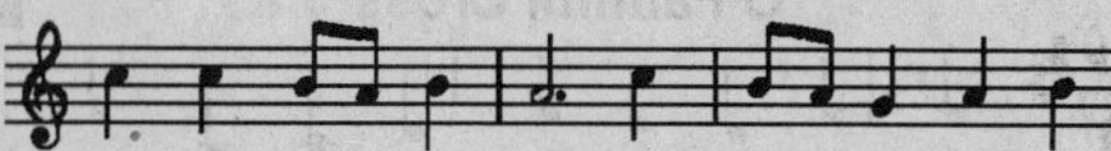

1. viled, and put to scorn! Death's pal - lid hue comes
2. wor - thy though I be: Be - neath thy cross a -
3. to thy cross we cling. O give us strength to

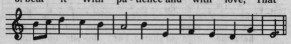

1. o'er thee, The glow of life de - cays, Yet
2. bid - ing For ev - er would I rest, In
3. bear it With pa - tience and with love, That

1. an - gel hosts a - dore thee, And trem-ble as they gaze.
2. thy dear love con - fid - ing, And with thy pre-sence blest.
3. we may tru - ly mer - it A glo-rious crown a - bove.

All Glory, Laud and Honour

16

St. Theodulph of Orleans, c. 820
Tr. J.M. Neale, 1854, alt.

St. Theodulph
M. Teachner, 1615

1. All glo - ry, laud, and hon - our To thee, Re-deem-er,

1. King, To whom the lips of chil - dren Made

Fine

1. sweet ho - san - nas ring. 2. Thou art the King of
3. The com - pa - ny of
4. The peo - ple of the
5. To thee be - fore thy
6. Thou didst ac - cept their

2. Is - rael, Thou Da - vid's roy - al Son. Who
3. an - gels Are prais - ing thee on high, And
4. He - brews With palms be - fore thee went; Our
5. pas - sion They sang their hymns of praise; To
6. prais - es, Ac - cept the pray'rs we bring, Who

D.C.

2. in the Lord's name com-est, The King and bles-sed One.
3. mor-tal men and all things Cre - a - ted make re - ply.
4. praise and pray'r and an - thems Be - fore thee we pre-sent.
5. thee now high ex - alt - ed Our mel - o - dy we raise.
6. in all good de - light-est, Thou good and gra-cious King.

17 Christ the Lord Is Ris'n Today

Jane E. Leeson, c. 1851,
based on Victimae Paschali

Victimae Paschali
Traditional

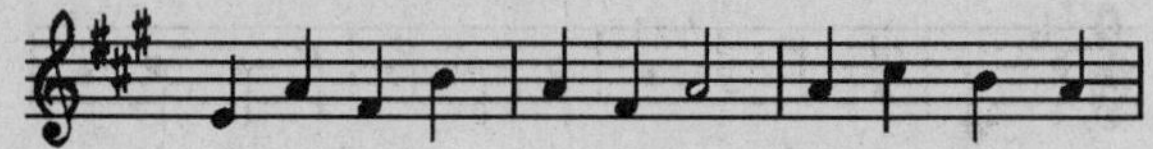

1. Christ, the Lord is ris'n to - day, Chris-tians, haste your
2. Christ, the vic-tim un - de-filed, Man to God has
3. Christ, who once for sin - ers bled, Now the first - born

1. vows to pay; Of - fer ye your prais - es meet
2. rec - on - ciled; When in strange and aw - ful strife
3. from the dead, Thron'd in end - less might and pow'r

1. At the pas - chal vic-tim's feet. For the sheep the
2. Met to - geth - er death and life; Chris-tians, on this
3. Lives and reigns for ev - er more. Hail, e - ter - nal

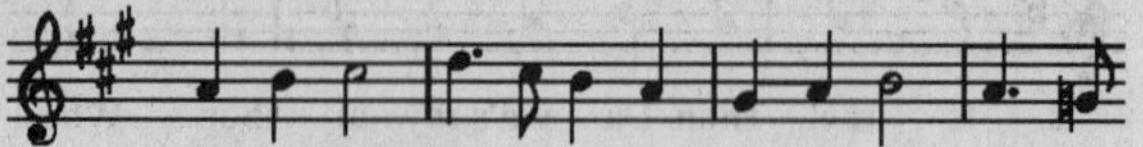

1. Lamb has bled, Sin-less in the sinners' stead; Christ, the
2. hap - py day Haste with joy your vows to pay. Christ, the
3. hope on high! Hail, thou King of vic- to - ry! Hail, thou

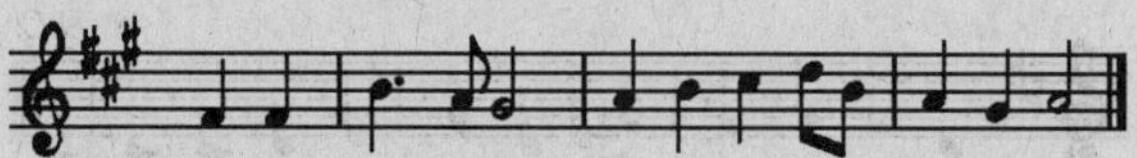

1. Lord, is ris'n on high, Now he lives, no more to die!
2. Lord, is ris'n on high, Now he lives, no more to die!
3. Prince of life a-dored! Help and save us, gra-cious Lord.

The Strife is O'er

18

Tr. F. Pott, 1861, alt.

Victory
Palestrina, 1591
Adapted W.H. Monk, 1861

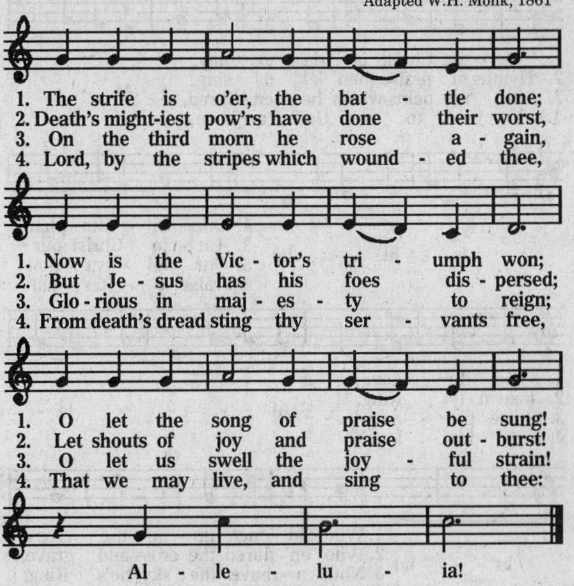
1. The strife is o'er, the bat - tle done;
2. Death's might-iest pow'rs have done their worst,
3. On the third morn he rose a - gain,
4. Lord, by the stripes which wound - ed thee,
1. Now is the Vic - tor's tri - umph won;
2. But Je - sus has his foes dis - persed;
3. Glo - rious in maj - es - ty to reign;
4. From death's dread sting thy ser - vants free,
1. O let the song of praise be sung!
2. Let shouts of joy and praise out - burst!
3. O let us swell the joy - ful strain!
4. That we may live, and sing to thee:
Al - le - lu - ia!

O God, Our Help in Ages Past

19

1.

O God, our help in ages past,
Our hope for years to come,
Our shelter from the stormy blast,
And our eternal home.

2.

Beneath the shadow of Thy throne,
Thy saints have dwelt secure,
Sufficient is Thine arm alone,
And our defence is sure.

3.

Before the hills in order stood,
Or earth received her frame,
From everlasting Thou art God,
To endless years the same.

4.

A thousand ages in Thy sight,
Are like an evening gone.
Short as the watch that ends the night,
Before the rising sun.

20 Jesus Christ Is Ris'n Today

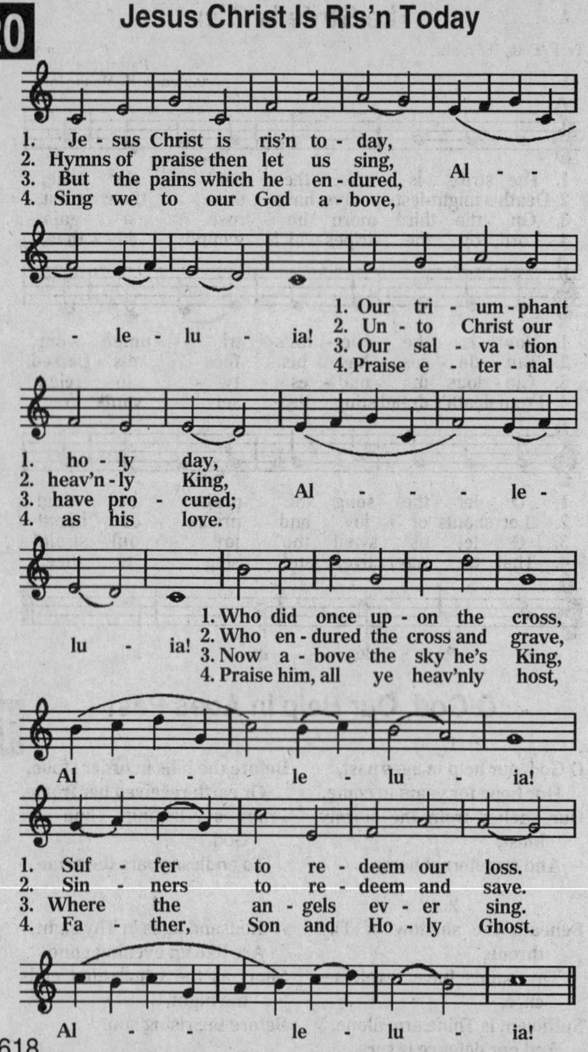
1. Je - sus Christ is ris'n to - day,
2. Hymns of praise then let us sing,
3. But the pains which he en - dured,
4. Sing we to our God a - bove,
Al - - le - lu - ia!
1. Our tri - um - phant
2. Un - to Christ our
3. Our sal - va - tion
4. Praise e - ter - nal
1. ho - ly day,
2. heav'n - ly King,
3. have pro - cured;
4. as his love.
Al - - - le - lu - ia!
1. Who did once up - on the cross,
2. Who en - dured the cross and grave,
3. Now a - bove the sky he's King,
4. Praise him, all ye heav'nly host,
Al - - le - lu - ia!
1. Suf - fer to re - deem our loss.
2. Sin - ners to re - deem and save.
3. Where the an - gels ev - er sing.
4. Fa - ther, Son and Ho - ly Ghost.
Al - - le - lu - ia!

That Eastertide with Joy was Bright

21

Verses 1, 2: tr. J.M. Neale, 1851 Lasst Uns Erfreuen
Verse 3: tr. J. Chambers, 1857, alt. Geistliches Kirchengesang, 1623

1. That East - er - tide with joy was bright, The
2. He showed to them his hands, his side, Where
3. To God the Fa - ther let us sing, To

1. sun shone out with fair - er light, Al - le -
2. yet those glo - rious wounds a - bide, Al - le -
3. God the Son, our ris - en King, Al - le -

1. lu - ia, al - le - lu - ia, When, to their long -
2. lu - ia, al - le - lu - ia, The to - kens true
3. lu - ia, al - le - lu - ia, And e - qual - ly

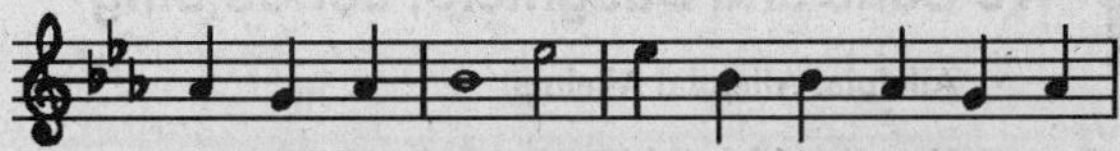

1. ing eyes re - stored, The glad a - pos - tles saw their
2. which made it plain. Their Lord in-deed was ris'n a -
3. let us a - dore The Ho - ly Spir - it ev - er -

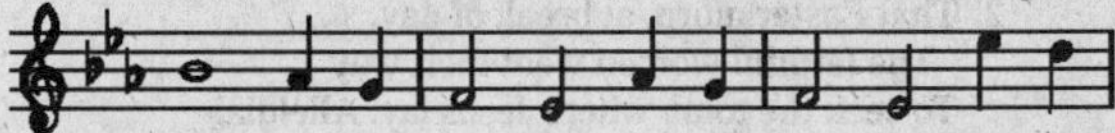

1. Lord, Al - le - lu - ia, al - le - lu - ia, Al - le -
2. gain, Al - le - lu - ia, al - le - lu - ia, Al - le -
3. more, Al - le - lu - ia, al - le - lu - ia, Al - le -

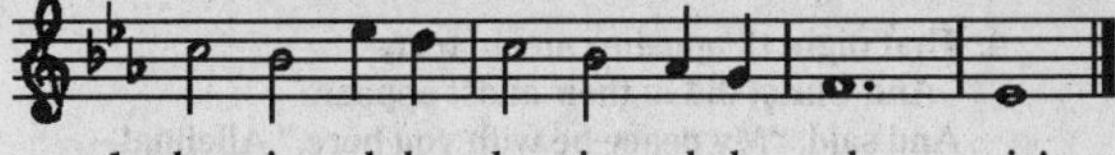

1. lu - ia, al - le - lu - ia, al - le - lu - ia!
2. lu - ia, al - le - lu - ia, al - le - lu - ia!
3. lu - ia, al - le - lu - ia, al - le - lu - ia!

22 At the Lamb's High Feast We Sing

1. At the Lamb's high feast we sing
   Praise to our victor'ous King.
   He has washed us in the tide
   Flowing from his opened side;
   Praise we him whose love divine
   Gives his sacred Blood for wine,
   Gives his Body for the feast,
   Christ the Victim, Christ the Priest.

2. When the Paschal blood is poured,
   Death's dark Angel sheathes his sword;
   Israel's hosts triumphant go
   Through the wave that drowns the foe.
   Christ the Lamb, whose Blood was shed,
   Paschal victim, Paschal bread;
   With sincerity and love
   Eat we Manna from above.

23 Ye Sons and Daughters, Let Us Sing

Alleluia! Alleluia! Alleluia!

1. Ye sons and daughters, let us sing!
   The King of heav'n, our glorious King,
   From death today rose triumphing. Alleluia!

2. That Easter morn, at break of day,
   The faithful women went their way
   To seek the tomb where Jesus lay. Alleluia!

3. An angel clothed in white they see,
   Who sat and spoke unto the three,
   "Your Lord has gone to Galilee." Alleluia!

4. That night th'apostles met in fear,
   And Christ did in their midst appear.
   And said, "My peace be with you here." Alleluia!

5. How blest are they who have not seen
   And yet whose faith has constant been,
   For they eternal life shall win. Alleluia!

All Hail, Adored Trinity

24

Verses 1, 2, 3: Anglo Saxon, 11th cent.
Praise God: Thomas Ken, 1709 Louis Bourgeois, 1551

1. All hail, a - dor - ed Trin - i-
2. Three Per - sons praise we ev - er-
3. O Trin - i - ty, O U - ni-
1. ty; All praise, e - ter - nal U - ni - ty:
2. more, And thee th'E - ter - nal One a - dore:
3. ty, Be pres - ent as we wor - ship thee;
1. O God the Fa - ther, God the
2. In thy sure mer - cy ev - er
3. And to the an - gel's songs in
1. Son, And God the Spir - it, ev - er One.
2. kind, May we our true pro - tec - tion find.
3. light Our prayers and prais - es now u - nite.

Sing We Triumphant Hymns of Praise

25

1. Sing we triumphant hymns of praise
To greet our Lord these festive days.
Alleluia, alleluia!
Who by a road before untrod
Ascended to the throne of God.
Alleluia, alleluia.
Alleluia, alleluia, alleluia!

2. In wond'ring awe His faithful band
Upon the Mount of Olives stand.
Alleluia, alleluia!
And with the Virgin Mother see
Their Lord ascend in majesty.
Alleluia, alleluia.
Alleluia, alleluia, alleluia!

26 Praise God from Whom All Blessings Flow

1. Praise God, from whom all blessings flow;
   Praise him, all creatures here below;
   Praise him above, ye heav'nly host;
   Praise Father, Son, and Holy Ghost.

2. All people that on earth do dwell,
   Sing to the Lord with cheerful voice;
   Him serve with mirth, his praise forth tell,
   Come ye before him and rejoice.

3. Know that the Lord is God indeed:
   Without our aid he did us make;
   We are his folk, he doth us feed,
   And for his sheep he doth us take.

4. O enter then his gates with praise,
   Approach with joy his courts unto;
   Praise, laud, and bless his name always,
   For it is seemly so to do.

27 Come, Holy Ghost

1. Come, Holy Ghost, Creator blest,
   And in our hearts take up your rest;
   Come with your grace and heav'nly aid
   To fill the hearts which you have made,
   To fill the hearts which you have made.

2. O Comforter, to you we cry,
   The heav'nly gift of God most high;
   The fount of life and fire of love,
   And sweet anointing from above,
   And sweet anointing from above.

3. To every sense your light impart,
   And shed your love in ev'ry heart.
   To our weak flesh, your strength supply:
   Unfailing courage from on high,
   Unfailing courage from on high.

4. O grant that we through you may come
   To know the Father and the Son,
   And hold with firm, unchanging faith,
   That you are Spirit of them both,
   That you are Spirit of them both.

O Holy Spirit, Lord of Peace

28

Tr. J. Chandler, 1806-76, alt.

Jeremiah Clark, 1709

1. O Ho - ly Spir - it, Lord of grace, E -
2. As thou in bond of love dost join The
3. All glo - ry to the Fa - ther be, All
1. ter - nal fount of love, In - flame, we pray, our
2. Fa - ther and the Son, So fill us all with
3. glo - ry to the Son, And Ho - ly Spir - it
1. in-most hearts With fire from heav'n a - bove.
2. mu-tual love, U - nite our hearts as one.
3. ev - er more While end - less a - ges run.

Creator Spirit, Lord of Grace

29

1. Creator Spirit, Lord of grace
   Make thou our hearts thy dwelling place
   And with thy might celestial, aid
   The souls of those whom thou hast made.

2. O to our souls thy light impart;
   And give thy love to every heart;
   Turn all our weakness into might,
   O thou the source of life and light.

3. To God the Father let us sing
   To God the Son, our risen king;
   And equally with thee adore
   The Spirit, God forevermore.

30 Now Thank We All Our God

M. Rinkart, 1586-1649
Tr. Catherine Winkworth, 1858

Nun Danket
J. Crüger, 1647

1. Now thank we all our God, With heart, and hand, and
2. O may this boun-teous God Through all our life be
3. All praise and thanks to God The Fa - ther now be
1. voic - es, Who won-drous things hath done, In
2. near us! With ev - er joy - ful hearts And
3. giv - en, The Son, and him who reigns With
1. whom his world re - joic - es; Who from our moth-er's
2. bless-ed peace to cheer us; And keep us in his
3. them in high - est heav - en, The one e - ter - nal
1. arms Hath blessed us on our way With
2. grace, And guide us when per - plex'd And
3. God, Whom heav'n and earth a - dore; For

1. count-less gifts of love, And still is ours to - day.
2. free us from all ills In this world and the next.
3. thus it was, is now, And shall be, ev - er - more.

31 We Gather Together

1. We gather together to ask the Lord's blessing;
He chastens and hastens his will to make known;
The wicked oppressing now cease from distressing:
Sing praises to his name; he forgets not his own.

2. Beside us to guide us, our God with us joining,
Ordaining, maintaining his kingdom divine;
So from the beginning the fight we were winning:
Thou, Lord, wast at our side; all glory be thine.

Holy, Holy, Holy

32

R. Heber, 1826, alt.

Nicaea
J. B. Dykes, 1861

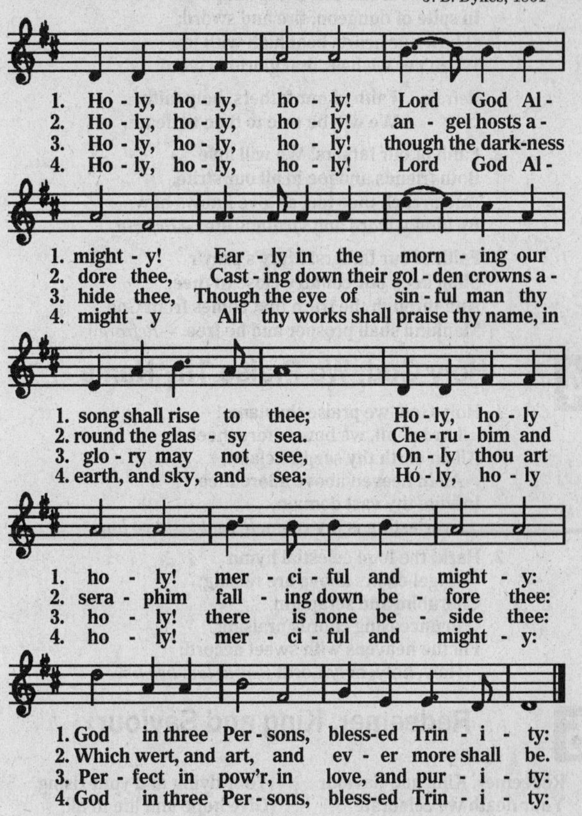
1. Ho - ly, ho - ly, ho - ly! Lord God Al -
2. Ho - ly, ho - ly, ho - ly! an - gel hosts a -
3. Ho - ly, ho - ly, ho - ly! though the dark-ness
4. Ho - ly, ho - ly, ho - ly! Lord God Al -
1. might - y! Ear - ly in the morn - ing our
2. dore thee, Cast - ing down their gol - den crowns a -
3. hide thee, Though the eye of sin - ful man thy
4. might - y All thy works shall praise thy name, in
1. song shall rise to thee; Ho - ly, ho - ly
2. round the glas - sy sea. Che - ru - bim and
3. glo - ry may not see, On - ly thou art
4. earth, and sky, and sea; Ho - ly, ho - ly
1. ho - ly! mer - ci - ful and might - y:
2. sera - phim fall - ing down be - fore thee:
3. ho - ly! there is none be - side thee:
4. ho - ly! mer - ci - ful and might - y:
1. God in three Per - sons, bless-ed Trin - i - ty:
2. Which wert, and art, and ev - er more shall be.
3. Per - fect in pow'r, in love, and pur - i - ty:
4. God in three Per - sons, bless-ed Trin - i - ty:

33 Faith of Our Fathers

1. Faith of our fathers, living still,
In spite of dungeon, fire and sword;
O how our hearts beat high with joy
When'ver we hear that glorious word!

Refrain: Faith of our fathers, holy faith,
We will be true to thee til death.

2. Faith of our fathers! We will love
Both friends and foe in all our strife.
And preach thee too, as love knows how,
By kindly word and virtuous life. *—Refrain*

3. Faith of our fathers! Mary's pray'r
Shall keep our country close to thee;
And through the truth that comes from God
Mankind shall prosper and be free. *—Refrain*

34 Holy God, We Praise Thy Name

1. Holy God, we praise thy name!
Lord of all, we bow before thee!
All on earth thy sceptre claim,
All in heaven above adore thee.
Infinite thy vast domain,
Everlasting is thy reign. *Repeat last two lines*

2. Hark! the loud celestial hymn
Angel choirs above are raising;
Cherubim and seraphim,
In unceasing chorus praising,
Fill the heavens with sweet accord;
Holy, holy, holy Lord! *Repeat last two lines*

35 Redeemer, King and Saviour

1.
Redeemer, King and Saviour
Your death we celebrate
So good, yet born our brother,
You live in human state.
O Saviour, in your dying
You do your Father's will,
Give us the strength to suffer
To live for others still.

2.
Your dying and your rising
Give hope and life to all.
Your faithful way of giving
Embraces great and small.
Help us to make our journey,
to walk your glorious way,
And from the night of dying
To find a joy-filled day.

To Jesus Christ, Our Sovereign King

M.B. Hellriegel

Ich Glaub An Gott
Mainz, 1900

36

1. To Je - sus Christ, our sov-'reign King, Who
2. Your reign ex - tend, O King be - nign, To
3. To you and to your Church, great King, We

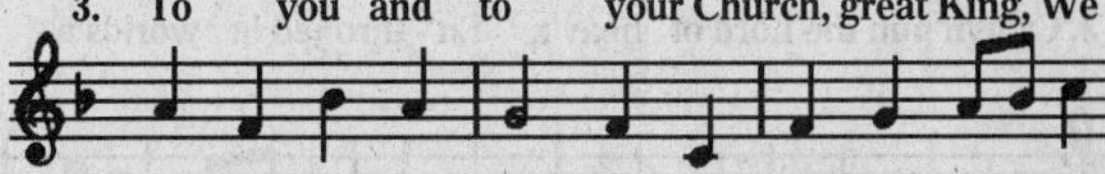

1. is the world's sal - va - tion, All praise and hom - age
2. ev - 'ry land and na - tion; For in your king-dom,
3. pledge our hearts' ob - la - tion; Un - til be - fore your

1. do we bring And thanks and ad - o - ra - tion.
2. Lord di - vine, A - lone we find sal - va - tion.
3. throne we sing In end - less ju - bi - la - tion:

Refrain:

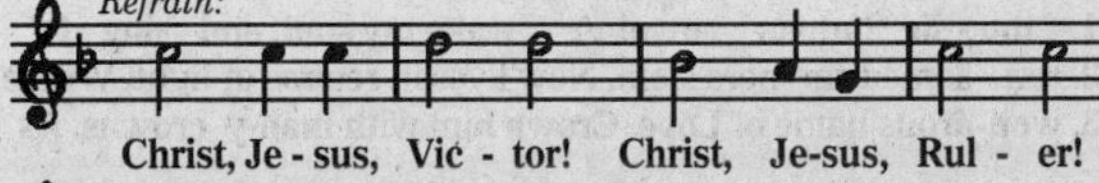

Christ, Je - sus, Vic - tor! Christ, Je-sus, Rul - er!

Christ, Je - sus, Lord and Re - deem - er!

O Lord, I Am Not Worthy

37

1. O Lord, I am not worthy,
   That thou shouldst come to me,
   But speak the word of comfort:
   My spirit healed shall be.

2. And humbly I'll receive thee,
   The bridegroom of my soul,
   No more by sin to grieve thee
   Or fly thy sweet control.

3. O Sacrament most holy,
   O Sacrament divine,
   All praise and all thanksgiving
   Be every moment thine.

38 Crown Him with Many Crowns

M. Bridges, 1851
and others

Diademata
G.J. Elvey, 1868

1. Crown him with man-y crowns. The Lamb up - on his
2. Crown him the Lord of Lords, Who o - ver all doth
3. Crown him the Lord of heav'n En - throned in worlds a -

1. throne: Hark, how the heav'n-ly an - them drowns All
2. reign, Who once on earth th'in - car - nate Word, For
3. bove; Crown him the King, to whom is giv'n The

1. mu - sic but its own! A - wake my soul, and sing Of
2. ran - somed sin -ners slain, Now lives in realms of light, Where
3. won-drous name of Love. Crown him with man-y crowns. As

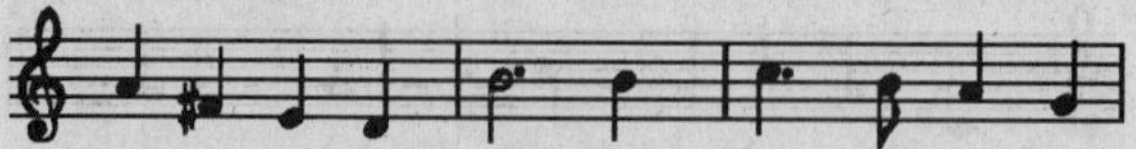

1. him who died for thee. And hail him as thy
2. saints with an - gels sing Their songs be - fore him
3. thrones be-fore him fall. Crown him, ye kings, with

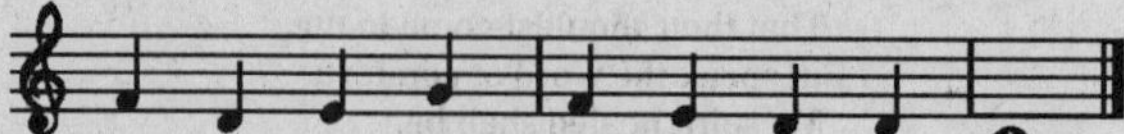

1. match-less King Through all e - ter - ni - ty.
2. day and night, Their God, Re - deem-er, King.
3. man - y crowns, For he is King of all.

Taste and See

Tune: James E. Moore, Jr., b. 1951

Text: Psalm 34; James E. Moore, Jr., b. 1951

Refrain

Taste and see, taste and see the good-ness of the Lord. O taste and see, taste and see the good-ness of the Lord, of the Lord.

Verses

1. I will bless the Lord at all times. Praise shall al-ways be on my lips; my soul shall glo-ry in the Lord for God has been so good to me.

2. Glo-ri-fy the Lord with me, To-geth-er let us all praise God's name. I called the Lord who an-swered me; from all my trou-bles I was set free.

3. Wor-ship the Lord, all you peo-ple. You'll want for noth-ing if you ask. Taste and see that the Lord is good; in God we need put all our trust.

D.C.

40 Lord, Who at Your First Eucharist Did Pray

Song I

W.H. Turton, 1881, alt. O. Gibbons, 1623

1. Lord, who at your first Eu - cha - rist did pray
2. For all your Church, O Lord, we in - ter - cede;
3. So, Lord, at length when sa - cra - ments shall cease,

1. That all your Church might be for ev - er one,
2. O make our lack of char - i - ty to cease;
3. May we be one with all your Church a - bove,

1. Grant us at ev - 'ry Eu - cha - rist to
2. Draw us the near - er each to each, we
3. One with your saints in one un - end - ing

1. say With long - ing heart and soul, "Your will be
2. plead, By draw - ing all to you, O prince of
3. peace, One with your saints in one un - bound-ed

1. done." O may we all one bread, one bod - y be
2. peace; Thus may we all one bread, one bod - y be
3. love: More bless-ed still in peace and love to be

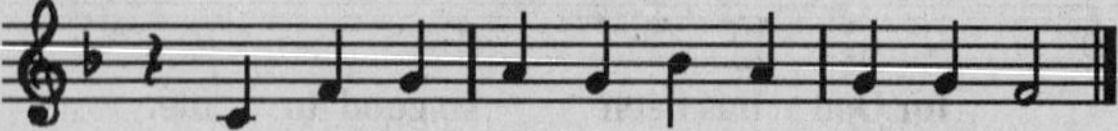

1. Through this blest Sa - cra-ment of u - ni - ty.
2. Through this blest Sa - cra-ment of u - ni - ty.
3. One with the Trin - i - ty in u - ni - ty.

Immaculate Mary 41

Anon. | Lourdes
Traditional Lourdes Melody

1. Im - mac - u - late Ma - ry, your prais - es we
2. In heav - en, the bless - ed your glo - ry pro -
3. Your name is our pow - er, your vir - tues our
4. We pray for our moth - er, the Church up - on

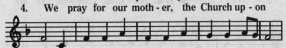

1. sing, You reign now in heav-en with Je - sus our King.
2. claim; On earth, we your chil-dren in - voke your fair name.
3. light, Your love is our com - fort, your plead-ing our might.
4. earth, And bless, dear-est la - dy, the land of our birth.

Refrain:

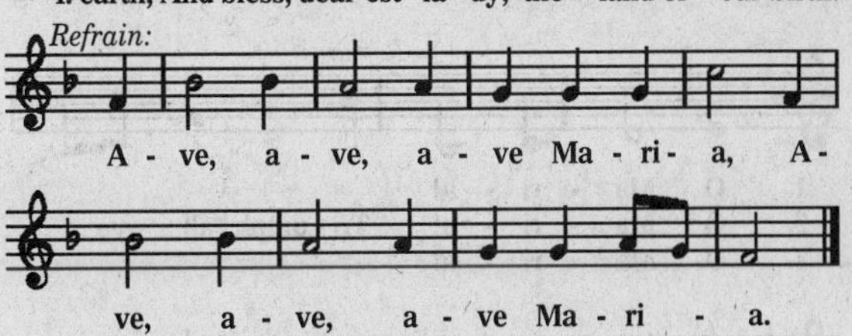

A - ve, a - ve, a - ve Ma - ri - a, A -
ve, a - ve, a - ve Ma - ri - a.

Hail, O Star of Ocean 42

1. Hail, O Star of Ocean,
   Portal of the sky!
   Ever Virgin Mother
   Of the Lord most high.

2. O by Gabriel's Ave
   Uttered long ago,
   Eva's name reversing
   Brought us peace below.

43 Hail, Holy Queen, Enthroned Above

Traditional

Salve Regina Caelitum
Traditional

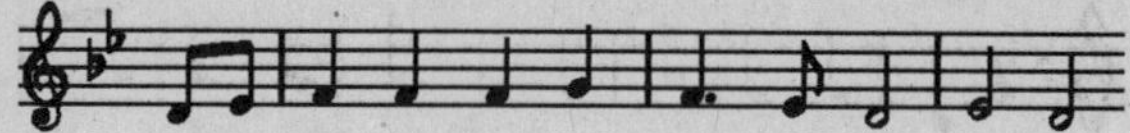

1. Hail, ho - ly Queen en - throned a - bove, O Ma -
2. Our life, our sweet-ness here be - low, O Ma -
3. We hon - our you for Christ, your son, O Ma -

1. ri - a! Hail, moth-er of mer - cy and of love,
2. ri - a! Our hope in sor - row and in woe,
3. ri - a! Who has for us re - demp-tion won,

Refrain:

1. O Ma - ri - a!
2. O Ma - ri - a! Tri - umph all ye
3. O Ma - ri - a!

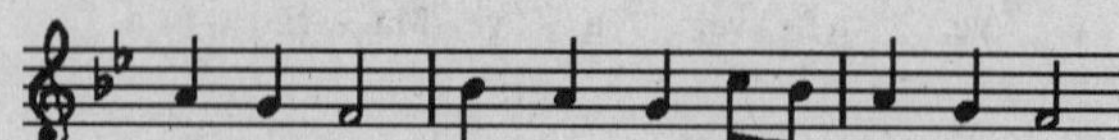

che - ru - bim, Sing with us, ye se - ra - phim,

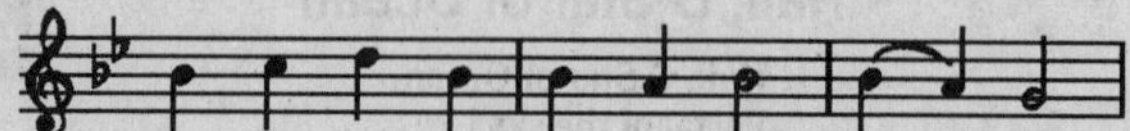

Heav'n and earth re - sound the hymn: Sal - ve,

sal - ve, sal - ve, Re - gi - na!

For All the Saints

W.W. How, 1864

Sine Nomine
R. Vaughan Williams, 1906

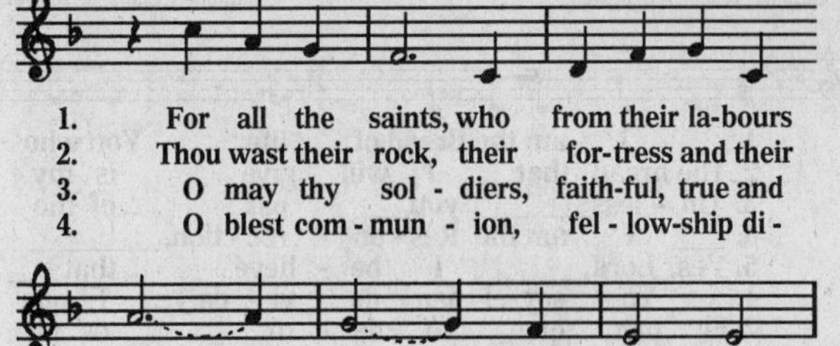

1. For all the saints, who from their la-bours
2. Thou wast their rock, their for-tress and their
3. O may thy sol - diers, faith-ful, true and
4. O blest com - mun - ion, fel - low-ship di -

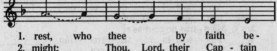

1. rest, who thee by faith be -
2. might: Thou, Lord, their Cap - tain
3. bold, Fight as the saints who
4. vine, We fee - bly strug - gle,

1. fore the world con - fess'd, Thy name, O
2. in the well-fought fight; Thou in the
3. no - bly fought of old, And win, with
4. they in glo - ry shine: Yet all are

1. Je - sus, be for ev - er blest. Al -
2. dark - ness drear, their one true light. Al -
3. them, the vic - tor's crown of gold. Al -
4. one in thee, for all are thine. Al -

1 - 4 le - lu - ia, al - le - lu - ia!

45

I Am the Bread of Life

Tune: BREAD OF LIFE, Irreg. with refrain;
Suzanne Toolan, SM, b. 1927

Text: John 6;
Suzanne Toolan, SM, b. 1927

1. ___ I am the Bread of life. You who
2. The bread that__ I will give is my
3. Un - less______ you___ eat of the
4. ___ I am the Res - ur - rec - tion,_________
5. Yes, Lord,______ I be - lieve that___
1. ___ Yo soy el pan de vi - da. El que
2. El pan que__ yo da - ré____ es mi
3. ___ Mien - tras no co-mas el__
4. ___ Yo soy la re - su - rrec - ción.__________
5. ___ Sí, Se - ñor, yo cre - o que___

come to me shall not hun - ger;__ and who be-
flesh for the life of the world,_____ and if you
flesh of the Son of Man_________ and___
I_________ am the life._______ If you be -
you_______ are the Christ,_______ the_____
vie - ne_a mí no ten-drá ham - bre.____ El que
cuer - po___ vi - da del mun - do,__ y el que
cuer-po del hi-jo del hom-bre,___ y___
Yo________ soy la vi - da.______ El que
tú e - res el Cris - to, ______ El_____

lieve in me shall not thirst.______ No one can come to
eat______ of this bread, ______ you shall__ live for
drink_____ of his blood,__ and drink____ of his
lieve _____ in____ me,_________ e-ven_ though you
Son___ of__ God,__ Who__ has__
cree_en mí no ten-drá sed._________ Na - die___ vie - ne_a
co - ma___ de mi car-ne_______ ten-drá___ vi - da_e-
be - bas__ de su san-gre y be-bas__ de su
cree_____ en_____ mí,_________ aun-que___ mu - rie-
Hi - jo de Dios,___ que vi - no al

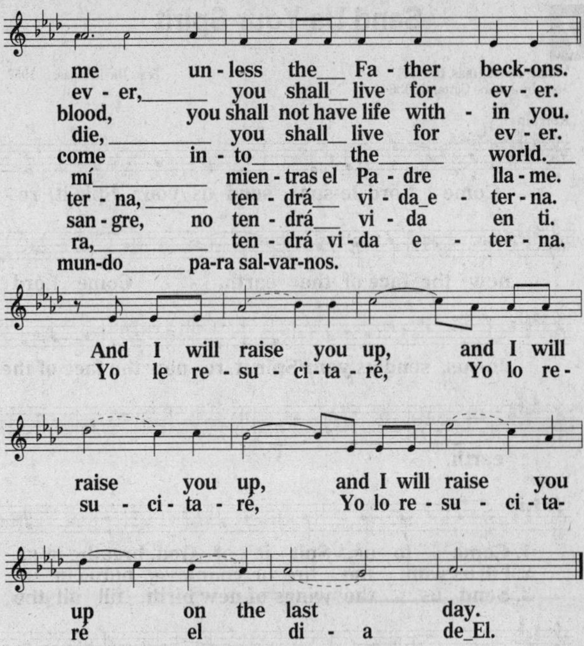

me un - less the___ Fa - ther beck-ons.
ev - er,______ you shall_ live for ev - er.
blood, you shall not have life with - in you.
die, __________ you shall_ live for ev - er.
come in - to__________ the_______ world.___
mí___________ mien - tras el Pa - dre lla - me.
ter - na, ______ ten - drá___ vi - da_e - ter - na.
san - gre, no ten - drá___ vi - da en ti.
ra,___________ ten - drá vi - da e - ter - na.
mun-do______ pa-ra sal-var-nos.

And I will raise you up, and I will
Yo le re - su - ci - ta - ré, Yo lo re -

raise you up, and I will raise you
su - ci - ta - ré, Yo lo re - su - ci - ta-

up on the last day.
ré el di - a de_El.

O Most Holy One

46

1. O most holy one, O most lowly one,
Loving virgin, Maria!
Mother, maid of fairest love,
Lady, queen of all above,
Ora, ora pro nobis.

2. Virgin ever fair, Mother, hear our prayer,
Look upon us, Maria!
Bring to us your treasure,
Grace beyond all measure,
Ora, ora pro nobis.

47

Send Us Your Spirit

Tune: David Haas, b. 1957
acc. by Jeanne Cotter, b. 1964

Text: David Haas, b. 1957

Refrain

*1. 2.

Come Lord Je-sus, send us your Spir-it, re - new the face of the earth. Come Lord Je-sus, send us your Spir-it, re - new the face of the earth.

Verses

1. Come to us, Spir - it of God, breathe in us now, we sing to - geth-er. Spir - it of hope and of light, fill our lives, come to us, Spir - it of God.
2. Fill us with the fire of your love, burn in us now, bring us to - geth-er. Come to us, dwell in us, change our lives, O Lord, come to us, Spir - it of God.
3. Send us the wings of new birth, fill all the earth with the love you have taught us. Let all cre- a - tion now be shak-en with love, come to us, Spir - it of God.

* *May be sung in canon.*

Praise to the Lord, the Almighty

J. Neander, 1950-80
Tr. Catherine Winkworth, 1863, alt.

Lobe Den Herren
Stralsund Gesangbuch, 1665

1. Praise to the Lord, the Al - might - y, the King of cre -
2. Praise to the Lord, let us of - fer our gifts at the
3. Praise to the Lord, who does pros-per our work and de -
4. Praise to the Lord, O let all that is in us a -

1. a - tion! O my soul, praise him for
2. al - tar. Let not our sins and of -
3. fend us; Sure - ly his good - ness and
4. dore him. All that has life and breath

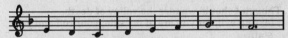

1. he is your health and sal - va - tion.
2. fen - ces now cause us to fal - ter.
3. mer - cy here dai - ly at - tend us;
4. come now re - joi - cing be - fore him.

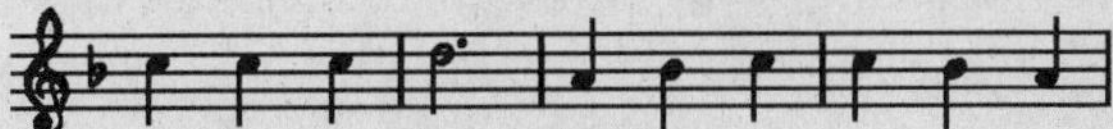

1. All you who hear, now to the al - tar draw
2. Christ the high priest, bids us all join in the
3. Pon - der a - new what the Al - might - y can
4. Let the A - men sound from his peo - ple a -

1. near; Join in pro - found ad - o - ra - tion.
2. feast, Vic - tims with him on the al - tar.
3. do, If with his love he be - friends us.
4. gain, As we here wor-ship be - fore him.

49 Psalm 23: Shepherd Me, O God

Music: Marty Haugen
Text: Psalm 23; Marty Haugen

Refrain

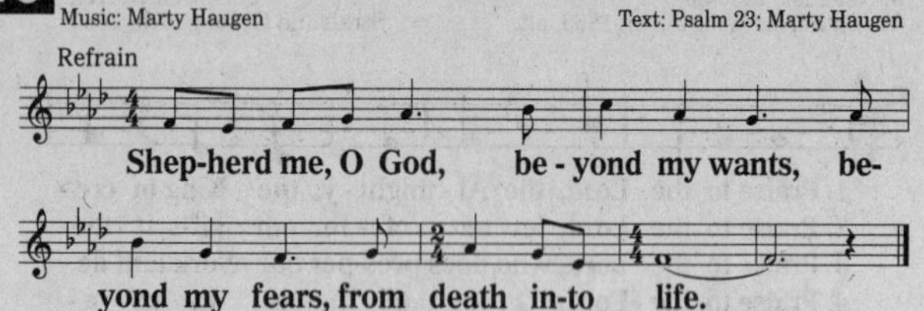
Shep-herd me, O God, be - yond my wants, be-
yond my fears, from death in-to life.

Verses

1. God is my shepherd, so nothing shall I want,
I rest in the meadows of faithfulness and love,
I walk by the quiet waters of peace.

2. Gently you raise me and heal my weary soul,
you lead me by pathways of righteousness and truth,
my spirit shall sing the music of your name.

3. Though I should wander the valley of death,
I fear no evil, for you are at my side, your rod and your staff,
my comfort and my hope.

4. Surely your kindness and mercy follow me all the days of my life;
I will dwell in the house of my God for evermore.

Amazing Grace

50

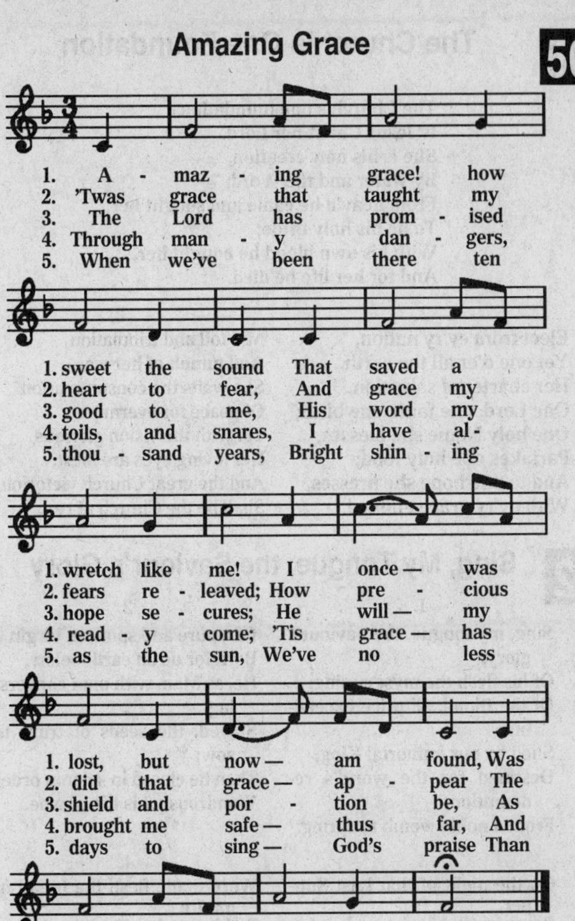
1. A - maz - ing grace! how
2. 'Twas grace that taught my
3. The Lord has prom - ised
4. Through man - y dan - gers,
5. When we've been there ten
1. sweet the sound That saved a
2. heart to fear, And grace my
3. good to me, His word my
4. toils, and snares, I have al -
5. thou - sand years, Bright shin - ing
1. wretch like me! I once — was
2. fears re - leaved; How pre - cious
3. hope se - cures; He will — my
4. read - y come; 'Tis grace — has
5. as the sun, We've no less
1. lost, but now — am found, Was
2. did that grace — ap - pear The
3. shield and por - tion be, As
4. brought me safe — thus far, And
5. days to sing — God's praise Than
1. blind, but now I see.
2. hour I first be - lieved!
3. long as life en - dures.
4. grace will lead me home.
5. when we'd first be - gun.

51 The Church's One Foundation

1.

The Church's one foundation
Is Jesus Christ her Lord.
She is his new creation,
By water and the Word;
From heav'n he came and sought her,
To be his holy bride;
With his own blood he bought her,
And for her life he died.

2.

Elect from ev'ry nation,
Yet one o'er all the earth.
Her charter of salvation,
One Lord, one faith, one birth;
One holy Name she blesses,
Partakes one holy food;
And to one hope she presses,
With ev'ry grace endued.

3.

Mid toil and tribulation,
And tumult of her war.
She waits the consummation
Of peace for evermore;
Till with the vision glorious
Her loving eyes are blest,
And the great Church victorious
Shall be the Church at rest.

52 Sing, My Tongue, the Saviour's Glory

1.

Sing, my tongue, the Saviour's glory,
Of his flesh the myst'ry sing;
Of the Blood, all price exceeding,
Shed by our immortal King,
Destined for the world's redemption,
From a noble womb to spring.

2.

Of a pure and spotless Virgin
Born for us on earth below,
He, as Man, with man conversing,
Stayed, the seeds of truth to sow;
Then he closed in solemn order
Wondrously his life of woe.

3.

On the night of that Last Supper,
Seated with his chosen band,
He the Paschal victim eating,
First fulfils the Law's command;
Then as food to his Apostles
Gives himself with his own Hand.

4.

Word made flesh the bread of nature
By his word to Flesh he turns;
Wine into his blood he changes
What though sense no change discerns?
Only be the heart in earnest,
Faith its lesson quickly learns.

(Tantum ergo)

5.

Down in adoration falling
Lo! the sacred Host we hail;
Lo! o'er ancient forms departing,
Newer rites of grace prevail;
Faith for all defects supplying,
Where the feeble senses fail.

6.

To the Everlasting Father,
And the Son who reigns on high,
With the Holy Ghost proceeding
Forth from each eternally
Be salvation, honour, blessing,
Might and endless majesty.
Amen.

Lord, Dismiss Us with Thy Blessing

53

1.

Lord, dismiss us with thy blessing;
Fill our hearts with joy and peace;
May we all, thy love possessing,
Triumph in redeeming grace:
O refresh us, O refresh us,
And the world its turmoil cease.

2.

Thanks to thee and adoration
For the scriptures' joyful sound,
May the fruit of thy redemption
In our hearts and lives abound;
Ever faithful, ever faithful
To the ways of truth be found.

The King of Glory

54

W. F. Jabusch — Israeli Folksong

Refrain: The King of Glory comes,
the people rejoices;
Open the gates before him,
lift up your voices.

1. Who is the King of Glory;
how shall we call him?
He is Emmanuel,
the promised of ages.

2. In all of Galilee,
In city or village,
He goes among his people
Curing their illness.

55 Praise the Lord of Heaven

T.B. Browne, 1844, alt.

Une Vaine Crainte
French Carol Melody

1.
Praise the Lord of heaven; / Praise him in the height!
Praise him, all ye angels, / Praise him stars and light;
Praise him, earth and waters, / Praise him, all ye skies;
When his word commanded, / All things did arise.

2.
Praise the Lord, ye fountains / Of the depths and seas,
Rocks and hills and mountains, / Cedars and all trees;
Praise him, clouds and vapours, / Snow and hail and fire,
Nature all fulfilling / Only his desire.

3.
Praise him, all ye nations, / Rulers and all kings;
Praise him, men and maidens, / All created things;
Glorious and mighty / Is his name alone;
All the earth his footstool, / Heaven is his throne.

56 To Christ the Prince of Peace

1. To Christ the prince of Peace
And the Son of God most high,
The Father of the world to come,
Sing we with holy joy.
Deep in his heart for us
The wound of love he bore;
That love wherewith he
Still inflames the hearts that him adore.

2. O Jesus, Victim blest,
What else but love divine
Could thou constrain to open thus
That sacred Heart of thine.
O fount of endless Life,
O Spring of Waters Clear,
O Flame Celestial,
Cleansing all who unto thee draw near.

Praise, My Soul, The King of Heaven 57

F. Lyte — John Goss

1. Praise, my soul, the King of hea - ven; To his feet thy
2. Praise him for his grace and fa - vour To our fa - thers
3. Fa - ther - like he tends and spares us; Well our fee - ble

1. tri-bute bring; Ran-somed, healed, re-stored, for-giv - en,
2. in dis - tress; Praise him, still the same for ev - er,
3. frame he knows; In his hands he gen - tly bears us,

1. Ev - er-more his prais - es sing: Al - le - lu - ia!
2. Slow to chide, and swift to bless: Al - le - lu - ia!
3. Res - cues us from all our foes; Al - le - lu - ia!

1. Al - le - lu - ia! Praise the ev - er - last - ing King.
2. Al - le - lu - ia! Glo - rious in his faith - ful - ness.
3. Al - le - lu - ia! Wide - ly as his mer - cy flows.

Praise the Lord, Ye Heav'ns, Adore Him 58

1. Praise the Lord, ye heav'ns, adore him
Praise him, angels in the height.
Sun and moon, rejoice before him.
Praise him, all you stars of light.
Praise the Lord, for he has spoken:
Worlds his mighty voice obeyed.
Laws which never shall be broken
For their guidance he has made.

2. Praise the Lord, for he is glorious,
Never shall his promise fail.
God has made his saints victorious.
Sin and death shall not prevail.
Praise the God of our salvation.
Hosts on high, his pow'r proclaim:
Heav'n and earth and all creation,
Praise and magnify his name.

59 Gather Us In

Tune: GATHER US IN, Irreg., Marty Haugen, b. 1950

Text: Marty Haugen, b. 1950

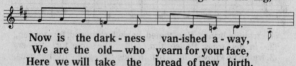

1. Here in this place new light is stream-ing,
2. We are the young—our lives are a mys-t'ry,
3. Here we will take the wine and the wa - ter,
4. Not in the dark of build-ings con - fin -ing,

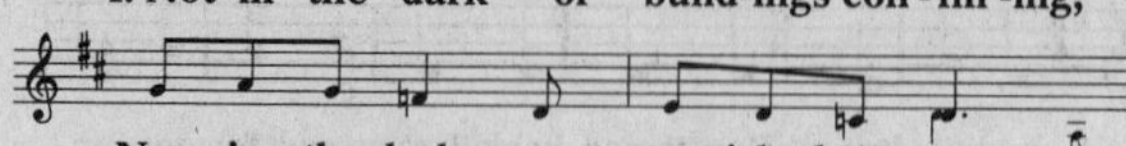

Now is the dark - ness van-ished a - way,
We are the old— who yearn for your face,
Here we will take the bread of new birth,
Not in some heav - en, light-years a -way, But

See in this space our fears and our dream-ings,
We have been sung through-out all of his - t'ry,
Here you shall call your sons and your daugh-ters,
here in this place the new light is shin-ing,

Brought here to you in the light of this day.
Called to be light to the whole hu-man race.
Call us a - new to be salt for the earth.
Now is the King-dom, now is the day.

Gath - er us in— the lost and for - sak - en,
Gath - er us in— the rich and the haugh-ty,
Give us to drink the wine of com - pas-sion,
Gath - er us in and hold us for ev - er,

Gath-er us in— the blind and the lame;
Gath-er us in— the proud and the strong;
Give us to eat the bread that is you;
Gath-er us in and make us your own;

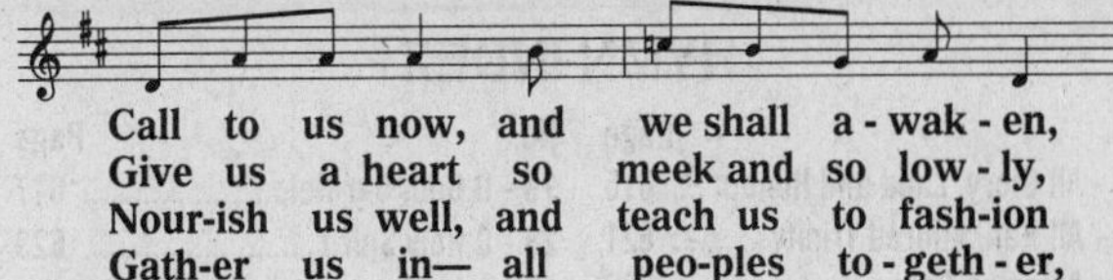
Call to us now, and we shall a - wak - en,
Give us a heart so meek and so low - ly,
Nour-ish us well, and teach us to fash-ion
Gath-er us in— all peo-ples to - geth - er,

We shall a-rise at the sound of our name.
Give us the cour-age to en - ter the song.
Lives that are ho-ly and hearts that are true.
Fire of love in our flesh and our bone.

Were You There

60

1. Were you there when they crucified my Lord?
Were you there when they crucified my Lord?
Oh! sometimes it causes me
To tremble, tremble, tremble.
Were you there when they crucified my Lord?

2. Were you there when they nailed him to the tree?
Were you there when they nailed him to the tree?
Oh! sometimes it causes me
To tremble, tremble, tremble.
Were you there when they nailed him to the tree?

3. Were you there when they laid him in the tomb?
Were you there when they laid him in the tomb?
Oh! sometimes it causes me
To tremble, tremble, tremble.
Were you there when they laid him in the tomb?

O Canada

61

R. S. Weir, 1908

O Canada! Our home and native land!
True patriot love in all thy sons command.
With glowing hearts we see thee rise.
The True North strong and free;
From far and wide, O Canada,
We stand on guard for thee.
God keep our land glorious and free!
O Canada! we stand on guard for thee.

A.B. Routhier

O Canada! Terre de nos aieux,
Ton front est ceint de fleurons glorieux!
Car ton bras sait porter l'epee,
Il sait porter la croix!
Ton histoíre est une epopee
Des plus briliants exploits.
Et ta valeur, de foi trempee,
Protegera nos foyers et nos droits.
Protegera nos foyers et nos droits.

HYMN INDEX

TREASURY OF PRAYERS

These prayers reflect the traditions of the Catholic Church. Individuals and families may find them helpful as they pray.

PRAISE AND THANKS

Blessed are you, Lord God:
blessed are you for ever.
Holy is your name:
blessed are you for ever.
Great is your mercy for your people:
blessed are you for ever. Amen!

Father, Son, and Holy Spirit,
we praise you and give you glory:
we bless you for calling us to be your holy people.

Remain in our hearts,
and guide us in our love and service.
Help us to let our light shine before others
and lead them to the way of faith.

Holy Trinity of love,
we praise you now and for ever. Amen!

We praise you, Father of all:
we thank you for calling us to be your people,
and for choosing us to give you glory.
In a special way we thank you for . . .

Cleanse our hearts and our lives
with your holy word
and make our prayer pleasing to you.
Guide us by your Spirit
as we follow in the paths of Jesus our brother.

All glory and praise are yours, Father,
for ever and ever. Amen!

Let us give glory to the Father
through the Son
in the Holy Spirit,
for God has made us his people, his Church,
and calls us to sing his praises.

All honor and glory and thanks are his,
and praise and worship belong to him.
To God be glory in his Church
for ever and ever! Amen!

Thanks for a beautiful day: *On a beautiful day we may thank God and praise him for his many gifts:*

Father of Jesus,
we praise you and give you glory
for the wonderful things you do for us:
for life and health,
for friends and family,
for this splendid day.

For these reasons, we pray as Jesus taught us:
Our Father . . .

MORNING PRAYERS

With our risen Lord. we praise our Father and offer our day and our work.

**In the ✠ name of the Father, and of the Son,
and of the Holy Spirit. Amen!**

Father, help your people.
Be with us as we pray.

MORNING PSALM:

We may pray one of these psalms, or last Sunday's responsorial psalm, adding the Glory (be) to the Father *at the end.*

Ps. 23—from Mass for Second Scrutiny (4th Sun. of Lent)
Ps. 95—from Mass for First Scrutiny (3rd Sun. of Lent)

Ps. 97—from Mass of the Nativity (at Dawn)
Ps. 116—from Mass for Holy Thursday

On Sunday, it is appropriate to use Ps. 118 from Easter Sunday Mass.
On Friday, it is appropriate to use Ps. 51 from Ash Wednesday Mass.

PSALM OF PRAISE:

One of these Psalms may be prayed, adding the Glory (be) to the Father *at the end.*

Ps. 46(47)—from Mass for Palm Sunday of the Passion
Ps. 67—from Mass of January 1
Ps. 96—from Mass of the Nativity (During the Night)
Ps. 98—from Mass of the Nativity (During the Day)

READING:

One of the first two readings from last Sunday, or another appropriate text from God's word.

A moment of silent prayer follows the reading.

Canticle of Zechariah Lk. 1.68-79

Blessed ✠ be the Lord, the God of Israel,
for he has looked favorably on his people and redeemed them.
He has raised up a mighty saviour for us
in the house of his servant David,
as he spoke through the mouth of his holy prophets from of old,
that we would be saved from our enemies and from the hand of all who hate us.
Thus he has shown the mercy promised to our ancestors,
and has remembered his holy covenant,
the oath that he swore to our ancestor Abraham,
to grant us that we, being rescued from the hands of our enemies,

might serve him without fear, in holiness and righteousness
before him all our days.
And you, child, will be called the prophet of the Most High;
for you will go before the Lord to prepare his ways,
to give knowledge of salvation to his people
by the forgiveness of their sins.
By the tender mercy of our God,
the dawn from on high will break upon us,
to give light to those who sit in darkness and in the shadow of death,
to guide our feet into the way of peace.

Glory to the Father . . . .

Or Glory to God in the highest *(see page 14) may be prayed or sung.*

Prayers for All People

Lord Jesus, we come to you for help:
Lord, have mercy.

Help us to love you more this day. ℟.
Teach us to see you in other people. ℟.
Help us to be ready to serve others. ℟.
Give us strength to carry our cross with you. ℟.
In moments of sorrow, be with us today. ℟.
Help us to do everything for the glory of your Father. ℟.
Help us to build the kingdom by our life today. ℟.

Other petitions may be added.

Lord Jesus, our brother,
hear our prayers for your people.
Help us to work with you today
to honour your Father and save the world.

Lord Jesus,
we praise you for ever and ever. Amen!

THE LORD'S PRAYER: *With Jesus and all his people on earth and in heaven, we sing or say:* Our Father . . . *(page 72).*

BLESSING: *The parents, one of the family, or all may say:*

May our loving God bless us,
Father, Son, and Holy Spirit. Amen!

All may share in a sign of peace and love.

EVENING PRAYERS

At the end of the day, we join Jesus and his Church in offering thanks to our loving God. A candle may be lighted.

**In the ✠ name of the Father, and of the Son,
and of the Holy Spirit. Amen!**

Father, help your people.
Be with us as we pray.

PSALMS:

We may pray one or two of these psalms, or last Sunday's responsorial psalm, adding the Glory (be) to the Father *after each psalm:*

Ps. 30—from Easter Vigil Service after Fourth Reading
Ps. 51—from Mass for Ash Wednesday
Ps. 104—from Mass for Pentecost Sunday
Ps. 130—from Mass for Third Scrutiny (5th Sun. of Lent)

READING:

One of the first two readings from last Sunday, or another appropriate text from God's word.

A moment of silent prayer follows the reading.

Canticle of Mary Lk. 1.46-55

My soul ✠ proclaims the greatness of the Lord,
my spirit rejoices in God my Saviour
for he has looked with favour on his lowly servant.

From this day all generations will call me blessed:
the Almighty has done great things for me,
and holy is his Name.

He has mercy on those who fear him
in every generation.

He has shown the strength of his arm,
he has scattered the proud in their conceit.

He has cast down the mighty from their thrones,
and has lifted up the lowly.

He has filled the hungry with good things,
and the rich he has sent away empty.

He has come to the help of his servant Israel
for he has remembered his promise of mercy,
the promise he made to our fathers,
to Abraham and his children for ever.

Glory to the Father.

Or we may sing the Holy, Holy, Holy Lord, *from page 23.*

Prayers for all people:

Let us pray to God our Father:
Lord, hear our prayer.
For the people of God everywhere. ℟.
For peace in the world. ℟.
For the people who are suffering. ℟.
For the sick and the dying. ℟.
For our family, friends, and neighbours. ℟.
For . . .

Other petitions may be added.

Prayer:

Blessed are you, Father of light,
Lord of all the universe:
in the name of Jesus our Lord we pray for your world.
Grant peace to your people,
strength to the weak,
courage to the downhearted,
and guidance to all in despair.
Send your Spirit to conquer evil,
and make your kingdom come among us.

Father, we ask this grace
through Jesus Christ our Lord. Amen!

THE LORD'S PRAYER: *With Jesus and all his people on earth and in heaven, we sing or say:* Our Father . . . *(page 72).*

BLESSING: *The parents, one of the family, or all may say:*

May our loving God bless us,
Father, Son, ✠ and Holy Spirit. Amen!

All may share a sign of peace and love.

BEFORE AND AFTER SCRIPTURE

Before:

Lord, open our hearts:
let your Spirit speak to us
as we read your word.

After:

Father, we thank you
for speaking to us today
through your holy word.

Or another prayer of thanks may be said (pages 647-648).

MEAL PRAYERS

When we are eating or drinking, or doing anything else, we can do it for the glory of God (1 Cor. 10.31). We may use these prayers or other familiar ones, or make up our own.

Before our meal:

Lord Jesus, our brother,
we praise you for saving us.
Bless ✠ us in your love
as we gather in your name,
and bless ✠ this meal that we share.

Jesus, we praise you for ever. Amen!

or:

Father of us all,
this meal is a sign of your love for us:
bless ✠ us and bless ✠ our food,
and help us to give you glory each day
through Jesus Christ our Lord. Amen!

After our meal:

Loving Father, we praise you
for all the gifts you give us:
for life and health,
for faith and love,
and for this meal we have shared together.

Father, we thank you
through Christ our Lord. Amen!

or:

Thank you, Father, for your gifts:
help us to love you more. Amen!

or:

Father, we thank you for your love
and for giving us food and drink.
Help us to praise you today
in the name of Jesus our Lord. Amen!

A PRAYER FOR OUR FAMILY

Blessed are you, loving Father,
ruler of the universe:

You have given us your Son as your leader,
and have made us temples of your Holy Spirit.

Fill our family with your light and peace.
Have mercy on all who suffer,
and bring us to everlasting joy with you.

Father,
we bless your name for ever and ever. Amen!

PARENT'S PRAYER

All praise to you, Lord Jesus, lover of children:
bless our family,
and help us to lead our children to you.

Give us light and strength,
and courage when our task is difficult.
Let your Spirit fill us with love and peace,
so that we may help our children to love you.

All glory and praise are yours, Lord Jesus,
for ever and ever. Amen!

PRAYER OF SORROW

Psalm 51: *from the Mass for Ash Wednesday.*

A prayer for mercy:

Lord Jesus, you have called us
to be children of light:

Lord, have mercy. **Lord, have mercy.**

Christ, you have suffered on the cross for us:
Christ, have mercy. **Christ, have mercy.**

Lord Jesus, you are the saviour of the world:
Lord, have mercy. **Lord, have mercy.**

Other prayers. We may sing or say Lamb of God *(see page 74), or* I confess to almighty God *(see page 12).*

JESUS PRAYER

We may use this simple prayer at any time.

Lord Jesus Christ, Son of God,
have mercy on me.

or:

Lord Jesus Christ, Son of God,
have mercy on us.

or:

Jesus, our Lord and our brother,
save us in your love.

MARIAN ANTHEM

Blessed are you, mother of my Lord,
for you have believed the word of God.

In faith and love,
you have pondered the words and actions of God
in your life and the life of God's people.

With Jesus we call you mother.
Pray for us,
and ask your Son to lead us to the Father. Amen!

PRAYER FOR PEACE

Lord Jesus Christ, we praise you:
bring peace into the world
by bringing your peace into the hearts of all.
Help us to turn away from sin
and to follow you in love and service.

Glory be yours, and honour,
for ever and ever. Amen!

A PRAYER FOR VOCATIONS

Heavenly Father, Lord of the harvest,
call many members of our community
to be generous workers for your people
and to gather in your harvest.
Send them to share the Good News of Jesus
with all the people of the earth.

Father,
we ask this prayer
through Christ our Lord. Amen!

THANKS FOR FAMILY AND FRIENDS

Blessed are you, loving Father,
for all your gifts to us.
Blessed are you for giving us family and friends
to be with us in times of joy and sorrow,
to help us in days of need,
and to rejoice with us in moments of celebration.

Father,
we praise you for your Son Jesus,
who knew the happiness of family and friends,
and in the love of your Holy Spirit.
Blessed are you for ever and ever. Amen!

FAMILY BLESSINGS

Family gathering: *When the family is gathered for a special occasion, a feast, a holiday, a reunion, or any other special time:*

Father in heaven,
we praise you for giving us your Son
to be our saviour and Lord.
Bless us all as we gather here today, [tonight,]
and let us live happily in your love.

Hear our prayer, loving Father,
for we ask this in Jesus' name. Amen!

Children: *Parents may bless their children each day, or on special occasions. These or similar words may be used:*

Simple form:

May God bless ✠ you, *N.*,
and keep you in love.

The child answers: Amen!

At bedtime:

Heavenly Father,
bless *N.*, and keep him/her in your love.
Grant him/her a good rest tonight,
and send your angels to protect him/her.
In the name of the Father, and of the ✠ Son,
and of the Holy Spirit.

The child answers: Amen!

PRAYER FOR A BIRTHDAY OF A FAMILY MEMBER

This prayer may be offered at a meal or birthday party:

Heavenly Father,
we praise you for all your gifts to us.
In a special way, we thank you for *N.*
Bless him/her on this birthday,
and keep him/her always in your love.

Bless us too, holy Father,
and this food with which we celebrate.
Help us all to praise you and give you glory
through Jesus Christ our Lord.

All answer: Amen!

PRAYER FOR A WEDDING ANNIVERSARY

N. and *N.*,
may God bless you and grant you joy.
May he deepen your love for each other.
May he bless ✠ you in your family and friends,
and lead you to unending happiness in heaven.

May almighty God,
Father, Son, ✠ and Holy Spirit,
bless us all, and keep us in his love for ever.

All answer: Amen!

WHEN VISITING A SICK PERSON

Heavenly Father,
look with mercy on *N.*,
and help him/her in this time of sickness.
Restore him/her to health, we pray,
through Christ our Lord.

All answer: Amen!

or:

Lord Jesus,
lover of the sick,
be with *N.* in his/her sickness.
Help him/her to accept this illness
as a sharer in your cross,
and bring him/her back to full health.

Lord Jesus,
we praise you,
for you are Lord for ever and ever.

All answer: Amen!

PRAYER FOR THE POPE

All praise and glory are yours, Lord Jesus:
you have made us your body, your Church,
and help us to bear fruit for our heavenly Father.

You chose St. Peter as the rock,
and sent him to feed your flock
and to strengthen his brothers and sisters.
Continue to help your Church
through the guidance of our pope,
and keep us faithful in your service.

Jesus, our brother,
you are Lord for ever and ever. Amen!

PRAYERS BEFORE MASS

Act of Faith

Lord Jesus Christ, I firmly believe that you are present in this Blessed Sacrament as true God and true Man, with your Body and Blood, Soul and Divinity. My Redeemer and my Judge, I adore your Divine Majesty together with the angels and saints. I believe, O Lord; increase my faith.

Act of Contrition

O my Saviour, I am truly sorry for having offended you because you are infinitely good and sin displeases you. I detest all the sins of my life and I desire to atone for them. Through the merits of your Precious Blood, wash from my soul all stain of sin, so that, cleansed in body and soul, I may worthily approach the Most Holy Sacrament of the Altar.

PRAYER AFTER MASS

Anima Christi

Partial indulgence (No. 10)

Soul of Christ, sanctify me.
Body of Christ, save me.
Blood of Christ, inebriate me.
Water from the side of Christ, wash me.
Passion of Christ, strengthen me.
O good Jesus, hear me.
Within your wounds hide me.
Separated from you let me never be.
From the malignant enemy, defend me.
At the hour of death, call me.
And close to you bid me.
That with your saints I may be
Praising you, for all eternity. Amen.

Indulgenced Prayer before a Crucifix

Look down upon me, good and gentle Jesus, while before your face I humbly kneel, and with a burning soul pray and beseech you to fix deep in my heart lively sentiments of faith, hope and charity, true contrition for my sins, and a firm purpose of amendment, while I contemplate with great love and tender pity your five wounds, pondering over them within me, calling to mind the words which David, your prophet, said of you, my good Jesus: "They have pierced my hands and my feet; they have numbered all my bones" (Ps 21.17-18).

A *plenary indulgence* is granted on each Friday of Lent and Passiontide to the faithful, who after Communion piously recite the above prayer before an image of Christ crucified; on other days of the year the indulgence is *partial (No. 22).*

Stations of the Cross

The Way of the Cross is a devotion in which we meditate on Christ's Passion and Death in order to put their meaning into our lives.

Heavenly Father, grant that I who meditate on the Passion and Death of Your Son, Jesus Christ, may imitate in my life His love and self-giving to You and to others. Grant this through Christ our Lord. Amen.

STATIONS of the CROSS

1. Jesus Is Condemned to Death

O Jesus, help me to appreciate Your sanctifying grace more and more.

2. Jesus Bears His Cross

O Jesus, You chose to die for me. Help me to love You always with all my heart.

3. Jesus Falls the First Time

O Jesus, make me strong to conquer my wicked passions, and to rise quickly from sin.

4. Jesus Meets His Mother

O Jesus, grant me a tender love for Your Mother, who offered You for love of me.

STATIONS of the CROSS

5. Jesus Is Helped by Simon

O Jesus, like Simon lead me ever closer to You through my daily crosses and trials.

6. Jesus and Veronica

O Jesus, imprint Your image on my heart that I may be faithful to You all my life.

7. Jesus Falls a Second Time

O Jesus, I repent for having offended You. Grant me forgiveness of all my sins.

8. Jesus Speaks to the Women

O Jesus, grant me tears of compassion for Your sufferings and of sorrow for my sins.

STATIONS of the CROSS

9. Jesus Falls a Third Time

O Jesus, let me never yield to despair. Let me come to You in hardship and spiritual distress.

10. He Is Stripped of His Garments

O Jesus, let me sacrifice all my attachments rather than imperil the divine life of my soul.

11. Jesus Is Nailed to the Cross

O Jesus, strengthen my faith and increase my love for You. Help me to accept my crosses.

12. Jesus Dies on the Cross

O Jesus, I thank You for making me a child of God. Help me to forgive others.

STATIONS of the CROSS

13. Jesus Is Taken down from the Cross

O Jesus, through the intercession of Your holy Mother, let me be pleasing to You.

14. Jesus Is Laid in the Tomb

O Jesus, strengthen my will to live for You on earth and bring me to eternal bliss in heaven.

Prayer after the Stations

JESUS, You became an example of humility, obedience and patience, and preceded me on the way of life bearing Your Cross. Grant that, inflamed with Your love, I may cheerfully take upon myself the sweet yoke of Your Gospel together with the mortification of the Cross and follow You as a true disciple so that I may be united with You in heaven. Amen.

THE HOLY ROSARY

Prayer before the Rosary

QUEEN of the Holy Rosary, you have deigned to come to Fatima to reveal to the three shepherd children the treasures of grace hidden in the Rosary. Inspire my heart with a sincere love of this devotion, in order that by meditating on the Mysteries of our Redemption which are recalled in it, I may be enriched with its fruits and obtain peace for the world, the conversion of sinners, and the favor which I ask of you in this Rosary. *(Here mention your request.)* I ask it for the greater glory of God, for your own honor, and for the good of souls, especially for my own. Amen.

The Five Joyful Mysteries

Said on Mondays and Saturdays [except during Lent], and the Sundays from Advent to Lent.

1. The Annunciation
For the love of humility.

2. The Visitation
For charity toward my neighbor.

3. The Nativity
For the spirit of poverty.

4. The Presentation
For the virtue of obedience.

5. Finding in the Temple
For the virtue of piety.

The Five Luminous Mysteries*

Said on Thursdays [except during Lent].

*Added to the Mysteries of the Rosary by Pope John Paul II in his Apostolic Letter of October 16, 2002, entitled ***The Rosary of the Virgin Mary.***

1. The Baptism of Jesus
For living my Baptismal Promises.

2. The Wedding at Cana
For doing whatever Jesus says.

3. Proclamation of the Kingdom
For seeking God's forgiveness.

4. The Transfiguration
Becoming a New Person in Christ.

5. Institution of the Eucharist
For active participation at Mass.

The Five Sorrowful Mysteries

Said on Tuesdays and Fridays throughout the year, and every day from Ash Wednesday until Easter.

1. Agony in the Garden
For true contrition.

2. Scourging at the Pillar
For the virtue of purity.

3. Crowning with Thorns
For moral courage.

4. Carrying of the Cross
For the virtue of patience.

INRI

5. The Crucifixion
For final perseverance.

The Five Glorious Mysteries

Said on Wednesdays [except during Lent], and the Sundays from Easter to Advent.

1. The Resurrection
For the virtue of faith.

2. The Ascension
For the virtue of hope.

4. Assumption of the BVM
For devotion to Mary.

3. Descent of the Holy Spirit
For love of God.

5. Crowning of the BVM
For eternal happiness.

VARIOUS PRAYERS

Prayer to St. Joseph

O Blessed St. Joseph, loving father and faithful guardian of Jesus, and devoted spouse of the Mother of God, I beg you to offer God the Father his divine Son, bathed in blood on the Cross. Through the holy Name of Jesus obtain for us from the Father the favor we implore.

For the Sick

Father, your Son accepted our sufferings to teach us the virtue of patience in human illness. Hear the prayers we offer for our sick brothers and sisters. May all who suffer pain, illness or disease realize that they are chosen to be saints, and know that they are joined to Christ in his suffering for the salvation of the world, who lives and reigns with you and the Holy Spirit, one God, for ever and ever.

For Religious Vocations

Father, you call all who believe in you to grow perfect in love by following in the footsteps of Christ your Son. May those whom you have chosen to serve you as religious provide by their way of life a convincing sign of your kingdom for the Church and the whole world.

For the Parliament

Father, you guide and govern everything with order and love. Look upon the assembly of our national leaders and fill them with the spirit of your wisdom. May they always act in accordance with your will, and may their decisions be for the peace and well-being of all.